THE RIGHT TO BE PROTECTED FROM COMMITTING SUICIDE

This book argues that suicidal people have the right to receive treatment and for reasonable steps to be taken to ensure that they are protected from killing themselves. Those suffering threats to life from mental health issues deserve the same protection as those who face threats to life from ill health or violence from others. The book explores the ethical and legal case for giving those beset with suicidal thoughts the treatment they need and for reasonable steps to be taken to prevent them attempting suicide.

Debates around suicide tend to be dominated by cases involving those with terminal medical conditions seeking assisted dying. But of those wishing to die, it is far more common to find middle aged men and young people oppressed by mental health and personal problems.

Too often the woeful failure in the funding of mental health services in the UK means that suicidal people are denied the support and help they desperately need. This ground-breaking book makes the legal and ethical case for recognising that the state and public authorities have a duty to provide and implement an effective suicide prevention strategy.

The Right to be Protected from Committing Suicide

Jonathan Herring

•HART•
OXFORD • LONDON • NEW YORK • NEW DELHI • SYDNEY

HART PUBLISHING

Bloomsbury Publishing Plc

Kemp House, Chawley Park, Cumnor Hill, Oxford, OX2 9PH, UK

1385 Broadway, New York, NY 10018, USA

29 Earlsfort Terrace, Dublin 2, Ireland

HART PUBLISHING, the Hart/Stag logo, BLOOMSBURY and the Diana logo are trademarks of Bloomsbury Publishing Plc

First published in Great Britain 2022

A catalogue record for this book is available from the British Library.

Library of Congress Cataloging-in-Publication data.

Names: Herring, Jonathan, author.

Title: The right to be protected from committing suicide / Jonathan Herring.

Description: Oxford, UK ; New York, NY : Hart Publishing, an imprint of Bloomsbury Publishing, 2022. | Includes bibliographical references and index.

Identifiers: LCCN 2022003650 (print) | LCCN 2022003651 (ebook) | ISBN 9781509949045 (hardback) | ISBN 9781509949083 (paperback) | ISBN 9781509949069 (pdf) | ISBN 9781509949052 (Epub)

Subjects: LCSH: Suicide—Law and legislation. | Suicide—Prevention. | Suicide victims—Legal status, laws, etc. | Assistance in emergencies—Law an d legislation. | Suicide—Law and legislation—Great Britain.

Classification: LCC K5178 .H47 2022 (print) | LCC K5178 (ebook) | DDC 362.28—dc23/eng/20220331

LC record available at https://lccn.loc.gov/2022003650

LC ebook record available at https://lccn.loc.gov/2022003651

ISBN: HB: 978-1-50994-904-5
ePDF: 978-1-50994-906-9
ePub: 978-1-50994-905-2

Typeset by Compuscript Ltd, Shannon
Printed and bound in Great Britain

To Joanna

ACKNOWLEDGEMENTS

I am very grateful for the support and help I have received in writing this book from the staff at Hart Publishing, especially Rosie Mearns from the editorial team, and copy editor Maria Skrzypiec.

While suicide is not the most cheerful of topics, in the writing of this book I have been sustained by the love and support of many friends, including Alan Bogg, Hannah Bows, Shazia Choudhry, Charlotte Elves, Charles Foster, Imogen Goold, Barbara Havelkova, Camilla Pickles, Chloe Romanis and Rachel Taylor. I also have the huge honour of supervising and mentoring some amazing doctoral and post-doctoral students who are such a source of inspiration, especially Marthe Goudsmit, Anne Lansink, Rachel Sloth-Neilsen, Petros Panayiotou, Saarah Ray, Shannon Russell, Chelsea Wallis and Suzanna Zaccour. But above all I am grateful for Kirsten, Laurel, Joanna and Darcy who make life at home so hilarious.

SOURCES OF LISTENING

Please note that there are many organisations should you want to talk through feelings raised by the issues discussed in this book. The Samaritans (www.samaritans.org) are available 24 hours a day 365 days a year.

CONTENTS

TABLE OF CASES

UK Cases

ECtHR Cases

1

Introduction

The idea for this book was sparked when I posed this question to my students: 'A person decides they want to die and seeks the help of their doctor. What does and what should the law say the doctor should do?' I had set them the standard kinds of reading on end-of-life issues that one would expect to find in a medical law course. I was astonished how many thought that the law should allow the doctor to facilitate the suicide, and expressed objection to the current law that forbade that. For most, the primary issue was about autonomy and whether the suicidal person had mental capacity to make their decision. If they did, their decision deserved respect and medical professionals should enable people to commit suicide. The current law's failure to permit that was a breach of their human rights. Of course, as soon as I asked whether they were proposing that this approach should be taken by a college doctor if a student approached them, they were adamant that they did not mean their answer to apply to that kind of case.

These interactions highlighted to me how the right to die has come to dominate in discussions about suicide and end-of-life questions. The importance of suicide prevention has been largely lost. In part this is because the litigation and debates, understandably, involve cases of people with terminal painful illnesses. Such cases dominate the students' reading and, no doubt, it was through that lens that the students were giving their initial response: they were assuming I was positing the case of a person with a terrible illness. But most suicides are not sought by people in such a situation. They are middle-aged men suffering the end of a relationship; students struggling with the pressures of exams; or teenagers bullied online. In such cases the human right to protection from suicide is what should dominate our discussions, not talk of the right to die.

This book argues in favour of a recognition of a right to be protected from committing suicide. This is *not* a book arguing against assisted dying in some circumstances. I, for one, would support changes to the law which would allow, for example, Tony Nicklinson,[1] who had 'locked in syndrome' and a long-established wish to die, access to assisted death. However, support for assisted dying in certain cases, is not necessarily incompatible with the idea that there is a right – I would argue a more profound right – to be protected from suicide. I will explore in

[1] *R (Nicklinson) v Ministry of Justice* [2014] UKSC 38.

Chapter 8 how these competing rights might be balanced. Of course, some readers will support the claim that there is a right to be protected from committing suicide which lies at the heart of this book, but not be happy with the arguments in Chapter 8. They may prefer there to be no circumstances in which assisted dying be permitted; or may prefer a more generous set of circumstances in which access to assisted dying is permitted; prefer a wider or differently formed proposal to that presented there. However, this book is not primarily about that issue. It is to reposition the right to be protected from suicide as a fundamental right, which should play a prominent role in end-of-life debates.

Suicide generates a range of different responses. Here are four approaches which broadly capture most views found in the literature:

(1) Suicide is a moral wrong. Life is an inherent good: a gift from God, if you like. To commit suicide is equivalent to murder: it is destroying the innate value in life and showing a lack of respect for the value of life. Clearly, completed suicide cannot be subject to a criminal sanction, but attempting, encouraging and assisting suicide should be seen as as much a crime as attempting, encouraging or assisting any other offence. That way the criminal law can deter suicide attempts.

    This view has few supporters today. We recognise now that those who have attempted suicide are often driven by forces outside their control and the ministrations of the criminal justice system are not what is needed for survivors of suicide attempts. Rather they need support and professional intervention. This has led to the second view, which finds much more support today.

(2) Suicide is typically the product of a mental disorder. We need to treat most suicides as manifestations of mental illness. The primary response to a suicide attempt should be to ensure that the person concerned receives the counselling and support they need. We need greater investment in clinical mental health services in order to provide the training professionals require to allow them to identify those liable to commit suicide and give them the support that is necessary.

    This view sees suicide as primarily a medical problem. It certainly highlights the failures of health care around mental illness. However, critics claim that it overly narrows the focus of causes of suicide. The next perspective offers an important addition.

(3) Suicide is a reflection of a sick society, not individual selves. We need to recognise the powerful social inequalities that blight lives and lead to suicide. As society causes suicide, it has an obligation to prevent it.

    This view sees suicide as a social problem. Suicide prevention is less about stopping individuals killing themselves, and rather about remedying the inequalities and exclusions which generate suicide and are reflected in suicide rates. This view sees suicide as something which should be stopped, which is an approach questioned by the fourth view.

(4) We need to respect people's private autonomous choices. Where a person has chosen to die, we need to respect that decision. It is easy for others to look on and determine that the decision was foolish or even immoral. However, at the end of the day 'whose life is it anyway?' While it might be appropriate to offer people support and therapy should they want it, it is not right for the state to be involved in seeking to intervene in private decisions. We should recognise a right to commit suicide and restrict active steps to intervene only where it is clear that a person does not want to commit suicide. This requires no longer making it an offence to assist a person to commit suicide and, indeed, ensuring there are the medical and legal facilities needed to make this happen.

Perhaps most people take a view somewhere between these schools of thought. There are some cases where suicide reflects a genuine autonomous decision, which deserves respect and facilitation, and others that are the product of the mental disorder and not fully autonomous, where suicide prevention is entirely appropriate. True, it is difficult to tell which cases are which, but determining whether a person has capacity to make a decision has become a well-known legal difficulty. Such an easy middle route has superficial attraction, but we need to know our starting point. Until we have taken a view on the relative harmfulness of suicide or likelihood of capacity, we cannot deal with hard cases. In other words, our starting point – whether that is that very few suicidal people have mental capacity, or that denying a person access to death is a serious wrong – will determine how we deal with the difficult cases.

This book does not seek to promote any one of the four views outlined above. In line with view (4) it accepts that there are cases where a suicide is the result of a free autonomous decision and should be respected and even enabled, although there are very few cases where that is true. This claim is explored in Chapter 8. Rather than emphasising the relevance of autonomy, I argue that the primary legal response to most potential suicide is to emphasise the right to be protected from suicide. I make this claim on two grounds. The first is that it is an aspect of the right to health and life. In so far as many suicide are connected to mental health or other health issues, the right to suicide intervention should be protected as part of the general right to health. The second is that suicide is commonly the product of socio-economic inequalities. There are strong connections between suicide and: poverty; toxic conceptions of masculinity; unemployment; and social exclusion. As society plays a role in creating an environment in which suicide can flourish, society has a special responsibility to protect citizens from committing suicide.

As those examples show, your approach to suicide can be clearly shaped by the image of suicide you start with. A particularly powerful example is Kevin Yuill's book, *Assisted Suicide: The Liberal, Humanist Case against Legalization.*[2] He centres his discussion around three suicides which he describes in some detail: Mohamed Bouazizi, a Tunisian street vendor who set himself on fire as

[2] K Yuill, *Assisted Suicide: The Liberal, Humanist Case against Legalization* (Palgrave, 2012).

a protest against government action; Thich Quang Du, a Buddhist monk who in 1963 gained international recognition after setting himself on fire in a political protest; and Arthur Friedman, who committed suicide in prison so that his son would not face humiliation at his trial. He goes on to see suicide as 'profound and meaningful, the most human of actions'.[3] He believes suicide can be 'inspirational, transcendent and the most beautiful and awe-inspiring act'.[4] He advocates making it easier for people to commit suicide so they can make these powerful statements. However, the suicides he focuses on are not typical suicides. A different book might start with more mundane, prosaic suicides: suicides of bullied teens or suicides of people whose benefits have been stopped. Such a book might reach very different conclusions about suicides. They certainly would not appear as grand public proclamations.

The book proceeds as follows. Chapter 2 will seek to define suicide. As often arises in such discussions, there is no single definition of suicide that can be provided but the discussion illustrates the debates around the nature of suicide. It also explores the statistics on suicide: its prevalence and the circumstances of those who commit suicide. Chapters 3 and 4 examine the causes of suicide. While suicide is a complex phenomenon and it is often inappropriate to identify a single cause, it is important to assess what factors are associated with and influence suicide. In Chapter 5 I set out some of the attempts that are, and can be, made to prevent suicide arising. Chapters 6 and 7 look at the legal responses to suicide, with Chapter 6 focusing on the human rights argument, and Chapter 7 looking at current interventions. Chapter 8 seeks to place the debates in the book in the context of the lively debates over assisted dying. The final chapter offers concluding thoughts.

[3] At 84.
[4] At 110.

2

The Definition of Suicide

I. Introduction

It should come as no surprise that there is no agreed definition of suicide. However, that creates problems because it makes gathering and comparing statistics on suicide difficult and generates confusion in debates over legal or ethical issues around suicide. The Institute of Medicine of the United States National Academies sees the ambiguity over the definition as a major impediment to suicide prevention:

> research on suicide is plagued by many methodological problems … definitions lack uniformity … [and] reporting of suicide is inaccurate [hence] …. a common language or set of terms in describing suicidal phenomena [is needed].[1]

Silverman emphasises the difficulties caused by the definitions issues in comparing academic studies:

> the suicide literature remains replete with confusing (and sometimes derogatory or pejorative) terms, definitions, descriptors, and classifications that make it difficult, if not impossible, to compare and contrast different research studies, clinical reports, or epidemiological surveys.[2]

Silverman[3] goes on to list some of the factors that could be taken into account in producing a taxonomy of suicide.

- **Timing**: imminent versus short-term versus long-term;
- **Duration**: acute versus chronic;
- **Frequency**: first attempt versus repetitive versus chronic;
- **Intensity**: low versus medium versus high;
- **Character**: unintentional versus intentional;
- **Intent to die**: present versus absent;

[1] S Goldsmith et al (eds), *Reducing Suicide* (The National Academics Press, 2002).
[2] M Silverman, 'Challenges to Defining and Classifying Suicide and Suicidal Behaviors' in R O'Connor and J Pirkis (eds), *The International Handbook of Suicide Prevention* (John Wiley & Sons, 2016).
[3] ibid.

- **Context**: impulsive versus planned;
- **Quality**: active versus passive;
- **Dosage**: nonlethal versus nearly lethal versus lethal;
- **Setting**: public versus semiprivate versus private;
- **Method**: firearm versus hanging versus jumping versus overdose;
- **Outcome**: injury versus non-injury versus death.

In large part the challenges posed by defining the term suicide are because it is used in different contexts and for different purposes. An ethicist may be primarily concerned with the moral character of the act.[4] As Michael Cholbi[5] notes 'views about the nature of suicide often incorporate, sometimes unknowingly, views about the prudential or moral justifiability of suicide and are therefore not value-neutral descriptions of suicide'. So, a person committed to the view that all suicide is unjustifiable is likely to have in mind a definition which only covers such unjustifiable acts. A theologian may be committed to a certain religious teaching about suicide and seek to align any definition with that. A public health expert may be focused on exploring what kinds of death can be addressed by suicide prevention policies and fashion a definition from that perspective. A loss adjuster determining whether a payment under a life insurance policy is due following a suicide, will have a different set of concerns again. The list goes on.

This difficulty in definition should not be overly concerning. There is agreement over the core concept: suicide is intentional self-killing. The debates tend to surround borderline cases.[6] Suicide is by no means alone in this definitional ambiguity; nearly any term of moral and public significance will be debated, particularly around its periphery. Terms such as murder, love and family are subject to similar definitional debates. Indeed, it would seem potentially stifling to the debates around families, for example, to insist that there is a perfect definition of family to be found if only we thought hard enough about it.[7] The debates on the definitions, when carried out explicitly, can clarify important theoretical issues.[8] What is more important than having a single 'correct' definition of suicide is being clear what are the primary debates people have around the definitions and ensuring that writers specify which definition is being used in their work.

[4] S Dowie, 'What is Suicide? Classifying Self-Killings' (2020) 23 *Medicine, Health Care and Philosophy* 717.

[5] S Cholbi, *Suicide: The Philosophical Dimensions* (Broadview Press, 2011) 2.

[6] M Silverman et al, 'Rebuilding the Tower of Babel: A Revised Nomenclature for the Study of Suicide and Suicidal Behaviors: Suicide-Related Ideations, Communications, and Behaviors' (2007) 37 *Suicide and Life-Threatening Behavior* 264; M Michaels et al, 'Suicide' in R DeBubeis and D Strunk (eds), *The Oxford Handbook of Mood Disorders* (Oxford University Press, 2017).

[7] A Gupta, 'Definitions' in E Zalta (ed), *The Stanford Encyclopedia of Philosophy* (University of Stanford, 2021).

[8] M Silverman, 'Suicide and Life-Threatening Behavior' (2006) 36 *Suicide and Life-Threatening Behaviour* 519.

This chapter will, therefore, focus on two key questions that arise in defining suicide, rather than seeking to promote a single definition. The first is the definition of intention, and whether non-intentional self-killings should be included within suicide. The second is whether and when cases where another person is involved in the killing – be that as an assistant or primary causer – are suicide: in other words, where the boundary between suicide and assisted suicide or euthanasia is drawn (if indeed it should be). Before developing these issues a little more, it may be helpful to set out some of the leading definitions, which will indicate how these different views can play out.

II. Popular and Official Definitions

Generally, suicide is understood as an act of intentional self-killing. For example, the UK Government[9] in one document defines suicide as 'a deliberate act that intentionally ends one's life'. But other official definitions sometimes suggest a broader understanding. The World Health Organization has defined suicide as 'the act of deliberately killing oneself'.[10] This definition notably limits suicide to acts and does not include omissions. Further, its reference to 'deliberately killing oneself' is somewhat ambiguous. It could be read to require simply that the act which kills oneself is done deliberately, without there needing to be a desire to cause death or as requiring a determination to die. The World Health Organization Regional Office for Europe has adopted a definition of suicide as 'an act with a fatal outcome which the deceased, knowing or expecting a fatal outcome, had initiated and carried out with the purpose of provoking the changes he desired'.[11] This definition focuses on knowledge or expectation of death, rather than intent.

A much-quoted definition is from Durkheim's *Le Suicide*:

> suicide is applied to all cases of death resulting directly or indirectly from a positive or negative act by the victim himself, which he knows will produce the result.[12]

There are two particularly notable features of this definition: it appears to cover both acts and omissions from the victim; and the focus is on knowledge that death will occur rather than intent to die.

As already mentioned, the context within which the term is used can impact on what definition is appropriate. A good example is palliative care, where the term suicide is often avoided. Instead, reference is made to the wish to hasten death (WTHD):

> The WTHD is a reaction to suffering, in the context of a life-threatening condition, from which the patient can see no way out other than to accelerate his or her death.

[9] Department of Health, *Preventing Suicide in England* (Department of Health, 2020).

[10] World Health Organization, *Suicide* (WHO, 2017).

[11] D De Leo et al, 'Definitions of Suicidal Behavior: Lessons Learned from the WHO/EURO Multicentre Study' (2006) 27 *Crisis: The Journal of Crisis Intervention and Suicide Prevention* 4.

[12] E Durkheim, *Suicide: A Study in Sociology* (Free Press, 1951 [1897]).

> This wish may be expressed spontaneously or after being asked about it, but it must be distinguished from the acceptance of impending death or from a wish to die naturally, although preferably soon.[13]

This terminology is used in palliative care to indicate that it is not so much a matter of choosing death over life, but rather a matter of the timing of death. The fact that this phrase is used might reflect a stigma that is still attached to suicide, or might be seen as a better way of framing end-of-life questions for patients or their families.

Another example of where the terminology of suicide is avoided is martyrdom. Bélanger et al define suicide as 'the psychological readiness to suffer and sacrifice one's life for a cause'.[14] A famous example is Mohamed Bouazizi, who burned himself alive in 2010 to protest at the Tunisian regime, which sparked the 'Arab Spring' uprisings. Cultural responses to martyrdom have changed. At one time martyrs were held up as inspirational figures, whose devotion (normally religious) shows they are willing to die for a greater purpose. However, increasingly martyrdom is treated with distaste, particularly where others are killed in the suicidal act: the fact that the language has changed back to 'suicide bombers' indicates as much. This again reflects the stigma that attaches to the terminology of suicide.

The collection of official statistics is another example of how context has an impact on the definition of suicide. The UK Office for National Statistics states that its definition of suicide 'includes all deaths from intentional self-harm for persons aged 10 and over, and deaths where the intent was undetermined for those aged 15 and over'.[15] This is a particularly opaque definition, and several issues are worth highlighting. First, the reference to 'includes' indicates that other deaths may count as suicide, but it is not explained what these are. Second, the fact there is a difference depending on age seems surprising. It reflects, perhaps, the stigma that is attached to suicide and a reluctance to ascribe that to children. The Office for National Statistics explains:

> Deaths from an event of undetermined intent in 10 to 14 year-olds are not included because although for older teenagers and adults we assume that in these deaths the harm was self-inflicted, for younger children it is not clear whether this assumption is appropriate. Deaths from an event of undetermined intent cannot be applied to children due to the possibility that these deaths were caused by unverifiable accidents, neglect or abuse.[16]

[13] A Balaguer et al, 'An International Consensus Definition of the Wish to Hasten Death and its Related Factors' (2016) 4 *PLoS One* 11.

[14] J Bélanger et al, 'The Psychology of Martyrdom: Making the Ultimate Sacrifice in the Name of a Cause' (2014) 107 *Journal of Personality and Social Psychology* 494, 469.

[15] Office for National Statistics, *Number of Suicides for Persons Aged 10 to 17, England and Wales, Registered Years 2001 to 2016* (ONS, 2018) 2.

[16] ibid, 3.

Apparent in this approach is a reluctance to call a death suicide in relation to children unless there is clear evidence that it was an intentional death. Third, the intent element of the definition focuses on whether the harm was intended, rather than death. That is a wider definition than is generally used. It could cover a case where a person intends to harm themselves, but specifically does not want to die. As suggested below, it may be that this definition is used because it is easier for statisticians to determine whether a person intended to harm themselves, than to determine whether they wanted to die.

The approach of the Coroners' Courts to suicide is interesting. When a person dies, if the death is not 'natural' then a coroner will be required to hold an inquest which will produce a verdict outcome. One of the possible outcomes is suicide. Until very recently, that verdict was only available if it was established beyond reasonable doubt (the standard required for a criminal conviction), whereas the other verdicts (such as accidental death) could be found on the balance of probabilities. Lang J explained:

> in order to return a verdict of suicide, the coroner or jury must be sure (i) that the deceased intended his own death; and (ii) that he did an act with that intention which caused his death.[17]

Given the issues discussed above about proving intent, it could be difficult for a coroner to produce a finding of suicide, particularly to a 'beyond reasonable doubt' standard. Indeed, the courts have taken the view that:

> If a person dies a violent death, the possibility of suicide may be there for all to see, but it must not be presumed merely because it seems on the face of it to be a likely explanation. Suicide must be proven by evidence [failing which] it is the duty of the coroner to find an open verdict.[18]

This approach seems based on the view that there is something stigmatic about suicide. It is something that should be reserved only for cases where we are quite clear what happened. Interestingly, this traditional approach was reversed recently by the Supreme Court in *R (Maughan) v HM Senior Coroner for Oxfordshire*,[19] where it was held that the ordinary, balance of probabilities was to be used in reaching a suicide verdict. Lady Arden emphasised that society 'needs to understand the causes and prevent suicides occurring'. This shift from seeing suicide as a stigmatic label to be reserved for proven cases, to using it to signal cases from which suicide prevention lessons could be learned, is revealing.

Having considered the broad issues around the definition of suicide, it is time to turn to a more detailed consideration of some of the specific issues.

[17] *R (Lagos) v Her Majesty's Coroner for the City of London* [2013] EWHC 423 (Admin).
[18] *R v London Coroner, ex p Barber* [1975] 1 WLR 1310.
[19] *R (Maughan) v HM Senior Coroner for Oxfordshire* [2020] UKSC 46.

III. The Mental State

One major area of dispute around the definition of suicide is whether or not suicide is limited to cases where there is intent to die. There are easy cases in which all agree. If a person after lengthy consideration decides to kill themselves and does so, this will be suicide by any definition. Similarly, a case where a person does not intend to die, but ends up terminating their life, such as where a person accidentally slips while walking on a cliff and falls to their death, will not be suicide on any reasonable definition. It is cases between these where there is more controversy. We need to unpack a little more the states of mind between a person who sets out to kill themselves and cases of pure accident.[20] It is possible to distinguish between various scenarios.

A. Pure Intent: Purpose to Die

Pure intent in simple terms is aim, purpose or wish. Hence, in a case of suicide this would be a case where a person sets out to end their life.[21] It would not, therefore, cover a rock climber undertaking a highly risky climb who falls to their death or a person who seeks to drink two bottles of whisky for a dare. In such a case the person may have foreseen their death – may even have been willing to take the risk of dying – but they were not acting for the purpose of dying. As Duff[22] has helpfully suggested, we can ask 'if the person had not died would they have regarded themselves as having failed?'. The rock climber will be thrilled if they survive their daring climb and so we can take it there was no (pure) intent to die. By contrast, the person beset by misery who seeks to end their life will be disappointed if they survive and so we can take it there was a (pure) intent to die.

While helpful as a broad guide, Duff's 'test of failure' must be treated with care. We can imagine a case where at the time of the act D wanted to die (eg they take a large dose of tablets) but then later changed their mind and decided they did not want to die. They would not regard survival as a failure. However, normally in legal terms intention is to be assessed at the time of the act. For a lawyer, it would be natural to ask – in a case of suicide (or attempted suicide) – whether the person had the intention to die, at the moment they did the act which led to death.

Supporters of restricting suicide to cases of pure intent often emphasise that relying on it helpfully excludes cases where most people would not instinctively see there being a case of suicide. When the Twin Towers were attacked on 11 September 2001, some people jumped from windows to escape flames and fell to their death. While they may well have known that they were jumping to their

[20] Silverman (n 2).

[21] D Hill, 'What is it to Commit Suicide?' (2011) 24 *Ratio* 192.

[22] A Duff, '"Thank God I Failed"' in H Hurd (ed), *Moral Puzzles and Legal Perplexities* (Cambridge University Press, 2021).

death, we can take it had they survived the fall they would have been delighted. Indeed, it seems particularly inappropriate to regard their act as suicide given that their aim or purpose was to save their lives. To many people, such cases intuitively fall outside the category of suicide.[23]

B. Death as a Necessary Means to a Purpose

In addition to cases of pure intent, some would include cases where death is a necessary means to achieve a further purpose. These would be cases where a person is not acting in order to die per se, but because of a further benefit that they see death as providing. This would cover a case where a person kills themselves in order to reach the afterlife, or a person who kills themselves in order to stop their pain. In these cases it is not death itself which is the goal, but some other consequence which they see as flowing from death. Brandt appears to include such deaths in his definition of suicide, and thus defines suicide as:

> doing something which results in one's death, either from the intention of ending one's life or the intention to bring about some other state of affairs (such as relief from pain) which one thinks it certain or highly probably can be achieved only by means of death.[24]

Those who believe these cases should be included within intent will argue that intent is about what a person aims to achieve; in these cases they aim to die, albeit only as a means to a secondary end. This could be put in terms of motive and intention. Criminal law has traditionally placed little weight on motive. The law is concerned to know that the defendant intended to steal, but is not interested in why they intended to steal. Similarly, for suicide our focus should be on the fact they intended death, even if death itself was not their motivation. In the context of suicide we might think it helpful to leave questions of why a person wanted to commit suicide as separate from the definition of suicide. Part of the reason for that is that it is hard enough to determine whether a person was aiming to die, let alone the reason for the death. Where a person has acted to die, it seems to introduce unnecessary complexity to distinguish cases where they wanted to die per se and wanted to die for a further motive. This means we can distinguish a suicide where a person took illegal drugs 'to stop the pain' and died as a result, from a case where a person took drugs 'to die and so stop the pain'. But we need not distinguish a person who took drugs 'to die' from a person who took then 'to stop the pain by dying'.

Some commentators would further distinguish cases where the end goal is inseparable from the purpose and those where it is not. Thus, for those who have

[23] E Torisky, 'Minimally Intentional Suicide and "The Falling Man"' (2015) 49 *Journal of Value Inquiry* 69.

[24] R Brandt, 'The Morality and Rationality Handbook for the Study of Suicide' in D Banatar (ed), *Life, Death and Meaning* (Rowman & Littlefield, 2010).

a religious belief, because the afterlife is only accessible to those who have died we might say that having the purpose of reaching the afterlife is inseparable from having the purpose to die. By contrast in the case of the person who wants to die in order to relieve pain, we might say these are separable. It is possible to end the pain without dying, while it is not possible to enter the afterlife without dying. This brings us close to the next view for discussion.

C. Oblique Intent: Death Inevitable, but not Purposed

Under this approach to the mental element of suicide, we include not just those where death is the aim of the person, but also cases where death is known to be the inevitable result of their act. In the literature this would commonly be seen as oblique intent. Examples of this may be a soldier who throws themselves on a grenade to save the lives of their fellow soldiers, or someone who jumps from high up on a burning building. Clearly in these cases the people do not want to die, nor is their death a necessary means to their end, but we might take it that death is inevitable (or nearly inevitable). A further well-known example might be the case of Captain Lawrence Oates in the 1912 Antarctic expedition.[25] He walked out into a blizzard because he had developed gangrene and was slowing the rest of his party down, and was aware that he would nearly inevitably die from the cold. 'I am just going outside and may be some time' were his famous final words. If we assume that he was aware that his death was virtually certain, then this seems a case of oblique intent. It would not be case of pure intent because we might presume he would have been thrilled if he had been rescued. Those who believe oblique intent should be included as a form of intent argue that if a person does an act knowing the outcome of it, they should be held to account for the consequence and not be permitted to claim that they did not want to produce the inevitable outcome of their act.

In these discussions we are seeing the borderline between intent and foresight. To some commentators this is a fundamental distinction: foresight must be kept separate from intent. Craig Paterson[26] thinks it is important to distinguish pure intent from the other state of mind. Telling someone bad news may mean that you foresee they will cry. It does not mean you intend them to cry. Indeed, you may deeply desire they will not cry and do everything you can to make sure they do not cry, but still they do. So, too, in a case of suicide there is a big difference between acting with the purpose of dying and acting foreseeing that you will die. To take the Twin Towers example: there is, on this view, all the difference in the world between jumping in order to die because life has lost its value, and jumping

[25] RA Duff, 'Socratic Suicide?' (1983) 83 *Proceedings of the Aristotelian Society* 35.
[26] C Paterson, *Assisted Suicide and Euthanasia: A Natural Law Ethics Approach* (Routledge, 2008).

to escape the fire, hoping that you might somehow survive, despite the inevitability of death. That distinction would be lost if oblique intent were included within intent in this context.

So put, the distinction between intent and foresight seems to be convincing. But in other scenarios it is less clear. Paterson considers the case of the person who refuses treatment because they fear they will be a burden on the family. He states:

> it is also a valid concern for the competent to altruistically assess what the burdens of treatment and care might entail for others. It is not unreasonable for persons to determine that they may not wish to place their families in the position of carrying the extended emotional and financial burden of treating and caring for them … Such altruism is, I think, permissible as a form of *self-sacrifice*, for the intention need only be to avoid the burdens associated with treatment and care, not the deliberate hastening of death.[27]

Here we see the danger that a moral assessment of the motives may impact on a determination of whether this is suicide. It looks, in Paterson's example, as though the person is wanting to die as a means of removing the burden, and so should be included within the meaning of intent, but Paterson is reluctant to reach that conclusion because of the 'good' motivation. This is all the more apparent when Paterson distinguishes a person taking a large dose of morphine to stop pain, realising they may well die as a result (which he sees as not suicide) and a person who takes the morphine in order to die and so stop the pain.[28] Here we might think the distinction between intent and foresight is becoming very thin. The person who does the act knowing they are going to die, but saying they are not wanting to die might be seen as self-deluding. 'If you don't want to die don't do the act which will kill you' we might say. And that might give us a distinction from the Twin Towers example, where that response does not work. If they don't do the act that will kill them (ie jumping from the tower) they will die.

Perhaps the conclusion is that in these cases where death is inevitable, but not desired, there are some cases that it seems appropriate to classify as ones of intent (if you know death will result from the act, why do it if you did not want to die?) and there are other cases that it does not (the person knew their act would kill them, but they felt they had no alternative). One solution is to take the approach that a person who acts knowing that death is inevitable will be taken to intentionally commit suicide, save in the case where they are acting to avoid death or another terrible outcome from another cause. In such a case their choice is between two deaths and it seems inappropriate to classify that as a decision to die.

[27] At 146.
[28] At 345.

D. Recklessness: Death is a Risk

At the outer reaches of possible definitions of suicide we have cases where it is not the purpose of the person to die, but they realise there is a risk they will die and take that risk anyway. For example, a person is climbing Mount Everest, aware of the high death toll the mountain has claimed, but is keen to attempt the ascent nonetheless. They are caught in a blizzard and die. Few would classify that as suicide. The person took the risk of death, but that is not how suicide is generally understood.

It can be useful to consider 'dare devil' suicides. These are cases where a person is undertaking an activity which has a risk of death, but death is not the desired outcome. This might cover cases of extreme sports, or engaging in pranks for a Youtube video. Breivik[29] suggests that within this category we can distinguish between three categories: pro-social risk taking, where the activities have a social benefit, firefighters being an obvious example; anti-social risk taking, where there are harms to society, especially in that others might be endangered by the activity; and ludic risk taking, where the individual is the only person whose life is in danger. He suggests that daredevil suicides should be limited to this third category. However, most commentators seem to think that these acts are not best categorised as suicides at all. They certainly seem to raise different kinds of issues to those associated with standard cases of suicide.

E. No Mental State

The approaches considered to date pre-suppose that we are able to identify the individual's state of mind.[30] It is notoriously difficult to determine a person's state of mind, even if they are alive and able to tell us.[31] It is even harder if a person is now dead and/or if their state of mind at the time of suicide was agitated or confused. It is not surprising, therefore, that some have suggested that it would be preferable to define suicide as self-killing, with no requirement for a particular mental state.[32] Beauchamp, for example, defines suicide in this way: 'an act is a suicide if a person brings about his or her own death in circumstances where others do not coerce him or her into action'.[33] That, however, seems to move suicide a long way from its natural definition. To describe a person who crashes their car or the mountaineer who slips by a crevasse as a suicide seems to include too wide a range of deaths within the concept.

[29] G Breivik, 'Can BASE Jumping Be Morally Defended' in M McNamee (ed), *Philosophy, Risk and Adventure Sports* (Taylor & Francis, 2007).

[30] Cholbi (n 5).

[31] Duff (n 25).

[32] S Dowie, 'What is Suicide? Classifying Self-Killings' (2020) 23 *Medicine, Health Care and Philosophy* 717.

[33] Paterson (n 26) 354.

F. Comparing the Approaches to Mental State

Some very fine distinctions are being drawn in these discussions on the mental state required for a suicide. So fine, in fact, that their use might be questioned. There may be few suicidal people whose thinking can be neatly classified in terms of the purpose, means to purpose, foresight and so forth, that such a philosophical analysis requires. It may well be that for many suicides the state of mind is a mixture of multiple and somewhat contradictory wishes and beliefs, making them not suitable for the fine-grained analysis that is required for the discussion presented here. But, as we have seen, abandoning any requirement for a state of mind and simply asking whether the person caused their own death seems to leave open too many cases (eg where someone crashes their car by accident and dies). So, it may be we stick to cases where the individual intended death, either as an end in itself or a means to an end, but leave other cases out. That is perhaps the closest we can get to the everyday understanding that a suicide occurs when someone kills themselves, wanting to die.

An alternative approach may be to try and break down suicide into different categories. We could, for example, distinguish self-murder (intention killing of self) and self-manslaughter (reckless killing of self).[34] There is an attraction in doing this because we have a detailed and reasonably clear set of laws on homicide (murder and manslaughter) which could be mapped for suicide. It would also mean that we could have congruence between the terminology used for killing oneself and killing others. If a person with a certain state of mind and set of circumstances can be held responsible for killing another, then that state of mind and set of circumstances should mean that there is no difference if the person they kill is themselves. So, it is claimed, if a drunk driver crashes a car and kills themselves and their passengers, we could refer to manslaughter of the passengers and self-manslaughter of the driver. However, I am not convinced this is a very helpful approach. The terms murder and manslaughter are used in criminal law to determine the correct level of blame that is attached to a defendant, and thereby the appropriate sentence they should receive. The definition of suicide seems to be seeking to do a different kind of thing: the blameworthiness of the suicidal person is not a key feature, as it is in homicide.

There is no ideal solution to determining the mental state required for suicide. As Morton Silverman[35] argues:

> it has long been recognized and debated that suicide intention is a multidimensional variable, characterized by different degrees of intensity/severity, and influenced by all possible aspects of human experiences (cultural, existential, spiritual, etc.). Reducing it to a dichotomic (yes/no) category may be pragmatic, but also a dangerous generalization, with potentially misleading implications, including the lowering of clinical attention and concern.

[34] Cholbi (n 5) 156.
[35] Silverman (n 2).

Lawyers, however, cannot get away with throwing their hands in the air and declaring it impossible to produce a definition. I suggest, therefore, that for legal purposes we define suicide as a case where a person intended to die, be that as an end in itself or as the means to another end. I accept that there will be cases which fall outside the definition that might be seen as appropriately classified as a suicide, but it is probably the best definition available as a general legal definition, without creating considerable complexity.

IV. Causation

It perhaps goes without saying that suicide requires someone to cause their own death. Clearly that requires a distinction between suicide ideation (someone contemplating committing suicide), attempted suicide (where a person puts their thoughts into action), and completed suicide. We might distinguish between preparatory acts, abandoned attempts, failed attempts, and interrupted attempts.[36] These are generally thought to be separable from self-harm where a person might injure themselves intentionally but without an intent to die. There may be links between the psychological motivations which lead to self-harm and suicide in some cases, but these should be kept separate because they often involve very different mental reasoning and raise separate issues.[37]

Assuming, however, that we have a death, there are still difficulties that can arise in determining whether a person has caused their own death. Of course, in some cases it is straightforward, such as a suicide by shooting. In others it is harder, as the following points demonstrate.

A. Ascertaining the Act

In some cases it may not be obvious that there is a particular act of the individual which leads to their death. Alcohol misuse, self-starvation or eating-disordered behaviour might lead to death, without there being a single incident that does so.[38] In such a case it seems sensible to take the approach the law takes to causation in criminal law generally: that we if we are clear that one of a series of A's acts caused a death, but we are not sure which one, we can still find that A caused the death.[39]

[36] K Posner et al, 'The Classification of Suicidal Behavior' in M Nock (ed), *The Oxford Handbook of Suicide and Self-Injury* (Oxford University Press, 2014).

[37] Silverman et al (n 6).

[38] J Hooley and S St Germain, 'Should We Expand the Conceptualization of Self-Injurious Behavior? Rationale, Review, and Recommendations' in Nock (n 36).

[39] J Muehlenkamp, 'Distinguishing between Suicidal and Nonsuicidal Self-Injury' in Nock (n 36).

B. The Involvement of a Third Party: Innocent Agents

Sometimes a suicidal person may seek to involve another in their act. Different scenarios may arise. Here we will discuss cases where a suicidal person manipulates or deceives another into killing them. For example, A tells B to give them a heavy dose of medicine, assuring them it is the normal, beneficial dose, but in fact it is a fatal one and A dies. That seems a case where A has used B to commit suicide. In traditional criminal law terminology B is an 'innocent agent' and is not responsible for their actions.[40] It is A who has caused B to so act. We would say a similar thing if B were a child or a person without mental capacity: they have become a tool for A to use. Such cases can be seen as homicide, rather than suicide.

C. Distinguishing Homicide and Assisting Suicide

In cases where a person has been involved in the death of another, they may have committed an offence of assisting suicide or of homicide. The distinction between these two crimes reflects the distinction drawn in criminal law between a person who is the 'principal' and the 'accessory'. The principal is the person who does the last free voluntary and informed act which is a significant cause of death. The accessory is someone who helps or encourages the principal to commit the crime. In a case where B asks Dr A to administer a fatal drug and Dr A does as requested, it will be Dr A's act which is the significant cause of death and so Dr A will be guilty of homicide, rather than assisted suicide. By contrast if B asks Dr A to give them some drugs, which B administers to themselves, then this will be a suicide: B was the principal (assuming B has capacity) and Dr A will be an accomplice. This approach seems to provide a relatively clear distinction, but it is worth highlighting two slightly trickier cases.

First, imagine B is paralysed and would like to take drugs themselves but cannot. They ask Dr A to administer them, and Dr A does so. At first sight this seems a straightforward case of homicide, with Dr A being the principal. However, some disabled activists have been keen to promote a role for personal assistants where the assistant's role is to enable the disabled person to do everything an able-bodied person can do.[41] Here, the personal assistant becomes 'a tool' for the disabled person to use, just as they might a prosthetic device, for example. Key to this model, the assistant is not meant to question or assess what they are asked to do; their role is allow the disabled person to do all that they could do without the impairment. There is clearly much to discuss about such a model but it might open

[40] P Alldridge, 'The Doctrine of Innocent Agency' (1990) 2 *Criminal Law Forum* 45.
[41] J Herring, 'The Disability Critique of Care' (2014) 8 *Elder Law Review* 2.

up an argument that Dr A is under a legal duty to comply with B's requests and should be treated as, in effect, an instrument for B to use, meaning that the case should be one of suicide, not homicide by Dr A.

Second, there may be cases where it is unclear if B is an 'actor'. For example, where A has abused their partner, B, causing them to commit suicide, is that a case of homicide or suicide? The case of *R v Wallace* is instructive.[42] Berlinah Wallace was charged with the murder of her ex-partner, Mark van Gongen, and applying him with a corrosive substance with intent (an offence under s 29 of the Offences against the Person Act 1861). She threw sulphuric acid on him, saying 'if I can't have you, no-one else will'. The acid attack caused awful injuries, leaving him disfigured, paralysed, and in constant pain. He travelled to Belgium, where euthanasia is permitted, and was given a lethal injection by doctors. The central issue for the Court of Appeal was whether the victim's decision to seek euthanasia or the act of the Belgian doctors in administering the lethal injection broke the chain of causation so that the defendant could not be said to have caused the victim's death. In other words was this a case of van Gongen committing suicide; or had Wallace caused his death; or had the Belgian doctors caused the suicide?

It was accepted that if the victim had simply died from his injuries, clearly Wallace would have caused the death. However, this was a case where the immediate cause of the death was not the injuries but the injection given by the doctors. Sharp LJ quoted one of the leading academic authorities on when an act will break the chain of causation:

> The free, deliberate and informed intervention of a second person, who intends to exploit the situation created by the first, but is not acting in concert with him, is normally held to relieve the first actor of criminal responsibility.[43]

The argument by the defence was that the Belgian doctors had performed a free, deliberate, and informed act, which had caused the victim's death. As a result, in this case the doctors caused the death. As they were acting in a way permitted by Belgian law, there was no offence committed.

Sharp LJ explained that the starting point in an analysis of causation was to decide whether there was 'but for' causation. In this case there clearly was: but for being disabled by the acid, the victim would not have sought euthanasia. There was no suggestion that prior to the attack the victim had been in any sense suicidal. She then went on to explore the closeness of the acts of the doctor and of the defendant. While accepting that there was a gap in time between them, the acts of the doctors were 'very closely, indeed inextricably, bound up with' the defendant's attack.[44] Further, it could not be said that the victim's decision to die was

[42] *R v Wallace* [2018] EWCA Crim 690.
[43] HLA Hart and T Honoré, *Causation in the Law* (Oxford University Press, 1985) 326.
[44] *R v Wallace* (n 42) para 60.

made with 'free and unfettered volition'.[45] The *novus actus interveniens* rule did not, therefore, apply and it could be said that the defendant's acid attack was a substantial and operating cause of death.

Sharp LJ thought it was also appropriate to consider whether the victim's response was reasonably foreseeable. She suggested that, if the jury decided that the throwing of the acid was a significant and operating cause of death, they should then ask themselves:

> Are you sure that at the time of the acid attack it was reasonably foreseeable that the defendant would commit suicide as a result of his injuries? In answering this question consider all the circumstances, including the nature of the attack, what the defendant did and said at the time *and* whether or not Mr van Dongen's decision to undergo voluntary euthanasia fell within the range of responses which might have been expected from a victim in his situation. If your answer is yes, your verdict on count 1 will be guilty. If your answer is no, your verdict on count 1 will be not guilty.[46]

The case was returned for a retrial. At the retrial Wallace was acquitted by the jury of murder or manslaughter. The jury is not required to give reasons and so we do not know why this was its conclusion. One might speculate that the jury determined that the suicide was not reasonably foreseeable on the facts of the case. Wallace was convicted for an offence under s 29 of the Offences against the Person Act (throwing corrosive fluid on a person, with intent to do grievous bodily harm) and given a life sentence for that.

This rather lengthy discussion shows the complexities that can surround causation in this area. Indeed, even with the Court of Appeal analysis there is some blurring whether the key test for causation is whether the defendant's act was a substantial and operating cause of the death, or whether the suicide was a reasonably foreseeable consequence of the defendant's act. Indeed, in the direction proposed by the Court of Appeal, it seems the jury should consider both questions. The problem is that it not difficult to imagine cases where the two questions would result in different answers.

D. Coerced Suicide

As the *Wallace* case, above, demonstrates, some suicides may be better classified as murder. These are suicides where a person is coerced to commit suicide. One case from the US involved Lori Drew, an adult neighbour of a 13-year-old girl, Megan Meier. Drew created a false MySpace account using the name of a boy, Josh Adams, to befriend the girl and then turn on her. He posted 'You are a bad person and everyone hates you' and other such messages. Megan Meier

[45] ibid, para 61.
[46] ibid, para 86.

hanged herself.[47] Drew was found to have violated the terms of use of MySpace but was not found guilty of any misdemeanour charge. Generally, such cases have not led to conviction in the US, even one where after a long campaign of abuse ended with the instruction to 'Drink bleach and die'.[48] However, more recently, the courts have shown a willingness to convict for involuntary manslaughter in such cases, particularly where there is a direct encouragement to suicide.[49]

English courts are much more open to prosecutions in such cases. First, there is the offence of assisting or encouraging suicide which can apply in such cases. Second, protection for freedom of speech is less strict in the UK than it is in the US, meaning that such cases are not seen as raising significant free speech issues. Third, as we have seen, if the act of the victim in committing suicide is not free, voluntary and informed, it is possible for the defendant to be charged with manslaughter. Certainly in cases of suicide following domestic abuse or bullying it becomes plausible to claim that the victim did not commit suicide in a free, voluntary and informed way, meaning that it is a case of homicide rather than suicide.

E. Acts and Omissions

A different issue is whether one can commit suicide by omission. Of course, suicide is usually associated with acts and there are relatively few omissions that would kill a person.[50] Perhaps the most common examples would be refusing life-saving medical treatment or refusing to eat or drink. We will put to one side the question of intent, and assume in these cases that the patient is refusing treatment as a result of a desire to die. The question is then whether a refusal of treatment, motivated by a desire to die, is suicide.

It may be argued, in the case of refusal of treatment, that the patient has been killed by the disease or condition, and not by the refusal to treat. A person who, for example, refuses cancer treatment and dies from the cancer would have the cancer recorded on the birth certificate. From such a perspective, the patient has allowed themselves to die, but that is different from actively killing oneself.

To some, these arguments miss the point. William E Tolhurst[51] argues that 'suicide is a matter of successfully implementing a course of action in order to bring about one's death'. On this view the method of suicide matters little – it is the intent

[47] *US v Drew*, Case No 2:08-cr-00582-GW (MD Ca) 28 August 2009.

[48] S Almasy et al, 'Sheriff: Taunting Post Leads to Arrests in Rebecca Sedwick Bullying Death' *CNN*, 16 October 2013, www.cnn.com/2013/10/15/justice/rebecca-sedwick-bullying-death-arrests/.

[49] ME Miller, 'Michelle Carter Can Face Manslaughter Charge for Allegedly Encouraging Boyfriend's Suicide, judge rules' *Washington Post*, 24 September 2015, www.washingtonpost.com/news/morning-mix/wp/2015/09/24/michelle-carter-can-face-manslaughter-charge-for-allegedly-encouraging-boyfriends-suicide-judge-rules/.

[50] Hill (n 21).5

[51] W Tolhurst, 'Suicide, Self-Sacrifice, and Coercion' (1983) 21 *The Southern Journal of Philosophy* 109.

to produce death which is key. Perhaps the point is best made by imaging a suicidal person who is trying to decide how to die: should they refuse treatment or take an excess of drugs? In such a case we might think that the method they happen to use to end their life is far less relevant than the fact that they wanted to die.

These kinds of arguments are familiar to those aware of the debates over the distinction between acts and omissions. The response of English law is to distinguish cases where there is a duty to act – where one is responsible for the outcome of the omission – and where there is no duty to act. Thus, a person who walks past a drowning child will face no criminal liability, unless they were employed as a lifeguard, or were the child's parent, in which case they would have a duty to act and be liable for that failure. That raises the potentially interesting question of whether a patient has a duty to receive treatment? The answer to that in English law seems to be a clear 'no', as there is a well-established right to refuse medical treatment or forced feeding. However, those rights only apply to those with capacity. There seems, therefore, good reason to determine that – at least in legal thought – killing oneself by failing to eat or consent to medical treatment is not suicide. This approach was taken by the European Court of Human Rights in *Jehovah's Witnesses of Moscow v Russia*,[52] where the court rejected an argument that a patient refusing a blood transfusion was tantamount to committing suicide. It was emphasised they were making a choice about medical procedures, not choosing death.

F. Near Death Cases

As already noted, some people suggest that the terminology of suicide is inappropriate in cases where a person is terminally ill and the question is more about selecting the time and manner of death, than a suicide.[53] That is certainly not, however, how homicide is normally treated. If X kills terminally ill P there is no debating whether X killed P on the basis that P was due to die soon. Such a case would still be homicide. Devlin J in *R v Adams* stated: 'a life shortened by weeks or months is just as much murder as one shortened by years …'. However, it might be noted that he speaks in terms of weeks. Some might read this as implying there may come a point where if the death is shortened by a few minutes then this will fall outside the law of murder, and so suicide. Indeed, that is one way of explaining why the people who jumped from the Twin Towers should not be seen as committing suicide.

A striking case is that involving Dr Michael Munro.[54] While it was not a case of suicide as such, it raises issues relevant to our discussion. Dr Munro was referred to the General Medical Council Fitness to Practise Panel. Two cases that he was overseeing involved ventilation being withdrawn from terminally ill premature

[52] *Jehovah's Witnesses of Moscow v Russia* Application No 302/02, (2011) 53 EHRR 4.

[53] American Association of Suicidology, *'Suicide' Is Not The Same As 'Physician Aid In Dying'* (AAS, 2017).

[54] J Goodman, 'The Case of Dr Munro: Are There Lessons to be Learnt?' (2010) 18 *Medical Law Review* 564.

babies. There was no complaint about this decision. As is common in such cases, the parents were present at the withdrawal of ventilation and were handed the baby to hold when ventilation was withdrawn. Unusually, in both cases following the ventilation withdrawal the babies commenced agonal gasping, which severely distressed the parents. Dr Munro administered pancuronium, which stopped the gasping but hastened death. The evidence suggested that without the pancuronium the gasping might have continued for several hours.

It might be argued that such a case was homicide. However, it is striking that neither set of parents complained about the doctor's conduct. The Procurator Fiscal determined that no criminal proceedings should be brought. The GMC imposed no sanction and confirmed Dr Munro's fitness to practise. The sympathetic reaction to this case may be based on the fact that the babies were due to die very soon and the remaining minutes or hours of their life were likely to be distressing to others, especially the parents, and possibly also to the babies themselves. This might raise questions where a person facing imminent death seeks an intervention which will shorten the life by a very short period of time.

Despite these points, I suggest that it is best to keep cases where an intervention shortens life as potential suicides or homicides. There is no clear line that can be drawn as to when the death is so imminent that it falls outside this category. These are better accepted as cases of suicide (or homicide) but as cases where the suicide (or homicide) is justifiable.

V. Conclusion

As this discussion has shown, producing a definition of suicide is not easy. There are practical problems, in that the person committing suicide is not able to explain their actions, and there are theoretical difficulties in distinguishing suicide from accidental death or homicide. The sad truth is that in many suicide cases there are confused, contradictory, muddled and complex explanations, which lawyers and others seek to place into categories. That is needed for legal classification, but it should never be supposed that it is a definitive statement about a person's state of mind. For the purposes of this book, the simplest definition seems the most appropriate. Suicide is the intentional killing of the self. Intention is to be understood as including cases where the death was the chosen means to achieve a different end and cases where a person kills themselves knowing they will die, unless they are seeking to avoid death. In terms of causation it requires proof that the person's acts were a significant cause of their death.

3

The Causes of Suicide

I. Introduction

In this chapter we explore the causes of suicide. It is rare for there to be a single cause of suicide. Indeed, in many cases there is considerable mystery surrounding the events that led to death. Claims that 'a cause' of suicide can be identified are rightly treated with considerable suspicion. To identify a single cause in a particular case is almost inevitably to involve a simplification. To seek a cause for all suicides is folly indeed. As Edwin Shneidman, a leading figure in suicide studies, has written:

> [s]uicide is not a disease. It is not like a stomach-ache or a headache or some special physiological state. Each suicide is sui generis. Its reasons, like the mind itself, cannot be categorized. Clinical labels are specious, and to build a profession on them is to put a skyscraper on sandy soil.[1]

That does not mean we should abandon the quest to find the factors linked to suicide and, in so far as we can, understand the different strands that wove together to create the desire for death.

This chapter starts by providing an overview of some of the statistics in relation to suicide. These can indicate at a large-scale level what factors appear to be correlated with suicide. It will then consider the attempts by psychologists and others to identify what causes a person to commit suicide. The primary focus of this chapter will be on what might be called 'individual' causes, those resting in the person themselves. In Chapter 4 we will look at the social and societal factors influencing suicide.

Right at the start it is important to acknowledge the danger of using statistics, particularly in the context of suicide, ie in assuming that a correlation is a cause. Headlines can make dramatic reading. Take, for example: 'Suicide-related internet use was found in 26% of deaths in under 20s'.[2] An uninformed reader may take from this that reading suicide-themed material on the internet causes death. However, that would be an error. We cannot conclude from the statistic that viewing suicide-related material causes suicide, any more than we can conclude

[1] Quoted in S Stefan, *Rational Suicide, Irrational Laws* (Oxford University Press, 2016) 320.
[2] The Samaritans, *Suicide Statistics Report* (The Samaritans, 2019).

from the fact most people who commit suicide own a mobile phone, that having a mobile causes suicide. Of course, such statistics could be a piece of evidence to suggest a causal link, but such causal links are notoriously difficult to establish and we would certainly need more information than that given in the headline. As the Patient Safety Group[3] reports notes 'Our understanding of which factors differentiate those who will have thoughts of suicide from those who will act upon those thoughts and attempt suicide is still elementary'. But that is not the only challenge in gathering suicides statistics. Before exploring the numbers, we will look at these difficulties in more detail.

II. The Problems with Gathering Suicide Statistics

The difficulties in obtaining accurate statistics on numbers of suicides are considerable. As seen in Chapter 2, the definition of suicide is much debated and without a clear definition it is difficult to obtain comparative data. Many definitions depend on factors which are difficult to prove, such as whether the individual was intending to commit suicide. There may also be questions as to the burden of proof to be satisfied before a death is recorded as a suicide. Should we record cases where it is shown beyond doubt that there was a suicide? Or shown on the balance of probabilities? Or is a serious possibility that the death was suicide sufficient? In part that answer depends on the purposes for which the data is collected and the attitudes towards suicide held by different parties. We might, for example, view a finding of suicide as producing a stigma which survivors will find hard to cope with, and so we should only record a suicide where on a tight definition it is proved beyond all reasonable doubt. Alternatively, we might want to record suicides so that such cases can be investigated to explore whether there are lessons to be learned in suicide prevention. From that perspective, if our aim is to find the causes of death and identify ways of preventing deaths, it matters less if the prevented deaths are suicide or accidents.

The more practical difficulty facing researchers is simply finding a source of statistics. In England and Wales a major source is findings of suicide by coroners at an inquest.[4] There are several problems in relying on these. First, the inquests can take months or even years and so finding the statistics for a particular year is not straightforward. For example, only 51 per cent of suicide deaths registered in 2019 actually occurred in that same year. The Office for National Statistics therefore records deaths *registered* in a particular year, rather than those occurring during that year. That is understandable, but it makes it harder to examine reasons for variation between the rates in particular years.

[3] Patient Safety Group, *Self-harm and Suicide in Adults* (Royal College of Psychiatrists, 2020).
[4] Office for National Statistics, *Suicide in England and Wales 2019* (ONS, 2020).

Second, there can be some strong incentives on coroners to deny that a death was suicide, particularly where that verdict is opposed by grieving friends and relatives. As mentioned in Chapter 1, in *R (Maughan) v Her Majesty's Senior Coroner for Oxfordshire*[5] the Supreme Court overturned a longstanding rule that a suicide verdict should only be returned if established beyond reasonable doubt. Rather, it would be sufficient if that was shown on the balance of probabilities. Lady Arden specifically raised the point about statistics:

> The reasons for suicide are often complex. It is important not to adopt a stereotypical attitude here as elsewhere. Society needs to understand the causes and to try and prevent suicides occurring. Statistics are the means whereby this can be done. If a criminal burden of proof is required, suicide is likely to be under-recorded. This is especially worrying in the case of state-related deaths. If there is an open verdict because the criminal standard of proof cannot be achieved, the circumstances of the case have to be analysed before it can be included in any statistics to show the true number of suicides. There is a considerable public interest in accurate suicide statistics as they may reveal a need for social and medical care in areas not previously regarded as significant. Each suicide determination can help others by revealing how suicide risks may be managed in future. I accept that to some extent policy makers and researchers can seek to mitigate the under-recording of cases by examining cases of open conclusions but they may not be able to do so accurately and lowering the standard of proof would be a more satisfactory way of getting accurate figures.[6]

This ruling will increase the number of suicides recorded and produce a more accurate finding, but that will make it harder to compare statistics before and after the ruling.

Third, there may be pressure on relatives and others to disguise suicides. In some countries, including England and Wales assisting suicide is unlawful and this may discourage openness about the circumstances of the death. In cases where a person has life insurance, that can be forfeited in a case of suicide and so again there is an incentive to disguise it.[7]

Fourth, as already mentioned, in many cases it is difficult to know whether a death is accidental or a suicide. A car drives into a tree at high speed or a person falls from a high cliff: these could be suicide or accident. This is all the more so if there are personal, legal, social or cultural factors encouraging a finding of accidental death rather than suicide. In part this is reflected in the fact that coroners' courts are increasingly using narrative verdicts, where the story of the death is told, rather than a single headline finding, making it harder for statisticians to know when to record to a suicide. These factors all mean that there is very probably significant under-reporting of suicide in England and Wales.

[5] *R (Maughan) v Her Majesty's Senior Coroner for Oxfordshire* [2020] UKSC 46.

[6] ibid, para 74.

[7] I Tøllefsen et al, 'The Reliability of Suicide Statistics: A Systematic Review' (2012) 12 *BMC Psychiatry* 9.

While everyone accepts that the current statistics are flawed, there is disagreement on whether they are of any use. As the Samaritans acknowledge:

> Researchers have different views about the reliability of suicide statistics and how, or even if, they can be used effectively. Some reject the use of official suicide statistics on the grounds of poor reliability; others argue that the statistics are still reliable enough to be used to establish trends over time.[8]

The point here is that even though the coroners' statistics may be under-reporting the numbers, they are still useful in establishing general increases or decreases. They may also provide indications of which groups are at risk of committing suicide. However, both of these points depend on whether the cases found as being suicides by coroners are a representative sample of all suicides. It may be, for example, that coroners are particularly reluctant to find that children have committed suicide because of the impact on the parents, or that particular forms of suicide – such as those in public places – are more reported to coroners than other suicides. These factors might mean that there is a distorted representation of suicide if one looks just at the cases considered by coroners. That said, it might be noted that any form of recording suicides is going to be problematic and open to arguments about under- or over-inclusion. However flawed, the official coroner statistics are probably better than any other source for high level statistics. Certainly, there is no alternative source which offers a more reliable set of statistics.

We can now consider some of the statistics on suicide rates, bearing in mind the limitations just discussed.

III. International Statistics

The leading source of statistics worldwide is the World Health Organization. Its report included the following eye-catching findings.[9] Suicide is a serious global public health issue. It is among the top twenty leading causes of death worldwide, with more deaths due to suicide than to malaria, breast cancer, or war and homicide. Close to 800,000 people die by suicide every year. World-wide, 10.5 people per 100,000 people killed themselves in 2016, although there is considerable national variance for that statistic (between 5 and 30). There is a notable gender difference, with the standardised suicide rate being 13.7 for males and 7.5 for females. WHO explains 'Globally, the age-standardized suicide rate was 1.8 times higher in males than in females … It is in high income countries where the gendered distinction is particularly notable (rising to three times as many men as women)'. Some 52.1 per cent of global suicides occur before the person has reached the age of 45. Suicide was the second leading cause of death for

[8] The Samaritans, *Suicide Statistics Report* (The Samaritans, 2019).
[9] World Health Organization, *Suicide: Global Health Estimates* (WHO, 2019).

those aged 15–29.[10] The age-standardised mortality rate for suicide decreased by 32.7 per cent worldwide between 1990 and 2016, from 16.6 deaths (15.2 to 17.6) per 100,000 in 1990 to 11.2 deaths (10.4 to 12.1) per 100,000 in 2016.[11]

Across the EU[12] 56,000 people died as a result of intentional self-harm in 2017, corresponding to 1.1 per cent of all deaths reported that year. Almost 8 in 10 of these suicides (77 per cent) were men. On average, there were almost 11 deaths from suicide per 100,000 inhabitants.

IV. Statistics for England and Wales

The Office for National Statistics is the leading source of statistics in the UK. Its study in 2020[13] found the following for England and Wales:

- in 2019, there were 5,691 suicides registered in England and Wales, an age-standardised rate of 11.0 deaths per 100,000 population;
- around three-quarters of registered deaths (4,303 deaths) in 2019 were among men, which follows a consistent trend back to the mid-1990s;
- the England and Wales male suicide rate of 16.9 deaths per 100,000 is the highest since 2000 and remains in line with the rate in 2018; for females, the rate was 5.3 deaths per 100,000, consistent with 2018 and the highest since 2004;
- males aged 45–49 years had the highest age-specific suicide rate (25.5 deaths per 100,000 males); for females, the age group with the highest rate was 50–54 years at 7.4 deaths per 100,000;
- despite having a low number of deaths overall, rates among the under 25s have generally increased in recent years, particularly 10- to 24-year-old females where the rate has increased significantly since 2012 to its highest level, with 3.1 deaths per 100,000 females in 2019;
- as seen in previous years, the most common method of suicide in England and Wales was hanging, accounting for 61.7 per cent of all suicides among males and 46.7 per cent of all suicides among females.

All of these were based on the figures of deaths registered as suicide. It is worth highlighting a few points about these 'headline statistics'.

First, when suicide and assisted suicide are discussed in the media typically this is presented as an issue of old people being kept alive longer than they wish or a patient suffering with a terrible medical condition. However, the statistics show

[10] After road accidents and before interpersonal violence, though among men interpersonal violence was the second most common cause.

[11] M Maghavi, 'Global, Regional, and National Burden of Suicide Mortality 1990 to 2016: Systematic Analysis for the Global Burden of Disease Study 2016' (2019) 364 *British Medical Journal* 194.

[12] Eurostat, *Just over 56 000 Persons in the EU Committed Suicide* (European Commission, 2019).

[13] Office for National Statistics, *Suicide in England and Wales 2019* (ONS, 2020).

that it is middle-aged men who are the largest category of suicides. Indeed in 2019 the male age group with the highest suicide rate (25.5 per 100,000) was those aged 45–49; and for women those aged 50–54 (7.4 deaths per 100,000).[14] There has been a growing number of deaths in the 10–24 age group, with the 2019 figure for men being 8.2 per 100,000, some 442 suicides and for women 3.1 (159 deaths). For men over 75 the figure is 13.9 per 100,000. Looking specifically at students, there were 4.7 deaths per 100,000 students, some 95 students in England and Wales.[15] This indicates that suicide among the elderly is, in fact, comparatively rare.

Second, the gender dimension is striking. Men account for around three-quarters of all suicide deaths registered in 2019, some 16.9 deaths per 100,000 men. For women the figure is 5.3 per 100,000.[16] Similar findings come from the EU statistics, where around 77 per cent of suicides were found to be men.[17]

Third, it is notable that only 28 per cent of suicides in the UK were of people receiving mental health care, questioning the assumed strong link between suicide and mental illness.[18] We will be returning to this point later.[19]

Statistics on attempted suicide can be even harder to obtain than statistics on suicide because – other than the potential suicide – no one else may ever become aware of a suicide attempt. One source of statistics is to ask people whether they have ever attempted suicide. There is evidence that the attempted suicide rate is 10–15 times more frequent that suicide.[20] In a disturbing study of over 10,000 17-year-olds in the UK, Patalay and Fitzsimons found that 7.4 per cent stated that they had attempted suicide, with 24.1 per cent reporting self-harm.[21] An international assessment calculated that, on average, 2.7 per cent of the world's population will attempt suicide at some point, with 9.2 per cent have suicide ideation.[22]

Sometimes statistics on suicide are linked with self-harm. This is probably unhelpful. Many people who harm themselves are not seeking to commit suicide. It is often a response to feelings of distress and is an attempt to alleviate them. However, there is certainly a correlation between self-harming behaviour and going on to commit suicide. Over half of those who commit suicide had

[14] ONS (n 13).

[15] G Iacobucci, 'Suicide Rates Continue to Rise in England and Wales' (2021) 370 *British Medical Journal* 3431.

[16] ONS (n 13).

[17] A Freeman et al, 'A Cross-National Study on Gender Differences in Suicide Intent' (2017) 17 *BMC Psychiatry* 234.

[18] University of Manchester, *The National Confidential Inquiry into Suicide and Safety in Mental Health*. (University of Manchester, 2019).

[19] Patient Safety Group (n 3).

[20] A Schmidtke et al, 'Attempted Suicide in Europe: Rates, Trends and Sociodemographic Characteristics of Suicide Attempters During the Period 1989–1992. Results of the WHO/EURO Multicentre Study on Parasuicide' (1996) 93 *Acta Psychiatrica Scandinavica* 327.

[21] P Patalay and E Fitzsimons, 'Psychological Distress, Self-Harm and Attempted Suicide in UK 17 Year Olds' (2021) 13 *British Journal of Psychiatry* 1.

[22] World Health Organisation, *Suicide* (WHO, 2021).

previously harmed themselves. Indeed, it seems that the risk of suicide is elevated by between 30 and 100 fold in the year after an incident of self-harm, compared with the general population.[23] One in 50 people who attend hospital as a result of self-harm will die by suicide within a year, and one in 15 within nine years.[24] Arensman, Griffin and Corcoran[25] have claimed that 'Engaging in self-harm is the strongest predictor of future suicidal behavior, both nonfatal and fatal'. That said, it must be emphasised that most of those who self-harm do not go on to commit suicide, and plenty of people who do commit suicide have no history of self-harm.[26] Much seems to turn on the extent to which the self-harm is an attempt at suicide, rather than a way of alleviating unwanted feelings.[27] Hence, those who self-harm through gunshot, hanging or asphyxiation, have higher rates of suicide than those who cut.[28]

In the UK, 6.4 per cent of respondents aged 16–74 in a 2014 survey reported that they had self-harmed.[29] However, the figures were much higher among younger people: 25.7 per cent of women aged 16–24 reported having self-harmed at some point, and about 9.7 per cent of men. A more recent survey found 24.1 per cent of 17-year-olds reporting self-harm in the previous 12 months.[30] Women's self-harm was mostly in the form of cutting. Clements et al[31] estimate that there are more than 200,000 hospital attendances following self-harm in England every year. However, few self-harmers seek medical attention and so it is hard to get a definitive picture.[32]

When thinking about self-harm, it is easy to forget that some self-harming behaviour is normalised. For example, 16.6 per cent of the adult population drink alcohol at 'hazardous levels' and a further 1.9 per cent at harmful levels;[33] 14.1 per cent of the adult population in the UK smoke;[34] 28.0 per cent of adults in England are obese and a further 36.2 per cent are overweight but not obese.[35]

[23] M Chan et al, 'Predicting Suicide Following Self-Harm: Systematic Review of Risk Factors and Risk Scales' (2016) 209 *British Journal of Psychiatry* 277.

[24] Office of National Statistics, *Adult Psychiatric Morbidity Survey: Survey of Mental Health and Wellbeing, England, 2014* (Office of National Statistics, 2016).

[25] E Arensman et al, 'Self-Harm: Extent of the Problem and Prediction of Repetition' in R O'Connor and J Pirkis (eds), *The International Handbook of Suicide Prevention* (John Wiley & Sons, 2016).

[26] Chan et al (n 23).

[27] S McManus et al, 'Prevalence of Non-Suicidal Self-Harm and Service Contact in England, 2000–14: Repeated Cross-Sectional Surveys of the General Population' (2019) 6 *Lancet Psychiatry* 573.

[28] C Haw et al, 'Suicidal Intent and Method of Self-Harm: A Large-Scale Study of Self-Harm Patients Presenting to a General Hospital' (2015) 45 *Suicide and Life-Threatening Behaviour* 732.

[29] ONS (n 24).

[30] Patalay and Fitzsimons (n 21).

[31] C Clements et al, 'Rates of Self-Harm Presenting to General Hospitals: A Comparison of Data from the Multicentre Study of Self-Harm in England and Hospital Episode Statistics' (2016) 6 *British Medical Journal* 9749.

[32] ibid.

[33] C Drummond et al, *Alcohol Dependence* (Health and Social Care Information Centre, 2014).

[34] Office for National Statistics, *Adult Smoking Habits in the UK 2019* (ONS, 2021).

[35] NHS, *Health Survey for England 2019* (NHS, 2000).

Whether a particular behaviour becomes classified as self-harm or not can depend on its social acceptability.

V. Suicidal Feelings

If it is difficult to find an accurate number of suicide attempts, it is even harder to locate statistics on suicidal feelings. Inevitably these depend on surveys of the population and people's self-reporting. Studies suggest that 20.6 per cent of the population of England have had suicidal thoughts at some point;[36] 5.4 per cent had in the previous year.[37] That differs significantly by gender, with 34.6 per cent of women and 19.3 per cent of men reporting suicidal feelings. It also varies by age, with 26.8 per cent of those aged 16–24 reporting suicidal feelings in their lifetime. What we cannot know, of course, is whether this reflects greater openness by women and younger people about talking about their experiences or whether it reflects genuine differences.

Ethnic background plays a role in rates of suicidal feelings. One British survey found that 21.6 per cent of white people reported having suicidal feelings, 20.7 per cent of Black British, and 13 per cent of those with Asian ethnicity.[38] Poverty and social exclusion are strongly linked to suicidal feelings, with 66.4 per cent of those in England receiving employment and support allowance experiencing suicidal feelings.[39] Another group with high rates of suicidal thought were students, with 42.2 per cent of UK students contemplating suicide at least once within the previous 12 months.[40] These kinds of statistics indicate the widespread nature of suicidal thoughts.

VI. Forms of Suicide

In England and Wales the most common methods of suicide were hanging, strangulation and suffocation, which are treated as one group of methods in the official statistics. Together they account for 61.7 per cent of all suicide attempts in 2019.[41] The second most common form of suicide was poisoning, accounting for 16 per cent of suicides for men. The National Confidential Inquiry into Suicide and Safety in Mental Health[42] found in relation to poisoning the main substances taken were

[36] Mental Health First Aid, *Statistics* (Mental Health First Aid, 2021).

[37] S McManus et al, *Suicidal Thoughts, Suicide Attempts, and Self-Harm* (NHS Digital, 2016).

[38] Office of National Statistics, *Self Harm and Suicidal Thoughts and Attempts* (ONS, 2017).

[39] McManus et al (n 37).

[40] U Akrama et al, 'Prevalence and Psychiatric Correlates of Suicidal Ideation in UK University Students' (2020) 272 *Journal of Affective Disorders* 191.

[41] ONS (n 4).

[42] *The National Confidential Inquiry into Suicide and Safety in Mental Health* (n 18).

opiates/opioids and, where it was known, the source was by prescription. Around 200 deaths a year result from jumping from a height or in front of a vehicle.

It is also generally found that there is a link between certain occupations and suicide.[43] Groups that have been seen as at particularly high risk are farmers, doctors, nurses, dentists, veterinarians, pharmacists, the military, seafarers and artists.[44] The normal explanation is that these jobs have the most ready access to the means of committing suicide.

VII. Seeking to Identify the Causes of Suicide

There has been significant research which seeks to give some insight into what factors might cause suicide. This research falls into three primary categories.

First, there are studies which seek to identify characteristics among those who have committed suicide. Of course, as already mentioned, the fact that a particular factor is prevalent at the time of suicide does not prove causation. Therefore, while it can be helpful to understand which factors are statistically linked to suicide, great care must be taken in explaining the relationship.

Second, there is evidence from those who have unsuccessfully attempted to commit suicide as to what motivated them. This might give greater insights into what leads people to commit suicide. However, such research also must be treated with caution: it may be that those who *survive* suicide are not representative of all those who *commit* suicide. Further, it may well be that people are not good at understanding their own reasons for their actions.[45]

Third, 'suicide autopsies' involve collecting information about a suicide from clinical and personal sources, such as medical records and interviews with family and friends, in an attempt to determine the cause of the suicide.[46] Of course, these rely on the causes being made manifest to others and carry the danger of retrospective assessment.

Notably, none of these sources can provide anything close to a definitive declaration about the cause of suicide. Nevertheless, it is notable that there seems to be a deep need to 'explain' a suicide. Perhaps that represents the assumption that suicide is illogical or bizarre. People go to extraordinary lengths to remain alive and we struggle, therefore, to understand why death is desired. Also, in many cases there is a concern by family members or friends that they were in some way to blame for a suicide or could have prevented it. Finding a cause which is outside their control might offer some reassurance. Most importantly, the desire to find a

[43] S Roberts et al, 'High-Risk Occupations for Suicide' (2013) 43 *Psychological Medicine* 1231.

[44] ibid.

[45] J Bantjes and L Swartz, 'What Can We Learn From First-Person Narratives? The Case of Nonfatal Suicidal Behavior' (2019) 29 *Qualitative Health Research* 1497.

[46] N Kapur and R Goldney, 'What Causes Suicidal Behaviour?' in N Kapur and R Goldney (eds), *Suicide Prevention* (Oxford University Press, 2019).

cause of suicide reflects a desire to reduce the rate of suicide. The better we understand what causes suicide, the more likely it is that we can put in place steps to reduce its occurrence.

It is important too to distinguish suicide ideation (serious contemplation of the idea of committing suicide) from planning or committing suicide. A 2017 US Government Report[47] estimated that only a third of those with suicide ideation develop a suicide plan, and of those only a third go on to make an actual attempt. As the report suggests, it seems that the risk factors for suicide ideation, suicide attempts and suicide deaths differ. For example, being a woman and having a recognised mood disorder are associated with suicide ideation, but when it comes to suicide deaths being male is more highly associated and mood disorders seem less statistically linked.[48]

There are multiple theories as to why people commit suicide. I will provide a brief overview of these, before focusing on some of the key ones. Common explanations for suicide include the following:

(1) biological theories: these typically see the causes of suicide as being the combination of genetic predispositions and external stressing events;
(2) sociological theories: these typically see the explanation of suicide as lying with society. They might seek to explain suicide in terms of a product of social forces and inequalities oppressing or isolating an individual;
(3) psychodynamic theories: these seek to find psychological explanations for behaviour. Popular ones include:
    (a) hopelessness theory: these theories see suicide as primarily motivated by a feeling that things will not and cannot improve from the current position;
    (b) psychache theory: the word psychache refers to a intense psychological pain, which is so great that suicide is seen as the only reasonable way to end the pain;
    (c) escape theory: this theory sees suicide as an escape from a state of affairs, where a person feels trapped in a bad situation and cannot see any way out of it;[49]
    (d) emotion dysregulation theory: this theory focuses on negative emotions, often produced by critical environments. Suicide is seen as a way to end the unpleasant emotion.
    (e) interpersonal-psychological theory: this sees suicide as involving the interaction between 'thwarted belongingness' (a sense of a lack of connection with others) 'perceived burdensomeness' (thoughts that one is a burden on others) and 'the acquired capacity to enact lethal pain', which results from repeated interaction with painful life events, reducing a fear of death or pain.[50]

[47] Centre for Disease Control and Prevention, *National Survey of Drug Use and Mental Health* (CDC, 2017).

[48] US Department of Health and Human Services, Office of the Surgeon General, & National Action Alliance for Suicide Prevention, *Suicide* (DHHS, 2012).

[49] E Selby et al, 'Comprehensive Theories of Suicidal Behaviors' in M Nock (ed), *The Oxford Handbook of Suicide and Self-Injury* (Oxford University Press, 2014).

[50] T Joiner, *Why People Die by Suicide* (Harvard University, 2005).

It is not possible in this chapter to give a complete analysis of the theories of the causes of suicide. Rather, the aim is to highlight the complex range of factors that are referred to in debates in suicidology. We will now explore in a little more detail some of the primary theories that have been developed around suicide.

VIII. Biological Theories

Most biological theories explain that there is a genetic risk component to suicide (a diathesis) which is aggravated by stressing events and leads to suicidal behaviours. Few people, if any, claim that it is the genetic component alone which causes suicide. Indeed, it has been hard to identify precisely what the genetic component is. Rather it is the combination of the genetic component with other factors. In biological terms, these other factors include dysregulation of the serotonergic system[51] or of the ventromedial prefrontal cortex.[52]

Supporters of the biological approach highlight studies which show there is a statistical link between these biological factors. A 1980s study by Egeland and Sussex[53] of Old Order Amish, an isolated religious community in Pennsylvania USA, found that there had been 26 suicides within the community in the past 100 years, but all within four families. This strongly implied a genetic component to suicide. Twin studies have also claimed to have shown a genetic link, with high suicide rates for twins even when they have been brought up in very different environments.[54] However, it is generally agreed that any genetic factors need to be combined with some external stressor event, because it is clear that not everyone with a particular set of biological factors commits suicide.[55] If, for example, we take serotonin dysfunction, which is commonly cited as linked to suicidal behaviour, the evidence suggests that only 2–6 per cent of those with abnormal serotonin levels will commit suicide.[56] This indicates that while there may be some link with biological factors (those percentages are certainly higher than those with normal serotonin levels), there are other much more significant factors at play.[57] That said, there is much more research to be done[58] and it

[51] These cause serotonin levels to differ from the norm.

[52] J Mann, 'Neurobiology of Suicidal Behaviour' (2003) 4 *Nature Reviews Neuroscience* 828.

[53] J Egeland and J Sussex, 'Suicide and Family Loading for Affective Disorders' (1985) 254 *Journal of the American Medical Association* 915.

[54] A Glowinski et al, 'Suicide Attempts in an Adolescent Female Twin Sample' (2001) 40 *Journal of the American Academy of Child and Adolescent Psychiatry* 1300; A von Borczyskowski et al, 'Suicidal Behaviour in National and International Adult Adoptees: A Swedish Cohort Study' (2006) 41 *Social Psychiatry and Psychiatric Epidemiology* 95.

[55] E Mościcki, 'Suicidal Behaviors among Adults' in Nock (n 49).

[56] J Bostwick and V Pankratz, 'Affective Disorders and Suicide Risk: A Reexamination' (2000) 157 *American Journal of Psychiatry* 1925.

[57] Selby et al (n 49).

[58] M Michaels et al, 'Suicide' in R DeRubeis and D Strunk (eds), *The Oxford Handbook of Mood Disorders* (Oxford University Press, 2018).

would certainly be wrong to determine that these biological factors play no part in suicide.[59]

IX. Sociological Theories

We shall be exploring in more detail in Chapter 4 the sociological understandings of suicide. A summary will be provided here. A primary source for these theories is Emile Durkheim's book, *Le Suicide*.[60] In it, he sees two societal forces that influence suicide: social integration and moral regulation. Social integration refers to the extent to which a person is connected with society as a whole, whether they feel a member of the wider community. Moral integration involves the extent to which society controls people's beliefs and behaviour through the law and social pressures.

Durkheim suggests that there are four types of suicide, reflecting the extremes of the ends of social integration and moral regulation:

(1) egotistic: this is where an individual has a deficiency of social integration. They do not feel relationships with others or their community. They may feel lonely or excluded by society and have little to contribute to their community;
(2) altruistic: this is where an individual has an excess of integration. They are fully committed to the wellbeing of their society. Suicide, for them, is appropriate if their death will promote the greater good of society. This might be a suicide bomber, or an older person who feels they are a burden to others;
(3) anomic: this is caused by a deficiency in moral regulation. This is taken to mean that society has failed to give the individual a sense of self-value or meaning for their life. The person cannot find or achieve goals. Durkheim suggested that this may be particularly common in time of poverty, where a person lacks any economic goal;
(4) fatalistic: this arises at the other end of the moral regulation spectrum where society is oppressive in imposing its standards on someone, and a person is overwhelmed by societal intervention. A prisoner who commits suicide rather than suffer an overbearing regime may be an example.

What is notable about the sociological approach is that it identifies explanations for suicide that are to be found, at least partly, outside the individual. Critics will argue that these external forces cannot be the sole explanation for suicide. For example, not all prisoners, nor those who are excluded by society, commit suicide. Clearly something is at play, in addition to these social factors play, it is

[59] L Fiori et al, 'Genetic and Neurobiological Approaches to Understanding Suicidal Behaviors' in Nock (n 49).

[60] E Durkheim, *Suicide: A Study in Sociology* (Free Press, 1951 [1897]).

claimed. But, as we have seen, the same can be said of the individual features: not all those with mental illness attempt suicide. Durkheim's approach can be seen as an attempt to marry to the societal and individual factors as explanations.

There can be links, too, between the sociological perspectives and the psychological perspectives. Loneliness is strongly linked to purposelessness in life,[61] which psychologists often refer to as linked to suicidal feelings. As we have seen, there are links between suicide ideation and those who are less integrated into society. It is, therefore, not surprising that notably higher rates are found among those who not married or in stable relationships than those who are. Perhaps surprisingly, there seems to be no difference between those who are separated/divorced or widowed and those who have never partnered,[62] although the time of relationship breakdown itself seems connected to suicide.[63]

It is worth noting that, in terms of suicide prevention, removing the sociological factors linked with suicide may be easier than identifying the biological factors. For example, there is a well-established link between firearm ownership and rates of suicide.[64] Restricting access to guns is far more achievable than, for example, reducing rates of depression.[65]

One concern with the sociological theories, which can apply also to the biological factors, is that they remove agency from the suicidal person. If suicide is seen as the result of inequalities in society or genetic factors, this deprives the individual of agency and respect for the decision they have made.[66]

With that last point in mind, it is worth highlighting another sociological perspective which sees suicide as a form of communication.[67] Suicide is a statement to society or those in relationship with the individual. This may be seen as a contrast to psychological theories, which see suicide as an attempt to resolve conflicts within the individual. Knizek and Hjelmeland[68] suggest that these the communications can be of various types, including: 'assertive', which are designed to convince the listener of their intent – eg this situation really is unbearable for me; 'expressive', which express a psychological condition – eg 'I love you too much and cannot bear to lose you'; and 'directives', which seek to influence behaviour, such as 'Don't leave me. If you do, I will kill myself'.

[61] K Cukrowicz and E Poindexter, 'Suicide' in C Richards and W O'Hara (eds), *The Oxford Handbook of Depression and Comorbidity* (Oxford University Press, 2014).

[62] Mościcki (n 55).

[63] R Evans et al, 'Gender, Relationship Breakdown and Suicide Risk: A Systematic Review of Research in Western Countries' (2016) 46 *Journal of Family Issues* 2239.

[64] Mościcki (n 55).

[65] S Abrutyn and A Mueller, 'Toward a Cultural-Structural Theory of Suicide: Examining Excessive Regulation and Its Discontents' (2018) 36 *Sociological Theory* 48.

[66] K Jaworski, 'Towards Ethics of Wonder and Generosity in Critical Suicidology' (2020) 34 *Social Epistemology* 589.

[67] B Knizek and H Hjelmeland, 'A Theoretical Model for Interpreting Suicidal Behaviour as Communication' (2007) 17 *Theory & Psychology* 679.

[68] ibid.

X. Psychological Theories of Suicide

Psychological theories seek the explanation of suicide in terms of people's management of internal conflicts. These often involve intense feelings of self-blame or pain which overwhelm the person.[69] Goldblatt[70] explains that 'a variety of intense, unpleasant affect states have been identified that are suicide inviting, including feelings of abandonment, self-hatred, rage, and anguish of intense degree'. He suggests that fantasies play a common role in suicide, stating 'Common fantasies about suicide include death as a means for rebirth; death as reunion; death as revenge, self-punishment, or atonement; death as escape; and death as assassination'. I will explain in a little more detail two of the most prominent theories.

A. Escape Theory of Suicidal Behaviour

Baumeister[71] developed this approach, which sees suicide as a form of escape from the problems of life. The significance of this perspective is that suicide (or death) is not seen in itself as having any gain but is simply a way of getting away from the problem. This is, then, in opposition to those theories which seek to see suicide in a slightly more positive light: as a new beginning, a resolution of a conflict, rather than an entirely destructive act.[72] For Baumeister, suicide is all about stopping unpleasant experiences. He suggests that suicide is often caused by a person's current circumstances falling short of their ideas for their life. That may be due to unrealistic expectations about life or an unlucky combination of events. The greater the discrepancy between the expectations for life and reality, the greater the likelihood of a suicide attempt. This is especially so where it leads to 'cognitive deconstruction' and a person loses faith in achieving their goals. This feeling, that hopes will never be achieved, causes a breaking down of the defences that keep feelings such as hopelessness, self-hatred and anxiety in check. To some it is better to understand this as a desire to escape from pain,[73] which can only be achieved by death.

B. Hopelessness Theory of Suicide

For Beck et al[74] the key factor in suicide is the perception of the unchangeable nature of one's dire position. It is the lack of power to change and gloom about

[69] A Brevard et al, 'Comparison of Suicide Notes Written by Suicide Completers and Suicide Attempters' (1990) 11 *Crisis* 7.

[70] M Goldblatt, 'Psychodynamics of Suicide' in Nock (n 49).

[71] R Baumeister, 'Suicide as Escape from Self' (1990) 97 *Psychological Review* 90.

[72] H Hendin, 'Psychodynamics of Suicide, with Particular Reference to the Young' (1991) 148 *American Journal of Psychiatry* 1150.

[73] E Shneidman, *The Suicidal Mind* (Oxford University Press, 1996) 4.

[74] A Beck, 'Beyond Belief: A Theory of Modes, Personality, and Psychopathology' in P Salkovskis (ed), *Frontiers of Cognitive Therapy* (Guilford Press, 1996).

the predictability which lead to suicidal thought. The sense of hopelessness can be broken down into a cognitive element (a belief about one's situation) and an affective element (how one feels about it). These lead to a motivational response where the suicidal thoughts are developed. There are clear overlaps with the escape theory here. The primary difference is that while the escape theory posits a clear decision to escape from the situation and pain one is in, the hopelessness theory sees it rather as a person being overwhelmed by hopelessness, with suicide being less of a positive resolution than a more unfocused response to the situation.[75] There is certainly some good evidence that hopelessness is a common feature of suicide.[76] As with many other theories, though, the difficulty is that a sense of hopelessness is experienced by many people who do not go on to attempt suicide.[77] In response to this point the next theory focuses on what 'tips' a person from being in a miserable state to developing suicidal thoughts.

C. Burdensomeness

Kleespies[78] argues that it is the perception that one is a burden on others which is particularly influential in suicidal feelings, especially where the individual feels they are not giving anything back to others in return. He argues that the combination of being a burden and not belonging as a member of society or communal group create powerful negative emotions.

Not everyone is convinced by his approach. Hjelmeland and Knizek[79] note that feelings of perceived burdensomeness and thwarted belongingness 'might be present to a certain degree in many people from time to time'. They also question whether the requirements of seeing yourself as a burden and a feeling you do not belong are consistent. As they put it, 'If you think no one cares about you, how can you perceive to be a burden (to them/whom)?'

D. Fluid Vulnerability Theory

This theory[80] highlights how people may have a baseline level of suicide risk but that this can be influenced by particular factors which heighten the risk

[75] M Linehan, *Cognitive-Behavioral Treatment of Borderline Personality Disorder* (Guilford Press, 1993).

[76] G Brown et al, 'Risk Factors for Suicide in Psychiatric Outpatients: A 20-Year Prospective Study' (2000) 68 *Journal of Consulting and Clinical Psychology* 371.

[77] Michaels et al (n 58).

[78] P Kleespies, 'Medical Illness, Suicide, and Assisted Death' in P Kleespies (ed), *The Oxford Handbook of Behavioral Emergencies and Crises* (Oxford University Press, 2016).

[79] H Hjelmeland and B Knizek (2020) 'The Emperor's New Clothes? A Critical Look at the Interpersonal Theory of Suicide' (2020) 44 *Death Studies* 168.

[80] Kleespies (n 78).

of suicide.[81] How the individual responds to the particular challenge or 'stressor' will mean the person either returns to their 'set point' or goes on to attempt suicide. This seeks to capture how a person's vulnerability to suicide may shift over time, and perhaps explains that – although we can identify vulnerabilities to suicide – it is much harder to identify who in that vulnerable group will actually go on to commit suicide.[82] As Klonsky et al put it:

> it is becoming clear that depression, hopelessness, most mental disorders, and even impulsivity predict ideation, but these factors struggle to distinguish those who have attempted suicide from those who have only considered suicide.

This background vulnerability, sometimes called diathesis, can result from a range of factors.[83] Harmer et al[84] suggest these can reduced to five primary kinds of factors:

(1) internal psychopathology (eg anxiety disorders; mood disorders; hopelessness; emotion dysregulation; sleep disturbances);
(2) demographic factors (eg age; education; employment; ethnicity; gender; marital status; religion; socioeconomic status);
(3) prior suicidal thoughts and behaviors (eg prior deliberate self-harm, nonsuicidal self-injury, suicide attempt, suicide ideation);
(4) external psychopathology (eg aggressive behaviors; impulsivity; incarceration history; antisocial behaviors; substance abuse);
(5) social factors (eg abuse history; family problems; isolation; peer problems; stressful life events).

They suggest these factors can work out as 'risk factors', which when combined with stressors mean that a person is more likely to seek suicide, and 'protective factors', which can mean that even when facing a severe stressor, a person is well placed to avoid suicide.

There is a further shift: from having suicide ideation (a wish to die) to forming a determination to act on that desire.[85] The significance of this point is that there are plenty of people with suicidal ideation who do not put it into effect. Joiner[86] emphasises that the capacity to commit suicide is not as straightforward as may be thought. He suggests that humans have a strong drive to self-preservation and that considerable emotional resources are required to engage in lethal self-injury.

[81] Sometimes known as the integrated volitional model: R O'Connor and O Kirtley, 'The Integrated Motivational–Volitional Model of Suicidal Behaviour' (2018) 373 *Philosophical Transaction of the Royal Society* 201.
[82] E Moscardini et al, 'Suicide-Specific Cognitions, Attentional Fixation, and Worst-Point Suicidal Ideation' (2020) 54 *Suicide and Life-Threatening Behaviour* 899.
[83] Mościcki (n 55).
[84] B Harmer et al, *Suicidal Ideation* (Statpearls, 2021).
[85] Joiner (n 50).
[86] ibid.

He suggests that this resistance to seeking death can be worn down through repeated exposure to painful experiences. However, as Eve Mościcki[87] writes:

> With few exceptions, there is nothing unique about most of the life events that may precede suicide, since most individuals experience similar events and do not attempt or die by suicide. Rather, it is the personal perception of the impact of the event that increases risk for nonfatal and fatal suicidal behaviors …, suggesting that the psychiatric response to the stressor must be taken into account.

It should also be noted that a further important factor in putting suicide ideation into effect is the access to means of suicide.[88] We shall be exploring this in Chapter 4.

E. The 'Three Step' Theory

An influential overarching theory of the road to suicide is Klonsky and May's 'three step' theory.[89] This suggests that first the psychological pain and hopelessness create and then maintain suicide ideation. This leads to the second stage of suicidal desire when the pain clearly outweighs the connectedness to others. Connectedness includes both relationships with others, but also the values and roles a person has in society which give them purpose or meaning. The third stage occurs where the capacity to attempt suicide is present. This can include access to lethal means but also knowledge.

As a broad scheme, this model has some empirical support for it and it has become subject to increasingly sophisticated development.[90] Baumeister,[91] for example, in exploring the first stage suggest that this itself can be broken down into three stages: first a person falls short of their own expectations and standards (which might cover a range of different areas of life); second, they blame themselves for these failures; third, they turn inwards and become absorbed by what they do not like about themselves. This approach contrasts with other theories, mentioned above, which see the primary issue related to perceived burdensomeness, rather than self-hatred, although those can be linked in some cases.

Having looked at some of the overarching theories, I will now explore some of the particular factors said to cause suicide.

[87] Mościcki (n 55).
[88] ibid.
[89] E Klonsky and A May, 'The Three-Step Theory (3ST): A New Theory of Suicide Rooted in the "Ideation-to-Action" Framework' (2015) 8 *International Journal of Cognitive Therapy* 114.
[90] K Dhingra et al, 'An Empirical Test of the Three-Step Theory of Suicide in U.K. University Students' (2019) 49 *Suicide and Life-Threatening Behaviour* 478.
[91] Michaels et al (n 58).

XI. Mental Illness

It is very often claimed that there is a strong link between suicide and mental illness.[92] A common view is that expressed by Eve K Mościcki:

> Over 90% of adult suicide deaths are associated with psychiatric disorders … In addition to the strong link with suicide fatalities, psychiatric disorders are also found in the large majority of persons who make serious suicide attempts … Mood disorders, principally major depression and bipolar disorder, are associated with approximately 50% to 60% of suicide fatalities among adult men and women.[93]

Similarly, Takahashi's research found:

> According to a survey done using the psychological autopsy method, 70–90% of those who committed suicide had evidence of some mental disorder when alive, and 60–70% were depressed … Patients with severe depression who meet the diagnostic criteria for melancholia are at a particularly high risk of suicide … The suicide rate in patients suffering from depression associated with delusions is extremely high.[94]

The UK Government has claimed that having a mental illness increases a risk of suicide by 10 per cent, compared with the general population.[95] Indeed, it has been claimed that every suicide involves a person with a mental disorder, whether diagnosed or not.[96]

Despite these confident claims, the link between mental illness and suicide is controversial.[97] For example, 98 per cent of those with mental disorders do not die by suicide.[98] Clearly, there are other very significant factors that are at play.[99] For example, although rates of depression are much higher among women than men, suicide is found far more commonly among men than women.[100] Further, the links between suicide and mental illness appear to vary significantly in different parts of the world.[101]

Those who emphasise that there is a link between suicide and a mental disorder accept that this is truer of some conditions than others. Cukrowicz and Poindexter[102] list the following as the most closely connected: 'mood disorders

[92] TR Insel and BN Cuthbert, 'Brain Disorders? Precisely' (2015) 348(6234) *Science* 499–500.
[93] Mościcki (n 55).
[94] Y Takahashi, 'Depression and Suicide' (2001) 44 *JAMA* 359, 359–60.
[95] HM Government *Preventing Suicide in England* (HM Government, 2020).
[96] Joiner (n 50).
[97] S Pridmore, 'Mental Disorder and Suicide: A Faulty Connection' (2015) 49 *Australian and New Zealand Journal of Psychiatry* 18.
[98] J Bertolote and A Fleischmann, 'Suicide and Psychiatry Diagnosis: A Worldwide Perspetive' (2002) 1 *World Psychiatry* 181.
[99] R O'Connor and N Nock, 'The Psychology of Suicidal Behaviour' (2014) 1 *Lancet Psychiatry* 73.
[100] Pridmore (n 97).
[101] A Rao et al, 'One Hundred Female Burn Cases: A Study in Suicidology' (1989) 7 *Indian Journal of Psychiatry* 330; J Zhang et al, 'Mental Disorders and Suicide among Young Rural Chinese: A Case-Control Psychological Autopsy Study' (2010) 167 *American Journal of Psychiatry* 773.
[102] Cukrowicz and Poindexter (n 61).

(eg MDD), personality disorders (eg borderline personality disorder), eating disorders (ie anorexia nervosa), schizophrenia, substance use disorders, and conduct disorder in adolescents'.

The difficulty with the studies that seek to draw a strong link between mental disorder and suicide is that many rely on 'psychological autopsies'. However, there are problems with this kind of methodology,[103] not least the difficulty in relying on the statements of others to diagnose an individual who cannot provide their own comments. Further, there is a concern that blaming mental illness for the suicide can be a comfort to relatives and friends, and so their contribution to the psychological autopsy may not be unbiased. They may instinctively find comfort in 'blaming' mental illness rather than addressing other explanations.

Traumatic events can be linked to suicide, especially when they have caused post-traumatic stress disorder (PTSD).[104] Childhood abuse and a history of sexual assault are linked with a risk of suicidal thoughts. In the popular imagination, being given a diagnosis of a serious illness is linked with suicide. However, there is only weak evidence for this. For example, overall rates of suicide ideation in cancer patients are comparable to the general population.[105] One cancer study found that of 4,722,099 patients diagnosed with cancer, 2,491 committed suicide within six months. That is 0.08 per cent of the sample.[106]

The debate over the role of mental illness in suicide is hard to resolve. It may not be particularly helpful. One person experiencing a desire to die is almost by definition suffering severe ill-health. To separate out the extent to which a person's conditions and situation are causing suicidal thoughts from the extent to which they are causing mental health issues, which in turn causes suicidal thoughts, is probably impossible.

XII. Alcohol

There is a surprisingly strong correlation between alcohol and suicide. Psychological autopsy studies have found that of adults who die by suicide between 25 and 50 per cent are intoxicated at the time of death.[107] Of course other drugs can be involved too. The most common explanation is that alcohol and drug use are linked to disinhibition and impulsive behaviour and so can facilitate the move from

[103] L Pouliot and D Leo, 'Critical Issues in Psychological Autopsy Studies' (2006) 36 *Suicide and Life-Threatening Behavior* 491; H Hjelmeland et al, 'Psychological Autopsy Studies as Diagnostic Tools: Are They Methodologically Flawed?' (2012) 36 *Death Studies* 605; S Shahtahmasebi, 'Examining the Claim that 80–90% of Suicide Cases had Depression' (2013) 1 *Frontiers in Public Health* 62.

[104] E Roberge et al, 'Suicide Following Trauma' in J Beck and D Sloan (eds), *The Oxford Handbook of Traumatic Stress Disorders* (Oxford University Press, 2019).

[105] Cukrowicz and Poindexter (n 61).

[106] K Henson et al, 'Risk of Suicide after Cancer Diagnosis in England' (2019) 76 *JAMA Psychiatry* 51.

[107] Mościcki (n 55).

suicide ideation to action. In passing, one US study found that coffee consumption reduces suicide risks.[108]

XIII. Religion

Religious faith can impact on suicidal behaviour. This is commonly explained on the basis that a belief that suicide can have consequences in the afterlife may provide a further deterrence from committing suicide. Alternatively, it may be that religious faith and being a member of a faith community provides comfort in the face of troubles. Notably, the extent to which religious faith protects against suicide seems proportional to the degree of involvement in religious activities.[109]

Bloshnich et al[110] found that being a Christian led to a 24 per cent reduction in the chance of suicide, and specifically being Catholic led to a 37 per cent reduction, when compared with agnostic or atheist belief. However, for those in the LGBT community, also having a religious faith increased the chance of suicidal ideation by 68 per cent and 77 per cent. Notably, those of a sexual minority who belonged to a religious group which supported their sexuality had a reduced risk of suicide, indeed with a lower risk than those with no faith.

XIV. Domestic Abuse

The statistics on domestic abuse and sexual assault are frighteningly high.[111] In one UK study, a third of female suicides were by victims of domestic abuse.[112] In another, 24 per cent of women escaping domestic abuse felt suicidal.[113] A study in Victoria, Australia found that 42 per cent of women who committed suicide had been victims of domestic abuse: 23 per cent had suffered physical violence, 18 per cent psychological violence and 16 per cent sexual abuse.[114] This link is not surprising, given well established link between being the victim of domestic abuse with depression, anxiety, PTSD, and alcohol and drug abuse disorders.[115]

[108] M Lucas et al, 'Coffee, Caffeine and Risk of Completed Suicide' (2014) 15 *World Journal of Biological Psychiatry* 377.

[109] D Sanchez et al, 'Association of Religious Activity with Male Suicide Deaths' (2020) 50 *Suicide and Life Threatening Behaviour* 449.

[110] J Blosnich et al, 'Questions of Faith: Religious Affiliations and Suicidal Ideation among Sexual Minority Young Adults' (2020) 50 *Suicide and Life Threatening Behaviour* 1158.

[111] M Hillbrand, 'Overlap between Suicidal Behavior and Interpersonal Violence' in Nock (n 49).

[112] S Walby, *The Cost of Domestic Violence* (DTI, 2004).

[113] R Aitken and V Munro, *Domestic Abuse and Suicide: Exploring the Links with Refuges' Client Base and Work Force* (University of Warwick, School of Law and Refuge, 2018).

[114] M MacIssac et al, 'Prevalence and Characteristics of Interpersonal Violence in People Dying from Suicide in Victoria, Australia' (2018) 30 *Asia-Pacific Journal of Public Health* 36.

[115] A Spirito et al, 'The Evaluation and Management of Suicide Risk in Adolescents in the Context of Interpersonal Violence' in P Kleespies (ed), *The Oxford Handbook of Behavioral Emergencies and Crises* (Oxford University Press, 2016).

A recent striking study in the US looking at suicides over a ten-year period in Kentucky, reported 26 per cent of suicides where the circumstances were known to have included intimate partner violence, and 43 per cent intimate partner problems.[116] Most of these cases were men, indicating that being a perpetrator of domestic abuse, as well as being the victim, is strongly linked to suicide. One strand of these cases are homicide-suicide cases, where a person has murdered their partner (and sometimes children) and then killed themselves.[117]

XV. Social Inequalities

A major theme in writing on causes of suicide is broader social forces. We will be looking at these in detail in Chapter 4. There are, for example, notable links between poverty and social exclusion and suicide risk. Other disadvantaged groups are linked to suicide. Data in the US suggests that adults aged 18–25 are at a three times higher risk of suicide than those aged 65 or over.[118] Further, there is a strikingly higher rate of completed suicide attempts among men than women, although it seems that for suicide attempts there are higher rates for women.[119] There are also statistical links between suicide and being part of the LGBT community,[120] disadvantaged ethnic minorities,[121] and being incarcerated.[122] All of this shows that focusing on personal issues – such as mental illness or drug use – risks individualising the causes of suicide and overlooking the way societal inequalities impact on suicide rate.

XVI. Conclusion

Having undertaken this review of the literature on the causes of suicide, it is perhaps a little dispiriting to read O'Connor and Kirtley's assessment that 'our ability to predict suicide is no better now than it was 50 years ago'.[123] Certainly we are a very long way from having a definitive test that can accurately predict who is likely to commit suicide. However, our understanding of suicide has improved. It is now clear that suicidal behaviour involves a complex interaction of social,

[116] S Brown and J Seals, 'Intimate Partner Problems and Suicide: Are we Missing the Violence?' (2019) 11 *Journal of Injury and Violence Research* 53.

[117] Hillbrand (n 111).

[118] Mościcki (n 55).

[119] Michaels et al (n 58).

[120] A Horowitz et al, 'Variation in Suicide Risk among Subgroups of Sexual and Gender Minority College Students' (2020) 50 *Suicide and Life Threatening Behaviour* 1041.

[121] K Johnson and R Rhodes, 'Ethnicity as a Factor' in S Youngner and R Arnold (eds), *The Oxford Handbook of Ethics at the End of Life* (Oxford University Press, 2020).

[122] Mościcki (n 55).

[123] O'Connor and Kirtley (n 81).

psychological, biological, social, interpersonal and cultural factors. Boldt[124] was correct to suggest:

> Scholars who seek a universal understanding of suicide (…) fail to appreciate the degree to which their logic and ideas are influenced by the unique cultural ground from which they grew (…) Despite their best efforts to achieve universal, culture-free theories, their perceptions are inevitably and profoundly shaped by ethnocentric, contempocentric, and egocentric values, experiences, concepts, prejudices, and so on.

It is also now clear that suicide cannot be explained primarily by the kinds of individual factors which have been the primary focus of this chapter. For any given characteristic – suffering depression, for example – there are far more people with that characteristic who do not go on to commit suicide than do. We can see that from the fact that suicide rates can vary widely around the world, in a way not correlated by mental illness. For example, between 2000 and 2012 the age-standardised suicide rate worldwide decreased by 26 per cent, but that was not consistent in all countries. It deceased by 69 per cent among women in Malta and increased by 416 per cent among men in Cyprus,[125] though there were no notable changes in rates of mental ill health in those countries. As the WHO concludes, suicide can only be explained by the 'interplay between biological, psychological, social, environmental and cultural factors'.[126]

Jesse Bering's book, *Suicidal – Why We Kill Ourselves*[127] explains that we must be 'acutely aware that we are social animals … whose mental machinery has evolved to be so finely attuned to the stuff of other people's thoughts that sometimes our very existence hangs in the balance of what we think others think of us'.[128] Whether this is a sign or cause of mental illness is perhaps beside the point; he urges us to create communities who value and appreciate each member. It is that thought which will be developed in the next chapter.

[124] M Boldt, 'The Meaning of Suicide: Implications for Research' (1988) 9 *Crisis* 93.
[125] World Health Organisation, *Suicide* (World Health Organisation, 2014).
[126] World Health Organisation, *Suicide* (2018) 2.
[127] J Bering, *Suicidal, Why We Kill Ourselves* (University of Chicago Press, 2018).
[128] ibid, 235.

4

Societal Responsibility for Suicide

I. Introduction

This chapter will explore the social landscape of suicide. There are two aspects to this: first, that suicides can gain meaning from societal context; second, and more importantly, that suicides reflect inequality and exclusion within society. Suicide is, therefore, a matter of social justice, akin to homelessness or poverty.[1] It is about power and privilege.[2] This chapter will explore societal responsibility for suicide. It will argue that in complex ways societal structures contribute significantly to rates of suicide. This is in contrast to the more common way of understanding suicide, which is to focus on individual factors impacting on the person, such as mental illness, which were discussed in Chapter 3.

This has two important consequences for the themes of this book. The first is that if society itself is responsible – or at least partly responsible – for suicide, then it has a duty to stop it, particularly where suicide reflects inequalities and power structures within society. The second is that it has significant impacts on suicide prevention. If the causes of suicide lie, at least in part, in society, then suicide prevention is as much about changing society as it is about changing the suicidal individual.

II. The Cultural Meaning of Suicide

Discussions of suicide come with assumptions about who commits it, why they do, and its moral status. But these questions, as we have seen in this book, are contested. Society creates a particular construction of what suicide is, which can tell us as much about society as it does about suicide itself.[3] It is perhaps more accurate to talk about constructions of suicide, which will vary depending on the context. Talk of 'assisted dying' immediately raises the image of an

[1] C Mills, *Decolonizing Global Mental Health* (Routledge, 2014); D Stuckler and S Basu, *The Body Economic: Why Austerity Kills* (Basic Books, 2013).

[2] S Canetto, 'Women and Suicidal Behavior: A Cultural Analysis' (2008) 78 *American Journal of Orthopsychiatry* 259

[3] S Fitzpatrick, 'Re-Moralizing the Suicide Debate' (2014) 11 *Journal of Bioethical Inquiry* 223.

older person in pain seeking relief from an undignified dying. When we talk of 'teen suicide' the assumption is that we are discussing a case of a young person with much to offer who is seeking suicide because, for example, they have been bullied online. But neither of these assumptions is necessarily correct. Perhaps they tell us as much about our guilt about the way old people are treated or our terror at the power the youth yield over the internet, as they do about suicide itself. In some cultures suicide has overtones of being a dignified act, with a person giving up their life for the greater good. In Japan, for example, seppuku – a ritual of suicide – reflects important cultural values of honour and self-esteem. In other cultures suicide is seen as a morally wrongful act. In yet other cultures suicide is unknown. Prior to the 1950s suicide was exceptionally rare within Indigenous communities in the US, but they now have some of the highest rates in the world.[4] As Heidi Hjelmeland makes clear:

> suicidal behaviour always occurs and is embedded within a cultural context and no suicidal act is conducted without reference to the prevailing normative standards and attitudes of a cultural community.[5]

What a suicide 'means', how it might be understood by the performer, and how it is reacted to by others, depend very much on the particular social context.

III. Social Causes of Suicide

Discussions of the causes of suicide are dominated by individual explanations, as seen in Chapter 3. The cause of suicide is seen to lie in a person's mental health; their psychological state; their relational difficulties; or particular tragedies that have happened to them. Yet, these overlook the broader impact of society on suicide.[6] Bold claims are made, such as that 'approximately 95 percent of people who die by suicide experienced a mental disorder at the time of death'.[7] Such claims led Margaret Pabst Battin[8] to write of the:

> uniform assumption that suicide is the causal product of mental illness, the normatively monolithic assumption seemingly so prevalent in contemporary times.

Given the focus on individual explanations of suicide, it is not surprising that the ethical and legal debates are dominated by discussions of autonomy. As Jaworski[9]

[4] Fitzpatrick (n 3).

[5] H Hjelmeland, 'Cultural Context is Critical in Suicide Research and Prevention' (2011) 32 *Crisis* 61.

[6] S Fitzpatrick et al, 'Suicidology as a Social Practice' (2015) 4 *Social Epistemology Review and Reply Collective* 44.

[7] T Joiner, *Why People Die by Suicide* (Harvard University Press, 2005) 191; T Joiner, 'Scientific Rigor as the Guiding Heuristic for SLTB's Editorial Stance' (2011) 41 *Suicide and Life-Threatening Behavior* 471.

[8] M Battin, *Ending Life: Ethics and the Way We Die* (Oxford University Press, 2005), 173.

[9] K Jaworski, 'The Gendering of Suicide' (2010) 25 *Australian Feminist Studies* 47, 50.

puts it, suicides are seen as 'the activities of a largely disembodied mind filled with masterful agency'. So understood, suicide prevention focuses on identifying people with particular mental health issues or in particular circumstances and intervening to stop them. Hence, psychotherapy or pharmaceuticals become the 'principal lines of defence' against suicide.[10] A striking example of this medicalisation is the use of brain imaging in an attempt to identify suicidal individuals.[11] This vividly portrays the problem of suicide as located in the brain of the individual and the solution to it is empowering people to deal with challenges they face, be that through medical intervention, or enabling suicide.[12]

In this chapter it will be argued that while in the past suicide was seen as a personal failing, even a sin, we should now understand it as a failing of society. We need to move beyond the assumption that suicide 'originates within the person'.[13] Instead we should look at broader structures, forces and oppressions within society which are reflected by suicide. As Button argues:

> … a political approach to suicide will invert all forms of moralism (religious and secular) about suicide today: suicide *is* debasing of humanity, but the debasement is not generated by individual annihilation but by prior distributions in the unequal opportunities afforded to a life of dignity. … To make suicide a subject of collective responsibility about which the members of a political society can and should be responsive, we should acknowledge that suicide is not simply a 'naturally' occurring social bad that is randomly distributed within a population but is something for which human agency (or the lack of human agency) plays a causal role.[14]

This important insight, which will be key to the discussions in this chapter, has significant ramifications.[15] These include that suicide prevention needs to be targeted at the broader inequalities facing society rather than individuals, and that the harm of suicide is not just in the individual loss, but the deeper inequalities within society.[16] Suicide is a matter of 'collective responsibility'.[17]

This becomes all the more apparent when it is appreciated that suicide is not randomly distributed among the population. It tracks disadvantages within society. For example, working-class men, welfare recipients, and Black children are

[10] Battin (n 8) 173.

[11] Hjelmeland (n 5).

[12] C Macdonald and J Naudin, 'The Construction of the Suicidal Self in Phenomenological Psychology' in M-L Honkasalo and M Tuominen, *Culture, Suicide and the Human Condition* (Berghahn Books, 2014).

[13] M Kral, 'Suicide and the Internalization of Culture: Three Questions' (1998) 35 *Transcultural Psychiatry* 221.

[14] M Button, 'Suicide and Social Justice: Towards a Political Approach to Suicide' (2016) 39 *Political Research Quarterly* 270.

[15] J Bantjes and L Swartz, 'The Cultural Turn in Critical Suicidology: What Can We Claim and What Do We Know' (2017) 41 *Death Studies* 512.

[16] J White, 'What Can Critical Suicidology Do?' (2017) 41 *Death Studies* 472.

[17] Button (n 14).

all featured highly in suicide statistics. Mills[18] has argued that austerity politics is directly related to suicide:

> people are killing themselves because austerity is killing them. Austerity suicides may be read as the ultimate outcome of the internalisation of eugenic and market logic underlying welfare reform driven by austerity. Such deaths make visible the slow death endemic to austerity.

A good example of the link between suicide and social inequality is how the high rates of suicide among younger members of the LGBTQI+ community are explained.[19] Traditionally these have been presented, particularly in the United States, as involving youngsters with 'troubled backgrounds' and 'vulnerable young people' with 'mental health issues'.[20] In fact, it seems far more plausible that it was society's oppression of LGBTQI+ individuals which created the issue. So understood, a more appropriate response to suicides within that community, rather than encouraging members to receive treatment or therapy, might be to challenge the heteronormativity and discrimination that such groups face.

Before exploring some of the more obvious ways in which societal pressures and circumstances influence suicide, it is important to understand how the self should be understood in a communal, relational way.

IV. Suicide and the Relational Self

Debates around the nature and cause of suicide reflect debates around the understanding of the self. The individualistic explanation of suicide and the standard legal response to it is based on a particular conception of the self. The law and much ethical discourse are premised on a self which is independent, autonomous and rational.[21] Hence, the law emphasises as key rights, autonomy, bodily integrity, privacy and liberty. Our right to be able to make our own choices over how to act and to only be subject to those responsibilities we choose to take, are seen as central pillars of economic, social, and legal structures. The role of the law in such a model is to protect the individual from unwanted intrusions and to protect liberty to pursue one's goal for one's life. In short, rights are about keeping other people away from you. It is this kind of understanding which sees the significance placed on respect for autonomy in the legal and ethical literature on suicide; the weight placed on factors such as mental health as the explanation of suicide; and

[18] C Mills, '"Dead People Don't Claim": Psychopolitical Autopsy of UK Austerity Suicides' (2017) 38 *Critical Social Policy* 302, 317.

[19] P Grzanka and E Mann, 'Queer Youth Suicide and the Psychopolitics of "It Gets Better"' (2014) 17 *Sexualities* 369, 372.

[20] ibid.

[21] J Nedelseky, *Law's Relations: A Relational Theory of Self, Autonomy and the Law* (Oxford University Press, 2014).

suicide prevention being dominated by attempts to identify 'suicidal individuals' and to restore them to a proper state of mind.

I have written elsewhere in support of a different understanding of the self,[22] ie an understanding of the relational self. On this view our selves emerge from our relationships with others and gain their meaning from our interactions with others. I highlight three particular aspects of the self which reflect this.

A. The Vulnerable Self

All human beings are vulnerable in nature. Society and the law may be organised around the image of the autonomous, self-sufficient and independent man, but the reality is that we are all deeply dependent on others; all vulnerable to disease; and all impaired in our decision making. Rather than identifying particular groups as falling short of the autonomous ideal, and therefore vulnerable, we should recognise our universal mutual vulnerability. And the fact that we are all vulnerable should be celebrated rather than decried. Our vulnerability requires us to reach out, co-operate and support each other – to pool resources and emphasise our need to be flexible and open to change. Far from being stigmatic, being vulnerable is an inherent part of being human and a source of much that is good.[23]

COVID-19 has highlighted the fragile status of all our bodies. It makes apparent what has always been true: our bodies are not static, immutable barriers against the world but are profoundly leaky and constantly changing. They are dependent on the environment and on other bodies. We are all acutely dependent on others for our physical and psychological wellbeing.

B. The Relational Self

The human self is profoundly relational. It is through our relationships that our selves are made.[24] As Baier puts it:

> [a] person, perhaps, is best seen as someone who was long enough dependent on other persons to acquire the essential arts of personhood. Persons are essentially second persons who grow up with other persons.[25]

We define and understand ourselves in terms of our relationships. It is our relationships that give our life meaning and constitute our identity. The story of our lives is told to, by and through those we interact with. That is why bereavement and

[22] J Herring, *Law and the Relational Self* (Cambridge University Press, 2020).

[23] D Bedford and J Herring, *Embracing Vulnerability: The Challenges and Implications for the Law* (Routledge, 2020).

[24] K Gergen, *Relational Being: Beyond Self and the Community* (Oxford University Press, 2011).

[25] A Baier, *Postures of the Mind* (University of Minnesota Press, 1985) 168.

relationship breakdown are two of the greatest sadnesses most people experience and have such an impact on the self. Talk of autonomy and writing the stories of our lies is a fiction.[26] We write our lives with others. We are more members of a choir, than solitary writers. Our decisions and life stories are bound up with and deeply connected to those of others.

C. The Caring Self

Given that we are vulnerable and we are relational, it is inevitable that caring is a core part of what it is to be a person. It is the highest moral value and central to our beings. Caring relationships are essential to our survival, our understandings of ourselves, and to the things we value. As Feder Kittay[27] writes:

> A world without care would not only be a dismal world, it would be a world in which great harm would be done. A world in which nobody cared about anyone else would be a world in which those who could not attend to their own needs (and that is all of us at some point in our lives) would be neglected.

We reach then the position that our value lies not in ourselves as isolated egos but in our caring relationships. As Reinders[28] puts it:

> Being loved by someone is what matters most in our lives. What we do not often think about, however, is the logic of this statement, and this logic is what I ask you to contemplate for a moment. If 'being loved' is the most important thing in our lives, then the most important thing is something we cannot do by ourselves or on our own. It's not a goal we can strive for, it is not something we can achieve. To be loved by someone implies that the most important thing in our lives is something we can only receive as a gift.

Caring relationships are, therefore, the hallmark of what it is to be a person.[29]

D. Suicide and the Relational Self

This way of understanding the self has some important messages for our understanding of suicide. As our human nature is to be vulnerable, relational and caring, it is clear that we are all profoundly dependent on others for our physical and psychological wellbeing. To imagine our health as being simply a matter of the state of our bodies or minds is profoundly mistaken. It is in creating healthy

[26] J Herring, *Relational Autonomy and Family Law* (Springer, 2017).

[27] E Feder Kittay, 'The Relationality and the Normativity of an Ethic of Care' in P Ivanhoe (ed), *The Oneness Hypothesis* (Columbia University Press) 120.

[28] H Reinders, 'The Power of Inclusion and Friendship' (2011) 15 *Journal of Religion, Disability & Health* 431, 441.

[29] J Herring, 'Relational Personhood' (2021) *Keele Law Review* 21.

societies and communities that we make health. It is for this reason that suicide is better understood as a social/communal issue, rather than in individual terms. Suicide is a symptom of a sick society, not of a sick person.

The social model of disability has much to teach us here. It demonstrates that it is wrong to assume that the root cause of disadvantages flows from a particular body and that the solution is to correct the 'misfit' body. Differences in bodies do not create disadvantage: it is the way society arranges facilities to privilege some bodies and not others that does so. There is great wisdom in this quotation from the National Aboriginal Health Strategy Working Party:

> Aboriginal health is not just the physical wellbeing of an individual but is the social, emotional and cultural wellbeing of the whole community in which each individual is able to achieve their full potential thereby bringing about the total wellbeing of their community.[30]

Further, suicide cannot be reduced to an individual event that is a choice just for the individual involved.[31] There is a well-established statistical link between the strength of a person's social network and suicide. Mäkinen writes:

> The number, duration, strength, and quality of social relations are all inversely related to suicide risk. People with marital, kinship, occupational, friendship, or other types of social ties are generally at lower risk of committing suicide than those who lack these ties, and people who commit suicide generally possess fewer social ties of any kind than others.[32]

Thus, issues such as social exclusion and discrimination can play an important part in explanations for suicide. It is important, too, to recognise the gendered factors that lead to female suicide, especially sexual abuse, domestic abuse and isolation in motherhood.[33] So seen, these female suicides are often the expression of violence against women, rather than an individual act.

In understanding the harms created by suicide, it is important that we are aware of the impact on those around the deceased. Families and friend of those who die through suicide have the grief normally associated with bereavement but report higher levels of rejection, shame, and stigma.[34] They will have in a real sense lost a part of themselves.[35] Research has found that a single death by suicide may

[30] Quoted in Department of Health (Australia), *Strategic Framework* (2013) 2.

[31] J Holmes, 'Suicide and Deliberate Self-Harm' in M Popili (ed), *Phenomenology of Suicide* (Springer, 2018).

[32] I Mäkinen, 'Social Dimensions of Suicide' in D Wasserman (ed), *Suicide: An Unnecessary Death* (Oxford University Press, 2016).

[33] S Mallon et al, 'An Exploration of Integrated Data on the Social Dynamics of Suicide among Women' (2016) 38 *Sociology of Health and Illness* 662.

[34] C Sveen and F Walby, 'Suicide Survivors' Mental Health and Grief Reactions: A Systematic Review of Controlled Studies' (2008) 38 *Suicide and Life Threatening Behaviour* 13.

[35] R Neimeyer et al, 'A Social Constructionist Account of Grief: Loss and the Narration of Meaning' (2014) 38 *Death Studies* 485.

touch approximately 135 people, a third of whom experience a severe life disruption as a result.[36] We cannot, therefore, reduce suicide to an individual decision or exercise of autonomy; it is a decision with a profound impact on others.[37]

Having set out the broad scope for arguing that suicide is best understood as a relational, communal issue, I will now explore some of the particular aspects of society which play a role in suicide.

V. Means

Clearly, access to means of suicide is an important factor in suicide risk.[38] The availability of firearms in the US makes them the most commonly used form of suicide in that country. They are rarely used in suicide in the UK. There is very strong evidence that restrictions on access to lethal weapons and other methods of suicide can have a dramatic effect on suicide rates.[39] For example, one study found, after controlling for other variables, that gun ownership accounted for 92 per cent of the variance between state suicide rates within the US.[40] We will be exploring this issue in much more detail in Chapter 7, but for now it is enough to note that how society organises access to guns; places barriers around high places; regulates access to medication, can dramatically affect the number and kinds of suicide that take place. This is a very obvious example of how society impacts on suicide.

VI. Poverty

There is extensive evidence of the link between being in poverty – particularly being in receipt of benefits – and being at risk of suicide.[41] Mills has argued that politics of austerity can explain the increase in suicides in the past two decades.[42] He sees the combination of poverty, shame and anxiety and a context of social dis-ease as forging a particular link to suicide. In their book, Stuckler and Basu[43] present a mass of new data revealing how, internationally, there have

[36] S Pollard et al, 'Suicide Contagion and Clusters' (2019) 47 *NSU Florida Faculty Articles* 21.

[37] H Parker, 'Survivors of Suicide' in M Nock (ed), *The Oxford Handbook of Suicide and Self-Injury* (Oxford University Press, 2014).

[38] E Mościcki, 'Suicidal Behaviours among Adults' in Nock (n 37).

[39] M Anestis and J Anestis, 'Suicide Rates and State Laws Regulating Access and Exposure to Handguns' (2015) 105 *American Journal of Public Health* 2049.

[40] M Anestis and C Houtsma, 'The Association between Gun Ownership and Statewide Overall Suicide Rates' (2018) 48 *Suicide and Life Threatening Behaviour* 204.

[41] Y Sawada et al, 'Socioeconomic Causes of Suicide' in Y Sawada et al (eds), *Economic Analysis of Suicide Prevention. Economy and Social Inclusion* (Springer 2017).

[42] Mills (n 18).

[43] Stuckler and Basu (n 1).

been over 10,000 additional suicides and an estimated million extra cases of depression since governments started introducing austerity programmes in 2007–2012. Case and Deaton,[44] focusing on the US, have documented 'deaths of despair'. Their focus was on the rise in mortality and morbidity of middle-aged white non-Hispanic men after 1998, a risk not matched by Hispanic men or African Americans. They suggest that in 2017 158,000 Americans died from 'deaths of despair'.[45] The striking increase was primarily due to suicide, accidental poisoning (such as opioid use) and liver disease (associated often with alcohol misuse). While the poisoning and liver disease would not normally be seen as suicide in the traditional sense, the authors group them with suicide as deaths resulting from acts driven by despair. They do not offer a simple explanation for this dramatic increase but list economic policies, healthcare policies and loss of social institutions as all playing important roles.[46]

In the UK there have been similar reports of suicide linked to reforms in welfare payments.[47] This is an issue governments refuse to address. The concern was graphically portrayed in 2017 with a protest outside Parliament with a banner 'Dead people don't claim', implying that the primary focus of austerity policies was to reduce the number of claimants. While it would absurd to claim this was literally the aim of the policies, it is at least arguable that the impact on the mental health of austerity claimants was a major factor in determining benefits policies. Attempts to discourage people from making welfare claims, by making the process of claiming difficult or shameful, reveal an attitude that suggests anything is permissible if it results in a drop in the number of claimants.

Certainly, some shocking stories emerged of suicide following interactions with welfare agencies. Tim Slater lost his employment and support benefit to assist with his blindness and agoraphobia, and was found fit to work. He hanged himself shortly afterwards.[48] Christelle Pardo jumped from a third-floor balcony with her baby after being informed that her jobseekers' allowance was being stopped.[49] Elaine Lowe was called in for a meeting to discuss her benefits, but became so worried that they were to be cut that she drowned herself, with her wrists covered in self-inflicted cuts.[50] No doubt each of these stories is complex, but what is particularly striking is that the DWP keeps no published record of suicides or

[44] A Case and A Deaton, *Deaths of Despair and the Future of Capitalism* (Yale University Press, 2020).

[45] ibid.

[46] A Case and A Deaton, 'Rising Morbidity and Mortality in Midlife among White Non-Hispanic Americans in the 21st Century' (2015) 112 *Proceedings of the National Academy of Science* 15078.

[47] Mills (n 18).

[48] ibid.

[49] See www.theguardian.com/commentisfree/2010/jan/07/mother-suicide-welfare-state, accessed 12 December 2021.

[50] See www.standard.co.uk/news/uk/suicide-bid-of-woman-who-feared-losing-her-incapacity-benefit-8761182.html, accessed 12 December 2021.

deaths linked to withdrawal of or reassessment of benefits.[51] This reflects the image of suicides being individual tragedies, rather than looking for the wider underlying social causes. Mills argues that:

> Many newspaper articles tell stories of long battles with the system, appeals processes, letters written to the DWP and medical reassessments that eventually ended in suicide. These articles hint at the affective and psychic life of austerity overlooked by statements about suicide rarely having a 'single cause'. Such statements fail to engage with the ways that austerity is lived and felt as affective force and atmospheric fear, a pervasive psychological and bodily anxiety, shame, and anger, differing in intensity at different times, and fatiguing the body – physically and psychologically wearing it out.[52]

The impact of COVID-19 on suicide provides an interesting case study of the sociology of suicide.[53] Standish and Weil predicted that the policies in response to the pandemic would lead to 'increased levels of psychological stress including anxiety, depression, fear and loneliness, unemployment and homecare/school burdens but also, domestic violence, racism, self-harm, suicide and even femicide'.[54] At the time of writing it is difficult to identify fully the impact of the pandemic on suicide-related issues. It seems as if the expected rise in suicide rates may not have occurred but there is evidence that self-harm and suicidal feelings may have. It was predicted that the required isolation and withdrawal of support would impact heavily on mental health. Certainly factors that are often linked to suicide, including use of intoxicants, economic hardships, social isolation and relationship breakdown, all seem magnified during the COVID-19 pandemic.[55] The Department of Work and Pensions did investigate 69 deaths, although that was only a small number of those it could have examined.[56] It has undertaken to create a 'serious cases panel' to explore more systematically cases with links to suicide.

Philippa Day committed suicide and was found holding a letter rejecting her request for an 'at home' benefits assessment after her benefits were cut.[57] She suffered unstable personality disorder and the responses to her benefit claims were said by her family to leave her feeling 'inhuman'. The inquest found that 28 errors had been made in the handling of her case. Errol Graham was found starved to death. He was seriously mentally ill and failed to attend a work capability assessment, as a result of which his benefits were stopped. At his death he was found to weigh four and a half stone and to have tried to use pliers to pull out his teeth.

[51] Mills (n 18).

[52] ibid.

[53] K Standish and S Weil, 'Gendered Pandemics: Suicide, Femicide and COVID-19' (2021) 30 *Journal of Gender Studies* 807.

[54] ibid.

[55] K Standish, 'A Coming Wave: Suicide and Gender after COVID-19' (2021) *30 Journal of Gender Studies* 114.

[56] A Haylan et al, *Suicide Prevention: Policy and Strategy* (House of Commons Library, 2021).

[57] A Homer, 'Deaths of People on Benefits Prompt Inquiry Call' *BBC News*, 10 May 2021, www.bbc.co.uk/news/uk-56819727, accessed 12 December 2021.

VII. Gender

Rates of suicide are significantly higher among men than women. The Office for National Statistics[58] explains, 'Generally, higher rates of suicide among middle aged men in recent years might be because this group is more likely to be affected by economic adversity, alcoholism, and isolation. It could also be that this group is less inclined to seek help'. That last point is commonly mentioned in discussions of gender and suicide. Men, it is said, find it harder than women to express their feelings and so keep them 'pent up'. They are expected to be strong providers, who do not talk about emotions. Further, it is often suggested that men are impacted by the 'crisis in masculinity'[59] meaning their role and identity is under challenge.[60] For example, the Samaritans report states:

> As a result of changes in the nature of employment and the labour market, in particular the 'feminisation' of employment (shift towards a more service-oriented economy) and the loss of jobs requiring heavy manual labour, men in lower socioeconomic groups now have less access to jobs that allow for the expression of working-class masculinity, and have thus lost a source of masculine identity and 'pride'. Working class men may struggle to 'reconstruct' their identity to fit the changing labour market situation. They may not take up jobs that do become available within the service economy because these conflict with their working class masculine identity.[61]

A survey by the Mental Health Foundation found only 24 per cent of men who experienced high levels of stress felt able to discuss this with a friend or family member.[62] Louise Kitchingham writes:

> In simple terms, toxic masculinity is the result of decades, perhaps centuries, of society teaching boys that they can't and shouldn't express emotion openly and that if they do, then they are weak and 'feminine'. These boys then internalise these feelings and grow into men who have been taught that they can't be anything less than 'masculine'.[63]

Powell claims that men have lost their place in society and this is directly linked to suicide:[64]

> Despite all the changes for women over the past decades, the role of men in society seems parked in the dark ages. Society still says, overwhelmingly, that a real man should get paid more than his wife/girlfriend, and should, indeed, be able to support them and

[58] Office for National Statistics, *Suicide Rates for Males and Females Remain Consistent with 2018* (ONS, 2020).

[59] Campaign against Living Miserably, *A Crisis in Modern Masculinity: Understanding the Causes of Male Suicide* (Campaign against Living Miserably, 2020).

[60] A Chandler, *Exploring the Role of Masculinities in Suicidal Behaviour* (The Samaritans, 2012).

[61] The Samaritans, *Men, Suicide and Society* (The Samaritans, 2018).

[62] Mental Health Foundation, *Only One in Four Men Feel Able to Talk to Friends and Family when Feeling Stressed* (Mental Health Foundation, 2021).

[63] See www.personneltoday.com/hr/world-suicide-prevention-day-why-we-should-redefine-masculinity/, accessed 12 December 2021.

[64] J Powell, 'Suicide, an Issue for Feminists', available at www.thecalmzone.net/2011/04/a-call-to-feminists/, (2011), accessed 12 December 2021.

> a family. A real man is always in charge. A real man is invincible [...] A real man can drink his weight in beer. A real man doesn't reveal anything personal. A real man will hide any personal pain – and be a hero for so doing. A real man doesn't talk.
>
> [...] Men die younger than women, across the age range, because help-seeking behaviour is, by definition, unmanly. So they don't go to their GP unless they have just sheared their leg off below the knee.

The theme of a toxic masculinity and crisis in masculinity with suicide is picked up by Poole:

> when it comes to gender politics it's constantly raining women, leaving men without a lifebelt, caught between the rocks of the traditional, socially conservative desire to protect women and children and the hard place that is the progressive, socially liberal drive to champion women and girls.[65]

A Samaritans Report stated:

> Men compare themselves against a masculine 'gold standard' which prizes power, control and invincibility. When men believe they are not meeting this standard, they feel a sense of shame and defeat. Having a job and being able to provide for your family is central to 'being a man', particularly for working class men. Masculinity is associated with control, but when men are depressed or in crisis, they can feel out of control. This can propel some men towards suicidal behaviour as a way of regaining control. Men are more likely to use drugs or alcohol in response to distress.[66]

This presentation of the problem of male suicide is certainly not without its critics.[67] One concern is that it presents masculinity as a problem for men, rather than acknowledging the problems that traditional masculinity poses for women. It also seems based on a cliched understanding of masculinity which it might be thought few men would identify with. There are also huge differences between different categories of men.[68] As Hill and Needham[69] argue:

> there are many types of men and diverse examples of masculinity and it is a changing concept as men are continually constructing gender. Attempting to understand men's emotional lives using singular and static constructions of man is therefore problematic as is employing binary categorisations of male and female emotions.

Nevertheless, it is clear that gendered identities are a source of confusion and complexity. It certainly seems that accounts of male suicide are associated with

[65] Quoted in A Jordan and A Chandler, 'Crisis? What Crisis? A Feminist Analysis of Discourse on Masculinities and Suicide' (2019) 29 *Journal of Gender Studies* 462, 472.

[66] The Samaritans (n 61).

[67] A Jordan, 'Postfeminist Men's Movements: The Campaign against Living Miserably and Male Suicide as "Crisis"' in A Jordan (ed), *The New Politics of Fatherhood* (Palgrave, 2019).

[68] A Chandler, 'Boys Don't Cry? Critical Phenomenology, Self-harm and Suicide' (2015) 25 *Feminism & Psychology* 124.

[69] T Hill and B Needham, 'Rethinking Gender and Mental Health: A Critical Analysis of Three Propositions' (2013) 92 *Social Science Medicine* 83.

feelings of failure or inadequacy. For example, Honkasalo[70] found that feelings of guilt and shame are prominent in suicide notes written by Finnish men. She cites the following as a typical example:

> Dear Anne. …
>
> I am disappointed with myself and my life. I am really a pitiful man. This is one reason why I think it would be better for you to live without me … Don't blame others for this, everything that took place is my fault. …

Indeed Garfield reports that 'men who hold more traditional beliefs about masculinity and male gender roles … report more problems with anxiety, depression, psychological stress, and maladaptive coping patterns'.[71] This does indicate that simply encouraging men to 'talk' might not be sufficient to address the deeper structural issues surrounding male suicide.

A different angle to look at this question from is to challenge the presentation of suicide as a particularly male activity.[72] Jaworski argues for a deeper analysis, asking 'whether the way we interpret gender differences in suicide has something to do with the living, with the researchers and practitioners working on suicide prevention, rather than those who want to die …'.[73] She suggests that the way suicide is portrayed – as a violent act against suffering – puts suicide in masculine terms.[74] That presentation may mean that suicides by women are not recognised as such. Various explanations are offered, including that there is a difference in the methods used, with men using means which are more likely to lead to death (such as guns) than women. This might lead to an under-reporting of female suicide. Some seek to explain that violent and physical means of suicide (as used by men) are more likely to be perceived as suicide, unlike the more passive means preferred by women.[75] Jaworski suggests that women's suicide is presented in terms of emotional turmoil, whereas for men it is 'pride and resistance against external circumstances such as economic hardship, severe physical illness and social isolation'.[76] In other words, although they may face the same crisis, women are seen to respond by becoming depressed and dependent whereas men assert their autonomy and physical strength. These explanations may even be seen to offer comfort to families and friends, but do not reflect an objective reality. Jaworski states: 'The existence of suicide as an act and an activity is sustained through a nexus of discursively interpreted corporeal signs, configured by gendered meanings and norms. When present, these materialise the deliberate taking of one's life'.

[70] M-L Honkasalo, '"When We Stop Living, We Also Stop Dying" Men, Suicide, and Moral Agency' in Honkasalo and Tuominen (n 12).

[71] C Garfield et al, 'A Review of Men's Health and Masculinity' (2008) 2 *American Journal of Lifestyle Medicine* 474, 475.

[72] Jordan and Chandler (n 65) 472.

[73] K Jaworski, 'The Gendering of Suicide' (2010) 25 *Australian Feminist Studies* 47, 72.

[74] ibid.

[75] ibid.

[76] ibid.

She suggests 'it means that suicide is a ritualised, repeated set of (gendered) norms, yet the workings of such norms are concealed behind intent'. Jaworksi's work has done much to show how gender norms can shape responses to suicide. Indeed, it is important to note that in studies looking at suicide intent there is little difference between men and women, with some studies finding that women have higher rates of suicidal ideation.[77] Indeed, Munro and Aitken claim 'that women – across all ethnic, racial and age groups – are significantly more likely than men to make suicide attempts'.[78]

Discussions of gender and suicide tend to focus on issues around male suicide. However, an important area is the connection between suicide and being a victim of domestic abuse.[79] Domestic abuse can be committed against both men and women, but sustained and serious abuse is predominantly male on female.[80] Sylvia Walby estimated that a third of female suicides were linked to domestic abuse.[81] Munro and Aitken[82] found that the link between domestic abuse and suicide was particularly strong when there was an:

> existence of personal and community support networks, the co-existence of depression, or drug or alcohol dependency, the type and duration of abuse experienced, and the ability to hold out hope for the future (often tied to the existence of children in the household).

These links between domestic abuse and suicide are important for this chapter. Domestic abuse itself is best understood as an expression of patriarchy.[83] Domestic abuse is sustained by patriarchy and sustains patriarchy. This is why there is increasing international recognition of the obligations of the state to protect victims of domestic abuse and offer resources for those who have escaped from abusive relationships. Part of these resources, I suggest, should be in ensuring that there is effective response to the suicidal feelings that emerge from being the victim of domestic abuse.

Less evidence has been collected on the links between sexuality and suicide, partly because sexuality is not recorded on data.[84] The data that exist do show increased risk for LGBTQI+ populations, especially in communities where there is a heightened discrimination against people on the grounds of sexuality,[85]

[77] A Freeman et al, 'A Cross National Study on Gender Differences in Suicide Intent' (2017) 17 *BMC Psychiatry* 234.

[78] V Munro and R Aitken, 'From Hoping to Help: Identifying and Responding to Suicidality amongst Victims of Domestic Abuse' (2020) 26 *International Review of Victimology* 29.

[79] ibid.

[80] J Herring, *Domestic Abuse and Human Rights* (Intersentia, 2021).

[81] S Walby, *The Cost of Domestic Violence* (Women and Equality Unit, 2004).

[82] Munro and Aitken (n 78).

[83] Herring (n 80).

[84] A Haas and M Mortali, 'Suicidal Behavior among Sexual and Gender Minority Populations' in E Rothblum (ed), *The Oxford Handbook of Sexual and Gender Minority Mental Health* (Oxford University Press, 2020).

[85] E Garcia-Vega et al, 'Suicidal Ideation and Suicide Attempts in Persons with Gender Dysphoria' (2018) 30 *Psicothema* 283.

particularly among younger people.[86] This again highlights how it is societal forces, rather than an individual characteristic, which are linked to suicide.

VIII. Age and Suicide

It is common to highlight the links between age and suicide.[87] However, too often this is put in individualistic terms. So it is said that suicide among older people is linked to them experiencing a loss of economic role, sense of loss of productivity and respect, especially within families.[88] Others highlight the 'indignities of aging', which make suicide 'understandable' as a cause of suicide among older people.[89] But that kind of language can reflect ageist assumptions about old age. The indignities and isolation which are often taken as a natural aspect of ageing should be seen as often the product of way society is structured and what is valued within society. The suicides among the isolated old are a product of an ageist society.[90]

Suicides among younger people cause particular concern.[91] The figures in the UK are shocking. In the Millennial study, 10.6 per cent of 17-year-old girls said that they had self-harmed with intent to commit suicide; 4.3 per cent of the boys had.[92] In 2018 there were 714 registered suicides among those aged 15–24, some 9.1 per 100,000 young people.[93] Esposito-Smythers et al[94] in their discussion explain that 'depression, disruptive behavior disorders, and substance use disorders place adolescents at high risk for suicidal behavior'. But this locates the source of the issue within individual young people. Such statistics should raise concerns about the pressures society puts on young people and how resources are allocated to them.[95] It is striking that, for example, there are huge waiting lists for mental health services for young people. It seems these pressures are particularly acute for those children living in poverty and with special educational and social needs.[96] The societal pressures, which are varied and complex, are clearly playing out in higher levels of mental health issues and suicide.

[86] R Cover, *Queer Youth: Suicide, Culture and Identity* (Routledge, 2012).

[87] M Gengasamy et al, 'Contemporary Characteristics and Lethality Correlates of Serious Suicide Attempts in Children and Adolescents' (2020) 50 *Suicide and Life Threatening Behavior* 714.

[88] E Apesoa-Varano et al, '"If You Were Like Me, You Would Consider It Too": Suicide, Older Men, and Masculinity' (2017) 8 *Society and Mental Health* 1.

[89] S Canetto, 'Suicide: Why Are Older Men So Vulnerable?' (2017) 20 *Men and Masculinities* 49.

[90] A Wand et al, 'The Nexus between Elder Abuse, Suicide, and Assisted Dying: The Importance of Relational Autonomy and Undue Influence' (2018) 18 *Macquarie Law Journal* 79.

[91] B Wagner, 'Suicidal Behavior in Children and Adolescents' (Yale University Press, 2009).

[92] P Patalay and E Fitzsimons, *Mental Ill-health at Age 17 in the UK* (UCL, 2000).

[93] RCPCH, *Suicide* (RCPCH, 2020).

[94] C Esposito-Smythers et al, 'Suicidal Behaviors among Children and Adolescents' in Nock (n 37).

[95] University of Manchester, *National Confidential Inquiry into Suicide and Homicide by People with Mental Illness* (University of Manchester, 2017).

[96] B Wagner, 'Nature and Scope of the Problem' in B Wagner (ed), *Suicide Behavior in Children and Adolescents* (Oxford University Press, 2009).

IX. Clusters

One of the most dramatic examples of the social aspect of suicide is 'suicide clusters'.[97] These are defined 'as two or more successive suicides delimited by time – and oftentimes also space – that occur beyond the probability of chance'.[98] There are a range of different forms of clusters. First, these are clusters which are linked to publicity around a particular suicide, typically of a celebrity;[99] for example, the suicide of comedian Robin Williams, which led to a 10 per cent increase in deaths by suicide.[100] The second is where there are a number of suicides connected to a particular place.[101] This separation is somewhat artificial: a suicide in school which sparks off suicides from other students in the school may have both features. The distinction seems to rest on what motivates others to copy the suicide: whether it is association with the person who has died or awareness of the place or form of suicide used. The third form of cluster is where a member of group commits suicide and others then follow that. This is particularly an issue where a family member commits suicide. Being exposed to the suicide of a family member or close friends significantly increases a person's chances of suicide.[102] The phenomenon is also particularly apparent in schools, colleges and the military.[103]

These suicide clusters can be explained in various ways. One is that the suicide of a close friend/relation or a celebrity can make suicide an option to ponder,[104] and even validate it as a possibility. This may be especially so where someone feels a close bond with the person who has committed suicide.[105] This demonstrates how the cultural and social context within which a person lives has a powerful link with suicide.

A particularly powerful example of this can be social media, which offers a microcosm of wider social pressures.[106] There are two primary issues here: first, bullying on social media, which can cause severe distress; second, the existence

[97] C Haw et al, 'Suicide Clusters: A Review of Risk Factors and Mechanisms' (2013) 43 *Suicide and Life Threatening Behavior* 97.

[98] S Abrutyn and A Mueller, 'Are Suicidal Behaviors Contagious in Adolescence? Using Longitudinal Data to Examine Suicide Suggestion' (2014) 79 *American Sociological Review* 211.

[99] Haw et al (n 97).

[100] Pollard et al (n 36).

[101] Haw et al (n 97).

[102] M Maple et al, 'Is Exposure to Suicide Beyond Kin Associated with Risk for Suicidal Behavior? A Systematic Review of the Evidence' (2017) 47 *Suicide and Life Threatening Behavior* 461.

[103] Haw et al (n 97).

[104] S Abrutyn et al, 'Rekeying Cultural Scripts for Youth Suicide: How Social Networks Facilitate Suicide Diffusion and Suicide Clusters Following Exposure to Suicide' (2020) 10 *Society and Mental Health* 112.

[105] M Yildiz et al, 'Suicide Contagion, Gender, and Suicide Attempts among Adolescents' (2019) 43 *Death Studies* 365.

[106] A Mueller, 'Does the Media Matter to Suicide? Examining the Social Dynamics Surrounding Media Reporting on Suicide in a Suicide-Prone Community' (2017) 180 *Social Science and Medicine* 152.

of social media which encourage suicide or provide information about ways in which suicide can be found.[107] In their systematic review, Daine et al[108] emphasise that internet use can have both a positive and negative effect on young people in relation to suicide. Positive effects can include the creation of intimacy and alleviation of loneliness and shame, which can combat suicidal feeling. It is also worth highlighting that in McTernan and Ryan's research[109] there were more websites about suicide prevention and education than there were sites promoting suicide. However, a recent US study of 413 videos about teenage suicide on YouTube determined that almost half (48.6 per cent) were educational and nearly a third (29.3 per sent) covered awareness/prevention of teenage suicide. Negative influence can be the normalising of self-harm, even sharing techniques of suicide and self-harm. Here we see can a culture which normalises and enables suicide having a direct link to the suicide rates.

X. Conclusion

As noted earlier, suicide is typically presented as an individual tragedy. It is seen as being caused by individuals facing challenging circumstances and mental health issues. On this approach, suicide prevention involves identifying suicidal individuals and seeking to stop them committing suicide. By contrast, this chapter has promoted the view that suicide should be seen as a matter of social justice.[110] A society in which there are significant numbers of suicides is a society that is deeply flawed society. The statistics shows us that such societies are those marked by: inequalities in health and financial provision; a lack of social inclusion; and failure to value each citizen.

Significantly for this chapter, the social understanding of suicide means that there is an obligation on society to prevent suicide. Society itself has created the conditions that lead to suicide and therefore has the duty to do what it can to prevent suicide. Suicide can be seen as having a political dimension.[111] A society that leaves individuals to their own devices and sees no responsibility towards them when they face challenges creates an environment where suicide will flourish, but it is also a society which will see suicide as an individual matter. A society that values each member and ensures an inclusive and supportive role for the

[107] R Sedgwick et al, 'Social Media, Internet Use and Suicide Attempts in Adolescents' (2019) 32 *Current Opinion in Psychiatry* 534.

[108] K Daine et al, 'The Power of the Web: A Systematic Review of Studies of the Influence of the Internet on Self-Harm and Suicide in Young People' (2013) 8 *PLoS One* e77555.

[109] N McTernan and F Ryan, *The Harmful Impact of Suicide and Self-Harm Content Online: A Review of The Literature* (National Suicide Research Foundation, Ireland, 2020).

[110] J Westefeld, 'Suicide Prevention: An Issue of Social Justice' (2020) 1 *Journal of Prevention and Health Promotion* 58.

[111] T Szasz, *Fatal Freedom: The Ethics and Politics of Suicide* (Syracuse University Press, 2002).

state will be one that should see lower suicide rates and a more proactive suicide prevention policy. The state's regulation of – and response to – suicide can say much about how the state understands its broader relationship to its citizens.[112] This brings us to how the law understands the obligations of the state to its citizens, which is discussed in the next chapter.

[112] D Sperling, *Suicide Tourism* (Oxford University Press, 2020).

5

Ethics and Suicide

I. Introduction

This chapter will explore the ethics of suicide. The debate is complex. In part this is because the questions it raises are profound. Camus claimed that 'There is but one truly serious philosophical problem, and that is suicide. Judging whether life is or is not worth living amounts to answering the fundamental question of philosophy'.[1] But the debate is also complex because in some writing there is a lack of clarity on precisely what question is being asked. 'Is suicide morally justified?' is a very different question from 'Is there a legal right to commit suicide?'. The question is made even more complex by the debates over the definition of suicide, discussed in Chapter 2. Indeed, how you define suicide can impact on whether you think suicides can be rational or justified. This means that answering a question such as 'is suicide irrational?' or 'is suicide ethically justifiable?' is highly problematic, because so much will depend on the particular definitions used and the precise nature of the question. At the end of this chapter I will seek to untangle the different questions that arise and particularly how they fit into legal responses. But the primary focus of this chapter will be on the ethical issues around suicide. I should emphasise that I am not here specifically considering the issues around assisted suicide or euthanasia, which are discussed further in Chapter 8, although clearly there is an overlap with them.

Before proceeding, it is important to acknowledge that when considering the ethical issues raised by suicide, emotional reactions have an important role. Chris Cowley[2] emphasises that the key elements of a reaction to suicide are horror, pity and mystery. Intellectual wrangling about suicide might not be the right starting point, he suggests. That view will be discussed later, but for now we focus on the traditional approaches to thinking through the ethics of suicide.

II. What is the Question?

For the purposes of this chapter, suicide is defined as intentional self-killing, as discussed in Chapter 2. I do not mean to pre-suppose that it is limited to cases

[1] A Camus, *The Myth of Sisyphus*, trans by J O'Brien (Penguin, 2000) 1.

[2] C Cowley, 'Suicide is Neither Rational nor Irrational' (2006) 9 *Ethical Theory and Moral Practice* 495, 501.

of wrongful self-killing, so that the ethical issues can be considered. As already mentioned, when thinking about ethical approaches to suicide it is important to be clear what question is being asked. There is a particular danger for lawyers and ethicists when discussing this issue. Lawyers tend to focus on what conduct should be prohibited by the law: what conduct is so bad that it should be punished using criminal law, or so negligent that liability under tort law is imposed? By contrast, ethicists often focus on what is the 'right thing to do'. If care is not taken, this can lead to ethicists and lawyers talking across each other. For example, just because something is unethical does not, of course, mean it should be unlawful. Sometimes behaviour which is ethically unproblematic may be illegal, although it would be rare for such a case to reach the courts.

Before exploring the ethical issues in more detail, it is helpful to provide the briefest overview of the intellectual journey of the ethical and moral responses to suicide. In the West, responses to suicide have been dominated by Christian thought. Although there is no explicit direction again suicide in the Bible, St Augustine thought it could be implied:

> God's command 'Thou shalt not kill,' is to be taken as forbidding self-destruction, especially as it does not add 'thy neighbour', as it does when it forbids false witness, 'Thou shalt not bear false witness against thy neighbour'.[3]

As church history developed, suicide became seen as a serious sin. St Thomas Aquinas explained that suicide was wrong because we are expected to love ourselves; that suicide harmed the community; and, perhaps most influentially, that life is a gift from God, meaning that it is for God to decide when a life was to end.[4] Harsh sanctions were imposed on those thought to have committed suicide, including desecration of the corpse and denial of a 'Christian burial'. In 1860 a man who had attempted to cut his throat was treated until he recovered, tried for attempted suicide, and then hanged.[5] While there was a vein of legal logic to this – suicide was murder of the self and therefore the death penalty used for murder should be applied – the outcome certainly seems somewhat bizarre. This negative attitude from Christian thinkers has existed from then until today, albeit it with some dissenting voices. Although, of course, the significance of religious thought in public discourse has considerably waned.

Signs of a more liberal approach might be found in David Hume's 'Of Suicide',[6] challenging the traditional religious arguments by saying that the church allowed people to change 'nature' by medical treatments, or diverting rivers for irrigation, and that suicide was no different a change to the natural course of events than

[3] St Augustine, *The Confessions of Saint Augustine* (Peter Pauper Press, 1949) Book I, ch 20.

[4] St Aquinas 1271, *Summa Theologica* in A Pegis (ed), *Basic Writings of Saint Thomas Aquinas* (Random House, 1945) Part II Q 64; Aristotle, *Nicomachean Ethics*, trans by R Crisp (Cambridge University Press, 2000 [c 330BCE]).

[5] J Droge and A Tabor, *A Noble Death: Suicide and Martyrdom among Christians and Jews in Antiquity* (Harper Collins, 1992) 7.

[6] D Hume, *Of Suicide* (Penguin, 2005 [1783]).

these. More significantly, he emphasised that in sickness our lives can become miserable and that continued existence is worse than death. It is this latter argument that has taken on significance in contemporary debates. The changes in attitudes towards suicide are revealed in the titles of leading works: 'From Sin to Insanity'[7] and 'From Satan to Serotonin'.[8] They reflect the shift from seeing suicide as a matter of moral blame to it being the subject of medical intervention. Nowadays the societal nature of suicide receives much attention too.

Today the public debates over suicide tend to focus on two sets of arguments. The first set is concerned with autonomy: when can a person autonomously decide whether to commit suicide? A popular view is that once it is determined that a person has made an autonomous decision to die, then that decision must be respected and they should be permitted to act as they wish, unless there are strong reasons not to. Some would take an even stronger line and suggest they should be enabled to satisfy their autonomous wishes. In other words, they should be given help to die, certainly if they cannot commit suicide without assistance. Of course, there are those who argue against this, who claim that no suicide – or very few at least – is autonomous (or sufficiently autonomous) to justify protection under principles of autonomy.

The second set of arguments surround whether if the decision to commit suicide is autonomous, whether nevertheless there may be a justification for interfering with a person's autonomous decision. Some will claim there never can be, because an autonomous decision which does not directly harm others must be respected. For others, the question is whether in a particular case the harms caused by the suicide are sufficient to justify interference. Here too we will discuss those who promote the sanctity of life view, which would argue that all suicides are wrong because they fail to respect the inherent value in life.[9] They might argue that respect for that principle certainly forbids assisting in a suicide, even if it is autonomous, and some would say justifies preventing a person from committing suicide.

Although these questions (Does the person have autonomy? Is there a good reason to interfere with their choice?) have been separated in this summary, they overlap in complex ways, as we shall see. For example, if you believe suicide is very harmful to the individual, that can (but may not) impact on whether you think the person is acting autonomously.

It is in fact rare these days to find people taking an absolutist view on suicide: that all suicides should be ethically permitted, or that no suicides should be ethically permitted. As is clear from this summary, the principle of autonomy plays a major role in the debates so we will start there, by explaining the principle of autonomy before unpacking some of the debates around it.

[7] J Watt, *From Sin to Insanity: Suicide in Early Modern Europe* (Cornell University Press, 2004).
[8] H Kushner, *Self-Destruction in the Promised Land* (Rutgers University Press, 1989).
[9] M Cholbi, *Suicide: The Philosophical Dimensions* (Broadview, 2011).

III. The Principle of Autonomy

At the heart of the principle of autonomy is the claim that we should be allowed to make decisions about what happens in our lives. It is not for the Government, or the great and the good, to control how people behave. Children are told what time to get up and how to speak, but adults should not be – at least, not unless there is a very good reason. A good reason would be that doing what they want to do will interfere with someone else's right to choose what they want to do. However, much you might like punching other people, that interferes with their right to live how they wish. Thus, your autonomous decision can be interfered with. But if you enjoy punching yourself, that can be an exercise of autonomy which is not hurting anyone else and so should be permitted. What would not be a good reason to interfere in autonomy is that the state thinks someone is making a bad choice. You might think the amount of time I spend reading articles on law a waste of time, my diet highly detrimental, and my use of money immoral, but I am not hurting anyone else (directly) by doing these things and so I should be free to use my time, digestion and money as I wish.

In part, the emphasis on autonomy reflects a profound belief that we should be 'authors of our lives'. Many people will agree with Isaiah Berlin, who stated:

> I wish my life and decision to depend on myself, not on external forces of whatever kind. I wish to be the instrument of my own, not of other men's act of will. I wish to be a subject, not an object; to be moved by reasons, by conscious purposes, which are my own, not by causes which affect me, as it were from outside.[10]

Dworkin[11] has argued this is particularly important because it means our lives can reflect who we are. Autonomy, he suggests:

> derives from the capacity it protects: the capacity to express one's own character – values, commitments, convictions and critical, as well as experiential, interests – in the life one leads.

The alternative, paternalism, means that one's life reflects the values and principles of others. And that sounds like a form of moral slavery.[12] The case in favour of respecting autonomy may be strengthened by considering the position of those without much freedom to choose how to live: slaves, those with profound disabilities, prisoners. Such people would be seen as having lost something of considerable value, perhaps even to be in a pitiable state.[13] People are respected as full citizens when they get to decide for themselves how to live: they are entitled to self-rule.[14]

[10] I Berlin, *Two Conceptions of Liberty* (Oxford University Press, 1968) 131.

[11] R Dworkin, *Life's Dominion* (Harper Collins, 1993) 38.

[12] L Swaine, *Ethical Autonomy: The Rise of Self-Rule* (Oxford University Press, 2020) 1.

[13] S Hitlin and H Won Kwon, 'Agency Across the Life Course' in J Mortimer and M Shanahan (eds), *Handbook of the Life Course* (Springer, 2016).

[14] Swaine (n 12) 1.

Support for autonomy also reflects a lack of confidence in the abilities of those in power to declare what is – or is not – in a person's best interests. With a lack of trust in expertise and a breakdown in agreed moral values, it has become highly controversial to declare what is or is not in someone else's interests. Too many of the confident declaration in the past of governments, doctors, bishops and the like about what was good, healthy or moral, are now looked back on with horror. We realise too that what might be good for one person might not be so for a different person, with different values and lifestyle. If no one can authoritatively decide what is good way of life for someone else, then we may as well let the person decide for themselves. Paternalism is troubling because it makes the object of paternalism a 'means to ends of the paternalist's making, rather than being recognized as the source of his or her own ends'.[15] Hence, we have the 'triumph of autonomy'.[16]

And it is easy to see how these arguments then become key in the ethics of suicide. To prevent a person who has autonomously chosen to commit suicide from doing so would be to compel them to carry on living when they do not want to. As David Benetar[17] puts it:

> Life would have been forced on them, and they would have to endure whatever life dished out to them. It is bad enough that prospective parents see fit to create people who, as a consequence, will suffer. It is worse still, once these people are created, to condemn a decision they might make to terminate their lives.

Indeed, he[18] argues 'because none of us could have consented to being brought into existence, it is especially important that each one of us at least have the option of ceasing to exist if he or she would rather not endure the hardships that life presents'. Famously, Ronald Dworkin has argued that not letting someone die when they want is a serious wrong:

> Making someone die in a way that others approve, but he believes a horrifying contradiction of his life, is a devastating, odious form of tyranny.[19]

Even suicide prevention strategies can be seen as part of the oppression of suicidal people. Alexandre Baril[20] argues that:

> based on the sanist silencing of suicidal subjects through the injunction to live and somatechnologies of life, suicidal people constitute an oppressed, stigmatised group whose claims remain unintelligible within society, law, medical/psychiatric systems and anti-oppressive scholarship …

[15] J Kleinig, *Paternalism* (Rowman and Allanheld, 1983) 38.

[16] C Foster, *Choosing Life, Choosing Death* (Hart Publishing, 2009).

[17] D Benatar, 'Suicide: A Qualified Defense' in J Stacey Taylor (ed), *The Metaphysics and Ethics of Death* (Oxford University Press, 2013).

[18] ibid.

[19] Dworkin (n 11).

[20] A Baril, 'The Somatechnologies of Canada's Medical Assistance in Dying Law: LGBTQ Discourses on Suicide and the Injunction to Live' (2017) 7 *Somatechnics* 201, 203.

The arguments here posit suicide prevention schemes as violence against suicidal people, seeking to impose on them an 'injunction to live'.[21] This can be reinforced by what is seen as broader oppression of those who are viewed as having 'mental health issues'.

As can be seen from the powerful expression of these views, they can lead to an argument that not only should an autonomous suicide not be prevented, it should be assisted. Normally autonomy is not seen as sufficient to justify state support. I may well want to holiday for a month in the Maldives, and while I should not be prevented from doing that, the state has no obligation to provide me with the means to do it. However, there seem to be cases where the autonomous decision relates to an issue which is so core to a person's identity and wellbeing – such as access to medical treatment, abortion or reproduction – that arguments for positive assistance can be made. While it may be assumed that the loss of a visit to the Maldives will not impact my identity or core values, denying me access to health treatment might well do so. Thus, it might be said that the strength of the autonomy claim is such that there is a case for requiring assistance to help people to die at the time and in the manner of their choosing. Such claims will be explored in Chapter 8.

Before moving on, we should note that those supportive of suicide prevention can rely on autonomy too. It might be argued that the person seeking suicide does not really want to commit suicide and their true autonomous desire is to live. Or that their momentary wish is to die but their deeper or longer-term autonomous decision is to live. In such cases, allowing suicide would be to disrespect autonomy, not to uphold it. We will be returning to that argument throughout this chapter, but next we need to consider in more depth the relationship between autonomy and welfare.

IV. Autonomy and Welfare

From what has been said so far, it might be expected that support for autonomy would require respecting a person's decision, regardless of whether it was for a person's welfare or could be seen as wise or not. Indeed, in most contexts that is precisely how it is applied. However, in the context of suicide, most of those who support assisted suicide argue that both autonomy and welfare are required. In other words, for suicide to be appropriate not only must the person autonomously choose to die, but there must be a good reason for their decision (eg they were close to death or suffering a terminal illness). There might be disagreement as to precisely what those welfare requirements are and precisely what role they play in moral reasoning. But few people would agree that a teenager bullied online, or a student fed up with the homophobia in their college, should

[21] G Wedlake, 'Complicating Theory through Practice: Affirming the Right to Die for Suicidal People' (2020) 9 *Canadian Journal of Disability Studies* 89.

be supported or enabled to end their life. Hence, a fairly standard view would be that it should be countenanced only if a person seeking to commit suicide is suffering unbearably and there is little or no hope for an improvement.[22] Of course, not everyone agrees and there are those who have argued that autonomy alone should be sufficient.[23] Some take the line that the arguments in favour of the principle of autonomy generally do not depend on any assessment of the wisdom of the decision and that should also be the approach taken for suicide. Davis and Mathison argue that it is impossible for another to assess someone's degree of suffering and we must accept the individual's own assessment that their life is not worth living:

> … what is morally relevant about suffering is that one judges continued life to be intolerable to her. … there are many other ways that life might be intolerable that do not involve pain in the ordinary sense, such as living a life that is inconsistent with one's values, or is otherwise judged to be no longer worth living. Importantly, judging that one's life is not worth living is not restricted to a prudential judgement. People care about living in accordance with their values, and the inability to do so is a significant source of distress. This is so even if one lacks physical suffering. On our view, it is possible to be prudentially well off while judging that something one values that requires death outweighs the prudential value of continued life ….

There are several issues behind this debate about the balance between welfare and autonomy.

A. The Reasons for Respecting Autonomy

There are two primary schools of thought on why autonomy deserves respect. The first is that autonomy is supported for instrumental reasons, ie that welfare is best promoted by allowing a person to make their own decisions. In short, imposing treatment that they do not want on people is unlikely to be beneficial. If I get to choose what flavour of yoghurt I will eat, it is likely to be a more beneficial decision than if a stranger or even a friend chooses for me. The second is that autonomy is an intrinsic good. Even if the choice I make is a bad one, it is my body, my life and my choice. It is a basic right of a person, independent of any welfare assessment.

For those who take the first view, that autonomy is supported as an instrumental good, there is scope for arguing that in a particular case, the welfare harm caused by the decision is so great that the normal assumption – that promoting autonomy promotes welfare – is overridden. As death is often seen as the most serious harm a person can suffer, we might see more scope than on other decisions,

[22] J De Haan, 'The Ethics of Euthanasia: Advocates' Perspectives' (2002) 16 *Bioethics* 154, 169.

[23] J Davis and E Mathison, 'The Case for an Autonomy-Centered View of Physician-Assisted Death' (2020) 17 *Journal of Bioethical Inquiry* 345.

for saying we can depart from the normal presumption that respecting autonomy promotes welfare.

Those who take the second view (that autonomy is an intrinsic good) will find it harder to justify treating suicide differently from other decisions. However, it might be argued that death so restricts the intrinsic good of autonomy, eg by severely limiting future options for autonomy, that we can intervene. If autonomy is an intrinsic good, we cannot use that to justify ending the intrinsic good of autonomy itself. We will return to this argument later.

These arguments, therefore, suggest that the harm of death is so great that the reasons for respecting autonomy do not apply with full strength in relation to suicide. We will be returning to this issue later in the chapter.

B. 'Risk Relative Capacity'

A second way in which welfare considerations can impact on autonomy is in relation to the assessment of capacity. This is the argument that different levels of capacity should be required, depending on the potential harmfulness of the decision being made. We might, for example, require a low bar to be set for capacity over trivial issues (do you want milk in your tea?) and a high bar for key issues (do you consent to amputation)?[24] This approach has an initial attraction, even though it does involve welfare considerations impacting on the capacity assessment. And it is not without judicial support. When deciding a case about forgoing life-sustaining treatment, Lord Donaldson of the English Court of Appeal said: 'The more serious the decision, the greater the capacity required'.[25]

In the academic literature, this approach – with different settings of the capacity bar depending on the degree of potential harm – is known as 'risk relative capacity'.[26] If this view is adopted it is clearly relevant to suicide as it is likely that suicide would be regarded as a significant issue for which the bar to capacity would be set high. 'Risk relative capacity' is a controversial approach. Many commentators feel that it is inappropriate, because a person either understands the issues or they do not, and the degree of risk should not affect an assessment of their comprehension. The concern is that under the guise of the capacity test, welfare considerations are being smuggled in. In other words, because a decision is deemed to be very dangerous, a person's decision is overruled because they are found to lack capacity. This looks like paternalism in disguise.

[24] D Strang et al, 'Capacity to Choose Place of Residence: Autonomy vs Beneficence?' (1998) 14 *Journal of Palliative Care* 25, 26.

[25] *Re T (Adult: Refusal of Medical Treatment)* [1992] 4 All ER 649, 662.

[26] J Herring, 'Entering the Fog: On the Borderlines of Mental Capacity' (2008) 83 *Indiana Law Journal* 1620.

To clarify the concept of risk relative capacity it is important to recall that on the standard approach capacity is determined in relation to a particular issue. This means that there is nothing unusual, even on the standard approach, of saying that a person may be able to consent to some matters, but not others. That might arise where one issue was straightforward and familiar to a person, while the other was complex and required considerable understanding. On that basis it could be readily concluded that a person might have capacity to determine whether they wanted milk in their tea but not to consent to complex surgery. Risk relative capacity departs from the standard approach in cases where a high-risk activity is relatively straightforward to understand or a low-risk activity is complex. In such cases, by lowering or raising the requirements of capacity using risk relative capacity, a different result might be found than using a standard capacity test for all issues whatever their dangerousness.

My concern with the risk relative capacity approach is that it involves a conflation of two issues: (1) whether a person has capacity to make a decision; and (2) whether or not a person's decision may ever be overruled on paternalistic grounds. If the real reason that we do not want to give effect to a person's decision is because we think it will cause too much harm, it is best to be open about that, rather than disguising the issue with a moveable capacity test. A well-known example is provided by Wilks,[27] who suggests that if we have two equally competent tightrope walkers who want to walk a tightrope, one with a net and one without, we might stop the one without a net from walking under the risk relative capacity, but not the one with a net. Even if their level of understanding was the same, the bar for capacity would be higher for the 'no net' walker. It seems that what is doing the work here in making this plausible is the danger involved, rather than levels of capacity. As Nancy Knauer[28] has argued, 'risk-relative capacity has the potential to become the ultimate self-fulfilling doctrine: those who exercise approved choices have capacity, whereas those who exercise socially undesirable choices lack capacity'.

A major aspect of the problem with the risk relative capacity approach is it that persists with the idea that capacity is an 'on/off' switch rather than recognising that it scalar. Rather than putting people into boxes marked 'with capacity' and 'without capacity', we can recognise the ways in which people can be to a greater or lesser extent autonomous. Not all autonomous decisions carry the same weight. To deal with that concern, the next alternative approach is preferable.

[27] I Wilks, 'The Debate over Risk-related Standards of Competence' (1997) 11 *Bioethics* 413.

[28] N Knauer, 'Defining Capacity: Balancing the Competing Interests of Autonomy and Need' (2003) 12 *Temple Political and Civil Rights Law Review* 321.

C. Balancing Capacity and Autonomy

Some commentators argue for a transparent weighing up of the strength of autonomy and the degree of welfare. As Wall and I have argued:

> … we should not assume that autonomy is an 'all-or-nothing concept'. A richly autonomous decision requires full protection and the patient has the right to have their refusal respected, however serious the consequences. Where, however, the decision is only marginally autonomous, then it may be sufficient to deserve respect in cases where what the patient wants to do something that is not particularly harmful. A weakly autonomous decision may, therefore, not be sufficient to justify doing an act that will lead to serious harm.[29]

Consider, for example, the law requiring the wearing of seatbelts. That does interfere with autonomy: you must wear one whether you like it or not. However, it is unlikely to be an issue you care very strongly about. It is hardly an issue that goes to the heart of your identity in the way that your religious beliefs might. The weight attached to autonomy is fairly light. Moreover, the belts will save you from death, a very serious harm. Comparing these issues, it should be clear that the welfare arguments win out.

It is helpful here to return to the arguments about why we think autonomy is important. We treasure autonomy and the power it gives us to shape our lives according to our own values. That we should be free to fashion our lives and live out our version of the 'good life' is seen as a fundamental aspect of humanity. Autonomy enables us to develop and express our characters and beliefs. Ronald Dworkin explains:

> [A]utonomy makes each of us responsible for shaping his own life according to some coherent and distinctive sense of character, conviction, and interest. It allows us to lead our own lives rather than being led along them, so that each of us can be, to the extent a scheme of rights can make this possible, what he has made himself. This view of autonomy focuses not on individual decisions one by one, but the place of each decision in a more general program or picture of life the agent is creating and constructing, a conception of character and achievement that must be allowed its own distinctive integrity.[30]

This shows us that the weight due to an autonomous decision does not just depend on the capacity I have, but also how core to my identity or beliefs it is. To show the difference, we might imagine a deeply religious person for whom their faith is key to their identity. We might well argue how capacitous this decision is: evidence for or against the existence of God is debated and complex. Inevitably they will not know all the information necessary to make the decision; maybe

[29] J Herring and J Wall, 'Autonomy, Capacity and Vulnerable Adults: Filling the Gaps in the Mental Capacity Act' (2015) 35 *Legal Studies* 698, 700.

[30] R Dworkin, 'Autonomy and the Demented Self' (1986) 64 *Millbank Quarterly* 4, 6.

they were raised in their religion and we might question whether or not they have freely chosen the religion; or maybe the comfort offered by faith is such that they have a terror of not believing. Consider the same person is an expert in yoghurt and has decided, after extensive research, that they like gooseberry yoghurt slightly more than any other flavour. Although the yoghurt choice is highly capacitous – they understand all the information and have thought deeply about the issue – maybe the religious decision is not: there is much to them which is a mystery about faith and they have not taken time to think deeply about faith; they have just accepted it. Nevertheless, we might assume it would be a far bigger interference in their selfhood to interfere with their faith than their yoghurt selection. That is because the faith issue goes to the heart of their identity, their life story, far more than the yoghurt selection.[31]

Another way of considering the issue is to say if a course of action is recommended by an expert, such as a doctor, then if the patient agrees to that we have less reason to question the patient's capacity. The doctor's advice gives them a good reason to agree. They can sensibly say 'I don't really understand all the issues, but I trust the doctor, and understand in broad terms what they are saying'. Indeed, this is the kind of reasoning we commonly use in decisions, especially those involving experts, whether this be a complex piece of plumbing, an investment decision, or purchasing a computer. It is when someone is saying they disagree with an expert, particularly when they do not have expertise themselves, that we might automatically question why and whether there are good reasons. Thus, in this context, if a person is wanting to die in circumstances when that decision seems not to accord with the opinions of experts, then we have reason to question their capacity. They need to do more to assure us that their autonomy is sufficiently rich for their decision to be respected, than in a case where their decision is in line with that of an expert and they have decided to follow the expert's opinion.

One important argument for the balancing approach is that we must accept responsibility for respecting the person's decision. If, as a result of our respecting the decision, the person is left in considerable pain or distress, which we could have easily prevented by an intervention, we need to have a good justification for why we did not provide that intervention. Respect for autonomy can be a sufficient justification, but only if that autonomy is rich full autonomy. Relying on autonomy where the person was mistaken about key facts; was thinking irrationally; was pressurised by others etc, will not provide a sufficient reason to justify them being left in a miserable state. In other words, we need to recognise both the

[31] Of course we might imagine another person who has religious beliefs which are utterly unimportant to them, while yoghurt eating is what gives their life meaning. For them we might assume the yoghurt choice is more fundamental to their identity than the religious decision.

dangers of not respecting an autonomous decision, but also of respecting a non-autonomous decision. Jesse Wall and I[32] have written:

> It is a terrible thing to be assessed as lacking capacity when you do not – to have others make decisions on your behalf and set aside your own wishes based on what they think is in your best interests. You lose control over your life. You are no longer in charge of your destiny.
>
> It is a terrible thing to be said to have capacity when you do not – to be left to cause yourself and those you love great harm on the basis that you know what you are doing and you are making your own choices, when in fact your decisions are not really yours. To have others harm you and to be told no protection is offered because you have chosen this harm, even though it is against your deepest values, is horrific.

This is true too when considering suicide. To ask whether the person had capacity to make the decision is not very helpful. We should ask whether the person's autonomy was sufficiently rich to justify respecting their decision. That is a far more useful question than to ask, than 'did they know enough to make the decision', which does not give us guidance as to how much they needed to know. As we argue, it is not obvious that the wrong done to a person who is incorrectly assessed as not having capacity is worse than the wrong to a person who is incorrectly assessed as having capacity. This will be seen as especially so in a case of suicide. It must be questioned whether respecting a decision to die that is based on a flawed understanding of the position or on an otherwise impaired autonomy is sufficient to justify this outcome. Indeed, as den Hartogh points out, the fact that many people rescued from a suicide attempt are very grateful for being stopped indicates that their settled, deep, autonomous wish was not to die.[33]

We need now to explore further the issues that arise in determining whether someone is sufficiently autonomous (whether they have capacity) to make the decision to die.

V. Capacity, Autonomy and Suicide

The arguments in favour of respecting autonomy are only effective when a person is autonomous, ie when they are in a position to make the decision.[34] If a person does not know the circumstances they are in, or is being forced to make a decision, then the decision being made is not 'theirs' or not about the position they are in. Respecting that person's decision will not be about the person being 'author of their lives', as others are manipulating their decision or they are not

[32] J Herring and J Wall, 'Autonomy, Capacity and Vulnerable Adults: Filling the Gaps in the Mental Capacity Act' (2015) 35 *Legal Studies* 698.

[33] G den Hartogh, 'Why Extra Caution is Needed in the Case of Depressed Patients' (2015) 41 *Journal of Medical Ethics* 588.

[34] T Grisso and P Appelbaum, *Assessing Competence To Consent To Treatment* (Oxford University Press, 1998).

where they think they are. For example, if a person refuses a medication because they are under a delusion it is 'from Satan' and will kill them, complying with that decision will not be allowing them to be 'authors of their own story' if they end up in severe pain or dead as a result. Indeed, such a person may be desperate to live and be willing to accept any medicine which is not 'from Satan'. It is important, therefore, that we distinguish between those decisions which can be taken as belonging to a person and can be taken as decisions about where their life is to go; and those decisions which are, for example, so ill-informed or so pressurised that they cannot be taken as a reflection of a person's desire for where they want their life to go. This is where the test for capacity comes in. It requires evidence that a person has sufficient understanding of their situation and freedom to make the decision. It is, therefore, a core pre-condition to claiming a right to autonomy that one is autonomous: one is in a position to be 'author of one's life' and make a decision which can be given effect. However, precisely how that test is formulated is controversial.

In English law, the general test for capacity is set out in section 2(1) of the Mental Capacity Act 2005:

> [A] person lacks capacity in relation to a matter if at the material time he is unable to make a decision for himself in relation to the matter because of an impairment of, or a disturbance in the functioning of, the mind or brain.

Section 3(1) of the same Act explains what is meant by a person being unable to make a decision for themselves:

> [A] person is unable to make a decision for himself if he is unable—
>
> (a) to understand the information relevant to the decision,
> (b) to retain that information,
> (c) to use or weigh that information as part of the process of making the decision, or
> (d) to communicate his decision (whether by talking, using sign language or any other means).

As this indicates, there are a number of ways in which a person may be said to be unable to make a decision. These can range from not understanding a key piece of information, to not being able to weigh up the different factors.[35] That legislative test has formed the basis of the MacArthur Competence Assessment Tool-Treatment (MacCAT-T), which is widely used in practice to assess capacity. The MacCAT-T criteria asks whether the patient has:[36]

(1) the ability to express a choice;
(2) the ability to understand information relevant to treatment decision-making;

[35] D Shaw et al, 'Assessment of Decision-Making Capacity in Patients Requesting Assisted Suicide' (2018) 213 *British Journal of Psychiatry* 393.

[36] Grisso and Appelbaum (n 32); T Grisso et al, 'The MacCAT-T: A Clinical Tool to Assess Patients' Capacities to Make Treatment Decisions' (1997) 48 *Psychiatric Services* 1415; P Appelbaum, 'Clinical Practice: Assessment of Patients' Competence to Consent to Treatment' (2007) 357 *New England Journal of Medicine* 1834.

(3) the ability to appreciate the significance of that information for one's own situation, especially concerning one's illness and the probable consequences of one's treatment options; and
(4) the ability to reason with the relevant information so as to engage in a logical process of weighing treatment options.

Those approaches are, however, based on legal principles. Ethicists tend to develop a richer account of what capacity requires. Jesse Wall[37] has argued that to act autonomously it must be shown that a person is able:

(1) to act free from undue interference or influence of others (the freedom condition);
(2) to exercise the capacity for rational thought and cognition (the competence condition); and
(3) to act according to the beliefs, values, and commitments that the person identifies or endorses as their own beliefs, values, and commitments (the authenticity condition).

This offers a far more nuanced approach to assessing capacity than the legal test.

We will now explore some of the precise issues in relation to capacity tests to better understand the debates over them.

A. Cause of Incapacity

Under the UK's Mental Capacity Act 2005, as was explained in *A Local Authority v TZ*,[38] the test of capacity in section 2(1) involves a 'diagnostic test' and a 'functional test'. Under the diagnostic test, it must be found that a person has an impairment or a disturbance in the functioning of the brain. Under the 'functional test', it must be determined whether, as a result of the disturbance, a person is unable to make the decision. Importantly, it must be shown that the inability to make the decision results from the impairment. Thus, patients with no mental impairment who refuse all treatment because of their religious belief that God will cure them will still have mental capacity. Even if the doctors try to argue that the patients do not properly understand the reality of their situation, that will not be because of a mental impairment.

This appears clearly to breach the United Nations Convention on the Rights of Persons with Disabilities. Article 12(2) of the Convention provides that people with disabilities may enjoy legal capacity 'on an equal basis with others in all aspects of life'. Yet here, if we have two people with delusions, the one whose delusion is as

[37] J Wall, 'Authentic Decision-Making and Depression' in C Foster and J Herring (eds), *Law and Depression* (Oxford University Press, 2018).
[38] *A Local Authority v TZ* [2013] EWHC 2322 (COP).

a result of a mental disorder is treated differently from the one whose is not. It is difficult to see, in ethical terms, why this should be so.

B. Presumption of Capacity

The Mental Capacity Act 2005, section 1 states:

> (2) A person must be assumed to have capacity unless it is established that he lacks capacity.
>
> …
>
> (4) A person is not to be treated as unable to make a decision merely because he makes an unwise decision.

This creates a clear presumption in favour of capacity. In other words, unless there is evidence to the contrary, an adult is presumed to have the capacity to make a decision. Generally this is seen as the correct approach for most issues.[39] I will focus on whether it should apply to suicide.

The issue, in other words, is whether the fact that a person is suicidal of itself rebuts the standard presumption of capacity. It might be argued that while it is reasonable to assume that most people who choose tea over coffee have capacity to make the decision, it is not reasonable to assume that those who wish to kill themselves are not in a position to make an autonomous decision. Of course, the claim need not be that all suicidal people lack capacity – just that a sufficient number lack capacity to mean the presumption of capacity is inappropriate. It might be added because we are discussing a presumption, an individual assessment could determine that, in fact, a person did have capacity to commit suicide.

This issue could be resolved by a matter of statistics. If, say, 99 per cent of those buying a flat white coffee have the capacity to do so, but only 22 per cent of those seeking suicide do so, it seems, as a matter of mathematics, reasonable to have a presumption of capacity for coffee purchase, but not in relation to suicide. Indeed, we might bolster that conclusion by saying that the 1 per cent of coffee purchases who are incorrectly presumed to have capacity and permitted to buy coffee are not going to do themselves much harm. By contrast, the 78 per cent wrongly presumed to have capacity to die by suicide will do themselves a serious wrong. These arguments seem convincing, but they all depend on the statistics and it is difficult to establish what these are, not least because of the lack of agreement over the test for capacity. While, therefore, I expect that the statistics would indicate the vast majority lack capacity, I accept that I cannot prove it.[40]

[39] I have argued it is not: J Herring, 'Peter Skegg and the Question No-one Asks: Why Presume Capacity?' in M Henaghan and J Wall (eds), *Law, Ethics, and Medicine: Essays in Honour of Peter Skegg* (Thompson Reuters, 2016).

[40] C Steward et al, 'A Test for Mental Capacity to Request Assisted Suicide' (2011) 37 *Journal of Medical Ethics* 34.

C. Foolishness

Even a person with autonomy can make a foolish decision. Indeed, there might be little point in having the principle of autonomy if it only respected wise decisions. The Mental Capacity Act 2005, section 1(4) states 'A person is not to be treated as unable to make a decision merely because he makes an unwise decision'. The word 'merely' is important there. Of course, the fact that a person makes a bizarre decision is evidence of a lack of capacity. If a person was found eating earth or hitting themselves, we would rightly question whether they were aware of what they were doing. There may be some good explanation, but we would be entitled to expect some explanation and, if there is no explanation, to assume a lack of capacity. In other words, absent some good reasons, there are certain kinds of conduct which are indicative of a lack of capacity. To put this point another way, in some contexts 'I felt like it' or 'no particular reason' is a reasonable explanation for a decision: choosing a flavour of ice cream, for example. For other forms of conduct, 'no particular reason' is not an explanation and, indeed, would indicate a lack of capacity: doing very dangerous activities or those that will cause the person a serious harm.[41] Suicide, it might be said, falls into that category. It is such a potentially harmful decision that we require convincing that the person undertaking it has capacity.

D. Information

In order for a person to be autonomous they need to understand the key information necessary to make the decision. Without knowing: the situation they are in; the alternative courses of action open to them; and the consequences of these decisions, the person is not fully deciding on the course of action that they want for their life. To take a straightforward example, if a person drinks poison believing it is water, and dies that is not an autonomous decision. They are not in the position they wanted to be in (having a thirst quenched) but in a place they did not want to be (dead). Another example would be a person who believed incorrectly that they had a terminal illness, and decided to end their life to avoid an imminent painful death, when in fact they were not ill at all. They were not 'master of their destiny' because they were completely mistaken about their position. It would, I suggest, be a gross misrepresentation of the principle of autonomy to require respect for such mistaken decisions. Indeed, if we take the core principle of autonomy being that the person should be in the position they would want to be as author of their lives, then in fact intervening to prevent the death in both these cases would be more in tune with respecting their wishes (would put them closer to the position they wanted to be in) than allowing them to act as they wish.

[41] J Werth et al, 'Requests for Physician Assisted Death: Guidelines for Assessing Mental Capacity and Impaired Judgment' (2000) 6 *Psychology, Public Policy and Law* 348.

A fundamental question about the informational aspect of capacity to commit suicide is whether we can know enough about death to choose it. Death is the 'great unknown'. If a patient consented to a medical treatment with no idea of what it would be like, it would generally be thought that such a person might lack capacity to make the decision. The difference with death, however, is that no one knows what death will be like. It is not as if there is some information which we could give to the patient, to make them more informed. In other words, the patient is as informed about death it is possible to be, which is not very informed at all. I suggest that as long as the patient knows they are selecting the 'unknown', then they have as much capacity as anyone can have in relation to the nature of death.

However, there are other issues relating to understanding around a suicide that may be significant. Amy Wenzel and Megan Spokas[42] list the follow perceptions as particularly associated with suicide: (a) hopelessness; (b) perfectionism; (c) burdensomeness; (d) low belongingness; and (e) unbearability. However, they note that it is the perception of these things rather than the reality which is linked to suicide. They state, 'empirical evidence suggests that people with suicidal ideation and those who have made a suicide attempt report being overly critical of themselves and having excessive concern about others' expectations for them'. We might say that such people are basing their suicidal decision on mistakes: for example, they think no one loves them, when in fact people do. Indeed, we might say that if they had an accurate perception of themselves then they would reach a different decision. Such mistakes appear common among those who commit suicide.[43]

Less straightforward will be cases where the suicidal person makes an error about the future. A person is diagnosed with cancer and on hearing that chemotherapy is the proposed treatment decides they would rather die. This decision may be based on an imperfect understanding of what undergoing chemotherapy is like. Or a patient with depression starts taking medication but it seems to be having little impact and they decide to terminate their lives. Here it is less straightforward that the person is going to end up in the position they are seeking to avoid. The chemotherapy might turn out to be as bad as the person expected; the depression might not be abated. We can separate out two issues here. The first is to distinguish a factual error from a non-factual one. An easier case is where the patient assumes that chemotherapy will lead to hair loss, and this is something they cannot live with, but in fact hair loss is not associated with the particular form of chemotherapy they are undertaking. Less clear are mistakes of prediction. For example, where the chemotherapy will lead to hair loss, but in

[42] A Wenzel and M Spokas, 'Cognitive and Information Processing Approaches to Understanding Suicidal Behaviors' in M Nock (ed), *The Oxford Handbook of Suicide and Self-Injury* (Oxford University Press, 2014).

[43] S Jager-Hyman et al, 'Cognitive Distortions and Suicide Attempts' (2014) 38 *Cognitive Therapy and Research* 369.

fact most patients cope with that far better than they think they will. The difficulty here is that we cannot be sure that the patient who seeks suicide because they cannot face hair loss is mistaken as to how they will feel about it when the time comes. It might be possible to rely on statistics about how patients generally react to hair loss and estimate that the majority of patients do not find hair loss as distressing as they expect. I suggest that these kinds of issues at least give a ground for querying the degree of autonomy. Blumenthal-Barby[44] suggests that there is substantial evidence that people are bad at predicting their reaction to future emotional events or their own future preferences. If a person is adamant that they will respond to a future event in a particular way, and there is good reason to doubt that, then the decision is sub-optimally autonomous.

E. Using Information to Make the Decision

Perhaps the most direct challenge to autonomy is to question whether people committing suicide weigh up the information sufficiently to make a decision.[45] For example, there is extensive evidence that although we believe we make decisions based on facts, in reality our decisions are influenced (often unknowingly) by many external factors. An important one is the way the questions are phrased. In one study, patients were offered two alternative treatments and were told of the percentages of people who survived the treatments; 18 per cent of people selected the first treatment. The same group were then offered the two treatments and were told the percentage of people who died (that is, the same statistic presented differently). This time, 44 per cent of people selected the first treatment.[46] In other words, although it may appear that a patient is exercising autonomy, and they believe they are, in fact the choice they make is influenced by the way the question is asked. But that is only one example of the myriad of ways our decisions are not the produce of our own rational thought processes. Conly[47] suggests that many decisions are the result of mistaken thinking:

> As has by now been discussed convincingly and exhaustively (notably by Nobel Prize-winning Daniel Kahneman and Amos Tversky), we suffer from common, apparently ineradicable tendencies to 'cognitive bias,' which means that in many common situations, our decision-making goes askew. These biases are many and varied, but they have in common that they interfere with our appreciation of even quite simple facts, and lead us to choose ineffective means to our ends.

We might like to think we are making rational decisions, but in fact we are being influenced by factors outside our control.

[44] J-S Blumenthal-Barby, 'Choice Architecture: Improving Choice While Preserving Liberty?' in C Coons and M Weber (eds), *Paternalism* (Cambridge University Press, 2013).
[45] Herring (n 37).
[46] Blumenthal-Barby (n 42).
[47] S Conly, *Against Autonomy* (Cambridge University Press, 2012).

Of course, this argument might lead us to decide to abandon placing weight on autonomy altogether. That would be a radical claim which would be too big a topic for this book. So instead, I will focus on whether this argument has particular resonance for suicide: that decisions to commit suicide have not involved sufficient 'use of the information'. Clearly, some suicides will fall within this definition: a case where a person responds suddenly to some overwhelmingly bad news, or is severely intoxicated, or responds to persistent voices in their head. I am not suggesting that suicides cannot involve a proper weighing up of the information.[48] As Benetar states:

> If one's end is to avoid those of life's burdens that can only be avoided by the cessation of one's life, then not only is suicide *a* rational action, it is *the* rational course of action.[49]

We might conclude that the kind of case where a suicide could be seen as using the relevant information would require one to appreciate that only the cessation of life will avoid life's burdens. That would require quite an extensive degree of understanding: of a person's present condition; the alternative treatment or sources of help; a reasonably sound assessment of how a person might feel in the future. That is rarely true of suicides.[50] Many suicides are conducted with the person having a limited awareness of their current position; what possibilities the future may bring; and the sources of help or treatment available. They are basing their decision on impulses or external suggestions, rather than using the facts available. Thomas Scanlon proposes that an autonomous person 'must see himself as sovereign in deciding what to believe and in weighing competing reasons for action'.[51] The many impulsive suicidal decisions, which are not based on a careful rational weighing of the evidence, will not fall within that definition.

F. Making a Decision: Self-Determination

A crucial aspect of autonomy is that a person use their own values to assess the relevant information. Mackenzie and Rogers refer to this as self-determination, the ability:[52]

> … to determine one's own beliefs, values, goals and wants, and to make choices regarding matters of practical import to one's life free from undue interference. The obverse of self-determination is determination by other persons, or by external forces or constraints.

[48] *R (Nicklinson) v Ministry of Justice* [2014] UKSC 38.
[49] D Benetar, *The Human Predicament* (Oxford University Press, 2017) 213.
[50] C Peisah et al, 'Biggest Decision of Them All – Death and Assisted Dying: Capacity Assessments and Undue Influence Screening' (2019) 49 *Internal Medicine Journal* 792.
[51] T Scanlon, 'A Theory of Freedom of Expression' (1972) 1 *Philosophy and Public Affairs* 204, 215.
[52] C Mackenzie and W Rogers, 'Autonomy, Vulnerability and Capacity: A Philosophical Appraisal of the Mental Capacity Act' (2013) 13 *International Journal of the Law in Context* 37, 40 ff.

Their point is that if this condition is not fulfilled then a person cannot really be taken to have chosen a course of action for themselves.[53] Others have imposed values upon them, or they are not able to use their values to make decisions for themselves. Imagine, for example, a woman who is in a relationship of domestic abuse. She has reached a position where she simply obeys her partner on every issue. In such a case, respecting her decisions is not respecting her autonomy; respecting her decisions would be to respect her partner's control over her.

The issue of self-determination extends beyond the case of a person dominated by another. Courts have been troubled by cases where a patient is in such a panic that they are unable to process information to reach a decision. In such cases, the patient will lack capacity to make the decision. For example, in *Mental Health Trust v DD*[54] a pregnant woman refusing to consent to a Caesarean section was able to understand the information relevant to the decision but due to her learning difficulties and autism spectrum disorder was found to be unable to weigh the information. Controversially, in *A Local Authority v E*[55] a 32-year-old woman who suffered from anorexia nervosa and other health conditions, including alcohol dependence and a personality disorder, was found by Jackson J to lack capacity to refuse treatment in relation to forcible feeding:

> [T]here is strong evidence that E's obsessive fear of weight gain makes her incapable of weighing the advantages and disadvantages of eating in any meaningful way. For E, the compulsion to prevent calories entering her system has become the card that trumps all others. The need not to gain weight overpowers all other thoughts.[56]

This kind of approach seems applicable in the context of suicide too. A person may be beset by unwanted thoughts, depression or terrors which mean there is no effective opportunity for making their own decision. A desire to 'end the pain' or avoid a feared situation may 'overpower' all other thoughts and prevent full self-determination.[57]

G. Self Government

Mackenzie and Rogers distinguish self-determination from self-government, which they describe as the ability:[58]

> … to make choices and enact decisions that express, or are consistent with, one's values, beliefs and commitments. Whereas the threats to self-determination are

[53] L Nordenfelt, *Rationality and Compulsion: Applying Action Theory to Psychiatry* (Oxford University Press, 2007).

[54] *Mental Health Trust v DD* [2014] EWCOP 11.

[55] *A Local Authority v E* [2012] EWHC 1639 (COP).

[56] ibid, para 49.

[57] J Brailovskaia et al, 'Thwarted Belongingness and Perceived Burdensomeness Mediate the Association between Bullying and Suicide Ideation' (2020) 41 *Crisis* 136.

[58] Mackenzie and Rogers (n 52).

> typically external, the threats to self-governance are typically internal, and often involve volitional or cognitive failings. Weakness of will and failures of self-control are common volitional failings that interfere with self-governance.

As they indicate, the kind of issues that arise here are where a person has values but is not using them to make a decision, whether through a lack of control or weakness of will. Again this can commonly arise in suicide, where a person's suicide is the result of exhaustion or despair, which prevents them from properly applying their values or principles to the question at hand.

Jill Craigie,[59] considering cases of depression, argues that being able to consider one's future self is an important part of capacity:

> Caring about the interests of the future inhabitant of one's body, and having at least some grip on what those interests will be, seem like prerequisites for engaging successfully in these processes. And perhaps this offers part of an explanation about how decision-making can be compromised in the context of disorders such as depression and bipolar disorder. Very crudely, the idea would be that as part of a much bigger picture the capacities necessary for diachronic agency are not functioning properly and this undermines the constitution of the self.

Without that ability take into account one's future self, one cannot properly exercise autonomy. One way of putting this is that a person needs to have a sense of themselves across their life course.[60] They need to be not just thinking about the interests of the immediate self but the self in the future, in order to be able to weigh up the information relevant to suicide. This is perhaps easiest seen in cases with recurring conditions, such as bipolar disorder, where a patient has expressed gratitude for interventions made to limit their behaviour in previous manic episodes and we may imagine they will do the same if an intervention in made in their current situation. A life course perspective is helpful here. The individual is at a particular point of a journey and their decision is going to impact their future self significantly. We might try looking at the overall course of their life, where they want their story to go. Is this a momentary blip, which if respected will divert their life from the course they have generally sought for it? Or is this current decision in line with their life normally? As far as we can tell, is their future self going to be content with this decision?[61]

Richard Brandt has written:

> The person who is contemplating suicide is obviously making a choice between future world-courses: the world-course that includes his demise, say, an hour from now, and several possible ones that contain his demise at a later point … The basic question a person must answer in order to determine which world-course is best or rational for him to choose, is which he would choose under conditions of optimal use of information,

[59] J Craigie, 'Capacity, Value Neutrality and the Ability to Consider the Future' (2013) 9(1) *International Journal of Law in Context* 4.

[60] J Herring, *Law Through the Life Course* (Bristol University Press, 2021).

[61] ibid.

> when all of his desires are taken into account. It is not just a question of what we prefer now, with some clarification of all the possibilities being considered. Our preferences change, and the preferences of tomorrow are just as legitimately taken into account in deciding what to do now as the preferences of today.[62]

This kind of reasoning does not rule out regarding a suicidal decision as richly autonomous, where we can see it being in line with future selves. The future self of the love-sick teenager who wants to die will, we presume, if prevented from committing suicide, be very pleased that they were not permitted to act on their impulse. It seems far less straightforward in the case of a person with a terminal illness, where it will be far from clear whether their future self would want to be in that position.

H. Authenticity

Mackenzie and Rogers also refer to authenticity as an element of autonomy.[63] They explain what having authenticity means:

> [A] person's decisions, values, beliefs and commitments must be her 'own' in some relevant sense; that is, she must identify herself with them and they must cohere with her 'practical identity', her sense of who she is and what matters to her. Actions or decisions that a person feels were foisted on her, which do not cohere with her sense of herself, or from which she feels alienated, are not autonomous.[64]

The idea of authenticity is that we must see ourselves as being true to who we are – that our acts are of us, rather than due to external forces. Katharina Bauer[65] writes of how authenticity is about 'self-constitution', being true to one's beliefs and projects. It requires a person to be able to evaluate and re-evaluate who they really want to be and how to act in line with that. Mark Okrent says that humans are 'the animal who is capable of rationalizing our acts not only by altering them in the direction of greater success, but also by justifying them'.[66] We see this colloquially when someone is said to acting 'out of character' or as a result of stress or exhaustion. They are not 'being themselves'. Indeed, sometimes people say of a way they have acted 'that is not the kind of person I am'. Such comments can be treated with a degree of cynicism. The person who repeatedly steals from their employer cannot be seen as acting 'out of character' or declare that being a thief

[62] R Brandt, 'The Morality and Rationality of Suicide' in R Brandt (ed), *Morality, Utilitarianism and Rights* (Cambridge University Press, 1992) 66.

[63] Mackenzie and Rogers (n 52).

[64] Mackenzie and Rogers (n 52) 40.

[65] M Okrent, 'To be or Not to be Authentic. In Defence of Authenticity as an Ethical Ideal' (2017) 20 *Ethics, Theory and Moral Practice* 567

[66] M Okrent, 'On Being a Human Self' in M Burch et al, *Normativity, Meaning, and the Promise of Phenomenology* (Taylor and Francis, 2019).

is 'not who they really are'. But, there are other occasions where such talk does seem appropriate. A person who is known to always have a kind word for others, but on one occasions is insensitive, might be described as reflecting the stress they were under rather than being 'the real them'. They would not, given their underlying character, choose to act this way. We might see this as a feature of suicide attempts, especially where the suicide seems to 'come out of the blue'. Or not be consistent with how the person normally lived their life. By contrast we might imagine the acts of a person which completely reflect how they were: 'they are that kind of a person'. Their actions are in tune with the values and attitudes they seem to live by. So an autonomous act is authentic to the person: it fits with their beliefs, values and commitments. They were being themselves. That will, I accept, occasionally be true of a suicide.

The authenticity requirement highlights another aspect of capacity: to be autonomous, a person must have values and beliefs that they can use. Without any values or beliefs a person has no tools with which to make a decision. This might arise where a person has depression to such an extent that they find no meaning or value in the world. More controversially it may be that certain moral values if adopted are not consistent with authenticity and autonomy. I have in mind a person who thinks they are worthless. Such a perspective can be taken to mean they see they have no story to write. Wall explains

> Reasons for action are normative; they are the product of an evaluation of current and possible circumstances. To have a reason for action, rather than a pool of beliefs, desires, and preferences, is to identify some action (or inaction for that matter) as valuable or worthwhile, and to appreciate some consequence or outcome as valuable or worthwhile to you as the actor.[67]

Or, as Korsgaard[68] explains:

> Since you are a human you must take something to be normative, that is some conception of practical identity must be normative for you. If you had no normative conception of your identity, you could have no reason for action.

If you have a life which has no values and no actions which are worthwhile acting under, then autonomy has no meaning.[69] One has no reason for doing one thing rather than another, as there is no value in your or your decisions. You are not 'writing your life story' because it not worth doing so. Determining that there is a worthwhile decision and a beneficial outcome requires an understanding that the self matters. Wall explains:

> To act autonomously, according to this restatement, is to act according to the beliefs, values, and commitments that the actor identifies as their own beliefs, values, and commitments with reference to an understanding of the 'self 'as worthwhile', whose present and future circumstances matter. … Beyond requiring that a person constructs

[67] Wall (n 35).
[68] C Korsgaard, 'The Sources of Normativity' (1992) 12 *Tanner Lectures on Human Values* 112, 129.
[69] S Varga, *Authenticity as an Ethical Ideal* (Routledge, 2012).

> their sense of self through adopting and endorsing judgments, thoughts, and beliefs, we can also require that for a person to 'be themselves' by adopting a minimal concern for themselves and their circumstances.[70]

This seems clearly relevant in cases of people with a deep depression or sense of despair.[71] For example, it has been claimed that major depression impairs the ability to 'recognise the viability of other options when negatively perceiving the future or even have difficultly seeing a future'[72] or 'orient ourselves in time: drawing on our past in order to project ourselves into the future by way of decision taken now'.[73] This inability to appreciate future possibility and an impaired ability to have sufficient concern for the self could hamper a person's authenticity and hence their capacity for autonomy.[74]

I do not for a moment mean to suggest that those with major depression or other impairments cannot exercise authenticity, but rather they often do not, at least in relation to suicide.[75] It is rarely true that a person has chosen to become a depressed person or a person for whom joy has drained from life. It is true that it is hard to speak of a 'true self' lurking behind the depression, although that can be the case for some people; particularly where the depression comes in severe bouts.

Care does need to be taken with this argument. We need a theory of authenticity that allows for a change in values. A person who has lived in a particular faith community may lose their faith and decide to reject the values they previously lived by. Or, of course, a person may decide to convert to a faith and take on new values. It must be perfectly possible for an authentic person to do this. This needs to be distinguished from a case where a person's change of values has been forced upon them, be that through brainwashing or a result of illness. Jon Elster[76] suggests that we can consider whether a person's desire is inauthentic by asking whether it is shaped by 'irrelevant causal factors', but that does not really help define what is inauthentic. Even a simple view that values that emerge as a result of a illness or disease (such as anorexia) are not authentic, does not seem helpful because so much then depends on the definition of a disease. History is full of examples of personal values being improperly labelled as a disease, including same-sex desire and a slave wishing to be free. These are labelled as illness precisely for the purpose of undermining their validity.

[70] Wall (n 35).

[71] T Hindmarch et al, 'Depression and Decision-making Capacity for Treatment or Research: A Systemic Review' (2013) 14 *BMC Medical Ethics* 54.

[72] P Fernandez et al, 'Implications of Autonomy for Forensic Consequences of Extended Suicide' (2002) 9 *Psychiatry, Psychology and Law* 146, 148.

[73] G Owen et al, 'Temporal Inabilities and Decision-making Capacity in Depression' (2013) 14 *Phenomology and the Cognitive Sciences* 163, 179.

[74] C Elliot, 'Caring about Risk: Are Severely Depressed Patients Competent to Consent to Research?' (1997) 54 *Archives of General Psychiatry* 113.

[75] U Schuklenk and S van de Vathorst, 'Treatment-Resistant Major Depressive Disorder and Assisted Dying' (2015) 41 *Journal of Medical Ethics* 577.

[76] J Elster, 'The Possibility of Rational Politics' (1987) 28 *Journal of European Sociology* 67.

Leannart Nordenfelt[77] suggests that a want which is self-destructive or based on an irrational belief is not authentic. Hence, he suggests, the patient with anorexia who does not eat because they falsely believe they are fat, is not acting on an authentic value. This, however, depends on what is a rational belief. It assumes, for example, that 'being fat' is an objective fact we can value. By contrast, consider the comments of Darcel Taylor,[78] a person diagnosed with bipolar disorder, who writes:

> … I have no grand wish for death. I do not view suicide as a desire to end life or a dramatic way to go down in flames … When I have lost enough of myself to this disease as to become unrecognizable even to me, I will stop. I will go no further. This, I tell myself, is my earned choice.

Here it is accepted that the decision to commit suicide will not be an authentic realisation of their own self.

It is not easy to determine, therefore, which values are authentically chosen and which are not. It should be recalled that authenticity should be about being able to judge and choose between desires.[79] There needs to be a degree of reflection about them. Such an approach could allow for a case where a person could adopt values which they accept were not, initially as chosen. A feeling of worthlessness as a result of a depression may not be chosen. A person raised as Catholic might, for example, accept that these beliefs were instilled in them before they had the power to choose, but later make a clear decision to adopt the faith. An interesting example to consider is hypnosis.[80] Where a person is hypnotised against their will we can readily see their desire to act in a particular way as not being chosen. Where, however, a person seeks hypnosis to give up smoking, we might say that the new desire not to smoke (assuming the hypnosis is successful) is chosen, even if to some extent imposed without their direct control. So, in relation to suicide, we might ask whether the wish to die is one that is selected based on values chosen by the individual. A good example of where that did occur is Tony Nicklinson's suicide. He fully understood his condition and its prognosis, he thought carefully over the decision, consulted with others, and used the values he had followed for his life. That seems a clearly authentic decision, in sharp contrast with the person who suddenly turns to suicide after being bullied online or the ending of a relationship. Further, Michael Cholbi writes of cases where:

> the agent's capacity to care about her own happiness has been nearly ground into submission …. Agents do not simply calculate future goods and evils and opt for the good of death over the evils of life. Instead, the evils of life accumulate until the point

[77] Nordenfelt (n 51).

[78] Quoted in S Stefan, *Rational Suicide, Irrational Laws: Examining Current Approaches to Suicide in Policy and Law* (Oxford University Press, 2016).

[79] T Blikshavn et al, 'Four Reasons Why Assisted Dying Should Not Be Offered for Depression' (2017) 14 *Journal of Bioethical Inquiry* 151.

[80] M Sjöstrand and N Juth, 'Authenticity and Psychiatric Disorder: Does Autonomy of Personal Preferences Matter?' (2014) 17 *Medicine, Health Care and Philosophy* 115.

> that agents no longer feel a sense of attachment to their own happiness at all and are indifferent to their existence.

Such a case is not one of an authentic actor and their decision is, at best, protected only weakly by autonomy.[81]

I. Rationality

Another way of thinking about capacity and suicide is to consider what would be required for a rational decision to commit suicide. Siegel[82] suggests it would require the following

(1) the individual possesses a realistic assessment of his or her situation;
(2) the mental processes leading to his or her decision to commit suicide are unimpaired by psychological illness or severe emotional distress; and
(3) the motivational basis of his or her decision would be understandable to the majority of uninvolved observers from his or her community or social group.

Can it be said that a decision to die is irrational and therefore indicative of a lack of capacity? This question needs to be broken down into more precise claims.

First, it might be argued that the decision to end one's life is so obviously harmful that no rational person could reach such a decision. That is not a very convincing. As death, we presume, is the ending of experiences, it is not itself harmful, or is only harmful in so far as it deprives a person of future positive experiences. Where a person might reasonably believe there are no, or few, positive experiences (eg they are close to death) the harm of death may be very limited because they are losing out on good experiences. A person facing primarily pain and distress might rationally decide that to experience nothing is better than that. In any event, a person might reject the claim that death leads to nothingness and believe instead in afterlife. For them, it would not for them be irrational to prefer the afterlife to the current one in some situations.

Second, it might be said that committing suicide is irrational because death is unknown. This is a slightly different argument from the lack of information argument. Devine writes '... a precondition of rational choice is that one knows *what* one is choosing, either by experience or by the testimony of others who have experienced it or something very like it'.[83] This argument assumes that it is never rational to choose the unknown. That certainly seems questionable. First, it seems rational if we know that the alternative is something that definitely involves

[81] M Cholbi, 'Suicide Intervention and Non-Ideal Kantian Theory' (2002) 19 *Journal of Applied Philosophy* 245.
[82] K Siegel, 'Psychosocial Aspects of Rational Suicide' (1986) 40 *American Journal of Psychotherapy* 405.
[83] P Devine, *The Ethics of Homicide* (University of Notre Dame Press, 1990).

considerable pain.[84] Second, we do regularly try new things: foods we have not had, meeting new people. It does not in such a case seem irrational to try something simply because it has not been experienced before.[85] Of course, death is such a major change in our status it might be said we are normally willing to try new things precisely because if they do not turn out well we can return to our normal state. Again that is less plausible where the person is at the end of their life.[86] I am not, therefore, convinced that the unknowns of death make it necessarily irrational to select it – though this will apply only in limited circumstances.

Third, it might be argued that a particular decision to commit suicide is irrational. The difficulty here is that rationality is hard to judge, particularly in decisions which involve emotional and intellectual reasons. This is partly why we avoid judging whether a person seeking to marry is acting rationally.[87] It is simply too easy to use rationality as a basis to say you disagree with someone. Consider, for example, the fact that many opponents of Brexit would describe supporters of it as irrational; and many of its supporters would say the same thing about the opponents. While this is a fair point, it can be taken to extremes. There are some lines of reasoning which are simply irrational. 'The Bible is the word of God. The Bible tells me not to commit suicide. Therefore I will commit suicide' is clearly not a rational thought line. There is active contradiction between the lines of argument, at least if we take it that the Bible does not tell people to commit suicide. It may, however, be that blatant irrationality of this kind is rare. Cowley draws the conclusion:

> the fact that the concept of rationality 'runs out' (a) when I consider my own horrified reactions to the news of someone's suicide, and (b) when I consider the sort of things that I am inclined to say to the victim or his family about the act, means that the concept was not important in the first place; it cannot do the philosophical work expected of it.[88]

So, it may not be helpful in many cases to use irrationality as a ground for lack of autonomy.

J. Options

If autonomy is seen as a person selecting between options or writing their life story then there need to be options to choose between.[89] Swain[90] suggests that:

> personal autonomy requires an adequate number of valuable, viable options from which an agent can choose, even if the precise number of such options may be indeterminate.

[84] F Feldman, *Confrontations with the Reaper: A Philosophical Study of the Nature and Value of Death* (Oxford University Press, 1994).

[85] ibid.

[86] A Pilpel and L Amsel, 'What is Wrong with Rational Suicide' (2011) 39 *Philosophia* 112.

[87] J Hirsch, 'The Wish to Die: Assisted Suicide and Mental Illness' (2012) 16 *Journal of Social Work in End-of-Life & Palliative Care* 213.

[88] Cowley (n 2) 501.

[89] J Raz, *Morality of Freedom* (Oxford University Press, 1986).

[90] Swain (n 12).

> Options of this sort make possible the pursuit of goals and the expression of an agent's will in action.

And it is not enough for there simply to be options there must be meaningful good options. 'Sign the contract or I will shoot you' gives someone a choice, but it is not a meaningful one.[91] There must be choices that are viable for the individual. 'Sign the contract or eat pork' may be little better than the shooting option for a person whose religion teachings instruct them not to eat pork.

It is important too that the individual is aware of their options. A victim of domestic abuse who is so terrified of her abuser that she is convinced she must comply with his commands or be killed, is not exercising autonomy, even if someone might demonstrate that there were effective alternatives. To the victim of the abuse there are no meaningful options. By analogy, we can say that the person facing a desperate position or death is choosing between two valueless options.

A slightly different argument is that autonomy cannot be used to justify suicide, because suicide ends options. Respect for autonomy is based on the argument that we value the choices people have, so it cannot justify putting someone in a position where they have no choices. Greasley argues that in the same way that autonomy cannot be used to justify a person selecting to be a slave, it cannot use autonomy to justify death because 'Death spells the end of all good options because it spells the end of options, period'.[92] Raz[93] himself rather neatly deals with that argument by saying the option for ending life creates valuable options in the time leading up to death. In other words, the knowledge that you can end your life when you choose, means that you are freed from worries that life may become too painful or beset by worries.

K. Which Decision?

Many complex cases involving autonomy are ones where there are competing or conflicting decisions. An obvious case is a person wanting to eat healthily but then choosing to eat a cake. In such a case a person may well be assessed as having two apparently contradictory wishes: to eat healthily and eat the cake. Indeed, I suggest, in many difficult cases around autonomy the question is not so much whether the patient has autonomy or not, but which wish of the patient should we respect. Often this arises as a clash between a decision taken when a person has time to think through the issues and reflect on their values, and a momentary decision, taken on impulse.[94]

[91] J Raz, 'Right-Based Moralities' in J Waldron (ed), *Theories of Rights* (Oxford University Press, 1984) 191.

[92] K Greasley, 'R (Purdy) v DPP and the Case for Wilful Blindness' (2010) 30 *Oxford Journal of Legal Studies* 301.

[93] J Raz, 'Death in Our Life' (2013) 30 *Journal of Applied Philosophy* 1.

[94] T Wilson, *Strangers to Ourselves* (Harvard University Press, 2004).

This might be reasonably common in a case of suicide. Generally, in times of calm, when able to reflect on all the issues carefully, a person may be happy to continue living. But in a moment of crisis, or sudden deep despair, a person seeks suicide. If we are committed to respecting this person's autonomy, which decision do we respect? Which self is to write the story?[95] It certainly seems in these cases that it is the richer autonomous decision which deserves respect. Preventing an impulsive suicidal wish so that a richer autonomous decision can be made later seems entirely justified from an autonomy perspective. Indeed, as Hecht argues, 'There is much evidence that the vast majority of people who try to suicide, but survive, are glad they survived. Your pain right now doesn't give you the authority to kill off all your previous selves, with their plans, sacrifices, and accomplishments'.[96] From that angle, suicide prevention, far from challenging autonomy, in fact enhances it.

L. Conclusion on Capacity and Autonomy

The argument I have made in this section is that there are very few cases of suicide where a person's decision is richly autonomous. There are a wide range of factors which mean that in many cases of suicide a person's autonomy is impaired. I argued above that the best ethical approach involves weighing the harm to the individual with the richness of their autonomous desire. In most suicides there will be considerable harm and in most suicides the autonomy is too weak for it to justify the harm.[97] Often people are not sufficiently informed to make the decision; often they are not sufficiently rational to apply the information to their values; illness or misfortune can mean they lack the self-determination, authenticity and self-government to have autonomy in a rich sense. Indeed, I have suggested that in many cases where a person says they wish to die, it will be more autonomy-enhancing to intervene to prevent their suicide, particularly in cases where their current wishes clash with their deep-seated values and decisions; or where the suicidal decision is based on an incorrect factual basis.

VI. Autonomy Issues: Limits

This section will move on to another aspect of the debate. It will assume that it has been determined that a person is autonomous (has capacity) to decide to commit suicide. Are there, then, any reasons for not respecting that decision?

[95] C Bidart, 'How Plans Change: Anticipation, Interferences and Unpredictabilities' (2019) 41 *Advances in Life Course Research* 254.
[96] J Hecht, *Stay: A History of Suicide and the Philosophies Against It* (Yale University Press, 2014).
[97] Stefan (n 74).

A. What Does Respect for Autonomy Mean?

Before exploring that question a little further, it is necessary to clarify precisely what we are discussing. As already mentioned 'respecting' autonomy is a very vague idea. David Velleman[98] correctly points out that a response to a person's choice can be complex and does not necessarily involve respecting a current expression of opinion. If I come across my friend, who is in a dire financial state, offering to sell me their clothing, the correct response may be to offer them a financial gift, rather than going along with their plan. In one sense I have not respected their choice – they want to sell their clothing – but by offering an alternative I have expanded their options. The gift might increase the opportunity for self-determination (autonomy) to a greater extent than respecting a choice. The significance of this point is that, faced with a person seeking suicide, the most autonomy-enhancing action may be to offer alternative options. Of course, it may be that at the end of the day there are no options.

Further, it is important to note that the autonomous decision of another at best allows you to set aside the reasons against acting in the way they request. It does not impose an obligation on you to accede to these wishes. As soon as we put this in another context we can see this. Imagine David decides he wants to have sex with Michael. He has thought about this long and hard and researched the issue. Indeed, this seems a sensible decision: David fancies Michael and by all accounts Michael is an excellent lover. However autonomous we might think David's decision is, it places no obligation on Michael to have sex with David. It may create a permission for Michael to have sex with David, but it cannot produce an obligation. It does not necessarily even give you a reason to act in the way you do. In Madden Dempsey's discussion of consent, she explores a situation where A asks B to punch her. She imagines that A does so and is asked to justify his actions. If A were to say 'well, B asked me to do so', Madden Dempsey denies this is a sufficient reason. She explains:

> by simply noting the fact of B's consent, A has failed to point out any reason he had in favor of punching B. Rather, A has merely referred to a fact (B's consent) which impacts some of the reasons A had not to punch B in the first place.

It may not even create a permission where there are reasons not to engage in the behaviour which lie outside the wellbeing of the individual. Again this is clear once we look outside the area of suicide. If a friend decided, autonomously, to have an affair and asked you to facilitate it, that is very likely to be unjustifiable, not least because of the impact on your friend's spouse. Similarly, if a friend approaches you for assistance in suicide, the fact the decision has been made autonomously does not of itself justify your intervention.

[98] P Jewell, 'Rationality, Euthanasia, and the Sanctity of Life' (2005) *Australian Association for Professional and Applied Ethics* 1.

The approach here is supported generally in medicine. A patient who asks for a certain medication can be told by their doctor that the medication is not appropriate for them. However much the patient may want medication, the doctor is under no obligation to give it to them. In fact, if it will cause harm then he *must* not give the medication. Indeed, in that scenario we might even take it further and suggest that if the doctor knows that the patient wants harmful medicine, the doctor may be obliged to take steps to ensure that the patient does not get hold of it and to discourage the patient from seeking to find it.

B. Virtue Ethics

Virtue ethics requires us to consider how a virtuous person would respond to the situation. If we are faced with a friend who is feeling suicidal it is highly unlikely that our natural response would be to attempt to ascertain the extent of autonomy. Indeed, the rationality of their feelings seems irrelevant. As Cowley[99] puts it 'there is something unique in the nature of suicide that makes any attempted ascription of the concepts of either rationality or irrationality *otiose*'.[100] Instead, we will hold them close, and offer comfort, love and support. We may feel powerless and sad at their feelings. The rationality or autonomous nature of the decision seems a highly academic point to concentrate on. Cowley argues that the correct response to a desire of suicide is 'horror and pity' and an 'a humble acknowledgement of the profound mystery at the heart of any suicide'.[101] He accepts that in other areas of life a focus on autonomy may be appropriate, but in relation to suicide there is an 'intuitive unease' about focusing on rationality.

What is important and helpful about Cowley's intervention is that it focuses us back on what is a third party's correct response to a suicidal person. As mentioned in the previous section, a finding that the suicidal person is autonomous should not foreclose the ethical issue raised. Cowley contrasts two scenarios:

(1) Tom, who has learning difficulties, asks you to buy a birthday card for his sister with balloons on, as she likes balloons. In fact, he is mistaken: it is nowhere near her birthday and she hates balloons. However, if you know the sister would be delighted to receive the card, albeit with its imperfections, you may well help Tom out with his endeavour, even if the degree of Tom's autonomy is severely impaired.

(2) Simon, a professor at a university, has fallen in love with a student, Rajana. He wants to date Rajana and commence a relationship. You are aware that Simon is married, and if he has an affair he is likely to lose his job and his marriage. Simon asks you for advice on how to 'chat up' Rajana. Surely the correct thing as a good friend is not to accede to his autonomous wish?

[99] Cowley (n 2) 501.
[100] At 496.
[101] At 497.

The point of Cowley's examples here is that they demonstrate that, in determining how to respond to these scenarios, our response is not limited to an assessment of autonomy. Indeed, in relation to Simon, Cowley suggests that not only do you not assist Simon in his autonomously chosen 'life plan', you might actively dissuade him. Of course, as Cowley notes, there are limits. You are not permitted to lock him up or him or physically incapacitate him, but you might take reasonable steps to dissuade him.[102]

C. Protecting Only Some Autonomous Decisions

The right of autonomy is well recognised in many areas of the law. For example, in medical law it is well established that a patient has a right to decide to refuse medical treatment. As Peter Jackson J in *Heart of England NHS Trust v JB* stated:[103]

> anyone capable of making decisions has an absolute right to accept or refuse medical treatment, regardless of the wisdom or consequences of the decision. The decision does not have to be justified to anyone. In the absence of consent any invasion of the body will be a criminal assault. The fact that the intervention is well-meaning or therapeutic makes no difference.

Indeed, it would be a criminal offence to touch a person without their consent. Generally speaking, if a person has consented to a touching there will be no criminal injury unless a notable injury has occurred. Similarly, if the owner has consented to the damage to property there is no charge of criminal damage.[104]

There are some exceptions to the principle. Notably, under the Mental Health Act 1983 a person can be given treatment for a mental disorder without their consent, where necessary to protect the individual from themselves or others.[105] There is also the recently developed jurisdiction for 'vulnerable adults', who can be treated contrary to their wishes.[106] The Court of Appeal has confirmed the existence of the jurisdiction in *DL v A Local Authority*.[107] Munby J defined this group in the following way:

> [T]he inherent jurisdiction can be exercised in relation to a vulnerable adult who, even if not incapacitated by mental disorder or mental illness, is, or is reasonably believed to be, either: (i) under constraint; or (ii) subject to coercion or undue influence; or (iii) for some other reason deprived of the capacity to make the relevant decision, or disabled from making a free choice, or incapacitated or disabled from giving or expressing a real and genuine consent.

[102] Cowley (n 2) 501.
[103] *Heart of England NHS Trust v JB* [2014] EWHC 342 (COP), [12].
[104] See J Herring, *Criminal Law* (Oxford University Press, 2020) Ch 7 for the detail of the law.
[105] We will look at that further in Ch 7.
[106] For a detailed discussion of the jurisdiction see J Herring, *Vulnerable Adults and the Law* (Oxford University Press, 2016).
[107] *DL v A Local Authority* [2012] EWCA Civ 253, [72].

It applies to those who have mental capacity but whose autonomy is impaired. Where it is used the court will determine what is in the best interests of the person concerned. Hence in *DL v A Local Authority*, an elderly couple were removed from the care of their son. They had capacity and wanted to stay with him, but he was abusive and dominated their thinking. Removing them from his care was justified as enabling them to make a more autonomous decision about where to live.

In these jurisdictions we see an approach similar to that advocated earlier in this chapter about weighing up the richness of the autonomy behind the decision and the degree of harm performed. In both the Mental Health Act 1983 and the vulnerable adult jurisdiction we see the courts being willing to intervene in a capacitous decision because it is not sufficiently autonomous to justify allowing a person to do themselves serious harm.

Some argue that not all autonomous decisions demand respect. Keown claims:

> The capacity to choose brings with it the responsibility of making not just any old choice, but choices that do in fact promote, rather than undermine, human flourishing. Given the legitimate diversity of lifestyles and life-choices which are consistent with human flourishing, many choices are consistent with human well-being. We should, therefore, think carefully before restricting another's autonomy. But it is difficult to see why patently immoral choices, choices clearly inconsistent with human well-being, merit any respect. In other words, an exercise of autonomy merits respect only when it is exercised in accordance with a framework of sound moral values.[108]

It is a standard view that we can interfere in autonomous decisions that harm others. But here Keown is arguing that a decision which undermines the individual's flourishing should not be respected. Such a view is often based on the claim that autonomy in itself is not good, it is the fact that it tends, normally, to lead to flourishing lives which makes it good. If the justification for autonomy is based on flourishing, we can interfere with it when it does not promote flourishing. The challenge for Keown is whether he can find consensus on what are 'sound moral values' and which are 'consistent with human flourishing'. Supporters of autonomy may reply to Keown that it is that because we cannot agree on such issues that we must let people use their own moral values and determine what, for them, constitutes flourishing. Maybe we could interpret Keown's argument very narrowly and simply say that manifestly harmful decisions (decisions which the vast majority of society would accept to be harmful) do not deserve respect.

I would not agree with Keown that autonomy only requires respect for 'choices that do in fact promote, rather than undermine, human flourishing'. That creates too sharp a divide between choices that are protected and choices that are not. As already argued, an acceptance that autonomy is scalar and the extent to which a decision is autonomous is variable, opens up a more flexible approach, allowing autonomy to be weighed against the degree of harm. It is where the harm is serious

[108] J Keown, 'The Legal Revolution: From "Sanctity of Life" to "Quality of Life" and "Autonomy"' (1998) 14 *Journal of Contemporary Health Law and Policy* 253, 263.

that we need to take considerable care in determining what precisely it is that the patient wants and only accede to their wishes where there is a strongly autonomous decision to die.

D. Relational Autonomy: Obligations to Others

Another challenge to the pre-eminence of autonomy is that it overlooks other important values. There is a danger that autonomy ignores issues of obligations owed to others, the pursuit of community goals, notions of justice in healthcare decisions, and the importance of relationships in the lives of others.[109]

Some who are sympathetic to these concerns might decide to abandon autonomy altogether. But others argue that we need to find a new way of understanding it. One of the most popular of these is the notion of 'relational autonomy'.[110] At the heart of this approach is a rejection of the idea that we live our lives as unconnected individuals. The traditional notion of autonomy promotes the concept of an isolated patient deciding for himself what is in his best interests (the image of 'the male in the prime of his life'), whereas in fact we live lives based on interdependent relationships. We therefore need to recognise that, for most people, the question is not simply 'What is best for me?', but rather 'Given the responsibilities that I owe to those in relationships with me and the responsibilities owed to me by others, what is the most appropriate course of action?' We need a vision of autonomy that promotes the values of love, loyalty, friendship, and care.[111]

Mackenzie[112] has written:

> Feminist relational ethics rejects social atomism and understands persons as embedded in interpersonal and social relationships, and as shaped and constrained by intersecting social determinants, such as those of gender, race, class, sexuality, ability, and so on. In line with the agenda of relational ethics, relational autonomy theorists uphold the importance of personal autonomy, especially for women and other groups subject to historical and contemporary forms of social oppression. At the same time, relational autonomy theorists seek to analyse the ways that the development and exercise of personal autonomy is enabled or constrained by social relationships and by social norms, structures and institutions.

It should be acknowledged that 'relational autonomy' is a fairly broad umbrella term, and writers using it are not in complete agreement as to its meaning.[113]

[109] J Downie, 'Why Feminist Philosophy (Especially Sue Sherwin's) Matters: Reflections through the Lens of Medical Assistance in Dying' (2020) 13 *International Journal of Feminist Approaches to Bioethics* 21.

[110] J Herring, *Relational Autonomy and Family Law* (Springer, 2014).

[111] J Herring, *Caring and the Law* (Hart Publishing, 2013).

[112] C Mackenzie, 'Feminist Innovation in Philosophy: Relational Autonomy and Social Justice' (2019) 72 *Women's Studies International Forum* 144, 145.

[113] C Mackenzie and N Stoljar, *Relational Autonomy* (Oxford University Press, 2000).

There are two aspects to it. The first is that we should assess capacity relationally. In other words, rather than sitting a patient in a room with a psychiatrist to be tested as to their capabilities, we should ask whether a person, after discussion with friends and experts, and with support, can reach a decision. That is, in fact, how most people make decisions, with others, and so the 'lonely' assessment of capacity typically used by professionals is highly artificial. This approach would, however, acknowledge the ways that unhelpful pressures and relationships can impede a person's decision making. As Westlund[114] explains:

> self-governance is a relational capacity – at the very least causally, in the sense that the capacities and competencies that one must exercise in autonomous choice and action can only be developed in and through relationships with other agents, but perhaps also constitutively, in the sense that what makes a choice or action one's own cannot be explained without reference to some form of relationality.

Yet it is a mark of many, but not all, suicidal decisions that they are made alone.

The second aspect of relational autonomy is that it acknowledges that most decisions are relational ones. They involve co-operation with and engagement with others. It can, therefore, often make more sense about seeing the 'good life' for a group of people in connected relationships, rather than a 'good life' for a single person. This then creates difficulties in cases where the wishes of one person are in conflict with the wishes of the group. Anne Donchin writes 'Any conception of autonomy that fails to incorporate socially situated interpersonal relations rests on illusion'.[115] She goes on to explain:

> Respect for everyone's autonomy, however, entails long-term reciprocity and a collaborative arrangement that balances power relations equitably. Hence when conflict arises, respecting another's autonomy need not be an invitation to break off communication, back off, or opt out so much as to move engagement to a new level. Commitment to reciprocity and collaboration limit an individual's freedom to 'opt out' of a relationship, but they might possibly require opting out under extreme conditions.

On this view, seeing suicide as a personal decision, and a matter of what an individual does with their life, is misguided.[116] A person's death impacts on those around them and those they are in relationships with. It is a decision which impacts on others and can only autonomously be made with others. The question 'Whose life is it anyway?' invites the incorrect answer that it is the person's. On a relational understanding, our lives are intertwined. Suicide is in this sense a very social act. This then reflects the arguments of those such as Boldt,[117] who claim that suicide's meaning is found in cultural and social traditions, symbols

[114] A Westlund, 'Relational Autonomy and Practical Authority' in P Garavaso (ed), *The Bloomsbury Companion to Analytic Feminism* (Bloomsbury, 2018).

[115] A Dochin, 'Autonomy, Interdependence, and Assisted Suicide: Respecting Boundaries/Crossing Lines' (2000) 14 *Bioethics* 187.

[116] S Fitzpatrick, 'Re-Moralizing the Suicide Debate' (2014) 11 *Journal of Bioethical Inquiry* 223.

[117] M Boldt, 'The Meaning of Suicide: Implications for Research' (1988) 9 *Crisis: The Journal of Crisis Intervention and Suicide Prevention* 93.

and institutions. Suicide says something important about the community. So part of the response to the suicide must be whether we want to be the kind of society or family or circle of friends or university in which this suicide take place. There is more to that issue than autonomy because the community is affected.

Sidney Callahan argues that an approach which emphasises relationships will oppose suicide:

> Suicide cuts off the self from life and thereby ends all relationships with others. It exercises the individual's cognitive powers of agency to kill the whole embodied individual. An individualistic goal: to end a human life is espoused because it is judged a life 'unworthy of life.' This act upholds the logic of domination and ensures a complete 'triumph of the will.' Such acts of self-determined control of death proclaim the message that it is morally permissible to judge and choose to destroy a human life at will. Others can be encouraged to choose this course and commit suicide or ask for aid in dying. What is done to the self can be done to others.[118]

There seem to be two primary arguments here. The first is that suicide ends relationships and therefore is bad. That argument captures an important harm in suicide, but it does not provide an argument against all suicides. While caring relationships are good and to be nurtured, that does not mean that all relationships should be continued and that relationships should be continued regardless of the costs to the parties to the relationships. No ethics of care can seek to maintain an abusive relationship, for example. Where a person is in considerable anguish, preventing them from leaving the relationship through death would be a more extreme version of denying divorce to a person who wishes to leave an abusive marriage.

The second argument is that a person's suicide may impact on others and encourage them to commit suicide. There is again a degree of weight in this, but it seems too strong a claim to deny every suicide. A person may make it clear, or it may be clear, that their suicide is as a result of being in a highly unusual position. Further, whether a person can be required to continuing living as a result of a possible impact on others may be questioned. It might be argued that obligations to others mean that a person should not be permitted to commit suicide. For example, it might be said that a parent may have a duty not to commit suicide, due to their obligations to care for their children.[119] Here we need to be particularly alert to whether we are discussing what is ethically the best thing to do and what is ethically permissible; and further again which obligations should be enforced. It should be remembered there are limits on the burdens we expect parents to bear for the good of their children. For example, parents are not required to stay in an abusive relationship 'for the good of the children'; nor can parents be

[118] S Callahan, 'A Feminist Case against Self-Determined Dying in Assisted Suicide and Euthanasia' (2015) 25 *Feminism & Psychology* 109.

[119] Cholbi (n 9) 62.

required to provide bodily material, even if necessary to save their children's lives. The burden of remaining alive in considerable pain and misery requires a very strong justification and it is not clear that these communal obligations are sufficient. A parent who finds it too much to care for a child is permitted to hand the child over to the authorities to care for. It must follow that a parent is permitted to commit suicide, perhaps with some provision in place to care for children. It may be argued that the highest moral standard requires a person to remain alive for the good of the child – just as they might require a parent to give up their life to protect their child. However, these are not burdens the law would impose and would not be required of the 'minimally decent' person.[120] As Benatar[121] puts it:

> … it would be indecent to condemn those who, having deliberated carefully about the matter, decide that they no longer wish to endure the burdens of a life to which they never consented. They ought to take the interests of others, especially family and friends, into account. This is particularly true of those (such as spouses and parents) for whom obligations to others have been voluntarily undertaken. The presence of such connections and obligations will trump lesser burdens, morally speaking. However, once the burdens of life reach a certain level of severity (determined, in part, by the relevant person's own assessment of his life's value and quality), it becomes indecent to expect him to remain alive for the benefit of others.

E. The Badness of Death

One argument that might be raised to justify overruling an autonomous decision is to say that the harm of death is so great that this justifies a breach in autonomy. To consider this we need to explore two understandings of why death is a harm.

i. *Quality of Life*

A popular view is that death deprives the person of the goods of life they would have had if they continued living.[122] This view would have to accept that it is possible to imagine some cases where the death would not be a harm: that there are those who – as far as can be told – would suffer greater harms in the remainder of their life than could be outweighed by any goods.

One difficulty with this approach is how we determine what counts as goods or harms in this context. At the most simplistic level this might break down into those who see these goods in terms of subjective value or objective. Hence, taking

[120] D Jones et al, 'Final Conclusions on Final Solutions' in D Jones et al, *Assisted Suicide and Euthanasia: Lessons from Belgium* (Cambridge University Press, 2018).

[121] Benatar (n 17) 113.

[122] J Broome, 'The Badness of Dying Early' in F. Gamlund et al (eds), *Saving People from the Harm of Death* (Oxford University Press, 2019).

the subjective approach, Harris argues 'the value of our lives is the value we give to our lives'[123] while Smuts argues 'lives are worth living if they are high in various objective goods and low in objective bads'.[124] Further, there are debates about what count as goods or bads in this context. Is it just a matter of pain versus pleasure or the other values? For example, a person may accept that their remaining years may include more pleasure than pain, but believe that it would be undignified to continue their life or that their continued life will cause too much trouble for other people. Particularly once we get to the weighing up of hedonistic values and virtues it become particularly difficult to determine how much pain someone should suffer for an objective good. Indeed it is hard in such cases to determine why anyone else is better positioned than the individual to make this assessment. If we take the quality of life assessment, it is hard to avoid concluding that the individual should determine how best to weigh up the future goods and bads of their life.

However, there is a very important caveat to that. As argued above, when in a suicidal state people are rarely in a position to make the required assessment. They have made factual or assessment errors; their thinking is impacted by values that are not authentic to them; their current temporary wishes clash with their longer term values. In all these cases they have not been able to make an accurate assessment, weighing up the goods and bads of death. If we imagine coming across a friend who tells us that they are worth no more than a worm and that their life has nothing good in it, we would hardly reply 'Well your life is worth what value you give it and as you give your life no value then it has no value'. Rather, we would seek to point out all the positives in their life and attempt to change their self-assessment.

ii. Sanctity of Life

A prominent argument against suicide is the argument that it infringes the principle of sanctity of life. Sanctity of life approaches typically make three linked claims:

(1) that life has a value independent of the person's wishes or feelings;
(2) that value outweighs any negative values about the life, in particular the personal views and experiences of the individual;
(3) that it is always wrong to intentionally end a life.

It goes without saying that opponents may agree with some of these points and not all. It is worth separating these out. Before doing that, it should be noted that the sanctity of life argument – at least as traditionally understood – is highly significant in this debate. It alone of the arguments has the potential to mean all suicides

[123] J Harris, *The Value of Life* (Routledge & Kegan Paul, 1985) 111.
[124] A Smuts, 'To Be Or Never To Have Been: Anti-Natalism and a Life Worth Living' (2013) 17 *Ethical Theory and Moral Practice* 711.

are ethically unjustified. The other arguments that we see, for example focusing on the importance of virtue or obligations to others, provide arguments that some suicides are unjustifiable. However, they do not seem to render suicide unjustifiable in every case.

There are two key aspects to the sanctity of life doctrine that are worth separating out.

a. Life Has a Value Independent of the Person's Wishes or Feelings

This claim counters the view that the value of a life is found in the experiences and feelings of the person themselves. Rather, it claims that the value of life is intrinsic; life is of value in and of itself. This claim is significant because it means that a person's life has value even if they have no experiences (eg they are in a persistent vegetative state) or they are simply experiencing pain.

The most attractive feature of the sanctity of life claim is that the value of each person's life is equal. Because the value of life does not depend on individual experiences or feelings, the worth of a person's life cannot be reduced or increased. We are all equal. No one's life is 'worthless'. Given the sorry history of humanity, with plenty of examples of cases where a group of people have been said to be worth less than another group or are treated as dispensable, a theory which highlights the indestructible value in every human life has considerable appeal. Consider, for example, this shocking comment by a respected philosopher, who rejects sanctity of life:

> People […] have no reason to feel guilty about putting a Down's syndrome baby away, whether it's 'put away' in the sense of hidden in a sanitarium or in a more responsible lethal sense. It is sad; yes. Dreadful. But it carries no guilt. True guilt arises only from an offence against a person, and a Down's is not a person.
>
> There should be no moral guilt in killing a baby with Down's syndrome because 'a Down's is not a person'. Indeed, the 'real guilt' would be 'in keeping alive a Down's or other kind of idiot, out of a false idea of obligation or duty'.[125]

Such a view could be strongly rejected by those holding a sanctity of life view. Nearly all those holding the view that the value of a life lies in the experience of the individual would find such comments repugnant, but it would be less straightforward for them to explain why.

While sanctity of life commonly finds support among religious thinkers, it is not confined to those relying on a theological perspective. Dworkin claims that most people share the 'fundamental' idea that:

> … human life is intrinsically valuable, and worthy of a kind of awe, just because it is human life. They think that once a human life begins, it is a very bad thing – a kind of sacrilege – that it end prematurely, particularly through someone's deliberate act.[126]

[125] J Fletcher 'The Right to Die' (1968) April *Atlantic Monthly* 59, 59.
[126] Dworkin (n 11) 406.

The difficulty for the sanctity of life approach is in identifying where this intrinsic good comes from. If the good of life does not rest in the experiences of the person, what is it that generates the intrinsic value? There is a ready answer for those with religious belief: God gives value to human life. Because the life is precious to God, it is precious, independent of the person's feelings. However, that argument will not persuade those who are without faith.[127] Indeed, Emily Jackson[128] argues that the sanctity of human life principle only makes sense when grounded in a certain kind of religious belief. But for precisely that reason sanctity of life supporters will be wary of relying on such an explicitly religious basis for the doctrine.

Attempts have been made to overcome this problem from a non-religious perspective. Dworkin claims there is a shared awe in the 'miracle of human creation' which can – but need not – come from a conviction in God:

> Any human creature, including the most immature embryo, is a triumph of divine or evolutionary creation, which produces a complex, reasoning being from, as it were, nothing, and also of what we often call the 'miracle' of human reproduction, which makes each new human being both different from and yet a continuation of the human beings who created it.[129]

Hoffmann LJ in the Court of Appeal in *Bland*[130] explained this particularly well:

> … we have a strong feeling that there is an intrinsic value in human life, irrespective of whether it is valuable to the person concerned or indeed to anyone else. Those who adhere to religious faiths which believe in the sanctity of all God's creation and in particular that human life was created in the image of God himself will have no difficulty with the concept of the intrinsic value of human life. But even those without any religious belief think in the same way. In a case like this we should not try to analyse the rationality of such feelings. What matters is that, in one form or another, they form part of almost everyone's intuitive values. No law which ignores them can possibly hope to be acceptable.

Such views get close to claiming that simply by being a member of the human species a person has moral value. But it is hard to see why a biological link in itself generates moral value. As McMahan[131] argues, we would not think much of those who claimed that members of a particular racial group were superior to others, by virtue of any biological link.

It seems at this point in the argument that we are left with two uncomfortable views. On the one hand, as Singer indicates, we might take the view that it is capabilities such as rational thought that generate the value in life.[132] However, such

[127] L Gormally, 'Two Competing Conceptions of Human Dignity' in S Muders (ed), *Human Dignity and Assisted Death* (Oxford University Press, 2017).
[128] E Jackson, 'Secularism, Sanctity and the Wrongness of Killing' (2008) 3 *Biosciences* 125.
[129] Dworkin (n 11) 83–84.
[130] *Bland v Airedale NHS Trust* [1993] 1 All ER 821.
[131] J McMahan, 'Our Fellow Creatures' (2005) 9 *Ethics* 353.
[132] P Singer, 'Is the Sanctity of Life Ethic Terminally Ill?' (1995) 9 *Bioethics* 327.

a view would mean that humans who lack such capabilities would be treated as having less value. That would challenge the widely held view that all humans are of equal value. On the other hand, if we take the view that membership of the human species is itself sufficient, we struggle to identify where that value lies.

Paterson is clear that all human life has value, regardless of whether it has rationality or quality of life. He argues that *all* humans must be offered the 'rightful protection offered to the archetypal members of our species because of what they essentially are *irrespective of the particular circumstances of any given member*'.[133] Such a view might still have problems from an equality perspective. It seems to imply that an individual who lacks a particular capacity important to personhood is valued because the archetypal human has that capacity. That seems a somewhat precarious, and potentially offensive basis of value. It seems to imply 'we value you not for who you are but who you might have been'. Wicks suggests:

> the key requirement for an individual to qualify for the special legal and ethical protection given to human life was said to be integrative function of a human organism. Such integrative function will be governed by the brain and will require sufficiently developed lungs to supply oxygen to the major bodily organs.[134]

The two selected requirements – brain stem activity and lung functioning – are pretty much essential to being alive, so it might be thought that this is close to requiring a person to be an alive human being. That seems to offer little by explanation for why the operation of those organs generates any particular moral value.

Another school of thought will find value in human communities and relationships of care. Thus, a human has value if they are loved and cared for by others. This might create problems for those excluded from society, but even those on the margins of society are cared about by someone, unless we are imaging a hermit whose existence is unknown to the rest of humanity.[135]

At this point some authors simply claim that the value of human life is 'ineffable' – something that is beyond our comprehension, almost something that cannot be talked about. Indeed, that is sometimes how religion is presented, as an attempt to explain and explore that which cannot captured in traditional language and thought. Guy Bennett-Hunter has suggested that the meaning of life is an ultimate meaning, beyond words. He writes:

> Life is itself meaningful in virtue of being experienced as being in a relation of appropriateness to what is beyond itself. And it is only as determinately meaningless that what is beyond the human can, in a non-circular manner, function as the measure for all human meanings.[136]

[133] C Paterson, *Assisted Suicide and Euthanasia: A Natural Law Ethics Approach* (Routledge, 2008).
[134] E Wicks, *The Right to Life and Conflicting Interests* (Oxford University Press, 2010).
[135] J Herring, 'Relational Personhood' (2021) *Keele Law Review* 17.
[136] G Bennett-Hunter, 'Ineffability: Reply to Professors Metz and Cooper' (2016) 44 *Philosophia* 1267, 1268.

It is, of course, difficult to respond to an argument 'which cannot be spoken'. It certainly runs up against problems as to who can claim this value and what strength to accord it.[137] It seems to lose any value in discussion if it cannot be explained or weighed.

b. The Sanctity of Life Outweighs All Other Values

If we take it for now that there is some inherent value in human beings, there is then a question of how much that value counts, in particular whether it is sufficient to outweigh pain and distress suffered by the individual. It is a striking aspect of the literature that it tends to be assumed that if there is a 'sanctity value' this is of ultimate value and trumps all other considerations. Davis writes:

> I believe that each human life is of infinite value, and since infinity cannot be multiplied or divided, remaining implicit in its infinity, so too is all human life precious and worthy of protection, no matter how long or short it may be.[138]

This leads Keown to develop what is often seen as the core principle flowing from that sanctity of life approach:

> the principle of the sanctity of human life … holds that, because all lives are intrinsically valuable, it is always wrong intentionally to kill an innocent human being.[139]

However, it does not seem to flow from the claim that life has an intrinsic value that that value trumps all others. It certainly seems a plausible claim to make that life has intrinsic value, but that can be trumped by the experiences of the individual. Much depends on the source of the value. For example, if the value is seen as coming from the fact that each life is valued by the community, it seems this could be over outweighed if an individual is in considerable pain. So we might say 'yes, you are a valued member of our community and we want you to remain with us, but we recognise you are in such pain that is too much to expect of you'. In a religious version of sanctity of life, where it is the valuing of a life by God that gives the life value, it seems plausible that one might conclude that nothing could outweigh the value placed on a life by God, even the suffering of an individual. But even then it takes quite some confidence in one's assessment of God's view to require a person to suffer considerable pain as a result. I suggest, therefore, that even if one accepts some concept of the sanctity of life, it should not be seen as a trump value which defeats all other considerations in every case, making all suicides wrong.

[137] T Metz, 'Is Life's Meaning Ultimately Unthinkable?: Guy Bennett-Hunter on the Ineffable' (2016) 44 *Philosophia* 1247.

[138] A Davis, 'The Status of Anencephalic Babies: Should Their Bodies Be Used As Donor Banks?' (1988) 14 *Journal of Medical Ethics* 150.

[139] J Keown, *Euthanasia, Ethics and Public Policy: An Argument against Legalisation* (Cambridge: Cambridge University Press, 2002) 36.

Indeed it is striking that there is some acknowledgement of these points, even by ardent supporters of sanctity of life. The 1980 *Declaration on Euthanasia* by the Vatican's Sacred Congregation for the Doctrine of the Faith claimed that terminally ill patients can permissibly refuse life-preserving treatments in cases where these treatments 'would only secure a precarious and burdensome prolongation of life'. Keown, a leading proponent of the sanctity of life, rejects what he calls vitalism, which suggests that 'human life is an absolute moral value and that it is wrong either to shorten the life of an individual human being or to fail to lengthen it'.[140] He emphasises that it is acts or omissions done with the direct intent of causing death which are forbidden under the sanctity of life principle.[141]

VII. A Duty to Commit Suicide?

This chapter has largely been seeking to outline circumstances in which suicide might or at least should be ethically permitted. However, it might be argued that there are cases where there is a duty to commit suicide. Obviously, this will rarely arise, but it is not difficult to think of a suicide which might promote the well-being of others or save lives. A range of examples might be provided: the soldier falling on a grenade to protect comrades; the captured spy who takes their own life, fearing that they will be tortured into giving out the names of others, who would then be killed; the person who gives up all their organs to save others. All of these examples would be likely to generate the label 'heroic', indicating that they might be seen as exhibiting great virtue. They are not cases where there is a duty to act in this way.[142]

Hardwig[143] has argued that there is a moral duty to die where continuing to live puts a considerable burden on family members or loved ones. He makes it clear that he is not arguing that this should be a legally enforceable duty. There are, however, a number of concerns with this approach. There are many decisions a person may make which might cause a burden to their families: entering a same-sex relationship; getting a divorce; deciding to move house – all of these kinds of decision might cause an emotional or economic burden to family members and we would never consider that to be a reason to impose a duty not to do such things. Indeed, to take one of those examples, we would think it quite wrong for a gay person not to enter a public relationship for fear of how their family would respond. There are therefore limits on what we oblige others to do, whether legally or ethically, for the good of others. Only very rarely does it seem that death should be required.

[140] J Keown, 'Restoring Moral and Intellectual Shape to the Law after *Bland*' (1997) 113 *Law Quarterly Review* 481, 483.

[141] D Jones, 'An Unholy Mess: Why "The Sanctity of Life Principle" Should Be Jettisoned' (2016) 22 *The New Bioethics* 185.

[142] D Lester, 'Can Suicide Be a Good Death?' (2006) 30 *Death Studies* 511.

[143] J Hardwig, 'Is There a Duty to Die?' (1997) 27 *Hastings Centre Report* 34.

VIII. Duties Towards the Suicidal: Drawing the Threads Together

This chapter has argued in favour of a general ethical framework that requires a balancing of the degree to which a decision is autonomous and the harmfulness of that decision. It has been argued that, on this framework, suicides can be justified. The decision may be richly autonomous and the harm limited. However, those are rare cases. In many cases the decision is insufficiently autonomous to justify the harm of death; indeed, in many cases it would be more autonomy-enhancing for the suicide to be prevented. This then raises the question of what is the correct response to a suicidal person?

I would argue that in many cases autonomy justifies an intervention. If we think it is true (or likely to be true) that a person is not genuinely autonomous then we can stop them acting, particularly as the killing will end all their autonomy. The suicidal wish is the result of a momentary despair, and their settled autonomous wish would be to live. In other words, we have a clash been their current wish to die – which is not autonomous, or only weakly so – and their longstanding wish to live, which they would normally have. Such an approach would need to accept that there may be some cases where it is clear the suicidal wish is a firm, settled, fully autonomous decision, in which case the justification for intervention would fall away.

Those rejecting this approach might argue that it fails to sufficiently respect the autonomy of suicidal people.[144] Alexandre Baril[145] argues that:

> based on the sanist silencing of suicidal subjects through the injunction to live and somatechnologies of life, suicidal people constitute an oppressed, stigmatised group whose claims remain unintelligible within society, law, medical/psychiatric systems and anti-oppressive scholarship, including LGBTQ scholarship.

Wedlake[146] argues that the suicidal are silenced as mentally ill and medicalised as mad and this producing 'espistemic violence'. She writes:

> Suicidal people are, therefore, unable to speak to their suicidality because they are perceived as incompetent and irrational. Their voices are silenced, and their needs are determined for them; they are not given space to express their desire to die nor are they given a choice in whether to live or die.

She argues that:

> Restoring the epistemic agency of suicidal people requires validating and supporting the desire to die as legitimate and giving suicidal people agency in their decision to choose suicide or not. Silencing suicidality and failing to affirm the desire to die is an act of ableism which does little to actually improve suicidal people's lives.

[144] S Tack, 'The Logic of Life: Thinking Suicide through Somatechnics' (2019) 34 *Australian Feminist Studies* 99.
[145] Baril (n 20).
[146] Wedlake (n 21).

The difficulty with both these approaches is that there is no single 'voice' of the suicidal. There are those who have approached suicide and been persuaded not to or have been prevented from doing so, who are enormously grateful that their apparently autonomous wish was not respected. Indeed, for the reasons set out earlier in this chapter, I expect the large majority of suicidal people are not sufficiently autonomous to make such a decision. That does not mean there are no suicidal people who can be richly autonomous, and their views deserve respect. But that should not come at the cost of ignoring the true autonomy of the suicidal people who are not in a rich sense choosing to die.

One of the most determined arguments against suicide prevention is set out in Kevin Yuill's book *Assisted Suicide: The Liberal, Humanist Case against Liberalization*.[147] He starts with an argument against legislating to permit assisted suicide:

> The most important undermining factor of the autonomy argument for assisted suicide is inconsistency. Not one genuine justification for providing autonomy for some and not for others has or can be made. … If assisted suicide was really a right, it should surely be accorded to all. If we reject laws against assisted suicide as paternalistic, we should also reject laws preventing assisted suicide for all as paternalistic.[148]

He goes on to say that legalising assisted suicide allows doctors to 'colonize our most intimate thoughts and influence what should be the most personal decision ever made'.[149] His concern is that on most programs for assisted suicide the court will judge a person's reasons for suicide and that is an 'intolerable intrusion into what should be a private affair'. The problem with this argument is that unless we wish to make suicide available to people who do not genuinely wish to die, we need to restrict ready access to the means to commit suicide. He argues:

> Legalising assisted suicide reduces suicide to a medical choice. What should be profound and meaningful, the most human of human actions, loses its meaning. The question of whether 'to be or not to be' becomes a medical rather than a moral question.[150]

He is keen to allow suicide to be 'inspirational, transcendent and the most beautiful and awe-inspiring act'.[151]

Astonishingly, he argues that rather than legalising suicide we should 'make deadly drugs available to the public, albeit with warnings about what ingesting them will do and perhaps even a waiting period'.[152] People would be free to pass these drugs on to those who want them without fear of prosecution. People will then be free to make their 'dramatic choices' for themselves, without state intrusion and leaving room for moral judgement, Yuill believes.

[147] K Yuill, *Assisted Suicide: The Liberal, Humanist Case against Liberalization* (Palgrave, 2012).
[148] At 57.
[149] At 129.
[150] At 84.
[151] At 110.
[152] At 142.

It is striking that in making this proposal Yuill describes three suicides in some detail: Mohamed Bouazizi, a Tunisian street vendor who set himself on fire as a protest against government action; Thich Quang Du, a Buddhist monk who in 1963 gained international recognition after setting himself on fire in a political protest; and Arthur Friedman, who committed suicide in prison so that his son would not face humiliation at his trial. While these are examples of the kind of dramatic statements which Yuill is clearly keen to enable people to express, they are hardly representative of those who seek suicide. As we have seen in this chapter, rarely is suicide the 'deliberate, dramatic action of the highest import'[153] that Yuill writes about. Suicide is only exceptionally some grand moral statement; most often it is marked by despair, loneliness or exhaustion.

Once we see suicide as it actually occurs in real life, rather than the glamourised version Yuill presents, or the image presented in the media of the terminally ill person seeking relief from pain, then we can properly develop the general approach to suicide which should be seek to stop it.

IX. Conclusion

Wicks offers this summary of the appropriate response to suicide:

> 'In respect of a clear suicide attempt by a mentally competent adult, the state's negative duty not to infringe an individual's autonomy will outweigh its positive obligation to take reasonable steps to preserve life under the right to life …
>
> If, on the other hand, the individual is not capable of exercising autonomy due to mental incapacity, or if an individual thoughtlessly endangers his or her life, then the state should intervene to offer protection.[154]

That seems broadly correct. However, so much depends on what counts as being mentally competent and the broader context of the decision. It has been argued in this chapter that, given the gravity of the issue (death), we require a rich form of autonomy to justify it. That, I have argued, is a challenging test to satisfy and few suicidal decisions are sufficiently autonomously rich to fulfil that justificatory role.

[153] At 110.
[154] Wicks (n 130).

6

Human Rights and Suicide

I. Introduction

In this chapter I seek to set out the legal case for a right to be prevented from committing suicide. I will focus on the European Convention on Human Rights (ECHR) as this has been the focus of the debate in Europe, although many of the points raised could be made in other human rights documents. I will rely in particular on Article 2 (the right to life); Article 3 (the right to protection from torture and inhuman and degrading treatment) and Article 14 (protection from discrimination). The argument will be that the state is under a positive duty to prevent suicide and that a failure to do so infringes the human rights of the suicidal. However, there are limits on the extent of the duty that are imposed on the state. My argument will be that the current interpretations of the ECHR by the European and domestic courts acknowledge that right and that the broader jurisprudence of the courts support that development.

The human right to be prevented from committing suicide imposes duties on the state which can be broken down into four elements:

(1) a general duty to have in place policies that discourage suicide;
(2) a duty to have in place policies to protect particular groups from suicide;
(3) a specific duty to prevent individuals known to pose a risk from committing suicide;
(4) a duty to investigate and learn from cases of suicide.

It must be admitted that the law in this area is under development. Lord Mance in *Rabone*[1] referred to 'the uncertainty' around this area of the law. While it is beyond doubt that in certain circumstances the state is under a duty to prevent someone from committing suicide and that a failure to do so breaches that person's rights under Article 2, what is less obvious is whether this is a more general right that all suicidal people possess and the precise extent and nature of the obligations owed by the state.

Before exploring these issues further, it is striking to note the shift in the law's response to suicide. As we have seen, for a long time suicide was seen as a serious

[1] *Rabone v Pennine Care NHS Trust* [2012] UKSC 2.

crime.[2] The argument in this chapter, that one has a human right to be prevented from committing suicide, moves the issue from being suicide as moral wrong to see it as something engendering legal rights. Before exploring this further a fundamental theoretical question will be raised, which will be addressed as the argument of the chapter develops.

II. Rights and Duties

Underpinning the debates around the extent of rights to suicide prevention is a core question, which is yet to be conclusively addressed by the court. It is accepted that the state cannot take steps to prevent every suicide because to impose a duty to do so would be to impose an excessive burden on the state. Hence, there are conditions that must be satisfied before a state can be found to have breached those rights. But what is the nature of those conditions? In particular, which of the following statements best represents the current position:

(1) everyone has a right to be prevented from committing suicide. However, there are limits on when the state can be held to account for failing to prevent a suicide, that is the duties that flow from that right. The purpose of the limits is, on this vision, to ensure that the burden on the state is not overburdensome; or
(2) people only have a right to be prevented from committing suicide in certain circumstances, such as when they are in the care of the state. The limits of the duty create the structure for the right.

I will argue that the first represents the correct view: that all suicidal people have a right to be prevented from committing suicide. However, the duty on the state to meet these rights is limited by practical and theoretical considerations. It may be that in practical terms little turns on which approach is taken. However, the distinction is important for two reasons. The first is conceptual. Imagine a case where a suicidal person is not given services that would have prevented suicide because of a reasonable rationing decision. Under the first approach, we can accept that their rights were infringed, but it was not reasonable to impose the duty upon the state. That requires a focus to be on why the suicide was not stopped and whether there were sufficiently good reasons for the failure to intervene. By contrast, the second approach asks whether there were good reasons to impose a duty on the state to intervene.

The second reason why the distinction is important is more practical. In borderline cases, if the starting point is that there is a right to suicide, but the duty on the state might be limited to ensure that obligations on the state are not

[2] J Tucker, 'The Geometry of Suicide Law' (2015) 43 *International Journal of Law, Crime and Justice* 432.

too onerous, then the focus becomes whether the burden is so great that the right cannot be protected by imposing a duty. If, however, the burden defines the right then it seems less is required of the burden to show that the right should not apply in these cases.

It is not completely clear from ECHR case law which view is taken. The terminology used in *Mammadov v Azerbaijan*[3] and many other cases is that the duty to prevent suicide only arises if the state was, among other things, reasonably aware of the risk to life. However, the court always expresses this in terms of the limits of the state's duty, rather than the limit of the individual's right. In other contexts, the court talks in terms of behaviour that is – or is not – covered by the scope of the right (eg in terms of the right to respect for private life). That way of expressing it, in terms of the duty rather than in terms of the right, seems to support the view there is a broad right to suicide prevention, but there are limits on the duty that arises from it. Or, putting that another way, the state cannot be held to account for every breach of an Article 2 right.

The argument seems appropriate in principle too. The fact the state did not know of the risk of death is a perfectly good reason to say they should not be held to have a duty to protect the right. That does not, however, seem to be sufficient reason to say that an individual's right has not been breached. Surely my rights have been breached regardless of the state of mind (knowledge) of another?

That seems a highly persuasive argument. There is, however, a somewhat technical argument against it. A standard jurisprudential view is that rights only exist if there is a corresponding duty (correlativity, as it is often known). David Lyons writes of the standard view on correlativity that:

> claims of individual rights need not be recognized unless backed by proof that corresponding obligations obtain. Such a doctrine of correlativity also forms part of the view that rights must be understood or analyzed in terms of duty or obligation.[4]

On this view a right can only exist in so far as there is a corresponding duty. However, that view is certainly not universal and is indeed questioned by Lyons himself, who gives many examples of rights without corresponding duties, such as a right of free speech or the right to turn right when facing a red light in some US states. Such rights, he says, do not impose duties on anyone.[5] Cohen[6] states:

> I have argued only that basic rights do not, as a conceptual or formal matter, necessarily impose second- or third party positive duties of protection or provision. There may very well be such duties, but they might not be correlated with basic rights. They might correlate only with derivative rights that arise by agreement or through special relationships. Alternatively, such duties might bind us all the time at varying levels of stringency, but the duties might not be enforceable as a matter of justice.

[3] *Mammadov v Azerbaijan* (2014) 58 EHRR 18.
[4] D Lyons, 'The Correlativity of Rights and Duties' (1970) 4 *Nous* 45.
[5] ibid.
[6] A Cohen, 'Must Rights Impose Enforceable Positive Duties?' (2004) 35 *Journal of Social Philosophy* 364.

I will not go further into this more technical side of the debate. It certainly seems that, conceptually, it is not utterly improper to imagine a right with no corresponding duty.

III. The Positive Duty to Protect the Right to Life

Article 2 of the ECHR states:

> 1. Everyone's right to life shall be protected by law. No one shall be deprived of his life intentionally save in the execution of a sentence of a court following his conviction of a crime for which this penalty is provided by law.
>
> 2. Deprivation of life shall not be regarded as inflicted in contravention of this article when it results from the use of force which is no more than absolutely necessary:
>
> (a) in defence of any person from unlawful violence;
> (b) in order to effect a lawful arrest or to prevent the escape of a person lawfully detained;
> (c) in action lawfully taken for the purpose of quelling a riot or insurrection.

Article 2 is said to be one of the 'most fundamental provisions of the convention' and enshrines one of the basic values of a democratic society.[7] Without life, the other rights have little or no value. As the Malawi Supreme Court of Appeal states, 'The right to life is the mother of all rights'.[8]

To the uninitiated it might be thought that the right to life protected by Article 2 means simply that the state must not kill civilians. And, of course, it does mean that. However, it is now well established that the right extends beyond state killing.[9] As the European Court of Human Rights (ECtHR) in *Olewnik-Cieplińska v Poland* puts it:

> … [T]he first sentence of Article 2(1) enjoins the state not only to refrain from the intentional and unlawful taking of life, but also to take appropriate steps to safeguard the lives of those within its jurisdiction.[10]

This has become a familiar refrain in cases that consider Article 2.[11] A similar approach is taken in relation to Article 3: not only must the state not torture its citizens, it has a duty to stop other citizens inflicting torture on each other.[12] This

[7] *Giuliani and Gaggio v Italy* [2011] ECHR 513.

[8] *Khoviwa v R* [2021] MWSC 3.

[9] L-A Sicilianos, 'Preventing Violations of the Right to Life: Positive Obligations under Article 2 of the ECHR' (2014) 3 *Cyprus Human Rights Law Review* 117; M Baros, 'The UK Government's Covid-19 Response and Article 2 of the ECHR (Title I Dignity; Right to Life, Charter of Fundamental Rights of the EU)' (2020) 9 *Laws* 19.

[10] *Olewnik-Cieplińska v Poland* [2019] ECHR 612, para 117.

[11] *Fernandes de Oliveira v Portugal* (2019) 69 EHRR 8.

[12] *Opuz v Turkey* (2010) 50 EHRR 28.

interpretation is correct. If a citizen has a right to life or not to be tortured then those rights are as much interfered with, whoever is doing the killing.

However, as the court in *Olewnik-Cieplińska v Poland*[13] emphasised, it cannot be that the state is held responsible for every death:

> Bearing in mind the difficulties in policing modern societies, the unpredictability of human conduct and the operational choices which must be made in terms of priorities and resources, the scope of the positive obligation must be interpreted in a way which does not impose an impossible or disproportionate burden on the authorities. Not every claimed risk to life, therefore, can entail for the authorities a Convention requirement to take operational measures to prevent that risk from materialising.

As argued above, the right to life is infringed, whenever a person is killed in a way as defined in the article, but the ECtHR acknowledges that there is a limit on the extent to which the state can be held to account for that breach. Where, for example, the state authorities could not have known that X was about to take their life, they could not be held to account for that breach; but that does not mean that X's right to life was not infringed.

IV. Does Suicide Infringe the Right to Life?

The previous discussion made it clear that an attack by a third party infringes the rights in Article 2. But does that apply to suicide? Perhaps surprisingly the answer to this question has been assumed by the ECtHR to be 'yes', with little debate.[14] Thus, a person who commits suicide has their Article 2 right infringed as much as the person who is killed by another. The ECtHR appears to take the view that autonomy rights do not mean suicide does not infringe Article 2, but rather that Article 2 rights are to be balanced against the right to life case in a suicidal case and can also limit the duties expected of the state. It, therefore, rejects the view that a right to life only exists in so far as a person wants to be alive. I think the ECtHR are correct to take this view and will explain why.

In part, this debate raises the well-known jurisprudential arguments between those supporting a 'will theory' and those who support an 'interest theory' of rights. Under the will or choice theory, core to the concept of a right is that the right-holder can choose whether or not to enforce their rights.[15] Rights are about giving especial power or significance to certain choices. Therefore, a person 'cannot be described as a right-holder unless he or she is able to exercise a choice over the exercise of that right'.[16] For HLA Hart, freedom is at the heart of rights and so it

[13] *Olewnik-Cieplińska* (n 10) para 119.
[14] *Fernandes de Oliveira v Portugal* (n 11).
[15] H Steiner, *An Essay on Rights* (Blackwell, 1994).
[16] J Fortin, *Children's Rights and the Developing Law* (Cambridge University Press, 2003) 12.

must be in the nature of rights that an adult can decide to limit their rights.[17] This theory poses real challenges for those who cannot exercise a choice, including at least some children and those lacking capacity. Indeed, some critics of the choice theory have used the example of children to suggest that the theory is flawed.[18] Under the interest theory rights protect wellbeing. We identify the key things that are important for human thriving and protect those interests with rights. This theory would have no difficulty with the argument that those lacking capacity can have rights, even though they cannot choose whether to exercise them. Where a person does not want to have a key interest, protecting this would create a clash of rights (between the right to the interest and the right of autonomy) but would not mean that the right no longer existed. This debate is clearly relevant in this context. Under the will theory, if a person does not want their right to life then they can decide to reject the right and it has no effect in relation to them. Under the interest theory the right to life remains, even though a person may reject it, although that rejection may lead to other rights which need to be balanced against it. One of the main benefits of the interest theory is that it enables a more nuanced approach to the balancing of autonomy and interests than the apparently binary options the choice theory manifests. In Chapter 5 I argued that this careful balancing is the ethically superior way of dealing with issues around suicide, in particular because of the difficulties in defining autonomy and choice in this context.

Whatever the jurisprudential disputes, the courts have accepted – with little questioning – that suicide is engaged by Article 2. In *Pretty v UK* the ECtHR stated:

> [The right to life] is unconcerned with issues to do with the quality of living or what a person chooses to do with his or her life. To the extent that these aspects are recognised as so fundamental to the human condition that they require protection from State interference, they may be reflected in the rights guaranteed by other Articles of the Convention, or in other international human rights instruments. Article 2 cannot, without a distortion of language, be interpreted as conferring the diametrically opposite right, namely a right to die; nor can it create a right to self-determination in the sense of conferring on an individual the entitlement to choose death rather than life.[19]

The court went on to find that a right to commit suicide might be found in Article 8, which protects the right to respect for private life. It was not possible to use Article 2 as the basis for a right to commit suicide. Indeed, the courts have stated that Article 2 requires the state to put in place protections for vulnerable people who might commit suicide.[20]

This then take us to the position that under Article 2 the right to life applies to suicide and requires the state to put in place interventions to prevent suicide. As was held in *Pretty v UK*:[21]

[17] H Hart, 'Are There Any Natural Rights?' (1995) 64 *The Philosophical Review* 131.

[18] S Brennan, 'The Goods of Childhood and Children's Rights' in F Baylis and C McLeod (eds), *Family-Making: Contemporary Ethical Challenges* (Oxford University Press, 2014) 29.

[19] *Pretty v UK* (1997) 24 EHRR 423, para 121.

[20] *Haas v Switzerland* (2011) 53 EHRR 33.

[21] *Pretty v UK* (n 19) para 38.

> Article 2 (1) enjoins the State not only to refrain from the intentional and unlawful taking of life, but also to take appropriate steps to safeguard the lives of those within its jurisdiction.

Thus, in cases of suicide, the starting point is that Article 2 is engaged and the debates are about the extent to which there are limits on the duty of the state to intervene.

V. What Does the Duty Require?

The case law reveals that Article 2 applies in all cases where a person's life is under threat. However, the duties on the state are limited and involve weighing up potential conflicting rights under Articles 3 and 8. As was stated in *Banel v Lithuania*:

> the positive obligation [under Article 2] is to be interpreted in such a way as not to impose an excessive burden on the authorities, bearing in mind, in particular, the unpredictability of human conduct and the operational choices which must be made in terms of priorities and resources …. Accordingly, not every risk to life can entail for the authorities a Convention requirement to take operational measures to prevent that risk from materialising.[22]

The obligations on the state in a case of potential suicide can be separated into four different categories:

(1) the universal general duty: this is the duty owed to every citizen to have in place a legal and administrative system that protects people's lives, including from suicide;
(2) the particular general duty: this is a duty owed to particular groups of people at risk of committing suicide to put in place legal and administrative provisions to protect the lives of members of that group, including from suicide;
(3) the operational duty to take steps to protect the life of a particular individual who the state is aware is in danger of committing suicide;
(4) the duty to investigate suicides, particularly with a view to ensuring that lessons are learned so as to avoid future suicides.

Each of these will be considered separately.

VI. The Universal General Duty

The general duty is owed to everyone.[23] It requires the state 'to put in place a legislative and administrative framework designed to provide effective deterrence

[22] *Banel v Lithuania* [2013] ECHR 558.
[23] *Fernandes de Oliveira v Portugal* (n 11).

against threats to the right to life'.[24] To be clear, these do not require proof that the state knew that a particular person was at risk of suicide.[25] It is an obligation owed to everyone. The kinds of duties that might be required under this general duty include the following.

A. Legislative

Basic legislative interventions to protect the right to life are required. These include criminal offences that are designed to protect life. Clearly that would include a law against murder. Less straightforward is what is required for the law on assisting or encouraging suicide. The ECtHR in *Pretty v UK*[26] has made it clear that the law regulating suicide requires a balancing of rights. On the one hand there needs to be a protection of the right to life of the suicidal, and on the other hand there is a right to respect for private life, which includes decisions being made to end one's life. To be compliant with the Convention there needs to be a balance between these rights, although considerable discretion is permitted. It seems that the Convention requires there to be some kind of criminal offence which would prohibit A from coercing B into committing suicide, or taking advantage of B's vulnerability into committing suicide; but there must also be room for lawful assistance for suicide in some circumstances. This means that a state which had no offences against assisted suicide and/or permitted unregulated access to assisted suicide would breach the Convention; but so too would a state which prohibited assisted suicide under all circumstances. It seems that between these two extremes the ECHR leaves the details to the particular state. The Convention makes clear that the protection for Article 2 must have protections which are 'practical and effective'.[27] The obligation is not just to enact laws preventing suicide; they must also be enforced.

The legislation required may be more extensive than simply direct regulation of assistance or encouragement to commit suicide. Lady Hale, in *Rabone*, explained that it was necessary to have in place laws that deterred 'threats to life from any quarter'.[28] Applying this in relation to gun control laws, in *Kotilainen v Finland*[29] it was held that the state was required 'to put in place and rigorously apply a system of adequate and effective safeguards designed to counteract and prevent any improper and dangerous use of such weapons'. A failure to do this could lead to liability even where the death of the particular victim was not foreseen. While the decision was not specifically considering suicide, the reference to 'any improper

[24] See *Öneryildiz v Turkey* (2004) 41 EHRR 325, para 89, applying what the court said in *Osman v United Kingdom* (1998) 29 EHRR 245, para 115.

[25] *Eremiasova and Pechova v Czech Republic* [2013] ECHR 568, para 110.

[26] *Pretty v UK* (2002) 35 EHRR 1.

[27] Eg *Kotilainen v Finland* [2020] ECHR 635, para 6.

[28] *Rabone v Pennine Care NHS Trust* (n 1) para 76.

[29] *Kotilainen v Finland* (n 27) para 68.

and dangerous use' surely includes suicide. There is an obligation on the state to have in place regulations around tools of suicide to restrict access to them.

B. Administrative

There are also universal general administrative duties on the state to protect Article 2. In the context of this book I would argue that there is a duty to have a suicide prevention policy and to take positive steps to discourage suicide. This might include ensuring that when the media raise issues around suicide, information is given about support services for people, or ensuring that schools provide information about mental health and support services. It might require that there be appropriate funding for helplines and other sources of intervention for those feeling suicidal. There might also be an obligation to put in place mechanisms to make suicide harder at 'suicide hot spots', such as safety barriers and signs encouraging people to seek help.

VII. The Particular General Duty

It is well known that there are certain groups who are at risk of suicide and self-harm, such as victims of domestic abuse and victims of school bullying. In such cases the state has a duty to put in place reasonable provisions to ensure that those in the group do not commit suicide. This might include, for example, ensuring that information is provided to groups about talking services or other support services.

These kinds of duties arise particularly where someone is in the care of the state, such as in prison or a public hospital.[30] This includes ensuring there are appropriate policies and regulations in those fields. For example, in *Fernandes de Oliveira v Portugal*[31] it was explained that Article 2 required the state:

> to make regulations compelling hospitals, whether private or public, to adopt appropriate measures for the protection of patients' lives. That positive obligation also requires an effective independent judicial system to be set up so that the cause of death of patients in the care of the medical profession, whether in the public or the private sector, can be determined and those responsible made accountable.

There is specifically a requirement to adopt policies that minimise suicide risk and to take reasonable measures to prevent people in these groups harming themselves.[32] This obligation is different from the obligations we shall discuss shortly which arise in the case where someone is known to be at risk of committing

[30] *Mižigárová v Slovakia* Application no 74832/01, para 89.
[31] *Fernandes de Oliveira v Portugal* (n 11).
[32] *Eremiasova and Pechova v Czech Republic* (n 25).

suicide (the specific operational obligations). For example, in *Keller v Russia*,[33] a man jumped to his death from a police station window following his arrest for the theft of two bicycles. The court found a breach of Article 2 because, even though there was no evidence to indicate that this particular man was a known suicide risk, ensuring that people could not fall from windows was a 'basic precaution', and had not been put in place.[34]

A good example of these issues in practice is *Fernandes de Oliverira v Portugal*.[35] AJ (the deceased) had been admitted to a psychiatric hospital eight times between his first admission, aged 20, in 1984 and his death in 2000. His issues related to schizophrenia, major depression, and abuse of alcohol and prescription drugs. He left the grounds of the hospital without leave and jumped in front of a train. The court held that there was a general regulatory duty on hospitals to protect patients' lives. This ranged from ensuring that there were sufficient numbers of staff and that they were well trained. It may also involve investigation into deaths to ensure regulatory lesson were learned.

On the facts of the particular case, the court focused on whether the Portuguese Mental Health Act had appropriate provision for civil detention in case patients needed protection from suicide, and concluded that it did. The court also considered whether the hospital had general policies designed to protect people from self-harm, balancing protection and freedom. It was held that the policies, which included regular checks on the wellbeing of patients and, in some cases, restricting patients to their wards, were appropriate. It was held that this was in broad terms an appropriate set of regulations. As a separate matter, as we shall see, the court then considered whether there were specific duties to protect the life of AJ, but these were seen as a separate head of claim from the general duties owed to patients. Notably while the majority found the regulatory framework appropriate, that was heavily criticised in the dissenting speeches of Judge Pinto de Albuquerque and Judge Harutyunyan. They criticised the judgment as 'an ideologically charged minimalist approach to the State's obligations in the sphere of health care law', the effect of which was 'downgrading the level of Convention protection to an inadmissible level of State inertia'.[36] In particular, they found the legal regulation of voluntary patients to be inadequate and there was no suicide prevention strategy at the time of AJ's death. They noted:

> [I]n other words, in 2000 Portugal was in the pre-historic stages of suicide prevention of psychiatric inpatients. There was no legislation or regulation on what types of regimes could be applied, under what circumstances, by whom and until when. … To put it simply, in 2000 the HSC was in a legal black hole.[37]

[33] *Keller v Russia* [2013] ECHR 985.
[34] ibid, para 88.
[35] *Fernandes de Oliveira v Portugal* (n 11).
[36] ibid, para 2.
[37] ibid, para 13.

It is not necessary here to determine whether these criticisms of the Portuguese system are fair or not, but they highlight the kinds of issues that arise under this heading.

It is important to note too that in the case of these particular general obligations the question is whether the regulations and policies are appropriate. The fact that a professional failed to follow the guidance would not normally breach this aspect of the duty. As was explained in *Kotilainen v Finland*:[38]

> where a Contracting State has adopted an overall legal framework and legislation tailored to the protective requirements in the specific context, matters such as an error of judgment on the part of an individual player, or negligent coordination among professionals, whether public or private, could not be sufficient of themselves to make a Contracting State accountable from the standpoint of its positive obligation under Article 2 of the Convention to protect life.

That said, it important to note that the court will consider whether the regulations' protection of the right to life is concrete and not abstract. A regulatory framework which is not enforced may well be insufficient to meet the state's obligations.

Bearing in mind the strong link between being in receipt of benefits and suicide outlined in Chapter 4, it can be argued that this group should also be seen as a particularly vulnerable group to whom state obligations are owed. They are dependent on the state for the most basic needs and their vulnerability to suicide indicates that the state should have in place a set of policies designed to prevent suicide among this group.

VIII. Specific Operational Obligations to those in the Care of the State

Under this heading we deal with cases where the state is aware that a particular individual is at risk of suicide and fails to protect them. As it was put in *Fernandes de Oliveira v Portugal*:[39]

> article 2 may imply, in certain well-defined circumstances, a positive obligation on the authorities to take preventive operational measures to protect an individual from another individual or, in particular circumstances, from himself.

The precise scope of this duty is debated. Lord Dyson in *Rabone* accepted that there is a degree of uncertainty about the law:[40]

> Strasbourg proceeds on a case by case basis. The jurisprudence of the operational duty is young. Its boundaries are still being explored by the ECtHR as new circumstances are

[38] *Kotilainen v Finland* (n 27) para 68.
[39] *Fernandes de Oliveira v Portugal* (n 11).
[40] *Rabone v Pennine Care NHS Trust* (n 1) para 25.

> presented to it for consideration. But it seems to me that the court has been tending to expand the categories of circumstances in which the operational duty will be found to exist.

In *Daniel v St George's Healthcare NHS Trust*,[41] Lang J remarked that 'the application of the operational duty has developed incrementally'.

Above, I alluded to the ambiguity in the question we are asking here. Is it that all suicidal people have a right to be prevented from suicide (subject to any countervailing rights: see below page 127) but that there are limits on the circumstances in which the state is responsible for the breach of those rights? Or is it that there is only a right to be prevented from committing suicide in certain circumstances? In the argument which follows I will argue that the former is the better view. As stated by the ECtHR in *Öneryildiz v Turkey*,[42] Article 2 'lays down a positive obligation on States to take appropriate steps to safeguard the lives of those within their jurisdiction'. I base this argument particularly on the fact that the reasons given for restricting the duty are very relevant in deciding the scope of the duty, but they are not relevant to whether the right is infringed in the first place. If I am correct in this argument, the point becomes significant because if the starting point is that a person does have a right to be protected from suicide and the question is whether it is reasonable to impose the duty on the state to protect that right, it seems that prima facie the answer should be 'yes'. We need good reasons for a person's right not to be protected by the state.

Before exploring these issues further it will be useful to describe the decision in the Supreme Court Case of *Rabone v Pennine Care NHS Foundation Trust*,[43] as it provides a good example of the kind of cases in which these issues arise.[44] Melanie Rabone, aged 24, was prone to bouts of deep depression. She attempted suicide and was admitted to the respondent hospital, where she was assessed as being at high risk of suicide or self-harm. She attended voluntarily but the doctor who assessed her on admission noted that should she seek to leave the hospital she should be compulsorily detained. She was put under '15 minute observation', which should have meant that she was checked by staff every quarter of an hour. However, this did not occur and she was allowed to leave the hospital. She committed suicide by hanging herself from a tree. Her parents, the claimants in the case, brought an action for damages. There were various aspects of the claim, but the one most relevant for us is the claim under section 7 of the Human Rights Act 1998, claiming a breach of Article 2 of the ECHR. The Supreme Court accepted that the state owed an operational duty to take steps to protect Rabone from committing suicide.

[41] *Daniel v St George's Healthcare NHS Trust* [2016] EWHC 23 (QB).

[42] *Öneryildiz v Turkey* (n 24) para 71.

[43] J Wright, 'The Operational Obligation under Article 2 of the European Convention on Human Rights and Challenges for Coherence – Views from the English Supreme Court and Strasbourg' (2016) 7 *Journal of European Tort Law* 58.

[44] *Rabone v Pennine Care NHS Trust* (n 1).

There were reasonable steps that could have been taken and were not. The breach of Article 2 was, therefore, established. Damages of £7,500 were awarded to her parents.

What are the questions which arise when determining when a duty is placed on the state to prevent suicide?

A. Being under the Care and Control of the State

A common view is that an operational duty can only be owed to someone who is in the care and control of the state in some sense.[45] It is certainly true that many of the cases involving breaches of Article 2 and suicide have involved those under the care and control of the state. Examples of such cases include the following:

(1) prisoners and immigrants being kept in administrative detention;[46]
(2) psychiatric patients detained in a public hospital;[47]
(3) people conscripted to military service;[48]
(4) people receiving voluntary care in a psychiatric hospital.[49]

The reason why there is a particularly strong case for there being a duty when a person is in the care and control of the state was set out in *Fernandes de Oliveira v Portugal*:

> Where the authorities decide to place and keep in detention a person suffering from a mental illness, they should demonstrate special care in guaranteeing such conditions as correspond to the person's special needs resulting from his or her disability.[50]

They went on to say that this covers people in psychiatric institutions, whether voluntarily or involuntarily, as accepted in *Rabone*[51] and *de Oliveira*.[52] In *de Oliveria* it was suggested 'in the case of patients who are hospitalised … involuntarily, the Court … *may* apply a stricter standard of scrutiny',[53] although that was not mentioned in *Rabone*. The explanation for treating voluntarily and informal patients in the same way as in *Rabone* was that the differences between an 'informal' and detained patient are 'more apparent than real'.[54] They noted that an informal patient may in theory be free to leave but be detained if they tried

[45] Lord Rodger in *Mitchell v Glasgow City Council* [2009] AC 874, para 66.
[46] *Slimani v France* (2004) 43 EHRR 1068; *Keenan v United Kingdom* (2001) 33 EHRR 913.
[47] *Savage v South Essex Partnership NHS Foundation Trust (MIND intervening)* [2009] AC 681.
[48] *Kilinç v Turkey* [2005] ECHR 367.
[49] *Rabone v Pennine Care NHS Trust* (n 1).
[50] *Fernandes de Oliveira v Portugal* (n 11) para 113.
[51] *Rabone v Pennine Care NHS Trust* (n 1).
[52] *Fernandes de Oliveira v Portugal* (n 11).
[53] ibid, para 124.
[54] ibid, para 28.

to do so.[55] In *de Oliveria* it was argued that '[t]o say otherwise would be tantamount to depriving voluntary inpatients of the protection of Article 2 of the Convention'.[56]

However, none of that means that being in the care and control of the state is a requirement for the duty to arise. Lord Dyson in *Rabone* explained that:

> the operational duty will be held to exist where there has been an assumption of responsibility by the state for the individual's welfare and safety (including by the exercise of control). The paradigm example of assumption of responsibility is where the state has detained an individual, whether in prison, in a psychiatric hospital, in an immigration detention centre or otherwise ....

It would be wrong, however, to read Lord Dyson as saying the duty only arises in relation to those in the care and control of the state. He is discussing when the duty will paradigmatically arise and is not suggesting that it is a requirement for the duty. Later he summarises his view that 'there is such a duty to protect persons from a real and immediate risk of suicide at least where they are under the control of the state'. The words 'at least' make it clear he is not restricting the duty to those cases. Indeed, he makes it explicit that a duty can arise even though there is no state care and control. He explains:

> In circumstances of sufficient vulnerability, the ECtHR has been prepared to find a breach of the operational duty even where there has been no assumption of control by the state.[57]

Lady Hale explained that the Article 2 duties arose in *Rabone* not primarily because the patient was in the care of the state but because of the 'special vulnerability of people suffering from mental disorders, especially psychosis'.[58] She went on to argue that in the case law 'there is no suggestion that the operational obligation to prevent suicide is limited to prisoners and detainees.' Indeed:

> in the context of any public or private activity in which the right to life may be at stake, the state has a duty, if the authorities know or ought to know of a real and immediate risk to the life of a particular individual, to take such measures as might reasonably be expected of them to avoid that risk?[59]

In *HM Senior Assistant Coroner of City of Sunderland*[60] it was noted that Lord Dyson referred to: the state's assumption of responsibility and exercise of control;

[55] P Bartlett, 'The Right to Life and the Scope of Control: Fernandes de Oliveira v Portugal' 18 March 2018 https://strasbourgobservers.com/2019/03/18/the-right-to-life-and-the-scope-of-control-fernandes-de-oliveira-v-portugal/, accessed 13 December 2021.

[56] *Fernandes de Oliveira v Portugal* (n 11) para 84.

[57] *Rabone v Pennine Care NHS Trust* (n 1) para 23.

[58] *Fernandes de Oliveira v Portugal* (n 11) para 25 states: 'Persons with mental disabilities are considered to constitute a particularly vulnerable group who require protection from self-harm'.

[59] *Rabone v Pennine Care NHS Trust* (n 1) para 96.

[60] *R (Lee) v HM Assistant Coroner for Sunderland* [2019] EWHC 3227 (Admin).

vulnerability of the person; and the nature and degree of the risk as 'indicia' of when the duty might arise, rather than 'a battery of fixed tests'.

This demonstrates that the requirement of an assumption of responsibility is not a condition for Article 2 duties being found.[61] Indeed it was explicitly recognised in *Mammadov v Azerbaijan*[62] that an operational duty can arise in relation to a person who is not in the care of the state. The case involved a woman who was being evicted from a flat by the authorities. She was living there illegally. As a protest, she covered herself in petrol and set herself alight. The police were present but did not take steps to prevent her killing herself. The ECtHR held, significantly, that there was a potential breach of Article 2 rights, explaining that:

> in a situation where an individual threatens to take his or her own life in plain view of State agents and, moreover where this threat is an emotional reaction directly induced by the State agents' actions or demands, the latter should treat this threat with the utmost seriousness as constituting an imminent risk to that individual's life, regardless of how unexpected that threat might have been.

On the facts a breach was not found, as there was no evidence that the agents could have done anything to prevent the suicide. It might be argued that this case is unusual because it is one where the state's actions 'induced' the suicide. However, I would argue a careful reading of the dicta indicates that the approach is not restricted to such cases, the word 'moreover' suggesting that the inducement is an additional factor, rather than a requirement.

This is also apparent from *R (Lee) v HM Assistant Coroner for Sunderland*,[63] where the court ordered a rehearing because the coroner had only considered whether the state had assumed responsibility and control over a patient. The court said the coroner should also have considered the deceased's vulnerability and the level of risk of suicide in determining whether an Article 2 duty arose.

The conclusion I reach on reading the case law is that the standard view – that an Article 2 duty only arises in a suicide case where a patient is under the care and control of the state – is misguided. Where a patient is under the care and control of the state it is a particularly likely that there is a duty and a breach can be found, but it is not a requirement. The court will also look at the person's vulnerability, the knowledge of the public authorities, and all the other circumstances in determining whether that duty arises. That seems also to be the correct approach at a theoretical level. If we look at other Article 2 cases, where a person's life is in danger from a third party, it is well established that there are obligations to protect that person, where the death is foreseeable and where there are reasonable steps the state can take to protect the person. In *Osman v United Kingdom*[64] the police

[61] As their lordships noted, *Z v UK* (2001) 34 EHRR 97 involved Art 3, rather than Art 2, but they thought nothing turned on that.
[62] *Mammadov v Azerbaijan* (n 3).
[63] *R (Lee) v HM Assistant Coroner for Sunderland* (n 60).
[64] *Osman v United Kingdom* (n 24).

failed to protect a family from the threats of a person with mental health issues who went on to kill a member of the family. The court concluded that the state has a 'positive obligation … to take preventive operational measures to protect an individual whose life is at risk from the criminal acts of another individual'. That duty is not limited to people in the care of the state. I can see no reason why the scope of the duty should be any different in a case where a person is posing a threat to themselves rather than others. Of course, it might be thought more reasonable to use force to prevent a person from harming others than themselves. Or it might be thought that autonomy arguments would mean an intervention would be inappropriate. However, these arguments all go to what reasonable steps that can be expected, rather than whether there is a breach of the right in the first place or a duty arising under it.

B. 'Vulnerability'

As already mentioned, in her speech in *Rabone*, Lady Hale indicated it was Ms Rabone's vulnerability which generated the duty under Article 2. In *G4S Care and Justice Services Ltd v Luke*[65] it was held that 'the state's positive obligation to protect life …. entails an obligation to take positive steps to prevent a "real and immediate risk" to the life of a person in a recognised category of particularly vulnerable people from materialising'. As with being in the care of the state, I argue that vulnerability is not an actual requirement for the duty to arise as such, but rather an indica of when the duty is likely to arise. I offer two reasons for this. First, it might well be argued that any person who is at immediate risk of suicide is automatically a vulnerable person. Almost by definition, a person wanting to die is experiencing their life to be profoundly negative. It seems, therefore, to add little to say they must be vulnerable. Second, the case of *Mammadov v Azerbaijan*, mentioned above, where the woman attempted to commit suicide on being evicted, is a good example of a person who was not seen as 'vulnerable' until the suicide attempt. It was the fact that she was known to be on the point of suicide which was key – no particular reference was made to her being vulnerable prior to that point. I suggest that being in a particularly vulnerable group may well assist in showing that the Article 2 duty arises, but again it is not a requirement.

C. Knew or Ought to Know

From the above discussion I suggest we reach the position where the facts that a person is in the care and/or control of the state, or is especially vulnerable, are good indications that a duty is owed, but neither is a requirement. This leaves

[65] *G4S Care and Justice Services Ltd v Luke* [2019] EWHC 1648 (QB).

remaining the potential limitation on the duty that it is only owed to those who the state knows – or ought to know – were at risk of imminent suicide.

The case law does not indicate whether the knowledge element is relevant to both the question of whether the duty exists and whether or not it was breached.[66] That does seem to be implied in *Fernandes de Oliverira v Portugal*, where the court held:

> In a series of cases where the risk derived not from the criminal acts of a third party, but from self-harm by a detained person, the Court found that the positive obligation arose where the authorities knew or ought to have known that the person posed a real and immediate risk of suicide. Where the Court found that the authorities knew or ought to have known of the risk it proceeded to analyse whether the authorities did all that could reasonably have been expected of them to prevent that risk from materialising. Thus, the Court assesses whether, looking at all the circumstances of a given case, the risk in question had been both real and immediate.[67]

Similarly, Lord Dyson in *Rabone* writes that:

> It is clear that the existence of a 'real and immediate risk' to life is a necessary but not sufficient condition for the existence of the duty.

The other judges in *Rabone* likewise take that line, although Lady Hale focuses on the knowledge issue when discussing breach, rather than establishing the duty. Nevertheless, as the High Court in *R (Morahan) v HM Assistant Coroner for West London*[68] concludes in its careful reading of *Rabone* on this point, there seems a clear majority for seeing the knowledge question as a prerequisite for the duty to arise. I will criticise this approach below, but before doing so three points about the knowledge requirement should be emphasised.

First, the test is whether the authorities knew or *ought to* have known of the risk. This contains an objective element. An authority cannot deny the legal duty by saying it was not aware of the risk, if in fact it was a risk that it ought to know about.

Second, the risk must be 'a real risk'. This is a somewhat opaque term, but it indicates that more than speculation is required. The use of the word 'risk' implies that it does not need to be shown that there is more than a 50 per cent chance of suicide, for example. In *Rabone* the risk was described as 'substantial or significant risk and not a remote or fanciful one'.[69] There, the risk of suicide was quantified as being 5 per cent, 10 per cent and 20 per cent on successive days, and that was held to be sufficient.[70] That said, it is extremely difficult to assess suicide risk. As Bartlett notes:

> Predicting suicide (or violence – the same issue arises) of people with mental health problems is extremely difficult: suicide is an extraordinarily rare event, and risk

[66] *Hiller v Austria* [2016] ECHR 1028.
[67] *Fernandes de Oliveira v Portugal* (n 11) para 110.
[68] *R (Morahan) v HM Assistant Coroner for West London* [2021] EWHC 1603 (Admin).
[69] *Rabone v Pennine Care NHS Trust* (n 1).
[70] ibid, paras 35–38.

> assessment systems are of highly doubtful validity and accuracy …. The question as regards the scope of Article 2 is therefore how far, if at all, the scope of compulsion should be expanded to include yet more people who will not commit suicide, to ensure that we control an additional few that do.[71]

Third, the risk must be of an 'immediate risk of suicide'.[72] This is an important limitation. It is not enough to show a general concern that at some point the person may commit suicide, but that the suicide is expected in the near future. Nor is it enough just to show that there was a risk of harm – the risk must be of death.[73] In *Rabone* the phrase 'present and continuing' was suggested as capturing the idea of 'immediate'.[74] This perhaps makes it clear that the risk may be ongoing over a period of time and still be immediate. In *Renolde v France*[75] the deceased had a psychotic disorder with delusion, regularly attempted suicide and was found to be at immediate risk for the 18 days after a suicide attempt. By contrast, in *Keenan v United Kingdom*[76] the prisoner was known to be mentally ill and from time to time to be at risk of suicide, but that was not enough to suggest an immediate risk of suicide.

Fernandes de Oliveira v Portugal[77] listed a number of factors that could indicate a real and immediate risk:

(1) whether the person had a history of mental health problems;
(2) the gravity of the mental condition;
(3) previous attempts to commit suicide or self-harm;
(4) suicidal thoughts or threats; and
(5) signs of physical or mental distress.

We need to return to the question of whether the knowledge requirement is an element that establishes the existence of the duty or feeds into whether there is a breach of the duty.

The most detailed discussion in the case law explicitly on that question is in *R (Morahan) v HM Assistant Coroner for West London*,[78] where it was held that the knowledge requirement was an element of the duty. The explanation Popplewell LJ gave is as follows:

> This is consistent with principle because the article 2 operational duty is not one to take steps in the abstract, but rather to take steps to avert a specific risk to life; until the specific risk to life has been identified, it is impossible to answer the duty question. Just

[71] Bartlett (n 56); M Large et al, 'The Validity and Utility of Risk Assessment for Inpatient Suicide' (2011) 19(6) *Australasian Psychiatry* 507.
[72] *Kotilainen v Finland* (n 27) para 68.
[73] *G4S Care and Justice Services Ltd v Luke* (n 65) paras 74–75.
[74] *Rabone v Pennine Care NHS Trust* (n 1).
[75] *Renolde v France* (2008) 48 EHRR 969.
[76] *Keenan v United Kingdom* (n 46).
[77] *Fernandes de Oliveira v Portugal* (n 11) para 115.
[78] *R (Morahan) v HM Assistant Coroner for West London* (n 68).

> as in the domestic tortious law of negligence it is not sufficient merely to ask, 'Is there a duty' but rather, 'Is there a duty not carelessly to inflict a particular type of damage?', so too the article 2 operational duty must be examined and defined as a duty to take reasonable steps to avoid the specific risk to life which is relevant in the circumstances of a given case. So a risk of death from natural causes is not one which necessarily or ordinarily attracts the operational duty even for detainees. It is not all risks to life, or even all risks to life within limited categories, which attract the duty, but only real and immediate risks to life in those categories of which the state agent is or ought to be aware.[79]

I suggest that as a matter of principle the reasoning used here is flawed. Popplewell LJ draws an analogy with the law of tort. This, however, is a fundamentally different kind of law from a law based on human rights and the right to life. In terms of tort, the victim who has suffered a loss has to establish the basis that this loss was the result of a wrong. There is no independent claim based simply on the fact of a loss. By contrast, where a person has committed suicide that is per se a breach of Article 2. Their human rights have been infringed. The question is whether or not the state can be held to account for that breach. In tort law, a person is entitled to deny a responsibility in relation to a certain kind of wrong. The fact that a neighbour's car has been damaged is 'not my business' or certainly 'not within the scope of my responsibility'. However, the fact that a human right has been breached is automatically within the responsibility of the state. It may be that there is nothing the state could have done to prevent that breach, but any breach of a human right, especially something as fundamental as the right to life, is a core aspect of the concern of the state. In other words, if the state knew of the risk of suicide and could have stopped it and failed to do so (without a justification) there is no room for the argument 'this was not my business'. There is, however, room in tort law for me to say that although I could have saved my neighbour's car from damage it is not my business.

D. Conclusion on Scope Duties

It has been argued above that a careful reading of the case law does not limit the specific operational duty to prevent suicide to cases where a suicidal person is in the control of the state. Rather the key issue is whether the person is 'vulnerable' (which will be the case in nearly all suicides) and whether the state knew or ought to have known that there was a real (not fanciful) and immediate possibility of suicide. Of course, whether the person was in the care and control of the state and the extent to which the risk was known will be key in determining whether the duty was breached. However, I have criticised the law in this regard and argued it should be the position that the state owes a duty to all those who are suicidal and

[79] ibid, para 48.

the questions of whether the state knew or ought to have known should go to the issue of breach of the duty, rather than the establishment of the duty in the first place.

IX. Breach of the Duty

Having established the duty, the state is only required to take reasonable steps to protect a suicidal person's care. There is an important difference here between cases where there is a negative duty and where there is a positive one. In relation to Article 2 it is relatively easy to comply with the positive obligation not to kill citizens. What must not be done is clearly defined, and generally it will not require expense or effort to comply with that requirement – just as the law outlawing murder is not seen as an excessive curb on our freedoms as a citizen, it is not unduly burdensome for the state to avoid killing people. The issue is much harder in relation to positive obligations to save life. These can certainly be burdensome, expensive, and of uncertain extent.

I will start by describing the obligations that flow from the general duty and then explore some of the particular factors that will determine the extent of that duty. The key test is whether 'appropriate steps'[80] were taken to protect people's lives. However, to that should be added an oft-quoted passage from *Osman*,[81] where it was said the obligation must be interpreted 'in a way which does not impose an impossible or disproportionate burden on the authorities'.

We need to explore further some of the particular issues that can arise in determining the scope of the duty.

A. Rationing

The courts have accepted that it is not possible to do 'everything' to protect Article 2. There are necessary 'operational choices which must be made in terms of priorities and resources in providing public healthcare and certain other public services'.[82] Certainly it is acknowledged that sometimes funds cannot be used to meet the needs of all those who have calls on the state's resources. Where such an issue is raised the courts are likely to determine that the national authorities are in a better position to balance the competing demands on limited resources than the parties themselves.[83] That said, given that the issues involve the lives of citizens, the courts are likely to be most sympathetic to cases where the state is saying it had to

[80] *Osman v United Kingdom* (n 24).
[81] ibid.
[82] See also *Osman v United Kingdom* (n 24).
[83] *Pentiacova v Moldova* (2005) 40 EHRR SE23.

allocate its resources to determine which lives to save. A simple argument that it was too expensive to prevent this suicide is unlikely, on its own, to be persuasive.

B. Powers

An important issue in deciding what the state could reasonably be expected to do, is what powers the state has. Here there is a close relationship to the general group duty mentioned above and the personal operation duty mentioned here. For the group duty the court must consider whether the general set of powers is appropriate. If it is decided that those powers are appropriate, then when the personal operational duty is considered and it is asked what the state might reasonably have done, clearly it will be constrained by the powers and policies in place. This has been used to explain why there might be a difference between, for example, a patient who is voluntarily detained in mental health hospital and one who is compulsorily detained. The state may have fewer powers to restrict the freedoms of the former than the latter. In *de Oliviera* the majority stated:

> this duty, namely to take reasonable measures to prevent a person from self-harm, exists with respect to both categories of patient. However, the Court considers that in the case of patients who are hospitalised following a judicial order, and therefore involuntarily, the Court, in its own assessment, may apply a stricter standard of scrutiny.[84]

This is controversial. Notably there is no equivalent passage in *Rabone*. It might well be thought that if there was no power to detain a voluntary patient known to be on the point of committing suicide, the absence of that power is a breach of the general duties. Perhaps there is a small band of cases where it is reasonable for the regulations not to grant a power of intervention in a case of suicide, even though it would be reasonable to exercise that power if it existed. It seems, from *Oliviera*, that in such a case there would be no breach of a state's duty under Article 2.

C. State Responsibility

In determining what the duty requires the state to do, one factor is whether the state played a role in causing the suicide. Reference has already been made to *Mammadov v Azerbaijan*,[85] where police officers attempted to evict the applicant and his family from the accommodation they were living in. The applicant's wife set fire to herself. The claim was that the officers did not do enough to prevent the suicide. The court identified the key question as 'whether at some point during the course of the operation the state agents became aware or ought to have become

[84] *de Olivera v Portugal* [2019] ECHR 106, para 124.
[85] *Mammadov v Azerbaijan* (n 3).

aware' that there was a risk of suicide. That does seem to imply that where the state has induced the suicide – albeit unwittingly –the obligation on the state is heightened.[86]

D. Autonomy

A major issue in relation to the state's duty to prevent suicide is the extent to which the autonomy of the patient is a justification for not intervening. In other words, can the state say 'we did not prevent the suicide because to do so would interfere with the patient's autonomy'. Perhaps surprisingly, this has received little attention from the courts. It is an important argument, but it needs to be treated with care. It is helpful to separate out two different versions the argument might take:

(1) it might be argued that restricting the freedom of a suicidal person can increase suicidal feelings.[87] Hence, a balance has to be struck between restrictions which may impede access to means of suicide and restrictions which increase the chance of the removing the suicidal feelings. In *Hiller v Austria* it was noted that 'today's paradigm in mental health care is to give persons with mental disabilities the greatest possible personal freedom in order to facilitate their re-integration into society'.[88] This argument is not based on the promotion of autonomy as a value itself, but looking at the harms that might flow from a breach of autonomy, particularly in increasing suicidal ideation; or
(2) there may be an argument that the degree of intervention required to prevent suicide would be so invasive of a person's autonomy (and perhaps bodily integrity and dignity) that it should not be used. Here the argument seeks to highlight the value of autonomy itself.

The first argument as a matter of principle is uncontroversial. No one would support an intervention designed to prevent suicide which in fact increased the risk of it. The second is more complex. It requires a balancing of the right to liberty and bodily integrity and the right to life. There is a real tension there. Judge Pinto de Albuquerque and Judge Harutyunyan in *Fernandes de Oliveira v Portugal*[89] criticised the suggestion in the majority that protecting the liberty of patients overrode rights to suicide prevention:

> The argument that there is an emerging trend to treat persons with mental disorders under an 'open door' regime is not decisive […]. First, it only shows one side of the coin, because there is also a counter-trend to increase State obligations with regard to suicide prevention, which is totally neglected by the majority […] The core of the problem

[86] *Öneryildiz v Turkey* (n 24).
[87] P Sullivan, 'Should Healthcare Professionals Sometimes Allow Harm? The Case of Self-Injury' (2017) 43 *Journal of Medical Ethics* 319.
[88] *Hiller v Austria* (n 66) para 54.
[89] *Fernandes de Oliveira v Portugal* (n 11) para 115.

> today lies precisely in the inter-relationship between these two different trends of international health law and practice, which the majority do not even seek to consider. … The right to life prevails over the right to liberty, especially when the psychopathological condition of the individual limits his or her capacity for self-determination. It is nothing but pure hypocrisy to argue that the State should leave vulnerable suicidal inpatients in State-run psychiatric hospitals free to put an end to their lives merely in order to respect their right to freedom … Ultimately, this reflects a hidden social-welfare disengagement policy, which aims at the maximum commodification of health-care services and above all at the protection of health professionals in an untouchable legal bubble, shirking State responsibility for health-system and hospital-related death or serious injury under the Convention and consequently limiting the Court's jurisdiction in this area.[90]

While this passage makes some important points, it blurs together the two arguments above: that a 'disengagement' fails to ensure 'the right to life prevails over the right to liberty' and the argument that 'disengagement' is the most effective means of achieving the protection of the right to life. What makes the question harder is that the design of policies in, for example, a mental health unit needs to be appropriate for all parties. It is worth recalling that most patients, even though deemed a suicide risk, do not commit suicide. It is inevitable that a general policy is more often going to infringe autonomy than prevent suicide. For this reason Leigh[91] expresses concerns that the judgment in *Rabone* will lead to defensive practices, with more patients subject to compulsory detention.

In *Hiller v Austria*[92] it was said that the hospitalised person needs freedom, as it is 'desirable in order to preserve as much as possible their dignity and their right to self-determination'. In de *Oliveira*[93] we are told 'the authorities must discharge their duties in a manner compatible with the rights and freedoms of the individual concerned and in such a way as to diminish the opportunities for self-harm, without infringing personal autonomy'.[94] Lady Hale in *Rabone* explained:

> There is a difficult balance to be struck between the right of the individual patient to freedom and self-determination and her right to be prevented from taking her own life.[95]

She went on to state:

> Autonomous individuals have a right to take their own lives if that is what they truly want. If a person announces her intention of travelling to Switzerland to be assisted to commit suicide there, this is not, by itself, sufficient to impose an obligation under article 2 to take steps to prevent her.[96]

[90] ibid, para 21.
[91] B Leigh, 'A Bad Decision for Patients' (2012) 11 *Mind's Newsletter* 1.
[92] *Hiller v Austria* (n 66) para 54.
[93] *Fernandes de Oliveira v Portugal* (n 11).
[94] *Fernandes de Oliveira v Portugal* (n 11).
[95] *Rabone v Pennine Care NHS Trust* (n 1) para 107.
[96] ibid, para 108.

These dicta highlight the issue, the need to balance autonomy and rights to protection from suicide, but do little to indicate how that balance should be struck. Doing so, I would argue, takes us back to the ethical issues discussed in Chapter 5 and particularly the argument that we should not be trying to balance 'autonomy' as an abstract principle and the right to life. Rather, we need to consider how autonomous the individual was, recognising autonomy as a scalar concept, with the right to protection from suicide. Further, we need to recognise that in the case of many suicide attempts there are conflicting autonomies and assessing what the person wants is far from straightforward. Much depends on the richness of the autonomy and the degree of force used to secure the intervention. I suggest that certainly in most suicide attempts, where the attempt is only weakly autonomous, the right to protection should win out. In such cases only where the intervention amounted to torture and inhuman or degrading treatment, as prohibited by Article 3, do we get close to the point where the right to protection from suicide is defeated.[97]

These issues are well illustrated by the case of Kerrie Wooltorton.[98] She was 26 and had borderline personality disorder. She had on several occasions drunk antifreeze in suicide attempts, although she then went on to accept treatment to save her life. She prepared an advance directive and swallowed anti-freeze. She called for an ambulance and accepted pain relief. However, this time she refused the renal dialysis needed to preserve her life. She was assessed for capacity but simply said 'It's in the letter'. Although she refused to say anything else she was deemed to have capacity and her decision was respected and she died. At the inquest the coroner approved of the hospital's actions and indeed stated it would have been unlawful to intervene.

At first sight the case seems straightforward. She had refused treatment and the medical teams had to respect that. However, there must be questions about the extent to which she had capacity. She was unable to explain or express her reasons for suicide. She had called an ambulance and allowed herself to be admitted to hospital, indicating that her desire to die was not single minded. She had a history of requesting and being grateful for attempts to save her life. Where a person whose life could readily be saved is to be denied medical treatment on the basis of their autonomy, we need to be confident we have a completely reliable assessment of their autonomy and for that decision to be richly autonomous.

X. Duty to Investigate

The final duty under Article 2 that is imposed on the state is a duty to investigate the suicide. Article 2 has been interpreted as imposing an obligation to conduct

[97] *Jeanty v Belgium* [2020] ECHR 276.

[98] N Allen, 'The Right to Life in a Suicidal State' (2013) 36 *International Journal of Law and Psychiatry* 350.

an independent and impartial official investigation in all cases of death caused as a result of the use of force, including suicide.[99] The purpose of that investigation is to ensure the effective implementation of laws which protect the right to life and to hold the state to account for deaths within their responsibility. In *Jordan v United Kingdom*[100] the ECtHR explained that the purpose of the duty to investigate was 'to secure the effective implementation of the domestic laws which protect the right to life and, in those cases involving State agents or bodies, to ensure their accountability for deaths occurring under their responsibility …'. The duty to investigate does not apply to all suicides.[101]

In *R (Maughan) (Appellant) v Her Majesty's Senior Coroner for Oxfordshire (Respondent)*[102] the Supreme Court considered the question of the standard of proof before a suicide verdict could be reached by a coroner. The conclusion was that it was the balance of probabilities for all short-form conclusions. As mentioned in Chapter 2, a primary reason behind this was to improve the collection of suicide statistics and assist in determining whether lessons for suicide prevention had to be learned.

XI. United Nations Convention on the Rights of Persons with Disabilities

Increasingly, legal debates on suicide involve reference to the United Nations Convention on the Rights of Persons with Disabilities (CRPD). The Convention is designed to ensure that people with disability have full and equal enjoyment of all rights. It is worth quoting the three key rights:

> **Article 10: Right to Life**
>
> States Parties reaffirm that every human being has the inherent right to life and shall take all necessary measures to ensure its effective enjoyment by persons with disabilities on an equal basis with others.
>
> **Article 12: Equal Recognition before the Law**
>
> 1. States Parties reaffirm that persons with disabilities have the right to recognition everywhere as persons before the law.
>
> 2. States Parties shall recognize that persons with disabilities enjoy legal capacity on an equal basis with others in all aspects of life.
>
> 3. States Parties shall take appropriate measures to provide access by persons with disabilities to the support they may require in exercising their legal capacity.

[99] *Mammadov v Azerbaijan* (n 3); *R (Morahan) v Her Majesty's Assistant Coroner for West London* (n 68).

[100] *Jordan v United Kingdom* (2001) 37 EHRR 52, para 105.

[101] *R (Maguire) v HM Senior Coroner for Blackpool and Fylde* [2020] EWCA Civ 738.

[102] *R (Maughan) (Appellant) v Her Majesty's Senior Coroner for Oxfordshire (Respondent)* [2020] UKSC 46.

4. States Parties shall ensure that all measures that relate to the exercise of legal capacity provide for appropriate and effective safeguards to prevent abuse in accordance with international human rights law. Such safeguards shall ensure that measures relating to the exercise of legal capacity respect the rights, will and preferences of the person, are free of conflict of interest and undue influence, are proportional and tailored to the person's circumstances, apply for the shortest time possible and are subject to regular review by a competent, independent and impartial authority or judicial body. The safeguards shall be proportional to the degree to which such measures affect the person's rights and interests.

Article 14: Liberty and Security of a Person

1. States Parties shall ensure that persons with disabilities, on an equal basis with others:
   a. Enjoy the right to liberty and security of person;
   b. Are not deprived of their liberty unlawfully or arbitrarily, and that any deprivation of liberty is in conformity with the law, and that the existence of a disability shall in no case justify a deprivation of liberty.
2. States Parties shall ensure that if persons with disabilities are deprived of their liberty through any process, they are, on an equal basis with others, entitled to guarantees in accordance with international human rights law and shall be treated in compliance with the objectives and principles of this Convention, including by provision of reasonable accommodation.

It is worth adding that under Article 25 of the CRPD persons with disability have the right to the 'highest attainable standard of health without discrimination on the basis of disability'.

It is easy to see how the debates over suicide prevention can play into these rights. For those who emphasise the right of suicide prevention Articles 10 and 25 are highlighted. Those who suffer mental disabilities that cause them to wish to kill themselves have rights to life and rights to health treatment which require reasonable steps to prevent suicide and to receive suitable treatment. On the other hand, those sceptical of suicide prevention will argue that there is no reason to distinguish between the suicidal feelings of those deemed to have capacity and those with a mental illness or those deemed to be lacking in capacity. Article 12 gives equal protection before the law for autonomy rights, regardless of any assessment of mental capacity or health.

The CRPD gives rise to some important lessons for the debates in this chapter. First, it highlights that there are duties to promote the health and protect the life of those with mental illnesses. A failure to offer effective mental health care, including suicide prevention, is a serious breach of the rights of those with mental illness. Second, it is wrong to assume that those with mental illness are necessarily less autonomous than those without. In particular, it would be wrong to have increased suicide prevention for those with mental illness than is available to those without. However, I would suggest, the key to this is to assess carefully the degree of autonomy of all those who are suicidal. There should be no presumption that those with mental illness are less autonomous than others, and likewise there should be no assumption that those without mental illness are more autonomous. In Chapter 4 I set out the reasons to question the autonomy of most cases of suicide, regardless of their mental health.

XII. Conclusion and the Way Ahead

There is general agreement that the application of human rights to suicide prevention is in flux and there are competing pressures on the law as it develops. Three tensions, in particular, may be noted:

(1) a recognition of the importance of mental health and the need to treat mental ill health as seriously as physical health. If a person were seriously ill with a condition and needing medical treatment to save their life, it would require a strong justification not to give it to them. The failure to tackle suicide prevention can be seen as a failure to recognise the severity of mental illness or not to value the lives of the mentally ill;

(2) the importance of autonomy. While the argument is commonly made that suicide prevention is a breach of autonomy, this needs to be treated with care. In many cases of suicide it is difficult to detect precisely what is the autonomous wish of the person committing suicide; there may well be competing autonomies. Further, we need to recognise that autonomy is scalar and that few suicides will be of sufficient richness to deserve the fullest protection of autonomy;

(3) suicide is a breach of Article 2 rights and is, therefore, a responsibility of the state. There are limits on what the state can be expected to do as suicides can be hard to predict and there can be competing resources.

Our starting point should be that a suicide involves a breach of Article 2 of the ECHR. The state has an obligation to protect citizens from breaches of their human rights. There are limits as to what the state can do to protect those rights. In particular, the state only be expected to intervene when there is a serious immediate risk of suicide. Even then there are issues of resources and questions of autonomy that will impact on what the state can do. These, however, are explanations for why the state cannot be held to account for the breach, rather than denying that the rights of the citizen were infringed in the first place. In the next chapter we will look at some of the current law as it relates to suicidal persons, with these rights issues in mind.

7

The Current Law on Suicide

I. Introduction

This chapter will explore the current response of the law to suicide in the UK. It will focus on the response of criminal, mental health and mental capacity law. This chapter will not seek to explain the whole of the legal responses to suicide, but to illustrate the primary provisions that are of direct relevance to suicide.

A helpful summary of the law governing the end of life was provided by Lord Sumption in *R (Nicklinson) v Ministry of Justice*:[1]

> (1) In law, the state is not entitled to intervene to prevent a person of full capacity who has arrived at a settled decision to take his own life from doing so. However, such a person does not have a right to call on a third party to help him to end his life.
>
> (2) A person who is legally and mentally competent is entitled to refuse food and water, and to reject any invasive manipulation of his body or other form of treatment, including artificial feeding, even though without it he will die. If he refuses, medical practitioners must comply with his wishes … A patient (or prospective patient) may express his wishes on these points by an advance decision (or 'living will').
>
> (3) A doctor may not advise a patient how to kill himself. But a doctor may give objective advice about the clinical options (such as sedation and other palliative care) which would be available if a patient were to reach a settled decision to kill himself. The doctor is in no danger of incurring criminal liability merely because he agrees in advance to palliate the pain and discomfort involved should the need for it arise. This kind of advice is no more or less than his duty. The law does not countenance assisted suicide, but it does not require medical practitioners to keep a patient in ignorance of the truth lest the truth should encourage him to kill himself. The right to give and receive information is guaranteed by article 10 of the Convention. If the law were not as I have summarised it, I have difficulty in seeing how it could comply.
>
> (4) Medical treatment intended to palliate pain and discomfort is not unlawful only because it has the incidental consequence, however foreseeable, of shortening the patient's life …
>
> (5) Whatever may be said about the clarity or lack of it in the Director [of Public Prosecution]'s published policy, the fact is that prosecutions for encouraging or assisting suicide are rare …

[1] *R (Nicklinson) v Ministry of Justice* [2014] UKSC 38, [225].

It should immediately be noted that the first point in this list is potentially misleading. As we have already seen, the state may be under a duty under the Human Rights Act 1998 to protect a person from suicide, even if they have a clear desire to commit suicide. The Mental Health Act 1983 provides ample scope to intervene to protect the person from committing suicide, even where they have mental capacity. With that caveat, Lord Sumption provides a helpful overview of the law's response. We shall explore many of these issues as the chapter develops.

II. Criminal Law Offences Prohibiting Suicide or Assisted Suicide

The law's response to suicide is complex. At one time, suicide was a crime and, bizarrely, attempted suicide potentially carried a sentence of capital punishment.[2] Now, the focus is on those who assist or encourage suicide or cause another's death at their request, rather than the suicidal individuals themselves.

A. Suicide and Attempted Suicide as Crimes

The present law, as set out in the Suicide Act 1961, is that suicide and attempted suicide are not crimes.[3] The reasoning behind the decriminalisation of suicide was explained by Lord Sumption in *R (Nicklinson) v Ministry of Justice*:[4]

> The reason for decriminalising suicide was not that suicide had become morally acceptable. It was that imposing criminal sanctions was inhumane and ineffective. It was inhumane because the old law could be enforced only against those who had tried to kill themselves but failed. The idea of taking these desperate and unhappy individuals from their hospital beds and punishing them for the attempt was as morally repugnant as the act of suicide itself. It was ineffective because assuming that they truly intended to die, criminal sanctions were incapable by definition of deterring them.

As Lord Sumption indicates, it is wrong to suggest the decriminalisation of suicide recognised a right to kill oneself. Rather, it was about ensuring that suicidal people got the support they needed. Indeed, it was more about prevention of further suicide attempts, than indicating any kind of authorisation or approval of suicide. That is all the more clear when we realise that it is still an offence to encourage suicide.

[2] This was because suicide was seen as murder of the self: *R (Purdy) v DPP* [2009] UKHL 45, [5].
[3] Suicide Act 1961, s 1.
[4] *R (Nicklinson) v Ministry of Justice* (n 1) [212].

B. Assisting or Encouraging Suicide

The Suicide Act 1961 makes it an offence if someone intentionally 'does an act capable of encouraging or assisting the suicide or attempted suicide of another person'.[5] To understand further the offence of encouraging or assisting suicide, a number of issues need to be considered.

i. *What is Suicide?*

The general view seems to be that in law suicide involves someone intentionally killing themselves.[6] There are two main areas of controversy surrounding the legal definition of 'suicide'. The first is whether it includes omissions: if a person refuses life-saving treatment because they want to die, is this suicide?[7] While we have no explicit discussion of this, there are plenty of cases where the courts have authorised the withdrawal of treatment and even required hospitals to stop providing treatment in cases where patients have not consented to it.[8] In none of these has it been suggested this could amount to assisted suicide. It seems then that suicide, as understood in English law, requires an act by the person who dies.

The second is whether a person who acts knowing that death will result, but who is not acting for the purpose of dying, is committing suicide The courts are also yet to express a clear view on this. Lord Justice Thorpe, in *Secretary of State for the Home Department v Robb*,[9] argued that a prisoner who went on hunger strike and died as a result did not commit suicide. Thorpe LJ did not explain why. It may be because the hunger striker did not intend to die; rather, he wanted his complaints to be dealt with. Or it may be because Thorpe LJ thought that suicide required a positive act.

ii. *What is 'Encouraging' or 'Assisting' Suicide?*

For a detailed discussion of these terms, you should consult a book on criminal law.[10] Only a brief summary will be offered here. An example of assisting suicide would be providing equipment or advice that would help someone to commit suicide. Encouraging suicide involves urging or supporting another to commit suicide. The offence is committed if a person encourages or assists someone to commit suicide, whether or not they actually do so. To be guilty of the offence, the defendant must intend to encourage another to commit, or to attempt to commit, suicide. Hence, the writer of a novel who describes a suicide in a way

[5] The wording of the 1961 Act was amended by the Coroners and Justice Act 2009.
[6] See Ch 2.
[7] See Ch 2.
[8] *Re B (Refusal of Medical Treatment)* [2002] All ER 449.
[9] *Secretary of State for the Home Department v Robb* [1995] Fam 127.
[10] J Herring, *Criminal Law: Text Cases and Materials* (Oxford University Press, 2022) Ch 15.

that helps someone to commit suicide will not be guilty of the offence because (presumably) the writer did not intend to assist or encourage a suicide. However, a person who created a webpage urging people to kill themselves could be convicted even though the prosecution cannot show that any particular individual killed themselves after visiting the page.

In recent years, it has become clear that not every case of assisted suicide is prosecuted by the Crown Prosecution Service (CPS). Following the decisions of the House of Lords in *R (Purdy) v DPP*,[11] and *R (Nicklinson) v Ministry of Justice*[12] the CPS was required to produce and then amend a list of factors that will be taken into account when deciding when to prosecute in a case of assisted suicide. It produced the following, which provides arguments that would weigh in favour of prosecution and arguments that would weight against:

> **Public interest factors in favour of prosecution**
>
> A prosecution is more likely to be required if:
>
> (1) the victim was under 18 years of age;
> (2) the victim did not have the capacity (as defined by the Mental Capacity Act 2005) to reach an informed decision to commit suicide;
> (3) the victim had not reached a voluntary, clear, settled and informed decision to commit suicide;
> (4) the victim had not clearly and unequivocally communicated his or her decision to commit suicide to the suspect;
> (5) the victim did not seek the encouragement or assistance of the suspect personally or on his or her own initiative;
> (6) the suspect was not wholly motivated by compassion; for example, the suspect was motivated by the prospect that he or she or a person closely connected to him or her stood to gain in some way from the death of the victim;[13]
> (7) the suspect pressured the victim to commit suicide;
> (8) the suspect did not take reasonable steps to ensure that any other person had not pressured the victim to commit suicide;
> (9) the suspect had a history of violence or abuse against the victim;
> (10) the victim was physically able to undertake the act that constituted the assistance him or herself;
> (11) the suspect was unknown to the victim and encouraged or assisted the victim to commit or attempt to commit suicide by providing specific information via, for example, a website or publication;

[11] *R (Purdy) v DPP* [2009] UKHL 45.

[12] *R (Nicklinson) v Ministry of Justice* (n 1).

[13] The Guidance states: 'On the question of whether a person stood to gain (paragraph 43(6) see above), the police and the reviewing prosecutor should adopt a common sense approach. It is possible that the suspect may gain some benefit – financial or otherwise – from the resultant suicide of the victim after his or her act of encouragement or assistance. The critical element is the motive behind the suspect's act. If it is shown that compassion was the only driving force behind his or her actions, the fact that the suspect may have gained some benefit will not usually be treated as a factor tending in favour of prosecution. However, each case must be considered on its own merits and on its own facts.'

(12) the suspect gave encouragement or assistance to more than one victim who were not known to each other;
(13) the suspect was paid by the victim or those close to the victim for his or her encouragement or assistance;
(14) the suspect was acting in his or her capacity as a medical doctor, nurse, other healthcare professional, a professional carer [whether for payment or not], or as a person in authority, such as a prison officer, and the victim was in his or her care;
(15) the suspect was aware that the victim intended to commit suicide in a public place where it was reasonable to think that members of the public may be present;
(16) the suspect was acting in his or her capacity as a person involved in the management or as an employee (whether for payment or not) of an organisation or group, a purpose of which is to provide a physical environment (whether for payment or not) in which to allow another to commit suicide.

Public interest factors against prosecution

A prosecution is less likely to be required if:
(1) the victim had reached a voluntary, clear, settled and informed decision to commit suicide;
(2) the suspect was wholly motivated by compassion;
(3) the actions of the suspect, although sufficient to come within the definition of the offence, were of only minor encouragement or assistance;
(4) the suspect had sought to dissuade the victim from taking the course of action which resulted in his or her suicide;
(5) the actions of the suspect may be characterised as reluctant encouragement or assistance in the face of a determined wish on the part of the victim to commit suicide;
(6) the suspect reported the victim's suicide to the police and fully assisted them in their enquiries into the circumstances of the suicide or the attempt and his or her part in providing encouragement or assistance.[14]

The CPS made it clear that, in issuing these guidelines, it was not changing the law:

> This policy does not in any way 'decriminalise' the offence of encouraging or assisting suicide. Nothing in this policy can be taken to amount to an assurance that a person will be immune from prosecution if he or she does an act that encourages or assists the suicide or the attempted suicide of another person.[15]

The CPS emphasised that the list of factors provided had to be used with care:

> Assessing the public interest is not simply a matter of adding up the number of factors on each side and seeing which side has the greater number. Each case must be considered on its own facts and on its own merits. Prosecutors must decide the importance of each public interest factor in the circumstances of each case and go on to make an overall assessment. It is quite possible that one factor alone may outweigh a number of

[14] Crown Prosecution Service, *Suicide: Policy for Prosecutors in Respect of Cases of Encouraging or Assisting Suicide* (CPS, 2014).
[15] ibid, para 6.

> other factors which tend in the opposite direction. Although there may be public interest factors tending against prosecution in a particular case, prosecutors should consider whether nonetheless a prosecution should go ahead and for those factors to be put to the court for consideration when sentence is passed.[16]

This has certainly put the law in a somewhat uneasy state. We have a criminal offence, but if you commit it you may or may not be prosecuted, depending on the decision of a state official. John Spencer, is concerned about the constitutional principle:

> Is it really compatible with the rule of law that, when an Act of Parliament makes a certain form of behaviour a criminal offence, the DPP should in effect decriminalise it, in whole or in part, by saying when it will and will not be prosecuted? The orthodox answer … is 'no': once Parliament has created an offence, only Parliament has the authority to redraw its boundaries so that it catches fewer people in its net. For any other organ of the State to attempt to do so is to infringe the first rule of the constitution, which is the supremacy of Parliament.[17]

Responses to the guidelines have been mixed. For the 'anti-euthanasia' lobby, the guidelines are 'dangerous' and open the door, in effect, to legalising assisted suicide.[18] Penney Lewis is concerned that the guidance, in focusing on what the defendant did rather than the position of the victim, has fallen between two stools.[19] It fails to protect the vulnerable, while not guaranteeing non-prosecution in appropriate cases:

> The dangers sought to be addressed by the policy focus on the unscrupulous or even abusive family member or friend, and the healthcare professional or activist. The shift of focus away from the victim, and the desire to avoid the appearance of the creation of a regulatory regime, have opened the door to assisted suicide in cases which would not be permitted by most of the existing regulatory regimes, while exposing to the risk of prosecution those with much-needed expertise and those who agree with the victim's decision.[20]

What should, however, be remembered is that the guidance is not stating when a particular person should be given assistance, but rather whether a particular defendant should be prosecuted. Given that question it is less surprising that the focus of the guidance is on the defendant's state of mind.

Kate Greasley is concerned that the guidance offers a formal sanctioning of assisted suicide.[21] She prefers the position in law prior to *Purdy*, under which

[16] Crown Prosecution Service (n 14) para 39.

[17] J Spencer, 'Assisted Suicide and the Discretion to Prosecute' (2009) *Cambridge Law Journal* 495, 495.

[18] Christian Concern, *Euthanasia and Assisted Suicide* (Christian Concern, 2020).

[19] P Lewis, 'Informal Legal Change on Assisted Suicide: The Policy for Prosecutors' (2011) 31 *Legal Studies* 119.

[20] ibid, 120.

[21] K Greasley, 'R (Purdy) v DPP and the Case for Wilful Blindness' (2010) 20 *Oxford Journal of Legal Studies* 301.

assisters were often not prosecuted, even though officially they were guilty of an offence. Greasley gives two reasons for disliking the formal approach of the guidance:

> Firstly, it carries with it the unwelcome and inescapable symbolism of identifying kinds of life which may not be worth living. Second, it is a significant step towards the cultivation of a social environment in which controlled death is an accessible and normalized option, and in which both internal and external pressure to end one's life may consequently mount. Moreover, there is a clear reciprocal relationship between the first and second concerns. The symbolic statements made through permitting assisted death in certain circumstances may lead to a change in how severely disabled people and those around them view their condition and their options, in turn generating even greater potential for the social pressurization and manipulation of the vulnerable. It is my contention that what we have here is a strong argument for a legal policy of wilful blindness towards assisted suicide-tourism.[22]

In relation to the last point, the policy, in effect, means that relatives can take a seriously ill person to Switzerland, where they can be helped to die. On that, Charles Foster has acknowledged 'that there is something intellectually, if not morally, uncomfortable, about getting another country to do your dirty work'.[23]

Supporters of the guidelines argue that they provide a reasonable balance between the competing views. Given the wide range of circumstances in which assisted suicide can take place, it is not possible to provide absolute clarity. Perhaps that is the point. The state manages to avoid saying anything negative or positive about assisting suicide by leaving each case to be determined by applying a wide range of principles. That 'neutrality' lasts only so long as there is not a clearly developed approach. Arguably, it is becoming increasingly clear that relatives motivated by compassion and acting in line with their family member's wishes will not be prosecuted. Those who seek to influence people into committing suicide or those influenced by financial considerations are likely to be find themselves prosecuted. It is also clear that those who kill a relative, rather than assisting suicide, are certainly likely to face a prosecution for homicide, something we will consider next.

C. Homicide

The key difference between a case of homicide[24] and a case of assisting or encouraging suicide is that in a case of homicide the defendant's act has been a significant and operating cause of the death,[25] while in a case of assisting or encouraging

[22] ibid, 311.

[23] C Foster, 'Suicide Tourism May Change Attitudes to Assisted Suicide, but Not Through the Courts' (2015) 41 *Journal of Medical Ethics* 620, 621.

[24] Whether the crime will be one of murder or manslaughter will depend on the defendant's mental state. That will not be discussed in detail here.

[25] *R v Norris* [2009] EWCA Crim 2697.

suicide the victim has caused their own death but the defendant assisted or encouraged them in that. There are some cases where the distinction is obvious:

(1) the defendant who simply watches a stranger commit suicide has committed no offence unless they are under a particular duty to intervene. Their watching has not contributed to the death and neither have they by their mere presence encouraged or assisted an offence;
(2) the defendant who tells a friend what combination of mediation would have a lethal effect, will have encouraged or assisted suicide if that friend takes the medication and dies. As we shall see, there may be cases where they will be guilty of homicide, if the friend was not acting in a free, voluntary and informed way;
(3) the defendant who shoots a person at that person's request will be guilty of murder or manslaughter. The defendant's act directly caused the death. The fact that the victim asked the defendant to act in this way will be irrelevant.

In other cases, such as the following, the distinctions are less straightforward:

(1) The case law has drawn a fine distinction in cases involving drug administration between cases where the defendant gave the deceased drugs, which the deceased took and died; and cases where the defendant helped the deceased administer the drug. The former case is one of assistance, but the in the latter case they have actively participated in the act that caused the death (administration).[26]
(2) As already mentioned, if a person provides medication or other means of suicide, which is then used by the victim this will normally be seen as a case of, at worst, assisting or encouraging suicide. It is not murder because the deceased, in performing a free, voluntary and informed act of suicide, has caused their own death. However, we have had two recent cases showing that this can be a difficult test to apply. In *R v Rebelo*[27] a defendant who sold dangerous dieting drugs on the internet to a 'vulnerable woman' who had become addicted was found to have caused her death because her taking the drugs was not free, voluntary and informed. Similarly, in *R v Field*[28] a defendant who befriended an older man was said to have caused his death by giving him a large quantity of alcohol. The allegation was that he was after the victim's inheritance. The older man drank the alcohol and died. The Court of Appeal held that the victim's decision to drink was not 'informed' as he (incorrectly) believed he was with a friend who would summon help if needed. These cases make it easier for the prosecution to argue that a defendant who is giving a

[26] *R v Kennedy* [2007] UKHL 37.
[27] *R v Rebelo* [2021] EWCA Crim 306.
[28] *R v Field* [2021] EWCA Crim 320.

> person the means to commit suicide can be guilty of murder or manslaughter if they are acting for improper motives and the victim can be said to be acting in a way which is not free, voluntary and informed.

In a murder case, it is necessary to show that the defendant's act was a substantial and operating cause of the death. This means that the defendant's act does not need to be the sole cause of death, but that it must be a substantial cause of it.[29] So, if deceased had a terminal illness and the defendant gave them medication to 'push them over the edge' to death, then the defendant could be guilty even if the death was a combination of the medication and their poor health. Bridget Gilderdale, aged 55, was cleared of attempted murder of her 31-year-old daughter, Lynn Gilderdale. Lynn had severe conditions which meant she was paralysed from the waist down and unable to swallow. Lynn had previously attempted suicide and had asked for a Do Not Resuscitate notice to be placed on her medical records. On the night Lynn died, a number of acts were done to produce death including injections of morphine, the administration of pills into Lynn's nasogastric tubes, and the creation of an air embolism in Lynn's Hickman Line. Some were done by Lynn and some by Bridget.[30] A conviction of assisted suicide was found, with a suspended sentence. It seems that homicide was not found because it could not be shown beyond reasonable doubt that any of Bridget's acts were the substantial and operating cause of death.

The claim that if the defendant's act is an operating cause of death then they can face a charge of homicide is subject to two caveats. The first is that if the administration of the drug shortened the victim's life by only few seconds, this may not constitute a substantial cause of death. Devlin J stated in the trial of Dr Adams: 'If the acts done are intended to kill and do, in fact kill, it does not matter if a life is cut short by weeks or months, it is just as much murder as if it were cut short by years'.[31] The fact that the reference is to weeks and months, rather than hours or minutes, might indicate that a very brief shortening of life will not be sufficient to amount to homicide. But there is little authoritative case law on that proposition. The second caveat is that the courts are reluctant to find 'normal' medical treatment to have broken the chain of causation. Certainly, where a defendant has stabbed a victim, who has received medical treatment and died, the courts are likely to be convinced that the stabbing did not cause the victim's death only where the medical treatment was 'palpably wrong'.[32]

[29] *R v Cheshire* [1991] 3 All ER 670; *R v Mellor* [1996] 2 Cr App R 245.

[30] 'Kay Gilderdale Case: A Clear Verdict on the Law's Confusion on Assisted Suicide', The Guardian, 25 January 2010, available at www.theguardian.com/uk/2010/jan/25/kay-gilderdale-case-expert-view, accessed 19 December 2021; 'Mother Cleared of ME Daughter's Attempted Murder', *BBC Online*, 25 January 2010, available at news.bbc.co.uk/1/hi/england/sussex/8479211.stm, accessed 15 December 2021.

[31] Discussed in H Palmer, 'Trial for Murder' (1957) *Criminal Law Review* 365.

[32] *R v Cheshire* [1991] 3 All ER 670.

D. Defences to Homicide

A person committing homicide at the victim's request might be able to rely on a number of defences. The most likely is diminished responsibility,[33] particularly in a case in which the defendant has been caring for a terminally ill relative and is suffering from stress and exhaustion. It should be noted that diminished responsibility is only a partial defence and so, if successful, the defendant is still guilty of manslaughter. Significantly, this means that the defendant does not have to receive the mandatory life imprisonment that accompanies a murder conviction. However, there are limitations on the defence, which mean it is not as easily used as might initially appear. First, it must be shown that the defendant was suffering from a recognised mental condition. Therefore claiming that the burdens of care had caused stress or exhaustion would be insufficient; there would need to be evidence of a medically recognised condition, provided by an expert. Second, even if there was such a mental condition, it must have been shown to impact the defendant in one of three ways:

(1) to understand the nature of the defendant's conduct;
(2) to form a rational judgment;
(3) to exercise self-control.

This will be problematic for the person who decides after careful deliberation to help kill a sick relative. It more likely to be used with a person who suddenly breaks down and impulsively engages in an act of murder. Third, it must be shown the mental abnormality 'is a significant contributory factor in causing, D to carry out that conduct'.[34] So, even if the defendant could show that they had a mental condition and that this impacted on their rational judgement, it would need to be shown that it impacted on their judgement enough to be a significant contributory factor.

A second defence that a person who kills a relative who wishes to die may seek to rely on is loss of control.[35] This defence is by no means easy to plead in cases of 'mercy killing' homicide. First, it needs to be shown there was a loss of control. Any suggestion that the defendant acted in a pre-planned or thought through way is likely to lead to the defence failing. Second, it needs to be shown that there was a qualifying trigger, which involves showing that there was a fear of serious violence or that circumstances of an extremely grave nature caused the defendant to have a justified sense of being seriously wronged. This will be very hard to show in a case of euthanasia.[36] Even if a defendant is deeply distressed at the suffering of the victim, this is unlikely to generate a justified sense that they are being wronged (who is wronging them?). Third, it is necessary to show that a reasonable person

[33] Homicide Act 1957, s 2, as amended by the Coroners and Justice Act 2009.
[34] Homicide Act 1957, s 2(1B).
[35] Coroners and Justice Act 2009, s 54.
[36] *R v Zebedee* [2012] EWCA Crim 1428.

might have responded in the same way. In short, it is hard to see in a 'euthanasia' case that the loss of control defence will apply very often. A very rare example appears to be an unreported case where a defendant lost control on being told by a care home that pain relief could not be given to a terminally ill parent in pain, and killed the individual. The use of the defence could only be appropriate if the refusal to give pain relief gave the defendant a justified sense of being seriously wronged.[37] That would be most likely if the pain relief was being improperly denied.

A final defence which should be mentioned is that of suicide pact.[38] If the defendant killed the victim intending to go on and kill him or herself as part of a suicide pact, then he or she will have a defence to a charge of murder, but still be guilty of manslaughter.[39] The onus of proof on establishing that the killing was in the course of a suicide pact is on the defendant.

Suicides pacts are treated with suspicion by some, where one of the parties has survived. There is certainly a tension in the law. On the one hand many of the arguments that might apply to not prosecuting attempted suicide apply here too: the survivor needs care and support, not the trauma of a prosecution. However, Brenner has argued that surviving a suicide pact 'g[ives] rise to a presumption … that the participant may have entered the pact in less than good faith'.[40] The response to this situation requires a careful analysis of the facts. It may be that giving the judge a discretion in relation to sentencing – ranging, in theory, from a life sentence to a conditional discharge – allows the judge to respond to the particularities of the case.

At one time there was speculation that a person who killed someone who wanted to die might be able to rely on the defence of necessity. This defence is only available in very exceptional cases where the defendant claims that they are performing the 'lesser of two evils'. However, in *R (Nicklinson) v Ministry of Justice*,[41] the court refused to apply the necessity defence in the assisted dying context. Lord Neuberger in the Supreme Court decision[42] explained that the law offered no defence in cases of 'mercy killing':

> Mercy killing is a term which means killing another person for motives which appear, at least to the perpetrator, to be well-intentioned, namely for the benefit of that person, very often at that person's request. Nonetheless, mercy killing involves the perpetrator intentionally killing another person, and therefore, even where that person wished to die, or the killing was purely out of compassion and love, the current state of the law is that the killing will amount to murder or (if one or more of the mitigating circumstances are present) manslaughter.

[37] A Clough, 'Mercy Killing, Partial Defences and Charge Decisions: 50 Shades of Grey' (2020) 84 *The Journal of Criminal Law* 211.

[38] Homicide Act 1957, s 4.

[39] ibid.

[40] SW Brenner, 'Undue Influence in the Criminal Law: A Proposed Analysis of the Criminal Offense of 'Causing Suicide' (1982) 47 *Alabama Law Review* 62, 85–86.

[41] [2013] EWCA Civ 961, a decision by implication approved by the Supreme Court.

[42] *R (Nicklinson) v Ministry of Justice* (n 1) [17].

It is worth noting that although a murder conviction leads to a mandatory life sentence, there is some flexibility in setting the minimum sentence which must be served in prison. In *Inglis*,[43] even though a murder conviction was upheld in a case of mercy killing, the Court of Appeal set the minimum sentence at the unusually low level of five years, indicating its sympathy for the plight of the defendant, who had killed her disabled son, while recognising that she had committed a serious crime.

III. Criminal Offences for Failing to Prevent Suicide

Can a defendant be guilty of a crime for failing to prevent a suicide? Generally, in the criminal law, a defendant is not criminally responsible for an omission. Many criminal lawyers point out that a defendant who walks past a stranger drowning in a pond without offering help will not be criminally responsible for the stranger's death. As explained above, if a person simply watches another commit suicide, there is no crime. However, there are occasions on which those who fail to act may face a criminal prosecution. These are situations in which the defendant owes a duty of care to the victim.[44] These include where the defendant was a parent or partner of the victim; or where the defendant had a professional responsibility to take care of the victim. However, it is important to note that the defendant is only required to take reasonable steps to prevent suicide. This was a key issue in *R (Jenkins) v HM Coroner for Portsmouth*,[45] where the victim injured themselves but did not want medical help and was willing to die. Pitchford J held that there could be no liability for the friend for gross negligence manslaughter because the victim, who had mental capacity, had made it clear that he did not want medical help.[46] This indicates that where a parent or nurse or anyone with a duty of care does not seek intervention for a person seeking to die there will be no liability. That case must be treated with care. This is only true if the person has capacity. In many cases where a defendant comes across a suicidal person to whom they owe a duty of care it may not be apparent whether there is capacity. Interestingly, in *Jenkins* Pitchford J did consider whether the friend could be liable for not summoning help once the victim collapsed into unconsciousness. He concluded that the friend could not, but on the basis that by that point any medical help would have arrived too late to save the victim's life. This indicates that there may be a duty to summon help if a victim loses capacity during a suicide attempt or where there is good reason to believe the victim lacks capacity to make the decision.[47]

[43] *R v Inglis* [2010] EWCA Crim 2637.
[44] *R v Stone and Dobinson* [1977] QB 354.
[45] [2009] EWHC 3229 (Admin).
[46] See J Herring, 'The Legal Duties of Carers' (2010) 18 *Medical Law Review* 248 for further discussion of the issues raised.
[47] *A NHS Trust v X* [2014] EWCOP 35.

Even if it is demonstrated that there was a duty to intervene and a defendant failed to take reasonable steps to prevent the suicide, criminal liability will require proof that the defendant failed to intervene with the intention to kill the victim or where their negligence was sufficiently gross to justify a conviction for gross negligence manslaughter. This is likely to limit such convictions to particularly callous failures to intervene in cases of suicide. Cases where the defendant is making fun of the victim or is hoping to gain financially from their death might be the kind of cases where a conviction is possible. Another possible charge could be under section 44 of the Mental Capacity Act 2005, which created an offence of ill-treating or wilfully neglecting a person who lacks capacity, or whom the offender reasonably believes to lack capacity. That might be appropriate in a case where a person fails to look after a suicidal person who lacks capacity, but it cannot be shown their failure contributed to the death.

IV. Mental Health Law

In this section we shall explore the response of the Mental Health Act 1983 (MHA 1983) to suicide. We need here to distinguish between two important jurisdictions in England. The Mental Capacity Act 2005 (MCA 2005) deals with cases where a person lacks capacity to make a decision. Under this legislation, if a person lacks capacity others may make an assessment of their best interests and are authorised to act on their behalf. However, the legislation assumes that those with capacity who refuse treatment cannot receive that treatment. However, the MHA 1983 can be used to provide treatment for those with a mental disorder, whether or not they have capacity to consent/refuse.

While both these pieces of legislation are controversial, there is a clear tension between them. The MHA 1983 appears to infringe the primary principle behind the MCA 2005: that treatment should not be given to a patient with capacity without their consent. That principle, which is normally a hallowed one, and to be complied with even if without the intervention the patient or someone else will die, is set aside in the case of a mental disorder. It is, therefore, not surprising that where possible it is the MCA 2005 that that is used rather than the MHA 1983. We will start by looking at the MHA 1983, before considering the MCA 2005 in the following section.

Not only does the MHA 1983 appear to contradict the key principles underpinning the MCA 2005, it appears also to be discriminatory, being contrary to Article 12(2) of the United Nations Convention on the Rights of Persons with Disabilities (CRPD), which provides that people with disabilities should enjoy legal capacity 'on an equal basis with others in all aspects of life'.[48] Under such a view there is no reason to treat a person with capacity who has a mental health

[48] R Chadwick, 'Expertise Revisited' (2016) 30 *Bioethics* 549.

disorder any differently from those who do not. This looks very much like denying a person the right to make decisions about their body simply because of their medical condition.

Further, the MHA 1983 assumes that we can confidently distinguish between those who are 'mad' and those who are 'sane'. As Bartlett and Sandland argue:

> The centrality of a medical model of insanity is asserted, imposing a scientific order onto the profoundly un-ordered world of the mad. While madness is displayed in the form of a disease, sanity is a constraint, both physical and moral, into which the insane person is confined through pressure of the group, the sane. All this is a construction of the reasoned, and reflects the world of the reasoned; to the insane person, it is an alien landscape.[49]

History teaches us of the errors made in labelling who is sane and who is not.

Clearly there is much to discuss here that is beyond the remit of this book. There are two common justifications provided for infringing this principle: that to do so is necessary to protect the 'general public' from dangerous mentally ill people, and/or for the protection of the individual themselves. For the purposes of this book, the protection of the patient themselves from suicide is the key focus and we will concentrate on that.

The MHA 1983 should only be used in cases where a patient does not consent to treatment, and has the capacity to refuse consent. If they are consenting and have capacity, then that consent can be relied upon. The MHA 1983 is for cases where the patient does not provide consent. There are three primary routes into compulsory care: section 2, which allows for an assessment lasting 28 days; section 3, which permits treatment for up to six months; and section 4 for emergencies, which lasts 72 hours. Each of these will be discussed in turn.

A. Admission for Assessment (Section 2)

An application for an admission for assessment can be made by either the patient's nearest relative[50] or an approved social worker (ASW). Two registered medical practitioners must support the application.[51] If necessary, reasonable force can be used to transfer the patient to hospital. The MHA 1983, section 2(2), provides that:

> An application for admission for assessment may be made in respect of a patient on the grounds that—

[49] P Bartlett and R Sandland, *Mental Health Law* (Oxford University Press, 2007) 1.

[50] Under the MHA 1983, s 26, 'nearest relative' is defined as spouse or civil partner, cohabitants (who have lived together for at least six months), child, parent, sibling, grandparent, grandchild, uncle or aunt, nephew or niece. Where there are competing claims, those higher up the list have priority over those lower down the list. If within the same category, then those relatives of the full blood have priority over those of the half blood and older relatives take priority over their juniors. However, there is one way in which a relative can 'jump' to the front of the queue: if the patient is living with or being cared for by a relative, then that relative is the 'nearest relative' even if he or she is not at the top of the s 26 list.

[51] At least one of the two must have a mental health qualification.

(a) he is suffering from mental disorder of a nature or degree which warrants the detention of the patient in a hospital for assessment (or for assessment followed by medical treatment) for at least a limited period; and
(b) he ought to be so detained in the interests of his own health or safety or with a view to the protection of other persons.

For our purposes, several things are worth highlighting about this section. First, it can only be used where a person suffers a 'disorder or disability of the mind'. It is not sufficient to show that a person is suicidal. As we have seen, it is perfectly possible for a person to be suicidal without suffering from a mental disorder. That said, the definition of disorder is broad. The MHA 1983 Code of Practice lists the following as examples of mental disorders:

> affective disorders, such as depression and bipolar disorder;
>
> schizophrenia and delusional disorders;
>
> neurotic, stress-related, and somatoform disorders, such as anxiety, phobic disorders, obsessive compulsive disorders, post-traumatic stress disorder (PTSD), and hypochondriacal disorders;
>
> organic mental disorders, such as dementia and delirium (however caused);
>
> personality and behavioural changes caused by brain injury or damage (however acquired);
>
> personality disorders;
>
> mental and behavioural disorders caused by psychoactive substance use;
>
> eating disorders, non-organic sleep disorders, and non-organic sexual disorders;
>
> learning disabilities;
>
> autistic spectrum disorders (including Asperger's syndrome); and
>
> behavioural and emotional disorders of children and adolescents.

These days, greater attention is paid to evidence that a particular condition exists than was in the past. Indeed, there is a history of the MHA 1983 being used against those who are seen as 'immoral' or 'unusual' and this has led to being made clear that learning disability,[52] or alcohol or drug dependency, cannot be the sole basis for treating someone as having a mental disorder.[53] It might, nevertheless, be thought that the list is so extensive and flexible that nearly every case of suicide could be included. Notably, depression is clearly included as a mental disorder.

Second, the patient must be detained 'in the interests of his own health or safety or with a view to the protection of other persons'. This clearly covers a case of suicidal or self-harm behaviour. The only issue which might arise here is where a person has settled and persistent suicidal feelings, who could possibly claim that it is not in the interests of their own health to receive treatment, but it seems it would be very rare for that to be the case.

[52] Mental Health Act 1983, s 1(3), defines learning disability as 'a state of arrested or incomplete development of the mind which includes significant impairment of intelligence and social functioning'.

[53] Mental Health Act 1983, s 1(3).

Once admitted under section 2, patients can be kept in hospital for assessment for a maximum of 28 days. If a patient is to be kept for longer, that must be under the section 3 powers. A patient can apply to have their case reviewed by a mental health review tribunal during the first 14 days of detention. Treatment can be given only for a patient being assessed with their consent, unless there is an immediate and serious danger. This reflects the fact that section 2 is intended to be used for assessment purposes. If treatment is needed, then section 3, as discussed below, will be required. Sometimes admission under section 2 will take too long; if there is an emergency, section 4 can be used. We will consider this next.

B. Emergency Admission (Section 4)

If there is an emergency, a patient can be admitted under section 4 of the MHA 1983 for an assessment on the recommendation of one doctor that the section 2 grounds are made out. But that doctor must confirm that it is of 'urgent necessity' for the patient to be admitted and detained, and that waiting for a second doctor to confirm the need for an admission under section 2 would cause 'undesirable delay'. Remarkably, this doctor does not need to be a specialist in mental illness, although (if practical) it should be a doctor who knew the patient beforehand. The maximum length of time for which a person can be detained under section 4 is 72 hours. At the end of that time, the patient must be free to go, unless one of the other routes of admission has been invoked.

There are other options available in emergency suicide cases. Other provisions in the MHA 1983 can also be relied upon in emergencies. Under section 135, a Justice of the Peace may, upon the application of an ASW, require the detention in a place of safety for up to 72 hours of mentally disordered individuals who are being ill-treated, neglected, or not kept under proper control, or who are living alone and unable to care for themselves.[54] Section 136 of the MHA 1983 allows mentally disordered individuals found by police officers in public places to be removed to a place of safety (such as a hospital) for up to 72 hours if it appears to the police officer that they are in need of immediate care and control.[55]

These provisions are remarkably wide and seem to provide ample opportunity for the detention of a suicidal person.

C. Admission for Treatment (Section 3)

Unlike the other two grounds, the ground under section 3 of the 1983 Act is designed for longer-term detention. An application can be made by either the patient's nearest relative or an ASW.[56] Section 3(2) states:

[54] *Ward v Metropolitan Police Commissioner* [2005] UKHL 32.
[55] *Seal v Chief Constable of South Wales Police* [2007] UKHL 31.
[56] Where a social worker makes the application, the next of kin must be consulted.

> An application for admission for treatment may be made in respect of a patient on the grounds that—
>
> (a) he is suffering from mental disorder of a nature or degree which makes it appropriate for him to receive medical treatment in a hospital; and
>
> (b) it is necessary for the health or safety of the patient or for the protection of other persons that he should receive such treatment and it cannot be provided unless he is detained under this section; and
>
> (c) appropriate medical treatment is available to him.

Again, I will highlight several points that are of particular significance in the context of suicide.

First, as with section 2, it is not enough simply to show that a person is suicidal; it must be shown that they have a mental disorder.

Second, it must also be shown that the mental disorder is such as to make it proportionate for them to receive medical treatment. It may be in some cases that a person's mental condition is so beset that there is no real prospect of treatment. A long-term depression which has failed to respond to numerous attempted interventions could be an example. Yet, there are such a wide range of treatments that it might be thought rare that a person's suicidal state will conclusively be determined to be irresponsive to treatment. Section 145(4) is crucial here. It states that:

> Any reference in this Act to medical treatment, in relation to mental disorder, shall be construed as a reference to medical treatment the purpose of which is to alleviate, or prevent a worsening of, the disorder or one or more of its symptoms or manifestations.

This would appear to indicate that if no medical treatment is available to a patient, then they cannot be detained under the Act. Simply 'warehousing' a patient is not permitted under the MHA 1983. However, it might be claimed that preventing suicide is a form of treatment. The reasoning behind this is that if there is nothing that doctors can do to assist a patient, they should not be required simply to detain them, acting as a 'warehouse' for the untreatable. It is unlikely that simply detaining a person solely for suicide prevention would be classed as 'treatment', although that is not beyond debate. It is clear that simply feeding and looking after someone cannot be treatment. Section 145 defines treatment as including 'psychological intervention and specialist mental health habilitation, rehabilitation and care'. Much may depend on whether the courts give the word 'care' a broad or narrow meaning. The MHA 1983 Code of Practice emphasises that a person can properly receive care even if they cannot be cured.[57] Further, it adds:

> Purpose is not the same as likelihood. Medical treatment may be for the purpose of alleviating, or preventing a worsening of, a mental disorder even though it cannot be shown in advance that any particular effect is likely to be achieved.[58]

This seems particularly pertinent in the case of suicidal interventions. It reinforces the case for saying that there are few cases of suicidal people which will not be

[57] Department of Health, *Code of Practice: Mental Health Act 1983* (Department of Health, 2015).
[58] ibid, para 23.4.

capable of being brought within section 3. This is particularly because in *MD v Nottinghamshire Health Care Trust*,[59] Jacobs J held that treatment under section 145 did not have to render the patient less dangerous. It was enough if it prevented a worsening of symptoms.

D. Community Treatment Orders

When a patient is discharged, having been detained under the MHA 1983, the clinician can impose a community treatment order under section 17A of the Act. This will mean that the release is conditional. The order can be made if a clinician and a mental health professional agree that it is appropriate to make it, and that the following conditions in section 17A(5) are made out:

> (a) the patient is suffering from mental disorder of a nature or degree which makes it appropriate for him to receive medical treatment;
> (b) it is necessary for his health or safety or for the protection of other persons that he should receive such treatment;
> (c) subject to his being liable to be recalled as mentioned in paragraph (d) below, such treatment can be provided without his continuing to be detained in a hospital;
> (d) it is necessary that the responsible clinician should be able to exercise the power under section 17E(1) below to recall the patient to hospital;[60] and
> (e) appropriate medical treatment is available for him.

Conditions can be imposed on the patient, but these cannot be used to deprive a patient of their liberty.[61]

E. A Discussion of the MHA 1983 Provisions

The powers under the MHA 1983 are remarkably broad. They can involve breaches of key human rights (liberty of movement and bodily integrity) which would be unjustified in any other context. The justification offered by Lord Phillips MR in *R (B) v S*[62] was this:

> The MHA is primarily concerned with the compulsory detention of patients suffering from mental disorders in order that they may receive treatment for those disorders. The compulsory detention is justified because it is necessary in order to ensure that the patient receives treatment. Ensuring that the patient receives treatment is justified

[59] *MD v Nottinghamshire Health Care Trust* [2010] UKUT 59 (AAC).
[60] In considering this factor, s 17A(6) provides that 'the patient's history of mental disorder and any other relevant factors, what risk there would be of a deterioration of the patient's condition if he were not detained in a hospital' should be taken into account.
[61] *Welsh Ministers v PJ* [2018] UKSC 66.
[62] *R (B) v S* [2006] EWCA Civ 38.

> because this is necessary for the health or safety of the patient or for the protection of others.

But that barely seems a sufficient justification. If detentions and breaches of bodily integrity were justified in order to promote the health and safety of people then it seems these rights should be justified in a wide range of circumstances beyond those in the MHA 1983. Often, in a case of a patient who, with capacity, is refusing treatment it can be said to be necessary for their health to receive the treatment. There is no explanation as to why these fundamental rights are breached in the context of mental health but not in other contexts.

Nor does that quotation capture the idea that any intervention needs to be a proportionate response to the risk. Indeed the mere fact there is any risk is sufficient to justify an intervention.[63] Fanning notes that, while risk is at the heart of the legislation, it is not defined. He suggests this means:

> The task of defining, identifying and evaluating the risks which warrant compulsory intervention therefore falls exclusively within the professional domain of expert decision-makers, such as registered medical practitioners, approved mental health professionals (AMHPs), psychiatric nurses, and so on. This means that in spite of the premium which the courts have placed on the importance of legal certainty where deprivations of liberty are concerned, there is no clearly prescribed threshold for compulsion under the MHA.

The problem, as Fanning elucidates, is that there is plenty of ambiguity here. What must the risk of harm be of, before the MHA 1983 is relevant? In the suicide context, must it be a risk of suicide, or self-harm? And if some form of self-harm, how serious must the harm be? What must the degree of risk be? Is a small chance of suicide sufficient? What must the chance be of the success of the compulsory intervention? The ambiguity here is likely to leave considerable discretion to the expert decision makers. Indeed, in many cases it is difficult to formulate an objective assessment of risk and it becomes a matter of professional intuition. Further, as Lord Rodger explained in *Savage*,[64] 'the level of risk for any particular patient [can] be expected to vary with fluctuations in his or her medical condition … Such decisions involve clinical judgment. Different doctors may have different views'.[65] This reveals the extent of professional discretion involved and the weakness of the legal limits on the powers. In other words, it would be a remarkable case where a doctor was found to have acted unlawfully in detaining a suicidal patient under the MHA 1983. It is hard to imagine, outside a case of malicious detention, that such a case would arise. That is reflected in how rare it is for a court to declare unlawful any kind of detention under the MHA 1983.[66]

[63] J Fanning, *New Medicalism and the Mental Health Act* (Hart Publishing, 2018).
[64] *Savage v South Essex Partnership NHS Foundation Trust* [2008] *UKHL* 74.
[65] Fanning (n 63) 74.
[66] *R v North West Thames Mental Health Review Tribunal, ex p Cooper* (1990) 5 BMLR 7 (QB).

The Code of Practice gives more guidance and invites decision-makers to consider the following:

- the evidence suggesting that patients are at risk of:
  - — suicide;
  - — self-harm;
  - — self-neglect or being unable to look after their own health or safety;
  - — jeopardising their own health or safety accidentally, recklessly or unintentionally; or
  - — that their mental disorder is otherwise putting their health or safety at risk;
- any evidence suggesting that the patient's mental health will deteriorate if they do not receive treatment, including the views of the patient or carers, relatives or close friends (especially those living with the patient) about the likely course of the disorder;
- the patient's own skills and experience in managing their condition;
- the patient's capacity to consent to or refuse admission and treatment (and the availability of the deprivation of liberty safeguards (DoLS)) [now Liberty Protection Safeguards];
- whether the patient objects to treatment for mental disorder – or is likely to;
- the reliability of such evidence, including what is known of the history of the patient's mental disorder and the possibility of their condition improving;
- the potential benefits of treatment, which should be weighed against any adverse effects that being detained might have on the patient's wellbeing; and
- whether other methods of managing the risk are available.[67]

This list of factors, which is no doubt appropriate, indicates the wide range of factors to be considered. This reinforces the claim already made that there are so many factors to be considered that it will be difficult to show that any decision to detain to prevent suicide is inappropriate.[68]

F. Is the MHA 1983 Discriminatory?

The CRPD provides a route to challenge the MHA 1983.[69] In particular, Article 14 of thr Convention states that people with disabilities should enjoy the right to liberty and security of person on an equal basis of those with others. As already indicated, the MHA 1983 – which allows treatment for those with a mental

[67] *Code of Practice: Mental Health Act 1983* (n 57) para 14.9.
[68] Fanning (n 63).
[69] A Nilsson, *Compulsory Mental Health Interventions and the UNCRPD* (Hart Publishing, 2021).

disorder without their consent – appears to be clearly in breach of this. As George Szmukler[70] argues:

> What is clear … is that any law that allows an interference with the rights of a person that is restricted to persons with a disability is discriminatory. … No matter how much other criteria are specified – whether the law additionally only permits the person's detention or involuntary treatment in the interests of the person or to protect others – in thus singling out a particular group of people with a disability for special interference, such legislation in the view of the committee breaches the Convention.

In line with this the CRPD committee has recommended that the UK 'Repeal legislation and practices that authorise non-consensual involuntary, compulsory treatment and detention of persons with disabilities on the basis of actual or perceived impairment'.[71] Peter Bartlett emphasises the wrong that is done to a competent person who receives mental health treatment against his or her wishes in this way:

> The violation of autonomy consequent on enforced treatment of a person with capacity is considerable. The introduction of psychiatric medication into an individual's body results in fundamental and substantial changes to the person's self. These changes are, of course, the objective of the treatment, and have social benefits. Many patients will also willingly consent to them, as they are perceived to have benefits to them too. That in no way alters the extraordinary nature of the intervention, however, and it is difficult to see that it should be provided to a patient with capacity who refuses it.[72]

However, it is too often assumed that the application of the CRPD would necessarily lead to the complete repeal of the MHA 1983 and the end of civil detention.[73] There are two reasons for this. First, it would be possible to fashion a law which provided for the civil detention of those who pose a risk to themselves (or others) which drew no distinction between those with or without a mental disability. Such a law would not breach the CRPD, at least on its face, although it would certainly be subject to other criticisms, particularly for being a severe interference in the civil liberties of the general population. Second, it is possible to argue that without any forms of civil detention for those suffering mental disabilities and who

[70] G Szmukler, 'The UN Convention on the Rights of Persons with Disabilities: "Rights, Will and Preferences" in Relation to Mental Health Disabilities' (2017) 46 *International Journal of Law and Psychiatry* 90.

[71] Committee on the Rights of Persons with Disabilities, *Concluding Observations on the Initial Report of the United Kingdom of Great Britain and Northern Ireland* (2017).

[72] P Bartlett, 'The Test of Compulsion in Mental Health Law: Capacity, Therapeutic Benefit and Dangerousness as Possible Criteria' (2003) 11 *Medical Law Review* 326.

[73] T Minkowitz, 'Abolishing Mental Health Laws to Comply with the Convention on the Rights of Persons with Disabilities' in B McSherry and P Weller (eds), *Rethinking Rights-Based Mental Health Laws* (Hart Publishing, 2010) 149; G Szmukler and B Kelly, 'We Should Replace Conventional Mental Health Law with Capacity-Based Law' (2016) 209 *The British Journal of Psychiatry* 449.

are suicidal there will be a breach of other provisions of the CRPD. For example, Article 10 states:

> States Parties reaffirm that every human being has the inherent right to life and shall take all necessary measures to ensure its effective enjoyment by persons with disabilities on an equal basis with others.

It could be argued that there is a need to balance the rights to protect life in Article 10 with that to protect from discrimination in Article 12, which could justify discriminatory treatment of the suicidal in a sufficiently strong case. Indeed, in line with the first argument there was provision for the civil detention of any suicidal person, regardless of their mental health status, this arguably would be compliant with the CRPD.

The CRPD Committee has addressed detention in mental health institutions, and it is worth quoting its views at length.[74] It states:

> D. Involuntary or non-consensual commitment in mental health institutions
>
> 10. Involuntary commitment of persons with disabilities on health care grounds contradicts the absolute ban on deprivation of liberty on the basis of impairments (article 14(1)(b)) and the principle of free and informed consent of the person concerned for health care (article 25). The Committee has repeatedly stated that States parties should repeal provisions which allow for involuntary commitment of persons with disabilities in mental health institutions based on actual or perceived impairments. Involuntary commitment in mental health facilities carries with it the denial of the person's legal capacity to decide about care, treatment, and admission to a hospital or institution, and therefore violates article 12 in conjunction with article 14.
>
> …
>
> 13. Throughout all the reviews of State party reports, the Committee has established that it is contrary to article 14 to allow for the detention of persons with disabilities based on the perceived danger of persons to themselves or to others. The involuntary detention of persons with disabilities based on risk or dangerousness, alleged need of care or treatment or other reasons tied to impairment or health diagnosis is contrary to the right to liberty, and amounts to arbitrary deprivation of liberty.
>
> …
>
> 15. The freedom to make one's own choices established as a principle in article 3(a) of the Convention includes the freedom to take risks and make mistakes on an equal basis with others. In its General Comment No. 1, the Committee stated that 'decisions about medical and psychiatric treatment must be based on the free and informed consent of the person concerned and respect the person's autonomy, will and preferences'. Deprivation of liberty on the basis of actual or perceived impairment or health conditions in mental health institutions which deprives persons with disabilities of their legal capacity also amounts to a violation of article 12 of the Convention. …

This strong interpretation is hard to justify. First, as has been argued throughout this book, the right to life – whether in the ECHR or the CRPD – includes, in many

[74] Committee on the Rights of Persons with Disabilities (n 71) 3.

circumstances, a right to be protected from suicide. The error in the reasoning of the committee, I suggest, is that the justifiable claim that we should treat those with mental disorders in the same way as those without mental disorders, means that the legal provisions for those without mental disorders is the model that should be adopted for both. But this does not follow. Equality could be achieved by opening civil detention to all suicidal people, regardless of the root cause of the suicidal feelings. Second, I very much doubt the interpretation given by the committee is in line with the view of the general public or those with mental disorders. If we return to a case like *Rabone*, we know that Ms Rabone, when the depression alleviated, was very grateful for the previous interventions she received, as many suicidal people are.[75] To claim it is respecting their autonomy and liberty to let them die when they, and all who know them, believe that generally they would seek intervention, seems to rely on a thin case of autonomy. A proper, richer understanding of autonomy, as outlined in Chapter 4, would see suicide prevention in many, but not all, cases as autonomy enhancing. The Mental Health Alliance[76] conducted a survey of 8,631 users and carers; 73 per cent agreed that it was 'sometimes necessary to restrict a person's human rights for their own safety'.

Indeed, it may be that if civil detention were prohibited there would simply be greater use of public order offences and other breaches of the criminal law to detain those with mental disorders causing threats to themselves or others. This would hardly increase the liberty or autonomy of such people. Further, as Melvyn Freeman et al ask, 'If a person having a severe exacerbation of affective or psychotic illness is not provided proven, effective treatment, can he or she be said to be receiving the highest attainable standard of health?'[77]

Perhaps the more likely reconciliation of the MHA 1983 and the CRPD would be a provision that allowed detention for all those who lack or have severely impair capacity. The argument would then be that the discrimination is not between those with a mental disorder and those without but between those with impaired capacity – whatever its cause – and those with fill capacity. For those who lack capacity we cannot respect their autonomy as they are unable to exercise it. There are, however, some who would question whether a distinction on the basis of mental capacity is discrimination in disguise. Indeed the CRPD prevents discrimination on the grounds of 'mental, intellectual and sensory impairments' and so it may be even a capacity-based distinction would be problematic under the CRPD. Even if that point is accepted, in many cases it will be very difficult to determine

[75] *Rabone v Pennine Care NHS Trust* [2012] UKSC 2. See S Priebe et al, 'Patients' Views and Readmissions 1 Year after Involuntary Hospitalisation' (2009) 194 *British Journal of Psychiatry* 49; G Owen, 'Retrospective Views of Psychiatric In-Patients Regaining Mental Capacity' (2009) 195 *British Journal of Psychiatry* 403.

[76] Mental Health Alliance, *A Mental Health Act Fit For Tomorrow* (MHA, 2017).

[77] M Freeman et al, 'Reversing Hard Won Victories in the Name of Human Rights: A Critique of the General Comment on Article 12 of the UN Convention on the Rights of Persons with Disabilities' (2015) 9 *Lancet Psychiatry* 844.

what the views of a person lacking capacity are.[78] As we have seen in Chapter 4, there are some cases where there is difficulty in interpreting what their decision is. For example, a person who wants to die because 'otherwise the Martians will kill them' could be understood to be saying that they would want to live if there were not Martians out to kill them. If we take it that there are not, we could understand that suicide prevention is in line with their views. Further, Jill Craigie has argued:

> When human agency is seriously compromised, preserving patient autonomy may sometimes require overriding a treatment decision to restore selfhood, on grounds that are not easily accounted for under the MCA without compromising the value-neutral aspirations of this area of law.[79]

G. Do Mental Health Interventions Work?

There is some dispute over how, if at all, involuntary admission impacts on suicide rates. While it is true that more patients commit suicide in psychiatric hospitals than anywhere else,[80] that is unsurprising. Normally, only the most suicidal people are admitted to hospital. Indeed, there are some studies reporting increased rates of suicide among involuntary admitted patients, as compared with similar patients not admitted,[81] particularly during the first seven days of involuntary hospital admission.[82] In an interesting study Ajit Shah[83] examined the impact of involuntary admissions on general suicide rates. This is a helpful way of looking at the question because it captures those who voluntarily received treatment only because of the threat of involuntary treatment. There were negative correlations between rates of involuntary admissions and general population suicide rates in both sexes. However, it is a mixed picture. Other studies looking at discharged patients did not find that hospitalisation increased suicide.[84] These studies are difficult to interpret because those involuntarily detained are likely to be suffering more severely than those attending voluntarily and so a higher rate may be expected. In other words, it is difficult to find a comparator group to compare.

[78] Fanning (n 63) 160–92.

[79] J Craigie, 'Capacity, Value Neutrality and the Ability to Consider the Future' (2013) *International Journal of Law in Context* 4.

[80] S Priebe 'Involuntary Hospitalization of Suicidal Patients: Time for New Answers to Basic Questions?' (2019) 19 *The American Journal of Bioethics* 90.

[81] I Hunt et al, 'Suicide within 12 Months of Mental Health Service Contact in Different Age and Diagnostic Groups. National Clinical Survey' (2006) 188 *British Journal of Psychiatry* 135; K Tolwinski et al, '"I Don't Want to Go on Living This Way": Desire for Hastened Death and the Ethics of Involuntary Hospitalization' (2019) 19 *The American Journal of Bioethics* 88.

[82] J Meehan et al, 'Suicide in Mental Health In-Patients and within 3 Months of Discharge. National Clinical Survey' (2006) 188 *British Journal of Psychiatry* 129.

[83] A Shah, 'The Relationship between the Use of Mental Health Act and General Population Suicide Rates in England and Wales' (2012) 4 *Journal of Injury and Violence Research* 26.

[84] E King et al, 'The Wessex Recent In-Patient Suicide Study, 2. Case-Control Study of 59 In-Patient Suicides' (2001) 178 *British Journal of Psychiatry* 537; W McKenzie and C Wurr, 'Early Suicide Following Discharge from a Psychiatric Hospital' (2001) 31 *Suicide and Life Threatening Behaviour* 358.

A different study of 100 countries found increases in general population suicide rates following the introduction of mental health legislation.[85] However, in another similar study no such link was found.[86] It is difficult to interpret these statistics. It may be that new legislation increases awareness of mental health and leads to a higher recording of suicide. Ajit Shah's study found no association between the general population suicide rate and rates of involuntary admission under the MHA 1983, section 4 and a negative correlation with admission under sections 2 and 3.[87] But other studies have found a positive link[88] or no link.[89] The time shortly after exit from compulsory treatment is a period when patients are at a high risk of suicide.[90] That could be seen as evidence that the in-patient care has not been an effective intervention, or that it simply delays the point of suicide.

The National Confidential Inquiry into Suicide found:

> During 2008–2018, 2,619 suicides (31% of general population suicides) were identified as patient suicides, ie the person had been in contact with mental health services in the 12 months prior to death. This represents an average of 238 patient suicides per year.[91]

Another way into studying the impact of intervention is to explore the rates of re-attempt following a suicide attempt. A major review of the evidence found that 6.7 per cent[92] of attempted suicides died by suicide in the following five years. Studies of suicide survivors show that most are grateful for the intervention, and view it as helpful: 71 per cent in one leading study.[93] However, there is also evidence that some people found the intervention humiliating.[94] In their assessment, Callaghan, Ryan and Kerridge[95] conclude that the risks of harm outweigh the benefits:

> Given the limits of suicide risk assessment, we argue that a public policy that allows involuntary preventative detention of competent persons thought to be at risk of suicide, places too great a burden on all persons living with mental illness to be justified. We

[85] P Burgess et al, 'Do Nations' Mental Health Policies, Programs and Legislation Influence Their Suicide Rates? An Ecological Study of 100 Countries' (2004) 38 *Australian And New Zealand Journal of Psychiatry* 933.

[86] Shah (n 83).

[87] ibid.

[88] Burgess et al (n 85).

[89] Hunt et al (n 81).

[90] V Moore, 'Leaving Hospital: A Step Too Far for Risk-Based Regulation?' (2020) 28 *Medical Law Review* 675.

[91] University of Manchester, *National Confidential Inquiry into Suicide and Safety in Mental Health Annual Report: England, Northern Ireland, Scotland and Wales 2021* (University of Manchester, 2021).

[92] I Parra-Uribe et al, 'Risk of Re-Attempts and Suicide Death after a Suicide Attempt: A Survival Analysis' (2017) 17 *BMC Psychiatry* 163.

[93] K Chesley and N Loring-McNulty, 'Process of Suicide: Perspective of the Suicide Attempter' (2003) 9 *Journal of American Psychiatry Nurses Association* 41.

[94] O Nyttingnesa et al, '"It's Unbelievably Humiliating" – Patients' Expressions of Negative Effects of Coercion in Mental Health Care' (2016) 49 *International Journal of Law and Psychiatry* 147.

[95] S Callaghan et al, 'Risk of Suicide is Insufficient Warrant for Coercive Treatment for Mental Illness' (2013) 36 *International Journal of Law and Psychiatry* 374.

suggest that we are better placed to serve the interests and respect the human rights of people with mental illness if we respect and support the right of persons to make decisions, rather than focussing on perceived vulnerabilities and calculations of suicide risk.

Similarly, Borecky, Thomsen and Duboy[96] conclude:

(1) that inadequate attention has been given to the harms resulting from the use of coercion and the loss of autonomy;
(2) that inadequate evidence exists that involuntary hospitalisation is an effective method to reduce deaths by suicide; and
(3) that some suicidal patients may benefit more from therapeutic interventions that maximise and support autonomy and personal responsibility.

It seems, then, that the evidence is mixed on whether coerced psychiatric intervention is effective. However, as Kay Wilson[97] argues, there are real problems with simply complying with the views of all, regardless of their capacity. Relying on examples of real cases, she says:

> mental impairment is likely to have distorted the thinking and diminished the autonomy of a person who tries to cut off their healthy right arm to quiet the voices in her head, a person who is starving to death that refuses to eat for fear of becoming obese, a woman who believed she would reach an enlightened state if she jumped off a building and landed with her head in the right place, a person who harms themselves as a distraction or outlet for their immediate psychological distress and pain without a thought for the consequences; or a woman who withdrew consent for a life-saving hysterectomy, because 'bad voices' and 'bad machines' were controlling her mind.

Kate Richards, in an auto-biographical account, explains the impact of psychosis and depression on her thinking:

> when I'm sick I believe the delusional stuff to the same degree that you might know and believe the sky is above and the earth is below. And if someone were to say to me that the delusional thinking is, in fact, delusional, well that's the same as if I assure you now that we walk on the sky. Of course you wouldn't believe me, and that's why it's sometimes so hard for people who are sick like this to accept treatment – to know that they even need treatment.[98]

Marie Failinger describes the impact that mental ill-health can have:

> [Persons with mental impairment] … may be oblivious to the ways that they themselves have changed, believing they are the same and the world outside has changed radically and that the trustworthy is now dangerous. Or, as in depression, they may be numb to the world outside themselves, while inside being stabbed over and over by pain, like a ceaseless knife.[99]

[96] A Borecky et al, 'Reweighing the Ethical Tradeoffs in the Involuntary Hospitalization of Suicidal Patients, (2019) 19 *The American Journal of Bioethics* 71.

[97] K Wilson, 'The Abolition or Reform of Mental Health Law: How Should the Law Recognise and Respond to the Vulnerability of Persons with Mental Impairment?' (2020) 28 *Medical Law Review* 3.

[98] K Richards, *Madness: A Memoir* (Penguin Group 2013) 174.

[99] M Failinger, 'The Paradox in Madness: Vulnerability Confronts the Law' (2012) 1 *Mental Health Law and Policy Journal* 127, 127.

Psychiatric treatment can relieve symptoms and improve mental function, although it is not always as effective as hoped. Emotional support and the teaching of coping strategies can also be effective in helping someone face challenging events. As explained by David Bilchitz:

> to focus on rationality, autonomy and independent activity as the sole source of value in life is to work with an impoverished conception of the worth of individual human life and what provides quality to human lives. To do so is to ignore and undervalue the spheres of our lives that are valuable and which are not constituted by high levels of rational functioning and activity. To do so is also todevalue the lives of those who are not able to act in these ways or contribute actively in the social sphere: those with severe psychosocial disabilities, or, even those who are unemployed.[100]

The difficult to which she is alluding is that because the bar for mental capacity under the MCA 2005 is set so low (as we shall see in the next section), it is arguable that some – if not all – such cases would be found to have capacity. Without some form of intervention along the lines of those under the MHA 1983 they would be left to die or suffer serious injury.[101] Thus, while with a more robust MCA 2005 we could conceive of doing away with the MHA 1983, with the current approach the MHA 1983 is still needed.[102]

V. Mental Capacity Law

It is a fundamental principle of medical law and ethics that, before treating a patient who has capacity, a medical professional should obtain the patient's consent.[103] It is the patient, rather than the doctor, who has the final say on whether a proposed treatment can go ahead.[104] As Peter Jackson J in *Heart of England NHS Trust v JB* stated:[105]

> anyone capable of making decisions has an absolute right to accept or refuse medical treatment, regardless of the wisdom or consequences of the decision. The decision does not have to be justified to anyone. In the absence of consent any invasion of the body will be a criminal assault. The fact that the intervention is well-meaning or therapeutic makes no difference.

[100] D Bilchitz, 'Dignity. Fundamental Rights and Legal Capacity: Moving Beyond the Paradigm Set by the General Comment on Article 12 of the Convention on the Rights of Persons with Disabilities' (2016) 32 *South African Journal of Human Rights* 410, 428.

[101] P Chin, 'Detention, Capacity, and Treatment in the Mentally Ill – Ethical and Legal Challenges' (2019) 28 *Cambridge Quarterly of Healthcare Ethics* 752.

[102] See further the discussion in J Craigie and L Bortolotti, 'Rationality, Diagnosis, and Patient Autonomy in Psychiatry' in J Sadler et al (eds), *The Oxford Handbook of Psychiatric Ethics* (Oxford University Press, 2021).

[103] R Chadwick, 'Expertise Revisited' (2016) 30 *Bioethics* 549.

[104] E Jackson, 'From "Doctor Knows Best" to Dignity: Placing Adults Who Lack Capacity at the Centre of Decisions about Their Medical Treatment' (2018) 81 *Modern Law Review* 247.

[105] [2014] EWHC 342 (COP).

This means, that unless the case falls within the MHA 1983 above, a patient with capacity has the right to refuse treatment. That is much less significant in the particular context of suicide than it might be in other others because in a case of refusal to accept medical interventions designed to protect a patient from suicide, these can, in most cases, be given under the MHA 1983. The main category of cases where they would not be, is where the suicide ideation is not as a result of a mental disorder. If a person with suicidal ideation is going to be given interventions under the MCA 2005, this can occur in two ways. The first is if the person has capacity and consents. This is uncontroversial. The second is where a person is found to lack capacity and it is in their best interests to receive the intervention. It is this second category which is far more controversial. But first, we will look at when a person has capacity to refuse treatment, before considering the best interest approach.

A. The Mental Capacity of the Suicidal

This section will examine when a suicidal patient will have mental capacity under the MCA 2005. I will not be exploring when in ethical terms a person should be found to have capacity, as that is explored in Chapter 3. One of the issues that will become apparent is that the test for capacity under the MCA 2005 has, I would argue, a very low bar for capacity meaning that many suicidal patients who lack the capacity to exercise autonomy in ethical terms will nonetheless be found to have capacity under the MCA 2005.[106]

i. The General Test for Capacity

The general test for capacity is set out in section 2(1) of the MCA 2005:

> [A] person lacks capacity in relation to a matter if at the material time he is unable to make a decision for himself in relation to the matter because of an impairment of, or a disturbance in the functioning of, the mind or brain.

Section 3(1) explains what is meant by a person being unable to make a decision for themselves:

> [A] person is unable to make a decision for himself if he is unable—
>
> to understand the information relevant to the decision,
>
> to retain that information,
>
> to use or weigh that information as part of the process of making the decision, or
>
> to communicate his decision (whether by talking, using sign language or any other means).

[106] C Stewart et al, 'A Test for Mental Capacity to Request Assisted Suicide' (2011) 37 *Journal of Medical Ethics* 34.

As this indicates, there are a number of ways in which a person may be said to be unable to make a decision. They can range from not understanding a key piece of information, to not being able to weigh up the different factors.

Capacity under the MCA 2005 is assessed at the time of the case and in relation to the particular issue at hand. As Baker J put it in *A v P*:[107]

> Capacity is both issue-specific and time-specific. A person may have capacity in respect of certain matters but not in relation to other matters. Equally, a person may have capacity at one time and not at another. The question is whether at the date on which the court is considering the question the person lacks capacity in question …

So the question is always whether a person has capacity to decide a particular question at this particular time.[108] An assessment that a person lacks the capacity to decide to end their life is not, therefore, an assessment the person lacks mental capacity to make other decisions. Indeed, it is possible to determine that they lack capacity to end their life, but are able to make all other decisions for themselves. Clearly much could be said about the capacity test, but my focus will be on the questions that tend to arise around suicide.

ii. The 'Generous' Approach to Capacity

The MCA 2005, particularly as interpreted by the courts, takes a generous approach to assessment of capacity. In other words it clearly prefers to err on the side of finding capacity even though a patient lacks capacity, as opposed to finding a lack of capacity when in fact capacity exists. We can see this in several provisions. First, under section 1(2), 'a person must be assumed to have capacity unless it is established that he lacks capacity'. In other words, the burden is on those who seek to claim that a patient lacks capacity. If the evidence on capacity is unclear, then the healthcare professionals should proceed on the basis that a patient has capacity.

Second, section 1(4) of the MCA 2005 states that: 'A person is not to be treated as unable to make a decision merely because he makes an unwise decision'.[109] Peter Jackson J in *Heart of England NHS Foundation Trust v JB*[110] emphasised:

> The temptation to base a judgment of a person's capacity upon whether they seem to have made a good or bad decision, and in particular on whether they have accepted or rejected medical advice, is absolutely to be avoided. That would be to put the cart before the horse or, expressed another way, to allow the tail of welfare to wag the dog of capacity. Any tendency in this direction risks infringing the rights of that group of

[107] *A v P* [2018] EWCOP 10.

[108] That said, of course, for major procedures a patient will be unconscious at the time of the operation and so their earlier consent will be relied upon: J Lindberg et al, 'Temporising and Respect for Patient Self-Determination' (2019) 45 *Journal of Medical Ethics* 161.

[109] Despite the clear statement of this principle, commentators have claimed that judges have done exactly this to ensure that patients receive the treatment they need: J Harrington, 'Privileging the Medical Norms: Liberalism, Self-Determination and Refusal of Treatment' (1996) 16 *Legal Studies* 348.

[110] *Heart of England NHS Foundation Trust v JB* [2014] EWHC 342 (COP), at [7].

> persons who, though vulnerable, are capable of making their own decisions. Many who suffer from mental illness are well able to make decisions about their medical treatment, and it is important not to make unjustified assumptions to the contrary.

Third, Baker J in *PH and A Local Authority v Z Ltd & R*[111] has explained that

> [the] courts must guard against imposing too high a test of capacity … because to do so would run the risk of discriminating against persons suffering from a mental disability.

Similarly, in *A v P*[112] Baker J emphasised that the court should avoid what he called the 'protection imperative':

> [T]he danger that the court, that all professionals involved with treating and helping P, may feel drawn towards an outcome that is more protective of her and fail to carry out an assessment of capacity that is detached and objective.

These three points put up quite a barrier against using the MCA 2005 in borderline cases of incapacity. It would be wrong to exaggerate the height of that barrier. For example, the word 'merely' in section 1(4) is important. It is perfectly legitimate to use the fact that the decision is unwise as part of a finding of incapacity – it just cannot be used as the sole factor. There is a careful line to be walked between not allowing the reasoning 'This decision is irrational, therefore the patient lacks capacity', but permitting the reasoning 'This decision is irrational because the individual is not able to properly weigh up the different issues'.[113] So, the fact that, in many cases, the wish to commit suicide will be 'unwise' can be taken into account in making the assessment of incapacity, so long as it is not the sole factor. The Code of Practice explains that the fact a person 'repeatedly' make unwise decisions, putting them at risk of harm can be used to determine that lack of capacity as can a decision which is 'out of character'.[114] This gives some scope for relying on a suicidal wish as an important part of determining a person lacks capacity. Nevertheless, it would be hard to rely on this argument when there are consistent appeals to seek suicide. It also makes it absolutely clear that it would be improper to assume that all suicidal patients lack capacity.

It is also worth noting that a patient should not be treated as lacking capacity 'unless all practical steps to help him' to reach capacity 'have been taken without success'.[115] Section 4(4) of the MCA 2005 states:

> He must, so far as reasonably practicable, permit and encourage the person to participate, or to improve his ability to participate, as fully as possible in any act done for him and any decision affecting him.

[111] *PH and A Local Authority v Z Ltd & R* [2011] EWHC 1704 (Fam), at para 16 (xi).

[112] *A v P* (n 108) para 15.

[113] See J Savulescu and R Momeyer, 'Should Informed Consent be Based on Rational Beliefs?' (1997) 23 *Journal of Medical Ethics* 282, who insist that a patient's decision must be based on rational belief if it is to be respected.

[114] Department of Constitutional Affairs, *Mental Capacity Act Code of Practice* (TSO, 2007) para 2.11.

[115] See ibid, para 2.7 for a further discussion of what might be involved.

This suggests that before making a capacity or best interests assessment time should be taken to enable the person to gain capacity. This might be used in a case where a person is suicidal but in the throes of a psychotic episode or mental health emergency, which is expected to pass soon and they may then be in a better state of mind to determine whether they want to die. It may well be, therefore, that under the MCA 2005, interventions are permitted to enable a person to gain capacity.

Overall, therefore, we see that the courts are reluctant to find no capacity unless there is clear evidence of a lack of capacity. Doctors are warned not to find a lack of capacity because they believe a suicide to be foolish, or because of any natural urge to protect people from harm.

iii. The Diagnostic Test and the Functional Test

As was explained in *A Local Authority v TZ*,[116] the test of capacity in section 2(1) of the MCA 2005 involves a 'diagnostic test' and a 'functional test'. Under the diagnostic test, it must be found that a person has an impairment or a disturbance in the functioning of the brain. The MCA 2005 Code of Practice lists the following as examples of conditions that might involve an impairment or disturbance of the functioning of the brain:

> conditions associated with some forms of mental illness;
>
> dementia;
>
> significant learning disabilities;
>
> the long-term effects of brain damage;
>
> physical or medical conditions that cause confusion, drowsiness or loss of consciousness;
>
> delirium;
>
> concussion following a head injury; and
>
> the symptoms of alcohol or drug use.[117]

Under the 'functional test', it must be determined whether, as a result of the disturbance, a person is unable to make the decision. Importantly, it must be shown that the inability to make the decision results from the impairment.[118] Thus, patients with no mental impairment who decide to commit suicide because of their religious belief that God will reward them in the afterlife them will still have mental capacity. Even if the doctors try to argue that the patients do not properly understand the reality of their situation, that will not be because of a mental impairment. Peter Bartlett has made a powerful case that this breaches the CRPD.[119] As already

[116] *A Local Authority v TZ* [2013] EWHC 2322 (COP). See also *PC v City of York Council* [2013] EWCA Civ 478.

[117] Department of Constitutional Affairs (n 115) para 4.12.

[118] *An NHS Trust v CS* [2016] EWCOP 10; *Wandsworth CGC v IA* [2014] EWHC 990 (COP).

[119] B Clough, '"People Like That": Realising the Social Model in Mental Capacity Jurisprudence' (2014) 23 *Medical Law Review* 53.

noted, Article 12(2) of the Convention provides that people with disabilities may enjoy legal capacity 'on an equal basis with others in all aspects of life'. Yet here, if we have two people with delusions, the one whose delusion is as a result of a mental disorder is treated differently from the one whose delusion is not.[120] It seems hard to explain why we need to respect the non-autonomous decisions to die of those who lack capacity due to non-mental health reasons. It may be that here the Article 2 obligation comes in to protect those who are non-autonomously determining to commit suicide, whatever the source of that capacity. The jurisdiction to do this would need to be found outside the MCA 2005.

As Jillian Craigie and Lis Bortolotti[121] note:

> In the area of psychiatry it is much more common for patients to reject their diagnosis than in other areas of medicine; and there is an accepted problem of people successfully deceiving psychiatrists as to their symptoms, with there being less objective evidence to rely on than with other conditions.

This demonstrates the challenges a doctor may face in determining whether a patient does have a mental disorder and, if so, whether it has led to the decision. Craigie and Bortolotti found that there are also complex interactions between culture and conditions. They go on to note that there is considerable irrationality in people not affected by psychiatric diagnosis and that there is a difference in the quality of the irrationality when there is a diagnosis – indeed, some mental disorders improve qualities of 'rationality'. This makes it all the harder to satisfy the diagnostic test required by the MCA 2005.

We see here, therefore, a further potential barrier to using the MCA 2005 in the case of suicidal people. The requirement is that a mental condition be shown and it be established that this has led to the inability to make the decision. This is challenging, especially in the case of the suicidal, where determining a person's state of mind and the cause of that is complex.

iv. Capacity: Understanding the Relevant Information

It is surprising to many that to have capacity all that is required is that the patient must understand 'in broad terms the nature of the procedure which is intended'.[122] Macur J in *LBL v RYJ*,[123] explained that 'it is not necessary for the person to comprehend every detail of the issue … it is not always necessary for a person to comprehend all peripheral details'. As explained in Chapter 3, it is not straightforward to determine what knowledge a person needs to be able to make an autonomous decision to die. However, under the MCA 2005 a bare understanding of what death is seems sufficient.

[120] Although it is arguable that the person with the disability is treated more favourably in that he or she can be protected by the MCA 2005.

[121] Craigie and Bortolotti (n 99).

[122] *Chatterton v Gerson* [1981] 1 All ER 257, 265.

[123] *LBL v RYJ* [2010] EWHC 2664 (Fam), [24].

It might be thought unlikely that a person lacks capacity to understand the decision to die, unless there is some kind of delusion. Even then it may be restricted to cases where a patient is utterly mistaken about their current state of health. A good example of the reluctance to find that lack of information leads to a lack of capacity is *Re C (Adult: Refusal of Treatment)*.[124] C was a patient at Broadmoor, who had been diagnosed as suffering from paranoid schizophrenia. One of his delusional beliefs was that he was a great doctor who had a 100 per cent success rate with patients with damaged limbs. He suffered an injury to his foot, which became gangrenous. He was told that there was an 85 per cent chance that he would die without an amputation. C opposed the treatment, believing that God did not want him to have his foot amputated. Although he accepted that the doctors believed he was going to die, he did not agree with them. Thorpe J held: 'I am satisfied that he has understood and retained the relevant treatment information, that in his own way he believes it, and that in the same fashion he has arrived at a clear choice'.[125] This indicates that a decision based on delusions is unlikely to be found to lack capacity.

v. Capacity and the Ability to Use the Information to Make a Decision

To have capacity, the patient must not only understand the information, but also be able to use the information, weigh it, and be able to make a decision. This is more likely to be the basis for an assessment that a suicidal person lacks capacity. It may be claimed that even if they are aware of the key facts, they are in such a distressed or disturbed state that they cannot weigh up those facts. MacDonald J warned against being too ready to use this approach, arguing in *Kings College Hospital NHS Foundation Trust v C and V*[126] that: '… the question for the court is not whether the person's ability to take the decision is impaired by the impairment of, or disturbance in the functioning of, the mind or brain but rather whether the person is rendered unable to make the decision by reason thereof'. The reference to an inability to make a decision severely restricts the potential use of this basis for establishing a lack of capacity.[127] A case of depression, for example, might impede or impair a person's reasoning, but is unlikely to render them unable to make a decision.

vi. Conclusion on Mental Capacity and Suicide

As we have seen, the MCA 2005 takes a 'generous approach' towards mental capacity and it will be challenging to establish a lack of capacity, even in a case of

[124] *Re C (Adult: Refusal of Treatment)* [1994] 1 WLR 290 (FD).
[125] ibid, at 294.
[126] *Kings College Hospital NHS Foundation Trust v C and V* [2015] EWCOP 80, para 15.
[127] Confirmed in *WBC Local Authority v Z* [2016] EWCOP 4.

suicidality.[128] This approach might well be questioned. As Jesse Wall and I have written:

> It is a terrible thing to be assessed as lacking capacity when you do not – to have others make decisions on your behalf and set aside your own wishes based on what they think is in your best interests. You lose control over your life. You are no longer in charge of your destiny.
>
> It is a terrible thing to be said to have capacity when you do not – to be left to cause yourself and those you love great harm on the basis that you know what you are doing and you are making your own choices, when in fact your decisions are not really yours. To have others harm you and to be told no protection is offered because you have chosen this harm, even though it is against your deepest values, is horrific.[129]

This is particularly true in relation to suicide. If we wrongly assess the suicidal person as having capacity when they do not, and a preventable suicide occurs this is a very serious wrong – perhaps the most serious wrong imaginable. When they are prevented from committing suicide because it is wrongly assumed they lack capacity, a wrong is done – but unlike in the first case it is reversible (they can commit suicide shortly). As argued in Chapter 3, where the courts are dealing with issues of long-term harms, such as suicide, a high standard should be expected for autonomy. This is not, as Baker J suggests, to discriminate against those with a mental disability, but to ensure all of their rights, such as the right to life and right to torture are protected; and indeed their right of autonomy to ensure the view they currently express is a genuine exercise of their will.

B. The Inherent Jurisdiction and Vulnerable Adults

For those who are concerned about the apparent difficulty in finding capacity among the suicidal, some hope may be offered by the inherent jurisdiction developed by the courts to deal with 'vulnerable adults' – that is, adults who are found officially to have capacity, but who are nevertheless thought to need protection.[130] Although the MCA 2005 appeared to suggest that those who have capacity are treated under the general law, the courts have invoked the inherent jurisdiction of the court, described by Lord Donaldson as 'the great safety net'[131] to protect vulnerable people.

[128] G Richardson, 'Mental Capacity in the Shadow of Suicide: *What* Can the Law Do?' (2013) 9(1) *International Journal of Law in Context* 87.

[129] J Herring and J Wall, 'Autonomy, Capacity and Vulnerable Adults: Filling the Gaps in the Mental Capacity Act' (2015) 35 *Legal Studies* 698.

[130] See J Herring, *Vulnerable Adults and the Law* (Oxford University Press, 2016) for a discussion of the case law.

[131] *Re F (Mental Patient: Sterilisation)* [1990] 2 AC 1.

The Court of Appeal has confirmed the existence of the jurisdiction in *DL v A Local Authority*.[132] Munby J has defined this group in the following way:

> [T]he inherent jurisdiction can be exercised in relation to a vulnerable adult who, even if not incapacitated by mental disorder or mental illness, is, or is reasonably believed to be, either: (i) under constraint; or (ii) subject to coercion or undue influence; or (iii) for some other reason deprived of the capacity to make the relevant decision, or disabled from making a free choice, or incapacitated or disabled from giving or expressing a real and genuine consent.[133]

Much more could be said about this jurisdiction, but it seems to provide a helpful safety net for those who, while technically having capacity, have severely impaired autonomy. This is particularly helpful in the case of suicidal people. Notably the courts have been particularly willing to use the jurisdiction where they perceive that a person is temporarily impaired in their autonomy (eg because they are in an abusive relationship) but that with intervention (eg removing them from the relationship), they will become able to exercise autonomy. The same may be so in plenty of suicidal cases, where the patient is in a crisis, but with intervention may be brought to a state of mind where a richer autonomy can be exercised. While the jurisdiction has been used in a sparing way, it does provide a legal basis to offer protections in line with the general thrust of this book.

C. Best Interests and Suicide

If a person lacks capacity then a best interest assessment must be made. Section 4 of the MCA 2005 states that, in deciding what is in a patient's best interests, the court or deputy must consider all the relevant circumstances. The MCA 2005 Code of Practice states:

> When working out what is in the best interests of the person who lacks capacity to make a decision or act for themselves, decision makers must take into account all relevant factors that it would be reasonable to consider, not just those that they think are important. They must not act or make a decision based on what they would want to do if they were the person who lacked capacity.[134]

If, therefore, a suicidal person is found to lack capacity, an assessment needs to be made as to what intervention – if any – will promote their best interests. At first sight, it might be thought that it would nearly always be in a person's best interests to be prevented from committing suicide. That said, there could be a case where

[132] *DL v A Local Authority* [2012] EWCA Civ 253.
[133] *Re SA (Vulnerable Adult with Capacity: Marriage)* [2005] EWHC 2942 (Fam), [77].
[134] Department of Constitutional Affairs (n 115) para 5.7.

they were in agonising pain which could not be alleviated, when it would, on an objective assessment be best not to intervene to stop the suicide. However, that conclusion is not as obvious as it might at first appear. That is because, in interpreting the best interests test in recent years, considerable weight has been attached to the current and past interests of the person concerned. In other words there has been a 'subjectification' of the best interests test. This was well captured in *Aintree University Hospitals NHS Foundation Trust v James*,[135] where Lady Hale stated:

> The purpose of the best interests test is to consider matters from the patient's point of view. That is not to say that his wishes must prevail, any more than those of a fully capable patient must prevail. We cannot always have what we want. Nor will it always be possible to ascertain what an incapable patient's wishes are. … But in so far as it is possible to ascertain the patient's wishes and feelings, his beliefs and values or the things which were important to him, it is those which should be taken into account because they are a component in making the choice which is right for him as an individual human being.

As that quotation indicates, it is part of respecting the patient and treating them in a humane way that we attach weight to their views, even though the patient lacks capacity. It may be that the number of cases where the defendant's long-standing values and beliefs will be in line with allowing them to commit suicide will be very small.

A second reason why it is not straightforward that suicide is contrary to the patient's best interests as understood in the law, is that if P opposes intervention, then this opposition may render the intervention ineffective and there may seem little to gain from it. That may be rare, but no doubt there are cases where that is so.

A third reason, would be if the only way to prevent the suicide required such drastic measures that it involved a high degree of force;[136] in such circumstances it may be that the intervention cannot be justified.[137] In *A NHS Trust v X*,[138] in refusing to order a hospital to feed nutrition to a woman with anorexia nervosa against her wishes, it was said:

> Articles 3 and 8 of the ECHR are particularly prominently engaged; repeated forcible feeding over a long period of time against her clearly expressed wishes, most especially with the use of physical restraint, is likely in my judgment to amount to inhuman or degrading treatment, certainly it would amount to a severe interference with her private life and personal autonomy.

It would not be difficult to imagine some interventions designed to prevent suicide reaching this kind of level.

[135] *Aintree University Hospitals NHS Foundation Trust v James* [2013] UKSC 67.
[136] The Liberty Protections Safeguards in the MCA 2005 must be followed.
[137] J Herring, 'Entering the Fog: on the Borderlines of Mental Capacity' (2008) 83 *Indiana Law Journal* 1620.
[138] *A NHS Trust v X* (n 47).

D. Advance Decisions and Suicide

Advance decisions are an important way for patients to control what happens to them when they lose capacity. Typically, they are entered into by a person who fears that they may lose capacity in the future and who wants to dictate how they are treated. In our context they are particularly relevant in cases where a person signs an advance decision before committing suicide, indicating that they do not want to receive treatment. Indeed, one study showed that 2.5 per cent of patients who presented to hospital with self-poisoning and then died had a purported advance decision in place.[139]

An advance decision is defined in section 24 of the MCA 2005:

> 'Advance Decision' means a decision made by a person ('P'), after he has reached 18 and when he has capacity to do so, that if—
>
> at a later time and in such circumstances as he may specify, a specified treatment is proposed to be carried out or continued by a person providing health care for him, and
>
> at that time he lacks capacity to consent to the carrying out or continuation of the treatment, the specified treatment is not to be carried out or continued.

A number of key points should be noted about this definition. First, the advance decision is effective only if the patient has capacity when they made it. Second, the advance decision is to be relevant only if the patient lacks capacity to consent to the treatment. Thus, if a patient has signed an advance decision refusing to consent to treatment for a suicide attempt, but when brought to hospital they consent, with capacity, then the advance decision should be ignored.[140] Third, the definition of advance decisions allows only 'negative' decisions: decisions to refuse treatment. An advance decision cannot be used to compel a medical professional to provide treatment. Hence, an advance decision could not ask doctors to 'finish me off if my suicide attempt fails'. Fourth, if the advance decision does reject life-saving treatment, that rejection must be in writing, signed by the patient and witnessed by a third party.[141] This is an important restriction in the case of advance decisions used by people as part of a suicide attempt. It should, however, be noted that if the note is not signed, although the advance decision is not binding, it can be taken into account in making a best interests assessment (see section V.C above). Fifth, an advance decision can be rendered invalid if the decision has been withdrawn or the patient 'has done anything else that is clearly inconsistent with the directive in the advance decision'. For example, if the patient has signed an advance decision asking for no medical treatment and then taken pills in a suicide attempt, if they were then to telephone a doctor asking for help this might be seen as conduct inconsistent with their directive.

[139] N Kapur et al, 'Advance Directives and Suicidal Behaviour' (2010) 34 *British Medical Journal* 4557.
[140] MCA 2005, s 25(3).
[141] ibid, s 25(6).

Looking at this list of circumstances in which an advance decision might not apply, it is tempting to think that there is plenty of opportunity for a medical professional to determine that the advance decision should not prevent medical treatment following a suicide attempt. Indeed, there is even a defence to any legal proceedings for doctors who treat a patient after mistakenly concluding the advance decision did not apply.[142] We might, therefore, conclude that an advance decision is only likely to prevent a doctor providing treatment following an attempted suicide where it is thought to clearly represent the settled and informed decision of the patient. In particular this is because, although a medical professional who wrongly withholds treatment from a patient who needs it could well face legal proceedings, it is hard to imagine a doctor who intervenes and saves the life of a suicidal patient facing any legal proceedings.

E. Summary on the Current Approach of the MCA 2005 to Suicide

Some caution needs to be exercised before setting out a definitive view on whether a suicidal person is likely to be found to have capacity, as there are relatively few cases where the capacity of a suicidal person is considered in depth. It would seem likely that the standard approach is that a suicidal person would be found to have capacity. As long as they understand the current position they are in, in broad terms, and understand that the act they will do will cause death; as long as they can weigh the factors and make a decision; and communicate that decision, they are likely to be found to have capacity. As argued above, and in Chapter 3, I think that is far too low a bar for capacity to commit suicide and fails to protect the autonomy rights and rights to life of suicidal people. It is possible that if the courts come to assess this question they will accept that a slightly different approach could be taken in relation to suicide or the courts could rely on inherent jurisdiction

VI. Suicidal Children

A series of distressing cases have appeared before the courts involving children and young adults. A good example is *Re X (A Child) (No 5)*.[143] The young woman, X, was subject to a Detention and Training Order and was detained in a secure unit. She was due to be released, but had serious mental health problems and had made several determined suicide attempts. A care order was made by the court, but the local authority had not been able to find a suitable setting for her. The

[142] L Quinlivan et al, 'Advance Decisions to Refuse Treatment and Suicidal Behaviour in Emergency Care: "It's Very Much a Step into the Unknown"' (2019) 5 *British Journal of* Psychology 50.
[143] *Re X (A Child) (No 5)* [2017] EWHC 2141 (Fam).

evidence was clear that without a suitable placement there was a very high chance of her committing suicide. Sir James Munby spoke in the strongest terms about the failure to find suitable accommodation:

> If this is the best we can do for X, and others in similar crisis, what right do we, what right do the system, our society and indeed the State itself, have to call ourselves civilised? The honest answer to this question should make us all feel ashamed.[144]

He concluded that if there was no supportive and safe placement, 'we, the system, society, the State … will have blood on our hands'. Eventually, following the judgment, a placement was found.[145]

The case highlights a tension with the law surrounding care orders. While the court determines when a care order can be made in relation to a child, it has only limited powers to control how a child in care is looked after by a local authority. It cannot, as this case demonstrates, require that a local authority house a child in a particular form of accommodation.

The case is in striking contrast to much contemporary legal thinking around suicide. It is notable that Sir James Munby was driven by the need to protect the troubled young woman from suicide. There was no real discussion of autonomy and, indeed, the issues around rights to liberty carried little weight given the imperative to protect from suicide.[146] While just shy of her 18th birthday, it is striking how once adulthood is reached a rather different set of values can come into play.

VII. Conclusion

This chapter has focused on the MCA 2005 and the MHA 1983 as they relate to suicide. In relation to the MCA 2005, it has highlighted how generally that legislation sets the bar for capacity at a fairly low level, meaning that many suicidal people will be able to satisfy it. By contrast, the MHA 1983 is readily available for such cases. It is easy to see how the two statutes can be seen as being in tension with one another: the MCA 2005, with its focus on the importance of autonomy, and the MHA 1983, with its paternalistic justification. It is not surprising that many commentators have called for the MHA 1983 to be abolished and instead replaced with a system focusing on autonomy. The mental disability discrimination critique of the MHA 1983 is powerful. As Fanning has argued:

> In a liberal, democratic society governed by the rule of law, the deprivation of a person's liberty should be contingent on the satisfaction of a set of fixed, objectively justifiable legal criteria and [be] executed in accordance with a fair and reviewable process.

[144] ibid.
[145] ibid.
[146] General comment No 36 (2018) on Article 6 of the International Covenant on Civil and Political Rights, on the right to life.

> Medicalism, with its looser criteria and deference to professional discretion, is not instinctively amenable to these standards.[147]

As Fanning goes on to conclude, 'People with mental illnesses are in fact more likely to pose a risk of harm to themselves than to others – and even then these risks are low'.

More fundamentally, it fails to provide for protection of autonomy. The Centre for Disability Law and Policy, Galway[148] has argued

> Even though we think that the person who refuses mental health treatment because they believe that the psychiatrist is an assassin is not making a decision based on all the right information, we still – for adults at least – accept that they have a dignity of risk [*sic*] to make the wrong decisions sometimes.

But I have argued above proper respect for autonomy a strict assessment of what autonomy requires and a careful listening to the person involve. In Chapter 3 I argued this required a careful listening to the person concerned and an attempt to understand their wishes in the context of their life story. Refusing the administration of an assassin should not be seen as refusing the administration of a psychiatrist.

This chapter has, however, been somewhat hesitant about the evidence that in patient care is highly effective in suicide prevention. In the next chapter we explore alternatives forms of suicide prevention and how they may be a more appropriate response to suicide.

[147] Fanning (n 63).

[148] Quoted in Northern Ireland Assembly, *Report on the Mental Capacity Bill* (Northern Ireland Assembly, 2016) at para 32.

8

Prevention of Suicide

I. Introduction

This chapter will explore what can be done to prevent suicide. The literature is extensive. It is replete with proposals of interventions which might possibly assist. But it is notoriously difficult to prove that any interventions actually work.[1] It is hard enough to identify a person who was intent on committing suicide, let alone to determine why they did not go ahead and do so. Even at the general statistical level, where a suicide rate has dropped it is enormously challenging to pinpoint a single cause for that decrease. The truth is that in many cases where a suicide has been prevented or the general suicide rate has dropped, it is a combination of a range of different interventions, including the efforts of the individuals themselves, which have played a role. Of course, just because an intervention is not proven to assist, does not mean it should not be used, especially when – as we shall see – many interventions have benefits in addition to any hoped-for reduction in suicide rates.

Suicide prevention has long focused on identifying people who are liable to commit suicide and putting in place measures designed to prevent them from doing so. However, more recently the focus has been on interventions aimed at the public. The development of these public health specific programmes to prevent suicidal behaviour can be traced back to 1996 and the publication of *Prevention of Suicide: Guidelines for the Formulation and Implementation of National Strategies*, produced by the WHO and the Economic and Social Council of the UN. Two years later the WHO launched the Suicide Prevention Programme, which emphasised: the treatment of mental disorder; restricting access to suicidal methods; and responsible media reporting as the primary means of suicide reduction. From these, a wide range of international and national organisations have sought to develop suicide prevention strategies. England has produced its suicide prevention strategy, first adopted in 2012[2] and regularly reviewed.[3] We will be exploring these, as well as other efforts, in the chapter below.[4]

[1] M Rudd, 'Inaccurate Conclusions Based on Limited Data' Electronic letter to the (2007) 11 *British Journal of Psychiatry* 1.

[2] HM Government, *Preventing Suicide in England: A Cross-Government Outcomes Strategy to Save Lives* (HM Government, 2012).

[3] ibid.

[4] M Nordentoft, 'Crucial Elements in Suicide Prevention Strategies' (2011) 84 *Progress in Neuropsychopharmacol and Biological Psychiatry* 848.

It should also be noted at the start of the chapter that much writing on suicide prevention assumes that an intervention that reduces suicide is 'a good thing'. Indeed, I have made that assumption in the opening paragraph above. Of course, as we have seen in Chapter 3, some will claim that in certain cases suicide will be a good outcome, or at least a permissible one, and so an intervention that is designed to prevent it would be inappropriate. This chapter will begin by addressing the question of whether interventions should be used. It will then go on to look at the interventions that are promoted. In broad terms these are generally divided into three categories: universal (aimed at the whole population); selective (aimed at particular groups of people); and individual (aimed at particular people who are thought to be at risk of suicide.)

II. The Case for Prevention

As already mentioned, it is generally taken for granted that seeking to prevent people from committing suicide is desirable. Don Richie, known as the 'Angel of The Gap' was said to have intervened in over 160 potential suicides at 'The Gap', a notorious suicide spot in Sydney. He was given the Order of Australia and received considerable praise for his dedication in talking people out of committing suicide.[5] It would seem odd, even offensive, to suggest that his attempts to talk people out of suicide were undesirable.

The case for suicide prevention is straightforward: it reduces deaths. It is estimated that over 800,000 people worldwide die each year by suicide, accounting for 1.4 per cent of deaths worldwide.[6] In England, one person dies every two hours as a result of suicide.[7] If we think of any other cause of death, a suggestion that we should seek to reduce the number of those deaths would be seen as inevitably good. It would seem, for example, absurd to suggest that we should not seek to reduce the number of people who die as a result of cancer or car accidents.

Autonomy is commonly used as an argument against suicide prevention. However, as argued in Chapter 3, there are good reasons for thinking that a decision to end one's life is not autonomous in many many cases. To respect a decision to die which is not autonomous could be a serious harm to the person and in fact undermine their autonomy. The number of suicide attempts is up to 30 times the number of successful suicides over time.[8] This might indicate, although it does not prove, that many people who attempt suicide do not resolve to try again via

[5] S Fitzpatrick and J River, 'Beyond the Medical Model: Future Directions for Suicide Intervention Services' (2018) 48 *International Journal of Health Services* 189.

[6] G Zalsman et al, 'Suicide Prevention Strategies Revisited: 10-year Systematic Review' (2016) 3 *Lancet* 643.

[7] HM Government, *Preventing Suicide in England: Fifth Progress Report* (HM Government, 2021).

[8] J Bertolote, 'Prevention of Suicidal Behaviors' in M Nock (ed), *The Oxford Handbook of Suicide and Self-Injury* (Oxford University Press, 2014).

more reliable method. Indeed, many are grateful that there has been intervention.[9] As one person who attempted suicide put it: 'From the moment I came round in intensive care, I knew that I wanted to be alive'.[10] Michael Cholbi argues:

> The basis of suicidal hopelessness, I contend, is that the agent's capacity to care about her own happiness has been nearly ground into submission. … In the case of many suicidal agents, it may be correct to say, with Kant, that they seek to end their misery, but this neglects the fact that their proper end is not to end their misery but to end their sense of normative listlessness.[11]

It should be noted that while suicide prevention tends to bring to mind a dramatic picture of a person being dragged from the edge of a cliff, it is often more subtle. Much of it might be said to involve 'nudging'. 'Nudging' is complex phenomena.[12] At its heart it is using circumstances, presentations and information to encourage people to act in a particular way. Sometimes this is very overt: at a supermarket a large poster advertises that cornflakes are half price. This is a clear encouragement to a person to buy cornflakes when they might not otherwise have purchased them. It may be slightly less obvious, with the cornflakes prominently displayed, in the hope that customers will select them because they are seen and easy to reach. Suicide prevention may be in terms of advertising services offering support, or offering practical help to people who are going through challenging times, or restricting access to means of committing suicide. These cases are less problematic in terms of autonomy because they are not directly forcing someone to act in a particular way but are encouraging them to make certain decisions. For these kinds of interventions, the concerns about autonomy are much less. A person is given information and practical interventions which might encourage a particular decision, but this is not compelling a person into acting in a particular way.

It is also significant that many suicide prevention policies, particularly those aimed at the general population, are beneficial for reasons other than suicide prevention.[13] A tragic example is the case of Lizzie Lowe, who was gay and raised in an evangelical church which opposed same-sex behaviour. She committed suicide, believing that God and the church could not love her as a lesbian. The church, shocked by the death, undertook a time of prayer and study, wanting there never to be another such an event in their church. As a result, it completely changed its attitude towards issues around sexuality and promoted an inclusive theology.[14]

[9] E van Wijngaarden et al, 'Still Ready to Give up on Life? A Longitudinal Phenomenological Study into Wishes to Die among Older Adults' (2021) 284 *Social Science and Medicine* 114.

[10] Anonymous, 'Suicide – My Story' in A Grant et al (eds), *Our Encounters with Suicide* (PCCS Books, 2013).

[11] M Cholbi, 'Suicide Intervention and Non-Ideal Kantian Theory' (2002) 19 *Journal of Applied Philosophy* 245.

[12] R Thaler and C Sunstein, *Nudge: The Final Edition* (Penguin, 2021).

[13] C Standley, 'Expanding our Paradigms: Intersectional and Socioecological Approaches to Suicide Prevention' (2020) 12 *Death Studies* 1.

[14] BBC News, 'Didsbury Church's Radical Change after Gay Girl's Suicide', www.bbc.co.uk/news/av/uk-england-manchester-45615029, accessed 29.10.2021.

Although the change was primarily spurred by a desire to prevent suicides, it also meant that the church was able to protect the mental health of LGBT evangelical Christians.

A further important point is that suicide causes considerable grief for the family members and friends left behind. There is ample evidence that this is in excess of the grief that is normally felt on bereavement. We have, therefore, a reason to prevent suicide: the reduction of severe emotional distress. I do not argue that this can simply outweigh the autonomous wish of the suicidal individual, but rather that it comes into play in (the many) cases where it is unclear how autonomous the wish to die is.

Suicide costs significant sums of money. A Royal College report in 2020 suggests that the UK annual cost of suicide is approximately £6.5 billion, but accepts that this is likely to be an underestimate.[15] Therefore, while suicide prevention costs money, it is likely that in purely economic terms it will be beneficial.

These points might show good reasons why the state should intervene. However, this book makes the case that there is a duty on the state to intervene. In part this comes from the fact that the state has a duty to ensure protection of people's human rights, but also from the fact that the state is often implicated in suicides. For example, as we saw in Chapter 3, economic policies and the resulting social exclusion are linked to suicide. As Mills claims:

> [P]eople are killing themselves because austerity is killing them. Austerity suicides may be read as the ultimate outcome of the internalisation of eugenic and market logic underlying welfare reform driven by austerity. Such deaths make visible the slow death endemic to austerity.[16]

III. The Case against Suicide Prevention

There are those who oppose suicide prevention. These can be separated into arguments of principle, and those who claim that suicide prevention is simply ineffective.

A. Principled Opposition to Suicide Prevention

It has been claimed that suicide prevention is oppressive of suicidal people. Baril[17] describes suicidism as:

> […] an oppressive system (stemming from non-suicidal perspectives) functioning at the normative, discursive, medical, legal, social, political, economic, and epistemic levels in which suicidal people experience multiple forms of injustice and violence.

[15] Patient Safety Group, *Self-Harm and Suicide in Adults* (Royal College of Psychiatry, 2020).

[16] C Mills, 'Dead People Don't Claim: A Psychopolitical Autopsy of UK Austerity Suicides' (2018) 38 *Critical Social Policy* 302.

He goes on to criticise the failure to listen to suicidal people and to develop 'non-coercive approaches to suicidality that could involve supporting some people's decision to die'. Other critics have complained of the medicalisation and 'psychiatrisation' of suicide, which strip the suicidal person of free will.[18] David Webb writes:

> In the current environment [...] talking about your suicidal feelings runs the very real risk of finding yourself being judged, locked up and drugged. Suicidal people know this and [...] will do their best to prevent it happening to them. We hide our feelings from others, go underground. And the deadly cycle of silence, taboo and prejudice is reinforced. [...] There is a fundamental flaw at the core of contemporary thinking about suicide; which is the failure to understand suicidality as it is lived by those who experience it.[19]

Thomas Szasz[20] claims that suicidal people are discriminated against. They are presumed to lack capacity and subjected to legal and social disadvantages of a kind which would never be used in relation to a non-suicidal person. His preferred response is to emphasise the liberty to commit suicide: people should be free to end their lives without the interference of the state. However, interestingly, he is opposed to positively assisting suicide. He believes that once the medical or legal establishment are controlling access to assistance in suicide, this would give them powers to determine who should – or should not – have access to these services. Suicide should be a private affair. By contrast Baril argues that 'the State should offer assisted suicide as one among several potential options, carefully guiding and counselling those who are contemplating this possibility'.[21]

Supporters of this kind of approach draw an analogy with disability discrimination. Just as ablism might say to a disabled person, 'you would be better off being "normal"', the 'suicidalist' response to the suicidal person, it might be argued, is 'you would be better off being "normal" and not feeling suicidal'. Our response to your suicidal feelings is to seek to eradicate them, just as an ableist response to disability is to seek to eradicate it.

These arguments are not convincing, for a number of reasons. A response to the disability analogy will illustrate my point. While there are plenty of people who (quite rightly) rejoice in their different bodies and conditions, there seem to be few who embrace their suicidal feelings. Indeed, by their very nature, the suicidal person wants their suicidal feelings to end. Thus, while quite understandably many parents with disabilities would be content if their child had a disability, I cannot believe there are any suicidal people who would wish those feelings on their children.

[17] A Baril, 'Suicidism: A New Theoretical Framework to Conceptualize Suicide from an Anti-Oppressive Perspective' (2020) 40 *University of Ottawa Disability Studies Quarterly* 1.

[18] Z Bayatrizi, *Life Sentences. The Modern Ordering of Mortality* (University of Toronto Press, 2008).

[19] D Webb, *Thinking About Suicide. Contemplating and Comprehending the Urge to Die* (PCCS Books, 2011).

[20] T Szasz, *Fatal Freedom: The Ethics and Politics of Suicide* (Praeger, 2002).

[21] Baril (n 17).

I agree with Baril, who says:

> Like Deaf, disabled and crip people who told us, in the past decades, that they don't want the 'ideal solution' that mainstream societies offer them (eg cochlear implants, cures, etc) but instead want their voices, perspectives, needs and claims respected and supported, suicidal people should not have imposed on them pre-conceived solutions devised by the majority of people who don't experience their reality but who nevertheless believe that they have the best solutions to offer.[22]

What I wonder, however, is whether Baril is talking about people with suicidal feelings, rather than those attempting suicide. Elsewhere Baril argues:

> Attempting to destigmatize suicide and to recognize it as one viable option among others – albeit one that requires considerable critical reflection with the support of relatives, friends, and healthcare professionals – may help a majority of suicidal people find solutions other than suicide along their exploratory journey of life and death. Simultaneously, the harm-reduction approach I suggest here may allow a small number of suicidal people who are determined to die to be accompanied while preparing their death.[23]

The quote is interesting because it acknowledges that only a small number of suicidal people are determined to die. Even they would choose not to be suicidal if possible. It is not clear that Baril is opposed to suicide prevention as such, but rather a more sensitive approach to those with depression and suicidal ideation. It is an argument for an approach based on listening, building relationships, coming alongside, rather than compulsory treatment.[24] It is misleading to suggest that suicide prevention normally involves restraint, as we will see as this chapter develops. In 2019 Lewitzka et al[25] published a thorough review of national suicide prevention programmes and found that medical intervention formed only a tiny proportion of the successful forms of intervention.

B. Ineffectiveness of Suicide Prevention

A rather different argument is that suicidal interventions are ineffective. Sullivan,[26] for example, considers the arguments against interventions for in-hospital patients designed to prevent self-harm. He suggests that such policies may be counter-productive and end up increasing, rather than decreasing, rates of self-harm, by depriving patients of control over their situation. There is, indeed, some evidence

[22] ibid.
[23] ibid.
[24] S Fitzpatrick, 'Epistemic Justice and the Struggle for Critical Suicide Literacy' (2020) 34 *Social Epistemology* 555.
[25] U Lewitzka et al, 'Are National Suicide Prevention Programs Effective? A Comparison of 4 Verum and 4 Control Countries over 30 Years' (2019) 19 *BMC Psychiatry* 158.
[26] P Sullivan, 'Risk and Responding to Self Injury: Is Harm Minimisation a Step Too Far?' (2019) 14 *Journal of Mental Health Training, Education and Practice* 1.

that medications to deal with depression and suicidal feelings may increase – rather than relieve – suicidal feelings.[27] However, it would be wrong to state that hospital detention and medication are always, or even mostly, counterproductive.[28] Indeed, the relatively low rates of suicide among in-patients in mental health establishment demonstrate that. Rather, it seems more plausible to express two concerns. The first is that for some patients, detention and/or medication is counter-productive, but we cannot predict who that will be. Second, there is a real concern about 'false positives'. In other words, the difficulties in predicting suicide mean that there are extensive deprivations of freedom of people who would not go on to commit suicide. Allen[29] notes that 60 per cent of suicides were categorised as low-risk suicides on the standard assessment. But only 3 per cent of those assessed as high risk do go on to commit suicide.[30]

C. Conclusions on the Case against Suicide Prevention

The concerns raised in the previous two sections are powerful points. However, they are primarily focused on detention and medically interventionist policies. While the most dramatic, these are a tiny portion of those with suicide ideation.[31] A major review by Gil Zalcman and colleagues[32] reviewed 1,797 studies into the effectiveness of various suicide interventions. They found the most effective to be: (i) restricting access to lethal substances, which had reduced suicides by 43 per cent as compared with 2005 figures; and (ii) putting in place barriers at hot spots for suicide, which reduced rates by 86 per cent. The efficacy in relation to pharmacological intervention was less clear, but a combination of pharmacological and psychological treatment was an important and useful part of prevention in a small number of cases.

Suicide prevention strategies based on community engagement, relationship building and respect appear far more effective than coercive ones. Indeed, it is striking that the six most successful methods of suicide prevention identified by the WHO were:

- the treatment of those with mental disorders;
- gun possession control;

[27] Bertolote (n 8).
[28] G Malhi, 'The Ethics of Suicide in Mental Illness: Novel Neuroscientific Perspectives' (2019) 19 *American Journal of Bioethics* 294.
[29] N Allan, 'The Right to Life in a Suicidal State' (2013) 36 *International Journal of Law and Psychiatry* 350.
[30] G Newton-Howes, 'Risk in Mental Health: A Review on and of the Psychiatrist' (2018) 13 *Journal of Mental Health Training, Education and Practice* 14.
[31] The Zero Suicide Alliance, *Evidence Review: National Approaches to Suicide Prevention Strategies and Policies* (ZSA, 2020).
[32] Zalsman et al (n 6).

- detoxification of domestic gas;
- detoxification of car emissions;
- control of toxic substance availability; and
- a toning down of reports in the press.

The anti-suicide prevention arguments are much much weaker against such interventions.

IV. Developing Suicide Prevention Policies

The WHO has called on suicide prevention to be prioritised through global and national suicide prevention policies. These need to take into account social, psychological and cultural factors.[33] It lists the following benefits of developing suicide prevention strategies:

- a national strategy not only outlines the scope and magnitude of the problem but, more crucially, recognises that suicidal behaviour is a major public health problem;
- a strategy signals the commitment of a government to addressing the issue;
- a cohesive strategy recommends a structural framework, incorporating various aspects of suicide prevention;
- a strategy provides authoritative guidance on key evidence-based suicide prevention activities – ie it identifies what works and what does not work;
- a strategy identifies key stakeholders and allocates specific responsibilities to them. Moreover, it outlines the necessary coordination among these various groups;
- a strategy identifies crucial gaps in existing legislation, service provision and data collection;
- a strategy indicates the human and financial resources required for interventions;
- a strategy shapes advocacy, awareness-raising and media communications;
- a strategy proposes a robust framework of monitoring and evaluation, thereby instilling a sense of accountability among those in charge of interventions;
- a strategy provides a context for a research agenda on suicidal behaviours.

The WHO emphasise how a successful suicide prevention strategy will not be seen simply as a matter for health care professionals, but include those involved

[33] World Health Organisation, *Suicide* (WHO, 2018).

in all areas of government. They highlight the need to reduce the stigma around suicide and increase awareness of the issues. Swedish suicide prevention policies are referred to by the WHO as being good practice. It lists the following:[34]

(1) promote good life opportunities for less privileged groups;
(2) reduce alcohol consumption in the population and in groups at high risk for suicide;
(3) reduce access to means and methods of suicide;
(4) view suicide as a psychological mistake;
(5) improve medical, psychological and psychosocial initiatives;
(6) distribute knowledge about evidence-based methods for reducing suicide;
(7) raise skill levels among staff and other key individuals in the care services;
(8) perform 'root cause' or event analyses after suicide;
(9) support voluntary organisations.

This list gives some indication of the breadth of suicide prevention measures that can and should be used. I will explore these further under the headings of: universal measures, targeted at the whole population; selective measures, targeted at particular groups; and individual measures, which are targeted at particular people.

V. Universal Interventions

Universal interventions are actions targeted at the general population, designed to discourage suicide. An example may be Suicide Prevention Day which aims to raise awareness and encourage conversations about the issue. We might also include attempts to place barriers at 'suicide hotspots' to discourage suicide. There may also be interventions which do not have suicide as the primary focus, but which will have benefits in relation to suicide production, for example, action tackling alcohol misuse will have a range of benefits, including suicide prevention.

One of the benefits of these universal interventions is that they can reach individuals who do not fall within the normal categories of being at risk. This is important because, as the National Confidential Inquiry into Suicide and Safety in Mental Health found, nearly three quarters of suicides occur in patients who did not have a recognised mental health disorder.[35] I will discuss in more detail three particular forms of intervention in this category.

[34] ibid.

[35] Patient Safety Group (n 15). See further B Ahmedani et al, 'Health Care Contacts in the Year before Suicide Death' (2014) 29 *Journal of General Internal Medicine* 870.

A. Restricting Access to Means of Suicide

The most obvious, and perhaps most effective, way to reduce suicide levels is to address the means used to commit it.[36] There is, for example, ample evidence that restrictions on gun ownership,[37] removal of hanging and strangulation points in psychiatric impact settings and prisons; and putting up barriers at high-risk locations, especially rail and underground networks, are highly effective methods of reducing suicide. These seem to be particularly effective in relation to 'impulsive suicides': 'acts of self-harm involving little preparation or premeditation'.[38] One study found 55 per cent of suicides to be impulsive[39] and 28 per cent to be of an intermediate level of impulsivity. Williams et al found that 40 per cent of suicide survivors contemplated suicide for less than five minutes before attempting it.[40] This highlights the way that restricting access to ready means for suicide can impact on rates significantly; the assumption that if the means are not readily available, the suicide ideation will pass, does indeed often seem to be correct.[41] An international comparison of studies found that control of access to analgesics created a 43 per cent decrease in suicide, and even higher percentages on restricting access to hot spots for jumping, with a reduction of 86 per cent in some studies.[42] Safety fences at the Eiffel Tower, Sydney Harbour Bridge and Empire State Building have all significantly reduced suicide rates.[43] Studies of these interventions found that they do not simply shift suicides to a different venue.[44] In South Korea there was an 11 per cent drop in the suicide rate after the most commonly-used pesticides for suicide were banned.[45] International comparisons and comparisons between US states found a strong link between the prevalence of gun ownership and rates of suicide.[46] In England there were notable reductions in suicide rates following

[36] HM Government, *Preventing Suicide in England: Fourth Progress Report of the Cross-Government Outcomes Strategy to Save Lives* (HM Government, 2019), although it is impossible to prove the correlation beyond doubt; S Shahtahmasebi, 'What Does a Statistician Know about Suicide and Suicide Prevention' (2018) 5 *Dynamics of Human Health* 1.

[37] J Pirkis et al, 'The Effectiveness of Structural Interventions at Suicide Hotspots: A Meta-Analysis' (2013) 42 *International Journal of Epidemiology* 541.

[38] E Lewiecki and S Miller, 'Suicide, Guns and Public Policy' (2013) 103 *American Journal of Public Health* 27.

[39] E Baca-Garcia et al, 'A Prospective Study of the Paradoxical Relationship between Impulsivity and Lethality of Suicide Attempts' (2001) 62 *Journal of Clinical Psychiatry* 560.

[40] C Williams et al, 'Impulsive Suicidal Behavior' (1980) 36 *Journal of Clinical Psychology* 90; E Deisenhammer et al, 'The Duration of the Suicidal Process: How Much Time is Left for Intervention between Consideration and Accomplishment of a Suicide Attempt?' (2009) 79 *Journal of Clinical Psychiatry* 19.

[41] Public Health England, *Preventing Suicides in Public Places* (Public Health England, 2020).

[42] Zalsman et al (n 6).

[43] J Lin and T Lu, 'Association between the Accessibility to Lethal Methods and Method-Specific Suicide Rates: An Ecological Study in Taiwan' (2006) 67 *Journal of Clinical Psychiatry* 1074.

[44] ibid.

[45] ibid.

[46] S Stefan, *Rational Suicide, Irrational Laws: Examining Current Approaches to Suicide in Policy and Law* (Oxford University Press, 2016).

the removal of carbon monoxide from household gas, and the introduction of catalytic converters to remove carbon monoxide from car exhaust fumes.[47] There was a 43 per cent reduction in the number of people dying from paracetamol poisoning between 1993 and 2009 following restrictions on the number of pills that could be put in a packet.[48] Barriers installed at the Clifton Suspension Bridge in Bristol in 1998 led to a halving of the number of suicides in the area.[49] Notably, these did not seem to lead to people simply using alternative methods to commit suicide.[50] This reinforces the view that many suicides do not reflect a settled desire to die. A major review found that 'limiting access to methods is one of the suicide prevention efforts with the most robust supporting evidence'.[51]

B. Social Media

There is widespread concern over the representation of suicide and encouragement of suicide within social media. In England the issue was brought to public attention following the death of Molly Russell, who committed suicide after accessing graphic suicide and self-harm content on social media sites.[52] It is difficult to prove a causal link between suicide and viewing suicide material online but a person's use of social media can give a clue about suicidal intent.[53] One survey of the general population aged 21 found that 9.1 per cent had searched for information about self-harm and 7.5 per cent about suicide.[54] In a study of young people, 1 per cent reported visiting a website that encourage self-harm or suicide. Those who visited such websites were found to be seven times more likely to think about taking their own life and 11 times more likely to think about self-harm, even adjusting for other known risk factors.[55] There does, therefore, appear to be a link between

[47] N Kreitman, 'The Coal Gas Story. United Kingdom Suicide Rates, 1960–71' (1976) 30 *British Journal of Preventive Social Medicine* 86; J Turvill et al, 'Change in Occurrence of Paracetamol Overdose in UK after Introduction of Blister Packs' (2000) 355 *The Lancet* 2048.

[48] K Hawton et al, 'Risk Factors for Suicide in Individuals with Depression: A Systematic Review' (2013) 147 *Journal of Affective Disorders* 1.

[49] O Bennewith et al, 'Effect of Barriers on the Clifton Suspension Bridge, England, on Local Patterns of Suicide: Implications for Prevention' (2007) 190 *British Journal of Psychiatry* 266.

[50] Stefan (n 46).

[51] J Florentine and C Crane, 'Suicide Prevention by Limiting Access to Methods: A Review of Theory and Practice' (2010) 70 *Social Science Medicine* 1626.

[52] M Savage, 'Health Secretary Tells Social Media Firms to Protect Children after Girl's Death', *The Guardian*, 26 January 2019, www.theguardian.com/politics/2019/jan/26/matt-hancock-facebook-social-media-suicide-self-harm-young-people, accessed 15 December 2021.

[53] Patient Safety Group (n 15).

[54] J Heron et al, 'Exposure to, and Searching for, Information about Suicide and Self-harm on the Internet: Prevalence and Predictors in a Population Based Cohort of Young Adults' (2015) 185 *Journal of Affective Disorders* 239.

[55] K Mitchell et al, 'Exposure to Websites that Encourage Self-harm and Suicide: Prevalence Rates and Association with Actual Thoughts of Self-harm and Thoughts of Suicide in the United States' (2014) 37 *Journal of Adolescence* 1335.

accessing such content online and suicidal or self-harm thoughts, especially for young people. It is, however, worth noting that in the Mars et al study, 81 per cent of those who accessed harmful sites also accessed helpful sites.[56] There certainly seems scope here for positive interventions to prevent suicide.

The broader media too has a role to play in suicide prevention.[57] The UK Government Suicide Prevention Strategy, published in 2012, noted 'two key aspects to supporting the media in delivering sensitive approaches to suicide and suicidal behaviour':

- promoting the responsible reporting and portrayal of suicide and suicidal behaviour in the media; and
- continuing to support the internet industry to remove content that encourages suicide and provide ready access to suicide prevention services.

The Samaritans have produced Media Guidelines for reporting suicide.[58] The Independent Press Standards Organisation (IPSO) has a Code of Practice, which states:

> When reporting suicide, to prevent simulative acts care should be taken to avoid excessive detail of the method used, while taking into account the media's right to report legal proceedings.[59]

C. Stigma

Suicide carries a stigma and that can discourage people from seeking help or admitting they are facing challenges. The past notions of suicide as something wicked and of a criminal nature still linger. Christine Morgan, a suicide advisor to the Australian Government identifies stigma as a major barrier to suicide prevention.[60] She argues that those with suicidal feelings have a sense of personal shame, and fear the stigma they will face if they open up to others; this deters them seeking help from others. The Campaign Group Live Through This writes:

> 'Suicide' is a dirty word in this country. It's a sin. It's taboo. It's selfish. It's not an easy topic to discuss and because we, as a culture, don't know how to approach it, it's easily swept under a rug. The problem is that suicide is a pervasive public health issue. I get

[56] B Mars et al, 'Predictors of Future Suicide Attempt among Adolescents with Suicidal Thoughts or Non-Suicidal Self-harm: A Population-Based Birth Cohort Study' (2019) 6 *Lancet Psychiatry* 327.

[57] M Sisask and A Värnik, 'Media Roles in Suicide Prevention: A Systematic Review' (2012) 9 *International Journal of Environmental Research and Public Health* 134.

[58] The Samaritans, *Media Guidelines for Reporting Suicide* (The Samaritans, 2020).

[59] IPSO, *Editors' Code of Practice* (IPSO, 2021) Art 5.

[60] K Murphy, '"Horrific" Level of Stigma: Biggest Barrier to Suicide Prevention is Discrimination', *The Guardian*, 19 November 2019, www.theguardian.com/society/2019/nov/13/horrific-level-of-stigma-biggest-barrier-to-suicide-prevention-is-discrimination, accessed 15 December 2021.

it: we're afraid of death. But avoiding it and pretending it doesn't exist is nothing more than wilfully perpetuating ignorance.[61]

D. Drinking Water

One radical suggestion is to add lithium to drinking water.[62] The suggestion from Jared Ng and colleagues[63] is based on the observation that in places where there is a naturally occurring level of lithium in the groundwater, there is a lower suicide rate. For example, a study looking at different counties in Texas found the suicide rate was 14.2 per 100,000 in low lithium areas and 8.7 in the relatively high areas.[64] It has also been found to have an impact on rates of violence and Alzheimer's disease.[65] This is particularly interesting as a means of suicide prevention, as many cases of suicide cannot be predicted and so giving this to the whole population is appropriate, given that it appears to have no serious side effects. There is a strong precedent for this, as fluoride is added to tap water for oral health. As bioethicist Jacob Appel concludes: 'If we are willing to ingest fluoride to prevent tooth decay, surely we can tolerate a trace of lithium to prevent suicides'.[66] Of course, there are difficulties with the proposal. It is unclear how much water needs to be drunk in order for it to be effective, and that will impact on how many people can benefit. More significantly, there is the question of whether people should have the option to choose what chemicals are in public water. There are, of course, many chemicals and it is not clear whether many people would specifically object to lithium.

E. Economic and Social Interventions

In Chapter 3 the links between suicide and economic deprivation were explored. It seems from that discussion that two areas are ripe for intervention. First, there are clearly issues around the way that those who are dependent on the state for financial support are dealt with by public authorities. As discussed in Chapter 3, it is clear that the system left those dependent on benefits feeling ignored, stigmatised and trapped. There is ample scope for improvement in those systems. Second, it seems

[61] See https://livethroughthis.org/.

[62] A Vita et al, 'Lithium in Drinking Water and Suicide Prevention: A Review of the Evidence' (2015) 30 *International Clinical Psychopharmacology* 1.

[63] J Ng et al, 'Adding Lithium to Drinking Water for Suicide Prevention – The Ethics' (2019) 12 *Public Health Ethics* 274.

[64] G Schrauzer, 'Lithium: Occurrence, Dietary Intakes, Nutritional Essentiality' (2002) 21 *The Journal of American College of Nutrition* 14.

[65] Ng et al (n 63).

[66] J Appel, 'Beyond Fluoride: Pharmaceuticals, Drinking Water and the Public Health', *Huffington Post*, 21 December 2009, https://fluoridealert.org/news/beyond-fluoride-pharmaceuticals-drinking-water-the-public-health/.

that public spending itself impacts on suicide rates.[67] Matsubayashi, Sekijima and Ueda[68] in their study of Japan concluded:

> These findings suggest that local suicide rates could be reduced when local governments increase their spending. The magnitude of the effect is not trivial. During our study period, the average male suicide rate for the middle-aged was 31.19, and a one-percent increase in government spending would translate to a reduction of the suicide rate per 100,000 by 0.078 cases, which translates to 0.36 cases of suicide in each prefecture and 17 suicides across the whole of Japan per year.

Clearly there are complex issues beyond the scope of this book to address around the extent and nature of economic provision, but it is clear that government financial support for citizens is an important part of suicide prevention.

Interestingly the 2019 UK Government review of suicide policy[69] recognises the importance of social effects. It accepts 'the well-documented adverse impact of periods of recession on suicide rates', noting that 'there is a strong relationship between unemployment and suicide in men, with studies examining suicides during the last recession finding a 1.4 per cent rise in suicide rates for every 10 per cent increase in unemployment in men'. It highlights the impact of debt, noting that those in debt are twice as likely to consider suicide as the general population.

In addition to economic interventions there are a wide range of social interventions that can combat suicide. These include interventions tackling loneliness,[70] meeting the needs of homeless people, debt[71] and drug/alcohol misuse. A report into the links between social deprivation and suicide in the UK concluded:

> There is a strong association between area-level deprivation and suicidal behaviour: as area-level deprivation increases, so does suicidal behaviour. Suicide rates are two to three times higher in the most deprived neighbourhoods compared to the most affluent.[72]

The 2019 Government review also highlighted social exclusion as a cause of suicide:

> Suicide is the second most common cause of death among people who are homeless or rough sleepers in England and Wales, with 13% of deaths among homeless people or rough sleepers in 2018 being due to suicide.

The review states that tackling inequalities is a priority in all aspects of the national suicide prevention policy.

[67] B Barr et al, 'Suicides Associated with the 2008–10 Economic Recession in England: Time Trend Analysis' (2012) 124 *British Medical Journal* 345.

[68] T Matsubayashi et al, 'Government Spending, Recession, and Suicide: Evidence from Japan' (2020) 20 *BMC Public Health* 243.

[69] HM Government (2021) (n 7).

[70] R Shaw et al, 'Living Alone, Loneliness and Lack of Emotional Support as Predictors of Suicide and Self-harm: A Nine-year Follow up of the UK Biobank Cohort' (2021) 279 *Journal of Affective Disorders* 316.

[71] The Samaritans, *Dying from Inequality* (The Samaritans, 2017).

[72] Ibid.

VI. Selective Interventions

Selective interventions are aimed at particular groups of people who are seen as being particularly prone to committing suicide. Examples of such groups may include: children whose parents are clinically depressed; victims of sexual abuse; veterans; or those suffering bereavements.[73] It can also include groups of people who work in particular professions or work in places which have high rates of suicide, such as doctors, nurses and farmers.[74] The kind of interventions can include focused education and information campaigns, ensuring professionals take special care with such groups to determine whether there is a suicide risk.[75]

The Fourth Progress Report on the UK Government's Suicide Prevention Strategy identified 'young and middle-aged men, people in the care of mental health services, people in contact with the criminal justice system, specific occupational groups, such as doctors, nurses, veterinary workers, farmers and agricultural workers, and people with a history of self-harm'.[76] I will say a little more about a few groups where there has been particular concern.

A. Prisoners

There are considerable concerns over the high rate of suicide in prisons.[77] Suicide is the leading cause of death in prisons in the US.[78] In the 12 months to March 2021, there were 79 suicides in English and Welsh prisons[79] and 55,542 incidents of self-harm in the 12 months to December 2020. There were 566 incidents per 1,000 prisoners in the male prisoner population in the 12 months to December 2020, down 13 per cent from 653 incidents per 1,000 prisoners in the 12 months to December 2019. In recent years approximately one in 1,000 prisoners commit suicide.[80] Male prisoners die at 3.7 times the rate of the general population.[81] However, it is difficult to determine the extent to which this is linked to prison per se as opposed to the higher rates of mental ill health and substance abuse among prisoners generally.

[73] G Hadlaczky et al, 'Suicide Prevention Strategies' in R O'Connor and J Pirkis (eds), *The International Handbook of Suicide Prevention* (J Wiley and Sons, 2016).

[74] HM Government (n 36).

[75] D Ridge et al, 'How Men Step Back – and Recover – from Suicide Attempts: A Relational and Gendered Account' (2021) 43 *Sociology of Health and Illness* 238.

[76] A Haylen et al, *Suicide Prevention: Policy and Strategy* (House of Commons Library, 2020).

[77] L Favril et al, 'Factors associated with the transition from suicidal ideation to suicide attempt in prison' (2020) 63 *European Psychiatry* 101.

[78] R Canning and J Dvoskinm, 'Preventing Suicide in Detention and Correctional Facilities' in J Wooldredge and P Smith (eds), *The Oxford Handbook of Prisons and Imprisonment* (Oxford University Press, 2018).

[79] National Statistics, *Safety in Custody Statistics, England and Wales: Deaths in Prison Custody to March 2021, Assaults and Self-harm to December 2020* (National Statistics, 2020).

[80] Office for National Statistics, *Drug-related Deaths and Suicide in Prison Custody in England and Wales: 2008 to 2016* (ONS, 2019).

[81] ibid.

A government minister was questioned about suicide and self-harm in prison in September 2020 and explained that the government was taking the following steps:

> We have given over 25,000 prison staff better training to spot and prevent self-harm;
>
> We have refreshed our partnership with the Samaritans which supports the Listeners scheme, whereby selected prisoners are trained to provide emotional support to their fellow prisoners;
>
> We have also piloted improvements to Assessment, Care in Custody and Teamwork (ACCT), the multidisciplinary case management approach to supporting prisoners thought to be at risk of self-harm or suicide. We are currently planning the resumption of roll-out of the revised ACCT across the prison estate.[82]

B. Young People

Suicides of young people raise particularly strong emotions. The 2012 Suicide Prevention Strategy for England proposed an approach focused on children and young people, recommending a school-based prevention strategy to include:

- a co-ordinated school response to people at risk and staff training;
- awareness among staff to help identify high-risk signs or behaviours (depression, drugs, self-harm) and protocols on how to respond;
- signposting parents to sources of information on signs of emotional problems and risk;
- clear referral routes to specialist mental health services.[83]

The strategy adds that 'appropriate training on suicide and self-harm should be available for staff working in schools and colleges'. There is now extensive guidance for public authorities and educational establishments to avoid clusters of suicide which can occur when a death occurs in close communities such as schools and universities.[84] A suicide cluster is described as:

> a situation in which more suicides than expected occur in terms of time, place, or both. It is difficult to precisely define a cluster. A suicide cluster usually includes 3 or more deaths; however, 2 suicides occurring in a specific community or setting (for example a school) in a short time period should also be taken very seriously in terms of possible links and impacts (even if the deaths are apparently unconnected), particularly in the case of young people.[85]

[82] Haylen et al (n 76).
[83] HM Government (n 2).
[84] Public Health England, *Identifying and Responding to Suicide Clusters* (Public Health England, 2019).
[85] Ibid.

VII. Individual Interventions

Here we discuss cases where particular individuals are identified as being at risk and interventions are designed to prevent them committing suicide. The most standard form of personalised intervention is through mental health services. The 2017 National Confidential Inquiry into Suicide and Safety in Mental Health[86] found that the rate of patient suicide has reduced from 111.5 per 100,000 patients in 2005, to 63.7 per 100,000 patients in 2015. This indicates a degree of improvement in suicide intervention, although clearly there is more work to be done.

The range of personal interventions is extensive. We have seen in Chapter 7 that the Mental Health Act 1983 allows for the detention and treatment of patients with a mental disorder, and is used extensively with suicidal people. The Mental Capacity Act 2005 also provides for treatment of those who lack capacity. Less dramatic forms of care, through crisis resolution and home treatment teams, seek to provide interventions which do not involve detention. In fact the Patient Safety Group report[87] states '[Crisis Resolution and Home Treatment Teams] had become the default for acute mental health care because of the pressure on in-patient beds'. This may put 'a dampener' on the good news about reduced in-patient suicide rates, as there has been an increase in suicides among CRHT patients.[88] Indeed, there is a clear link between deaths within two weeks of discharge and being admitted for less than seven days. This certainly raises the concern that getting people out of hospital to free up beds quickly is being prioritised over patient safety.[89] The root problem, no doubt, is the lack of funding for mental health services.[90]

A survey of case notes of those who had committed suicide found:

- 14 per cent had an inadequate mental state assessment (mental state assessments should always include suicide);
- 26 per cent had an inadequate risk formulation;
- 38 per cent had an inadequate risk 'management plan'.[91]

These statistics could be seen as having two messages. One is the limited power of intervention. The fact that 62 per cent of patients who committed suicide had been appropriately assessed and given an adequate risk management plan is a powerful reminder that even with appropriate intervention the risk of suicide is very present

[86] L Appleby et al, *The National Confidential Inquiry into Suicide and Safety in Mental Health. Annual Report: England, Northern Ireland, Scotland and Wales* (University of Manchester, 2021).

[87] Patient Safety Group (n 15).

[88] L Bojanic et al, 'Early Post-Discharge Suicide in Mental Health Patients: Findings From a National Clinical Survey' (2020) 11 *Frontiers of Psychiatry* 502.

[89] Patient Safety Group (n 15).

[90] V Moore, 'Leaving Hospital: A Step Too Far for Risk-Based Regulation?' (2020) 28 *Medical Law Review* 675.

[91] MS Rahman et al, *Quality of Risk Assessment Prior to Suicide and Homicide: A Pilot Study* (University of Manchester, 2013).

and there are limits about what can be done to prevent suicide. The other message is that there are failures to put in place appropriate protections. While 86 per cent of patients who committed suicide had been appropriately assessed, 38 per cent then had not received an appropriate management plan.

Assessing the risk of suicide is extremely difficult.[92] One study found that 60 per cent of those who died from suicide after engagement with health practitioners had denied having suicidal thoughts.[93] The difficulty in assessing the risk of suicide is acknowledged in the Patient Safety Group Reports which states that:

> The current approach to risk assessment and responding only to those identified as 'high risk' is fundamentally flawed, and the use of terms such as 'low risk' or 'high risk' is unreliable, open to misinterpretation and potentially unsafe.

A safety plan can be an important response. This is 'an agreed set of activities, strategies, people and organisations to contact for support if someone becomes suicidal or if their suicidal thoughts get worse or if they might self-harm'.[94] Indeed the Royal College of Psychiatry suggests that all who have engaged in self-harm or suicidal thoughts should have a safety plan.[95] It should include:

- individualised strategies/activities to instil hope;
- calming/distracting activities;
- restriction of access to common means of suicide;
- contacts for social and crisis support.[96]

There is some evidence of growing success with such plans.[97]

A common form of intervention involves pharmacological intervention. The challenge is that these often take a long time to take effect: in relation to anti-depressant medication, a reduction of risk can take at least two months to manifest. Fawcett and Busch, for example, suggest that lithium carbonate can reduce suicide risk, but only when given for six months.[98] Further, severely depressed patients may not even respond to the medication.[99] Fawcett and Busch[100] suggest that around a third of severely depressed patients do not have a notable response to medication and a notable proportion – between 30 and 60 per cent – will experience a relapse

[92] M Senior et al, 'Identifying Predictors of Suicide in Severe Mental Illness: A Feasibility Study of a Clinical Prediction Rule (Oxford Mental Illness and Suicide Tool or OxMIS)' (2020) 11 *Frontiers in Psychiatry* 268.

[93] C McHugh et al, 'Association between Suicidal Ideation and Suicide: Meta-analyses of Odds Ratios, Sensitivity, Specificity and Positive Predictive Value' (2019) 5 *British Journal of Psychiatry* E1.

[94] Patient Safety Group (n 15).

[95] ibid.

[96] ibid.

[97] J Zonana et al, 'The Impact of Safety Plans in an Outpatient Clinic' (2018) 39 *Crisis* 304.

[98] J Fawcett and K Busch, 'The Pharmacologic Treatment of Suicidal Patients' in Nock (n 8).

[99] N Riblet et al, 'Strategies to Prevent Death by Suicide: Meta-Analysis of Randomised Controlled Trials' (2017) 210 *British Journal of Psychiatry* 396.

[100] Fawcett and Busch (n 98).

into a suicidal state, despite some initial success in response. While in the popular imagination medication can be seen as the solution to depression, it is certainly not an automatic solution and in cases of suicidal behaviour, it has been difficult to find conclusive proof of effectiveness.[101] While there are a growing range of products available, the suicidal feelings can remain for a period of time, and there is often disappointment that the medication appears to make no difference for some time, particularly when coupled with its side effects.

The issue of compulsory interventions has been discussed further in Chapter 7, but the evidence on the issue is complex.[102] While it certainly seems that compulsory admission to hospital does save lives, the difficulty is in identifying which people will – or will not – benefit from it.[103] This creates the risk of serious invasion of a person's human rights, which may be unnecessary or even exacerbate their mental health challenges. As Owens et al put it:

> There is now compelling evidence that suicide, being a low-frequency event, is very difficult to predict. The clinical methods for predicting suicide among patients have a very poor predictive capacity[104]

A further study found that 95 per cent of those assessed as at 'high risk' of suicide will not die by suicide and that half of all suicides in a group of patients were among those assessed as being at low risk.[105] These challenges and the increased risk of suicide following discharge[106] indicate the need to exercise great caution. While, of course, it is unsurprising that there are higher rates of suicide among those admitted to hospital and then released than among the general public, there must be a concern that the stigma and isolation created by compulsory detention exacerbates a risk of suicide.[107] One can certainly imagine the impact of a person who attempted suicide being told 'You're supposed to be an intelligent person. What on earth are you doing a stupid thing like this for?'[108]

[101] K Hawton et al, 'Pharmacological Interventions for Self-harm in Adults: Three Trials Indicated No Overall Improvements' (2015) 6 *Cochrane Database of Systematic Reviews* CD011777.

[102] D Wang and E Colucci, 'Should Compulsory Admission to Hospital Be Part of Suicide Prevention Strategies?' (2017) 41 *British Journal of Psychology Bulletin* 169.

[103] I Hunt et al, 'Suicide in Recently Admitted Psychiatric In-patients: A Case-Control Study' (2013) 44 *Journal of Affective Disorders* 123; E Agerbo, 'High Income, Employment, Postgraduate Education, and Marriage: A Suicidal Cocktail among Psychiatric Patients' (2007) 64 *Archives of General Psychiatry* 13777.

[104] D Owens et al, 'Fatal and Non-fatal Repetition of Selfharm' (2002) 181 *British Journal of Psychiatry* 193; M Large and C Ryan, 'Disturbing Findings about the Risk of Suicide and Psychiatric Hospitals' (2014) 49 *Social Psychiatry and Psychiatric Epidemiology* 1353; R Mulder et al, 'The Futility of Risk Prediction in Psychiatry' (2016) 209 *British Journal of Psychiatry* 271; M Chan et al, 'Predicting Suicide Following Self-harm: Systematic Review of Risk Factors and Risk Scales' (2016) 209 *British Journal of Psychiatry* 277.

[105] M Large et al, 'Meta-analysis of Longitudinal Cohort Studies of Suicide Risk Assessment among Psychiatric Patients: Heterogeneity in Results and Lack of Improvement over Time' (2016) 11 *PLoS ONE* 6.

[106] Bertolote (n 8).

[107] G Newton-Howes and R Mullen, 'Coercion in Psychiatric Care: Systematic Review of Correlates and Themes' (2011) 65 *Psychiatric Services* 465.

[108] Patient Safety Group (n 15).

The 2020 Royal College of Psychiatry Report notes variation in the experiences of those who attempt suicide: 'Although some report being treated with respect and compassion, others have felt belittled or ignored'. The report noted that 'at-risk patients are not being identified and/or offered the mental health treatment that could have prevented their death'.[109] Indeed, it concludes 'that the current approach to risk assessment is fundamentally flawed'.[110] As the report notes, this is becoming increasingly common:

> We note that increasingly, practitioners working with patients who are at elevated risk of suicide think in terms of mitigating the risk rather than managing it. We link this to the importance of Safety Plans being co-created with the patient, which encourages communication with family and friends.[111]

The way ahead requires an approach based on co-operation and mutual communication.

VIII. Problems in Preventing Suicide

Suicide prevention is extremely complex to put into practice. First, as we have seen, it can be extremely hard to assess the level of suicide risk.[112] In particular, patients can deny suicidal feelings for a range of reasons. A second difficulty is that patients have a right to refuse treatment. While the Mental Health Act 1983 permits compulsory detention and treatment, this itself creates risk. It is also not really an effective response as the reduction in risk from taking anti-depressant medication may not occur for the first two months. Third, studies have shown that the vast majority of suicides are facing a number of challenges. Finding solutions and approaches to all of the difficulties a person is coping with can be very difficult.[113]

It is enormously difficult to assess the success of suicide prevention schemes. It can be very hard to identify why an individual does not commit suicide or why a suicide statistic has dropped. There is also an ethical issue of whether it is appropriate to have a control group of suicidal people who do not receive an intervention, making the standard model of randomised control trials ethically dubious.[114] It is worth noting, for example, that in the UK one in five adults has reported

[109] ibid.
[110] ibid.
[111] ibid.
[112] PM Kleespies, 'Medical Illness, Suicide, and Assisted Death' in PM Kleespies (ed), *The Oxford Handbook of Behavioral Emergencies and Crises* (Oxford University Press, 2016).
[113] E Townsend et al, 'Self-Harm and Life Problems: Findings from the Multicentre Study of Self-harm in England' (2016) 51 *Social Psychiatry and Psychiatric Epidemiology* 183.
[114] D Sisti and S Joffe, 'Implications of Zero Suicide for Suicide Prevention Research' (2018) 320 *JAMA* 1633.

considering suicide and one in 15 has taken steps towards suicide.[115] Only a small proportion go on to commit suicide. Indeed, around a half of those who attempt suicide seek help afterwards. Around a quarter seek help from GPs and a quarter from hospitals or specialised services. Large et al suggest in their meta-analysis of studies that it was not possible to identify a single clinical risk factor as a sufficiently accurate basis for interventions. Ward-Ciesilski and Linehan,[116] writing in 2014, state:

> To date, there have been only 46 randomized, controlled trials (RCTs) of treatments designed specifically to target suicidal behaviors. Of these trials, only a fraction of them have been shown to effectively reduce these target behaviors.

The difficulties in finding an effective prevention lead Susan Stefan[117] to say:

> The current model of suicide prevention is not working, in part because it is focused too specifically: too much on the individual instead of the environment, too much on preventing the moment of self-destruction rather than what led up to that moment. The public health model is cheaper and more effective than the medical model, in both fiscal and emotional terms.

The claim that suicide prevention in terms of hospital admission and medical intervention does not work seems an exaggeration. There are clearly cases where the interventions have saved lives; the concern is that too often cases are missed which do not receive interventions; there are too many cases where the intervention was not needed, and breached the human rights of a person who would not have committed suicide; and cases where the intervention could not have helped. This leads me to call for a reliance on a wider source of suicide intervention; a focus on continuing to improve the quality of the intervention; and a more collaborative approach with patients to decrease the negative impacts of the intervention. This last point was captured by Laura Delano:[118]

> Instead of saying 'You feel suicidal, let's stop it,' they should say, 'What does it mean?' Therapists shouldn't say 'I have answers,' but 'I'm with you while you work out your answers'.

I suspect that is how many practitioners will handle these interventions.[119] We would do better to focus on prevention before a crisis point is reached. A core starting point is emphasising basic mental health care. Allegretti claims:

> The public's understanding of mental health has increased recently with more high profile and other individuals opening up about their personal struggles with their

[115] M Large et al, 'Can We Usefully Stratify Patients According to Suicide Risk?' (2017) 359 *British Medical Journal* 4627.
[116] E Ward-Ciesielski and M Lindhan, 'Psychological Treatment of Suicidal Behaviors' in Nock (n 8).
[117] Stefan (n 46).
[118] ibid.
[119] C de Albuquerque Green et al, *A Matter of Life or Death* (King's College London, 2020).

mental health. This increased profile has not yet fully translated into improved responsiveness of social care mental health services to meet needs and we still hear stories about people with mental health problems receiving no help at all, leading to hundreds of thousands of lives put on hold or ruined, and thousands of tragic and unnecessary deaths.

IX. Current Approach in the UK

The Government has over the past decade been seeking to develop a coherent approach to suicide prevention. The first major cross-Government strategy was published in 2012. In 2016 a national ambition was set to reduce suicides by 10 per cent by 2020. This has not been achieved; in fact the suicide rate has increased, not decreased. By 2019 the suicide rate was 10.8 per 100,000, an increase from 9.5 in 2016. There is now a Minister for Patient Safety, Suicide Prevention and Mental Health, who has the job of overseeing the multi-sector response to suicide.

While England has an overall suicide prevention plan, responsibilities for its implementation are divided between Clinical Commissions Groups (CCGs) and NHS England. NHS England commissions services for specialist psychiatric services (such as eating disorders or personality disorder services). Other mental health services, including in-patient community teams, are commissioned by CCGs.[120]

Preventing Suicide in England seeks to capture the wide range of what might be required to challenge suicide:

> The factors leading to someone taking their own life are complex. No one organisation is able to directly influence them all. Commitment across government, from Health, Education, Justice and the Home Office, Transport, Work and Pensions and others will be vital. We also need the support of the voluntary and statutory sectors, academic institutions and schools, businesses, industry, journalists and other media. And, perhaps above all, we must involve communities and individuals whose lives have been affected by the suicide of family, friends, neighbours or colleagues.[121]

As this makes clear, suicide prevention is rarely reducible to a single policy, but involves a wide range of different policies. The Report summarises the key interventions most commonly referred to:

1. Reduce the risk of suicide in key high-risk groups
2. Tailor approaches to improve mental health in specific groups
3. Reduce access to the means of suicide
4. Provide better information and support to those bereaved or affected by suicide
5. Support the media in delivering sensitive approaches to suicide and suicidal behaviour
6. Support research, data collection and monitoring.[122]

[120] Patient Safety Group (n 15).
[121] HM Government (n 7).
[122] ibid.

Update reports provide details on progress. The 2019 *Fourth Progress Report of the Cross-Government Outcomes Strategy to Save Lives* highlighted the following areas as requiring more work:[123]

- ensuring the effectiveness of every local authority suicide prevention plan;
- ensuring every mental health trust has a zero-suicide ambition plan for mental health inpatients by the end of 2019;
- implementing the Prison Safety Programme across the prison estate;
- improving data collection at local and national level, and harnessing technology to identify those most at risk of suicide and self-harm.

The report also highlights the widely acknowledged problems around the transition from child and adolescent mental health services (CAMHS) to adult services and describes them, to put it politely, as 'uncomfortable'.[124]

A. Zero-Suicide Ambition

Perhaps the best know suicide prevention programme is the zero-suicides ambition. There are between 81 and 91 deaths by suicide in NHS in-patient services in England each year.[125] In 2018 the Government announced a zero-suicide ambition for mental health in-patients, requiring NHS mental health organisations to draw up plans to achieve zero suicide, including:

- asking that all suicides by mental health patients be reported and published more quickly;
- requiring NHS Trusts to 'strengthen the package of suicide prevention measures' they have in place;
- ensuring that there are thorough investigations after all suicide attempts, with a focus on learning from errors; and
- encouraging a 'cultural shift within mental health services' so that suicides are not viewed as inevitable.[126]

Zero-suicide policies first emerged in 2001 in Detrioit in the US.[127] It was reported to reduce suicide rates from 89 per 100,000 mental health patients to 16 between the years 2001 and 2013,[128] with the target of zero suicide being reached in most recent years. When that is compared with the US national average figure of 230 per 100,000, the Detroit figures look extremely impressive. Similar schemes elsewhere

[123] HM Government, *Preventing Suicide in England: Fourth Progress Report of the Cross-Government Outcomes Strategy to Save Lives* (HM Government, 2019).
[124] ibid.
[125] Patient Safety Group (n 15).
[126] Haylen et al (n 76).
[127] R Hackman, 'Detroit Tackles Suicide Taboos Head on', *The Guardian*, 18 February 2015.
[128] ibid.

have reported notable reductions.[129] It became adopted more broadly in the US as part of the National Action Alliance Suicide prevention with seven essential elements:

1 lead: create a leadership-driven, safety-oriented culture committed to dramatically reducing suicide among people under care. Include survivors of suicide attempts and suicide loss in leadership and planning roles;
2 train: develop a competent, confident, and caring workforce;
3 identify: systematically identify and assess suicide risk among people receiving care;
4 engage: ensure every individual has a pathway to care that is both timely and adequate to meet his or her needs. Include collaborative safety planning and restriction of lethal means;
5 treat: use effective, evidence-based treatments that directly target suicidal thoughts and behaviours;
6 transition: provide continuous contact and support, especially after acute care;
7 improve: apply a data-driven Quality Improvement approach to inform system changes that will lead to improved patient outcomes and better care for those at risk.[130]

The zero-suicide policy has been adopted as a general policy for NHS England.[131] It might be thought uncontroversial to promote such a policy. However, the Royal College of Psychiatry report concludes:

> On balance, although the 'zero suicide' approach has generated enthusiasm for radical and system-wide attempts to reduce suicide, and provides a model and framework to engage many different stakeholders, there is not currently sufficient evidence to be confident that it is an effective or sustainable approach, or that there are no potential unintended consequences associated with it. Further research and evaluation are needed in different populations and settings to clarify these issues.[132]

Concerns about the zero-suicide approach focus on two key issues. The first is that it means that a suicide is automatically seen as a failure and hence something to be avoided at all costs. There is no room here for a suicide which is appropriate. Also, it may set up professionals and organisations to fail. The second issue is that it can dominate the thinking of a trust to the exclusion of other factors and policies. It might, for example, mean that excessive steps are taken to avoid suicide[133]

[129] N Stapelberg et al, 'Efficacy of the Zero Suicide Framework in Reducing Recurrent Suicide Attempts: Cross-Sectional and Time-to-recurrent-event Analyses' (2020) 12 *British Journal of Psychiatry* 1.
[130] US Department of Health and Human Service, *About Zero Suicide* (USDHHS, 2021).
[131] D Fearnley, *The Zero Suicide Policy Challenges*, www.england.nhs.uk/blog/david-fearnley, accessed 15 December 2021.
[132] Patient Safety Group (n 15).
[133] P Karlsson et al, 'Skepticism towards the Swedish Vision Zero for Suicide: Interviews with 12 Psychiatrists' (2018) 19 *BMC Medical Ethics* 26.

or too many resources are diverted away from other health care initiatives. These are valid concerns, but neither of them should lead to a rejection of the policy. It emphasises the value in rejecting suicide as an inevitable outcome. It encourages Trusts to try out new methods of suicide prevention and to learn from each death to explore new ways of preventing similar events.[134]

X. Conclusion

A European study found that 73 per cent of suicides could be prevented if all EU countries matched the country with the lowest suicide rates.[135] That would include 600 fewer children committing suicide and around 40,000 fewer adult deaths. We can, and should, be doing much better at suicide prevention.

This chapter, however, has emphasised that the kind of prevention that is commonly thought of when this topic is discussed is the dramatic detention and forced treatment of suicidal people. However, that is one of the least effective methods of suicide prevention. Far more striking reductions in suicide can be found in general measures, such as restricting access to means of suicide; improving access to and funding of mental health; economic and social measure to combat social inclusion; and facilities for groups at particular risk of suicide. Many such interventions not only prevent suicide, but also produce wider social benefits.

Sadly, much of the debate around end-of-life decisions in the academic literature, media and legal materials does not discuss these issues. Instead, the arguments focus on the provision of euthanasia and assisted dying. We turn to these in the next chapter.

[134] S Usborne, 'The Bold New Fight to Eradicate Suicide' *The Guardian* 1 August 2017.

[135] D Stone et al, 'Intentional Injury Mortality in the European Union: How Many More Lives Could Be Saved?' (2006) 12 *Injury Prevention* 327.

9

Euthanasia and Suicide

I. Introduction

This book's focus has been on the right to suicide prevention. I have largely avoided the debates on euthanasia and assisted dying, although clearly many of the points made are relevant to that too. In this chapter I will explore how the right to suicide prevention impacts on the debates around euthanasia and assisted dying. In doing this, I only briefly rehearse the now very familiar arguments on those subjects. I hope to highlight two points. The first is that we need to recentre the debates around end-of-life care. We need to address the questions that are raised whenever a person wants to die. The focus on the terminally or progressive conditions miscues the debate. The second is that an effective suicide prevention strategy, combined with other policies, strengthens rather than weakens the case for a reform of the current law in England.

This chapter will start with the briefest overview of the primary positions that are taken on the assisted dying/euthanasia debate. I will then highlight some of the issues raised by the themes of this book. In this chapter the terminology assisted dying will be used to refer to euthanasia or assisted suicide.

II. The General Debate on Assisted Dying

The primary argument in favour of taking a permissive approach to assisted dying is the principle of autonomy (see Chapter 3). We can separate out the 'autonomy only view' and the 'autonomy plus view'. The 'autonomy only view' suggests that once it is determined that a person with capacity wishes to die, they have the absolute right to die.[1] Even though other people may take the view that that their decision is foolish or immoral, it must be respected. Generally, those who take this view argue that the law should ensure that the means to suicide must be made available to people who have the capacity to decide to die and if a person is unable to commit suicide themselves then euthanasia should be available.[2]

[1] J Davis and E Mathison, 'The Case for an Autonomy-Centered View of Physician-Assisted Death' (2021) *Journal of Bioethical Inquiry* 345.

[2] K Yuill, *Assisted Suicide: The Liberal, Humanist Case against Liberalization* (Palgrave, 2012). Some argue that euthanasia should be available even to those who could commit suicide but prefer not to kill themselves.

The 'autonomy plus view' holds that the law should permit assisted dying only where the person is autonomous and a further condition is met, such as the person is close to death; or has an incurable illness. Those who take this view might have two different reasons for the additional requirements: that they confirm the determination that the patient has made an autonomous decision; or that they provide an independent good reason for the decision, which when combined with autonomy provide us with sufficient reason to permit the assisted dying. In practice, there may be little to distinguish the two explanations for the additional requirements. A person who wishes to die for a trivial reason (eg their favourite football team had just lost a match) would not be permitted access to assisted dying on either view. The reasoning may differ: the weakness of the reason means that we doubt the autonomy or there is insufficient additional reason to autonomy to require assistance. Either way, the outcome is the same: there must be no assisted dying. In theory, a difference between the two 'autonomy plus' views could open up in a case where a person wished to die for a trivial reason, but supplied extensive evidence that it was a fully autonomous one.

Less commonly, arguments in favour of euthanasia and assisted dying are made in terms of beneficence in certain cases: that death is beneficial for the patient. These are most likely to be relied upon if a patient lacks capacity and so we cannot rely on the patient's own assessment of the benefit of continued life.[3] Frances Kamm[4] says 'when death is a lesser bad and pain relief a greater good for the same person … a doctor is morally permitted to intentionally cause death, or assist in its being intentionally caused, when it alone can stop pain'. The argument can be bolstered by acknowledging that death is going to come at some point and, rather than choosing death over life, a doctor in such a case is determining which is the best life out of the two alternatives: a shorter less painful life or a longer painful life. Indeed Kamm[5] goes further and claims 'doctors have a moral *duty* to intentionally cause the patient's death or assist in its being intentionally caused when death is a (least) lesser bad and pain relief is a greater good for the patient or when death is imminent anyway and causing it alone can stop the patient's pain'. Occasionally the argument for assisted suicide is put in terms of justice: it is better to focus our limited resources on those patients who want medical treatment than on those who do not want them.[6]

Opponents of assisted dying tend to rely on two kinds of arguments. First, there is the claim that the principle of sanctity of life means that it is never justifiable to intentionally end a person's life. We discussed this principle in Chapter 3. As noted in that chapter, one of the difficulties with the principle – at least in its absolutist form – is that it is difficult to develop an entirely secular version of it.

[3] Hence euthanasia is permitted in some countries for very sick babies.

[4] F Kamm, *Almost Over* (Oxford University Press, 2020) and J Savulescu, 'Autonomy, Interests, Justice and Active Medical Euthanasia' in M Cholbi and J Varelius (eds), *New Directions in the Ethics of Assisted Suicide and Euthanasia* (Springer, 2015).

[5] Kamm, ibid.

[6] Savulescu (n 4).

As the concept of sanctity of life raises some sensitive questions about what the value of life is, it is natural for the law to seek not to impose one particular viewpoint on everyone. That may explain why, among lawyers, less weight has been placed on the sanctity of life claims in recent years.

A second argument led by opponents is that legalising assisted dying will impact on the vulnerable and the wider societal response to old age and those with a disability. The obvious issue is a concern that relatives will pressurise an older person into seeking assisted dying, especially given the cost of care. The less obvious issue is that if euthanasia/assisted dying is permitted will that mean that older people or those with a disability will feel they need to consider the option and justify a decision not to take it: 'social permission to die can evolve into social pressure to die'.[7] It might also be claimed that if euthanasia or assisted dying is permitted, then fewer resources might be made available to care homes or services for the disabled.

A third argument is the claim of the 'slippery slope': that in practice permitting voluntary euthanasia will slip into involuntary euthanasia or allowing euthanasia to an ever increasing range of cases. There are fierce debates over the statistics here. This is not the place to resolve that. Certainly, it seems that those countries that have moved in the direction of permitting euthanasia to a narrow group of people have gradually extended the range of those to whom it can be offered. However, it might be said that this is a natural development, as the health services become more confident that the mental capacity assessment can be done in a reliable way.

It is worth noting that despite the ferocity of the debate around euthanasia and assisted dying there is widespread agreement on some things:

(1) attempted suicide (or suicide) should not be a crime. The International Association for Suicide Prevention:

> recommends the decriminalisation of attempted suicide on the grounds that this will reduce social stigma, help remove barriers to obtaining adequate mental health care, increase access to emergency medical services, foster suicide prevention activities, improve the well-being of people who are vulnerable to engaging in suicidal behaviours, and contribute to more accurate monitoring of suicidal behaviours;[8]

(2) at least some cases of assisted suicide should be a criminal offence and some should not. Everyone, I take it, agrees that a person who encourages a vulnerable person to commit suicide so they can film it for YouTube, or to gain an inheritance, deserves a criminal sanction of some kind;

(3) the administration of pain relief can be justified even if it is known to hasten death. I think there is widespread agreement that a person should not be denied pain relief due to the concerns raised against assisted dying.

[7] M Wente, 'Should Doctors Be Allowed to Kill' *The Globe and the Mail*, 19 September 2015, www.theglobeandmail.com/opinion/should-doctors-be-allowed-to-kill/article26428075/, accessed 15 December 2021.

[8] See www.iasp.info/, accessed 15 December 2021.

We should not lose sight of the significant common ground on this controversial issue, despite the extensive areas for debate. I will now focus on issues around the assisted dying debate that are impacted by the arguments raised in this book.

III. The Starting Point

One of the perils of law is that, by its nature, it creates rules of general application. When presented with a particular scenario, it is easy to respond that the law should, or should not, permit a certain a certain activity, but that may imply a general rule to apply to all cases. Hence it is that in both sides of the debate around euthanasia it is possible to come up with a scenario, real or imagined, where it is hard to deny 'well of course that person should be allowed access to assisted dying' or 'of course that person should not be allowed access to assisted dying'. The difficulty, and this is the skill of the lawyer, is in to draft a set of rules that works for all cases. It is surprising to read how often a person's view of what the law should be in this area is impacted by their personal experience of a relative dying. The fact that the law does, or does not, work well in a particular case does not tell us an enormous amount about what the law should be for the generality of cases. We need to look at many cases to determine what the law should be and how it should operate.

To deal with the problem that a single rule rarely provides the right outcome in all cases, it is common for the law to start with a general rule and then put in place exceptions to deal with cases where that is not appropriate. Consider, for example, the offence of dangerous driving. We might produce a number of alternative ways of drafting this offence. Here are two.

(1) it could be an offence to drive in a dangerous way;
(2) it could be an offence to drive at all, unless you can show you are doing so safely.

Several factors will impact on how the law responds. I will focus on one issue: the core message of the law. Thus, one of the reasons many people would reject option (2), is that it implies there is something wrong with driving itself: it is an act that requires a justification. Option (1) indicates there is no wrong in driving itself; it is only driving dangerously which is the problem. If you were stopped by the police and asked why you were driving 'I just felt like it' would be a perfectly good reason. Contrast this with a case where a person has punched someone. Then, it seems entirely appropriate to ask them 'why did do that?' and not find 'I just felt like it' a satisfactory reason. In criminal law, therefore, we typically, start by describing acts for which a person can be properly held to account or asked for an explanation. This is an important part of the message sending function of the law. It is setting out wrongs which we should not permit, unless we are confident can prove that we have a good reason. So one issue is whether assisted death or euthanasia is an act which requires a justification or whether it does not. I take it as generally uncontroversial that it does require a justification. It is a 'prima facie wrong' or 'an act which calls for a justification'.[9]

This, at last, brings us to one of the key issues in response to euthanasia and assisted suicide. Accepting, as indicated, that there are likely to be exceptions to any view presented, we need to determine our starting point. That is problematic, as it is far from obvious what a 'core case' is, or what the core message of the law is. The cases that have come before the courts in recent years and have received such considerable attention in academic circles involve those with serious medical conditions, such as Tony Nicklinson with locked-in syndrome. However, if we are thinking about how to respond in general to cases where a person wants to commit suicide we should look at the most common cases of suicide: a teenager bullied at school; a middle aged man sacked at work; someone beset by depression.

I suggest that the central legal message we should be sending out to people wishing to commit suicide is 'please don't'. The official response must be one offering care, comfort, and support. If the primary message from the law to those seeking death and those dealing with them is 'you have a right to kill yourself if you want' something has gone badly wrong. The right to suicide prevention and to medical and social treatment seems far more appropriate, for two reasons. First, in the vast majority of cases where a person wishes to die, this is not the kind of case where the kind of richly autonomous decision to die has been made and to which a positive response is appropriate. There is, therefore, good reason to take a lack of sufficient autonomy as the starting point. This argument was made in Chapter 3. Second, I think the harms done by having the wrong primary message are far worse where the primary message is 'you should have the right to die if you want' than where it is 'please let's talk and see what we can do to help you deal with the position you are in'. If our primary starting point is in favour of suicide prevention, then any permission for assisted dying will be an exception to the general rule.

The law must then determine the form of the justification. One issue is whether the burden should lie on the defendant to prove the justification exists or whether the prosecution should prove the lack of justification. Often, that depends on the ease with which the justifying evidence can be produced. Take the offence of drink-driving, for example. It would seem onerous to expect the defendant to prove they had not been drinking. In the nature of the activity that will be a difficult thing for the defendant to do that. It is more reasonable there to require the prosecution to prove the alcohol levels. By contrast, it might be thought reasonable to expect the defendant to produce evidence that they had a driving licence, assuming they will carry one with them or have one readily available at home to show. In other cases it might be the dangerousness of the activity which determines where the burden lies. For example, in the law of rape where the defendant has administered a 'stupefying substance' to the victim without consent before sex, the burden is on

[9] M Madden Dempsey and J Herring, 'Why Sexual Penetration Requires Justification' (2007) 27 *Oxford Journal of Legal Studies* 467.

him to prove there was consent.[10] Having engaged in such a risky activity, it seems reasonable – to say the least – to expect the defendant to have very good reason to believe the victim was consenting. Indeed, one might question in that particular scenario whether a defendant could ever have reasonable grounds.

Pulling these threads together in broad terms in relation to assisted dying, we could have four general structures for the law:

(1) people wanting to die have the right to die and access assisted dying, but that should be denied if there is evidence that they lack sufficient autonomy;
(2) people wanting to die have the right to die and access assisted dying, but only if they can demonstrate that they have sufficient autonomy;
(3) people wanting to die should have interventions designed to stop them doing that, although the state should provide assisted dying if there is evidence of sufficiently good reasons for doing so;
(4) people wanting to die should have interventions designed to stop them doing that, although the state should provide assisted dying if the individual demonstrates that there are sufficiently good reasons for doing so.

It seems to me that the fourth approach is the correct one. It makes it clear that for the majority of cases involving suicidal wishes the correct response is to offer intervention designed to stop them. I accept there needs to be the provision of assisted dying where people have made a richly autonomous decision to die and are in terrible pain or indignity, but that is properly understood as exceptional.[11] Opponents of that conclusion are likely to claim that such an approach fails to appreciate the right to die, so I need to address that further.

IV. The Right to Die

Some formulations of legal permissibility of assisted dying promote access to assisted dying as a right to die. As we have seen, there is limited acceptance of this within the European Court of Human Rights (ECtHR), where a right to determine when and how to die is interpreted as being part of the Article 8 right to respect for private and family life. The argument that there is a positive right to die is highly problematic.

As already noted, most advocates of the right wish to limit the right to certain categories of people, such as those with terminal illnesses or those in unbearable pain.[12] Further, most would limit the access to euthanasia to those who are able

[10] Sexual Offences Act 2003, s 75.

[11] W Pringle, 'Problematizations in Assisted Dying Discourse: Testing the "What's the Problem Represented to Be?' (WPR) Method for Critical Health Communication Research' (2020) 4 *Frontiers in Communication* 58.

[12] M Dees et al, '"Unbearable Suffering": A Qualitative Study on the Perspectives of Patients who Request Assistance in Dying' (2011) 37 *Journal of Medical Ethics* 727.

to satisfy various administrative hurdles. Indeed, the ECtHR has indicated that restrictions must be put on the right to die, to ensure the obligations under Article 2 are met.[13] This renders the 'right to die' a potentially misleading term: unlike most rights it is not available to everyone, but only those who satisfy the conditions. It may well be a right that is accessible to only a very small portion of those who would like to exercise the right. That makes this right highly unusual in the panoply of human rights. Others rights are readily available to all who seek to rely on them, or at least a clear majority.[14]

It may be more accurate, therefore, to refer to a liberty to die. A person is permitted to commit suicide free from state interference. However, it was argued in Chapter 4 that this is not an accurate statement of the law. The state has a positive duty to stop suicide in so far as it is possible and reasonable to do so. 'The Philosopher's Brief', penned by Ronald Dworkin et al in 1997 states that:

> a person's interest in following his own conviction at the end of life is so central a part of the more general right to make 'intimate and personal choices' for himself that a failure to protect that particular interest would undermine the general right altogether.[15]

Such a claim seems more plausible but does not make for a strong case requiring assisted suicide, or euthanasia. You are free to end your life, just as you are free to drink tea at 4pm; give generously to charity; or take up fencing. But you have no claim against the government or others to, for example, help you drink tea at 4pm.

It seems that to generate a positive right to assistance something more than merely personal choice is required. Perhaps the most plausible claim would be to dignity. However, as Margaret Battin[16] notes:

> Not all cases of suicide involve dignity, no matter how we define it; there are some, perhaps many, clearly catastrophic, needless, awful cases, but that does not yet tell us how to draw a line. Dignity, like beauty, may be to a large degree in the eye of the beholder, something to be admired and perhaps emulated, but not objectively real. Just the same, I think it is not only in the beholder's eye.

It may be that, although Battin is generally correct, we can identify a few cases where there would be consensus that to remain alive would be undignified. But those will be a small minority of cases of those where people wish to die. Further, as Cohen-Almagor[17] argues:

> The preservation of one's dignity involves, inter alia, listening to the patients' complaints, helping patients cure their diseases or at least assisting them in controlling pain,

[13] *Pretty* v *United Kingdom* [2002] 35 EHRR 1.

[14] D Mendelson and M Bagaric, 'Assisted Suicide through the Prism of the Right to Life' (2013) 36 *International Journal of Law and Psychiatry* 406.

[15] R Dworkin et al 'Assisted Suicide: The Philosopher's Brief', *The New York Review*, 27 March 1997 www.nybooks.com/articles/1997/03/27/assisted-suicide-the-philosophers-brief/, accessed 15 December 2021, p 5.

[16] M Battin, 'Could Suicide Really Be a Fundamental Human Right?' in S Muders (ed), *Human Dignity and Assisted Death* (Oxford University Press, 2017).

[17] ibid.

responding to their distress and anxieties, making an effort to relieve them, demonstrating sensitivity to the physical indignities that occur in severe illnesses, making the patient sense that he or she is a human being and not an infant, a case study or worse, a body that occupies a bed and consumes resources. Maintaining the patients' dignity requires physicians as well as the patients' families to help the patients retain at least some of their self-respect. The aim is to secure dignified living in severe health conditions. The liberal state has an obligation to protect the vulnerable. Protecting the vulnerable means caring for them.

V. Dealing with Hard Cases

It is common for criminal law to set out the definition of a crime, but then to find a case which technically falls within the definition of the offence, and where no defence is available, but where the defendant does not deserve a conviction. The criminal law has a range of ways of dealing with these cases. We create 'wiggle room' through prosecutorial discretion; the common sense of juries; providing minimal sentences; and the defence of necessity. This is because human life is complex. It does not fit into rigid boxes. A few statutory lines cannot produce a full assessment of blame or capture all the nuances of morally complex scenarios. This is true for all crimes, from battery through to murder. There is no breach of constitutional principle if the courts and prosecuting authorities use these devices to ensure there is no conviction in the rare case where the official response is inappropriate. Indeed, Parliament relies on these to make the criminal law workable. They are an acknowledgement of the limitations of language and an inability to deal in rules with all the minutiae of an individual case that are needed for an effective moral assessment. Without such devices, the individual defendant can bear the burden of the inevitably blunt nature of the law.

Applying this approach to our issue, I think we can start with a suicide prevention strategy as the primary response, while acknowledging that in exceptional cases assisted suicide or euthanasia can be appropriate. The ways above provide us some route to do this. One, currently used in English law on assisted suicide, is prosecutorial discretion, as seen in Chapter 5. This has some benefits. It maintains a clear statement against euthanasia or assisting suicide. The formal position is that assisting suicide is a crime, but it is recognised that persuing legal proceedings is sometimes inappropriate. It is therefore in a slight 'liminal' state between legality and illegality. It retains a taint of illegality. It continues to have a deterrent effect: a person will be reluctant to engage in euthanasia or assisted suicide unless they are fully confident that the discretion will be exercised in their favour. Some will argue that this sets the right tone for assistance in suicide. The difficulty with this approach is that a person cannot be sure in advance that they will not be prosecuted. They can look at the factors and confidently assess it is unlikely, but there is no security in that. Nor does it seem to allow for a case where the assistance of suicide is not only 'a wrong to be overlooked' but a positive good. As argued in Chapter 2, I believe there are a small number of cases that fall into that category.

The alternative is to create an excuse-based defence which states that if certain facts are shown, a defendant will not be guilty of a crime. This would result in a slightly different message being sent, as compared to the prosecution policy. In particular, it acknowledges that a wrong has occurred, although that wrong is either excused, or the wrong is counterbalanced by other considerations which make it justified, all things considered. An obvious example of an excuse in this context would be a person who has assisted a relative to die but is relying on diminished responsibility to claim they were not fully responsible for their behaviour. Here the defendant accepts that they ought not to act in the way they did, but they were not fully in control of what they were doing. There are good reasons to allow such defences, but they do not really go the heart of the issue: whether the assistance is good.

More interesting for these discussions is a claim of justification. Here the law is accepting that the act itself is wrong, but there are unusual countervailing reasons for allowing the act. For example, in *Re A*[18] doctors were permitted to separate conjoined twins, even though that would involve killing one conjoined twin, which would be murder, because not doing so would lead to both twins dying. There the court, in using the defence of necessity, was saying that murder is wrong, but in this particular case the alternative – of both twins dying – was even worse. Thus, if the law wanted to capture the message 'euthanasia and assisted dying' are wrong, but there may be exceptional circumstances in which this is justified, necessity might well capture that message. That seems to me close to what we are seeking.

Simon Gardner[19] has provided one of the best justifications for the defence of necessity. He argues against the view that necessity is available where the defendant is simply doing the lesser of two evils:

> It is much more comfortable to think of necessity in terms of the vindication of rights. That is, I should have the defence if, committing what would otherwise be an offence, I act to vindicate a right that is recognised by the law but not otherwise reflected in the offence's definition, and that is superior to any right or interest that the offence exists to protect and that I injure by my action; and no less aggressive course of action (ie no course of action likewise calculated to vindicate the right, but less injurious of the rights and interests protected by the offence) was open to me.

While not directly addressing the euthanasia issue, his approach could be used to explain why the human rights claim of a person seeking to end their life is sufficient to justify an exception in the application of the law in an unusual case.

The use of necessity would have a number of advantages. First, it retains the key message that euthanasia and assisted dying should (generally) not be done. Our primary focus is on suicide prevention. Second, it makes it clear that only exceptionally are these acts justified. Third, and most importantly, using necessity deals with the strongest arguments against liberalising the law on euthanasia and

[18] *Re A (Conjoined Twins)* [2000] EWCA Civ 254.
[19] S Gardner, 'Direct Action and the Defence of Necessity' (2005) *Criminal Law Review* 371, 378.

assisted dying, what might be called the 'vulnerability concern'. This is not that people will be pressurised by relatives into killing themselves, a concern which is realistic, though there is little evidence to suggest that it is a common problem. Rather, the better version of the 'vulnerability concern' is that by creating the option of a 'right to die', older people will need to justify to themselves why they are not taking that option. The creation of a choice thereby creates a pressure: 'why not buy this product' asks the crafty salesperson putting you in the position of justifying your decision not to buy. In the loneliness of the care home, with the ever-increasing financial burden, the older person would inevitably question why they choose to live, when they could choose to die. Kate Greasley has written of the dangers of:

> the cultivation of a social environment in which controlled death is an accessible and normalized option, and in which both internal and external pressure to end one's life may consequently mount.[20]

I believe, therefore, that the best structure for the law is to put suicide prevention as the primary legal response to requests for death. Assisted suicide and euthanasia are contrary to that primary response and should be unlawful. We can, however, fashion a defence of necessity which accepts that in rare cases assisted suicide or euthanasia can be permitted. That still leaves a question about how to formulate these 'necessity' justifications. A number of key themes emerge about the 'exceptions'.

A. Should the Law Set the Justifying Circumstances or Leave It to Discretion?

Most proponents of a regime which permit euthanasia or assisted dying suggest having in place a set of criteria which must be satisfied before access is provided. Typically these are set out in a statute and will involve proof that someone is terminally ill and/or they are suffering a serious medical condition and/or they are in unrelievable pain. A good example is the Assisted Dying Bill 2021 which, as introduced, proposed as follows:

> Assisted dying
>
> (1) Subject to the consent of the High Court (Family Division) pursuant to subsection (2), a person who is terminally ill may request and lawfully be provided with assistance to end his or her own life.
>
> (2) Subsection (1) applies only if the High Court (Family Division), by order, confirms that it is satisfied that the person—
>
> (a) has a voluntary, clear, settled and informed wish to end his or her own life;

[20] K Greasley, 'R (Purdy) v DPP and the Case for Wilful Blindness' (2010) 30 *Oxford Journal of Legal Studies* 301, 304.

(b) has made a declaration to that effect in accordance with section 3; and
(c) on the day the declaration is made—
    (i) is aged 18 or over;
    (ii) has capacity to make the decision to end his or her own life; and
    (iii) has been ordinarily resident in England and Wales for not less than one year.

The alternative to this would be to leave the precise criteria up to the decision makers, although there may be a list of factors or considerations to be taken into account. This might be similar to the approach currently taken under the Mental Capacity Act 2005, when the court makes a best interests assessment about whether to remove life-sustaining treatment. The formal legal test in such cases is simply one of best interests and the court will weigh up all the competing factors.

In choosing between these options there are two main considerations. The first is the messaging involved. If, for example, it was said that only people over the age of 90 could access assisted dying, this could be said to send a message that those over 90 should consider euthanasia and that it would be understandable that those of that age would want to die. This is the kind of argument commonly used by disability activists who oppose requirements that a person must have a disability if they are to be offered assisted dying. If we start, as this book as suggested we should, with a commitment to suicide prevention, then it becomes difficult to square this with a list of criteria which set out when assisted dying is appropriate. Specifically, it weakens the message to the group identified as eligible for assisted suicide that society wishes to offer them the support needed so they no longer seek suicide. An approach with a broad discretion sends no message to a particular group that suicide is appropriate for them.

The second consideration is whether the options provide a secure barrier against the 'slippery slope'. In other words, the concern is that if we set up a set of apparently stringent considerations, are we confident that over time these will not become looser? For example, the 'unbearable suffering' criterion in Dutch law has been loosened, through interpretation, to include psychological suffering, to such an extent that anyone wanting to die is likely to satisfy it.[21] In a similar vein it might be that concepts like 'suffering' are so subjective that it is difficult to prove the extent of suffering.[22] Clearly such a concern is present, but it is possible under either approach.

Third, there is a question of whether a set of criteria that must be satisfied creates too rigid a system. A good example is that of Tony Nicklinson who had 'locked in syndrome' and wished to die. The prognosis was that he would live many years and although there was physical suffering, it might not have been classified as

[21] M Verhofstadt et al, 'When Unbearable Suffering Incites Psychiatric Patients to Request Euthanasia: Qualitative Study' (2017) 211 *The British Journal of Psychiatry: The Journal of Mental Science* 238.

[22] T Lemmens, 'When a Theoretical Commitment to Broad Physician Aid-in-Dying Faces the Reality of Its Implementation' (2019) 19 *American Journal of Bioethics* 65.

severe. Yet he was determined he wished to die. Such a case in some ways seems the most compelling for assisted dying: he was facing years in a condition in which– after lengthy and careful consideration and experience – he did not want to live. He would not be able to use the Assisted Dying Bill, for example. An approach which has no fixed criteria would be more open to consider such cases.[23]

These factors lead me to suggest a system that does not over specify criteria, but rather takes each case on its own merits. I suggest three reasons for this. First, it avoids identifying a group that euthanasia/assisted dying is appropriate for, with the negative message that approach sends to people in that group and the conflict with suicide prevention policies. Second, as argued in Chapter 3, the correct approach requires a balancing between autonomy and the best interest assessment. This requires a flexible approach and careful weighing up that is not reducible to a set of fixed criteria. I accept that this comes at the cost of there not being a secure barrier against assisted dying and concerns over assisted dying. However, for some of the reasons indicated, I doubt whether the fixed criteria would be any more secure. It is the integrity of the decision makers which is the most secure foundation against this, rather than any formulation.

B. Who Should 'Police' the Exceptions?

There are three primary options here.[24] First, the approval of a court could be required to make the decision. Second, it could be left to doctors, as it is in The Netherlands. Third, a panel of mixed experts could be used. While the Assisted Dying Bill 2021 requires a judge in the Family Division to make the final assessment that assisted dying is permitted, it seems their role is limited to ensuring that the medical evidence is in place. It may be helpful to contrast the discretion given to a judge in a case involving children under the Children Act 1989 where a judge is given discretion, taking into account the listed factors, to determine what order will best promote the welfare of the child. In the case of the 2021 Bill, if the facts are made out then the judge must issue the court declaration.

One of the issues here is the extent to which assisted dying/euthanasia should be seen as a medical decision. In the Dutch system euthanasia is seen as a medical option to be offered as an alternative form of treatment and so is best left to the doctor-patient interaction. To others, that undermines the integrity of the physician/patient relationship.[25] Calkins and Swetz[26] argue that at the heart of that

[23] J Downie and S Sherwin, 'A Feminist Exploration of Issues around Assisted Death' (1996) 15 *St Louis University Public Law Review* 303.

[24] M Cholbi, 'Medically Enabled Suicides' in Cholbi and Varelius (n 4) 64.

[25] R Huxtable and J Ives, 'License to Kill: A New Model for Excusing Medically Assisted Dying?' in Cholbi and Varelius (n 4).

[26] B Calkins and K Swetz, 'Physician Aid-in-Dying and Suicide Prevention in Psychiatry: A Moral Imperative over a Crisis' (2019) 19 *American Journal of Bioethics* 68.

relationship is 'the clinician's role as healer and trusted advisor'. However, where, as discussed above, the issue is a prima facie serious wrong which is justified due to a human right, it seems this is better carried out by legal authorisation. It has the added benefit of offering greater reassurance to family and friends, and perhaps will also help doctors who feel uneasy about making the decision.

I recommend that we have a judicial form of assessment, but with a set of factors to be considered, rather than a set definition of a group of people for whom assisted dying should be available.

C. Gender and Assisted Dying

At several points in this discussion I have mentioned the risk of permitting assisted dying for vulnerable groups, but more needs to be said about that concern. First, it is worth emphasising, as Downie and Sherwin[27] do, that there can be concerns on both sides of the debate. First, we need to ensure that the oppressed are not coerced or channelled into assisted dying though lack of support and experiences of disadvantage.[28] Second, denying access to assisted dying can be seen by others as itself a form of oppression, particularly where that denial is reflecting oppressive forces, rather than a genuine difference in the justification.[29]

Bearing these in mind, there is a particular concern that the right to die has gendered implication. Susan Wolf[30] worries that given the structures within society women are more susceptible to depression, are less likely to be given effective pain management, and face difficulty obtaining quality healthcare. Bonnie Horgos writes:

> Yes, a woman absolutely has a right to die if she is terminally ill with six months to live. But a woman also has the right to adequate mental health care, and to live a society that believes her when she's been raped, or to be treated by a doctor that doesn't dismiss her symptoms. In the end, can we erase a woman's desire to die by offering her better mental health care? Can we dismantle a patriarchal system that leaves her with more options than death?[31]

Jennifer Parks notes:

> Feminist arguments can support conclusions either that gendered perceptions of women as self-sacrificing predispose physicians to accede to women's requests to die –

[27] Downie and Sherwin (n 23).

[28] G Tulloch, 'Feminism, Suicide and Assisted Dying: Reflections on Sandra Bem's Death' (2015) 25 *Feminism & Psychology* 113.

[29] T Sikka, 'Is Physician-Assisted Suicide a Feminist Issue? Barriers to Access: A Feminist Analysis of Medically Assisted Dying and the Experience of Marginalized Groups' (2021) 84 *OMEGA – Journal of Death and Dying* 4.

[30] S Wolf, 'Gender, Feminism, and Death: Physician-Assisted Suicide and Euthanasia' in S Wolf (ed), *Feminism and Bioethics* (Oxford University Press, 1996).

[31] B Horgos, 'Is Physician-Assisted Suicide a Feminist Issue?' (2019) *Lady Science*, 8 October.

> or that cultural understandings of women as not fully rational agents lead physicians to reject their requests as irrational.[32]

It may be that the correct response to these issues is to seek to tackle the underlying causes of the oppressions that impact on different groups. But we are left in the meantime in the uncomfortable position that – whatever the formulation – women will be disadvantaged.

Certainly, there would be concern among many feminists that the focus on individualised autonomy fails to appreciate the complex relational context within which these decisions are reached. We cannot focus simply on the image of the autonomous, self-sufficient patient. As Rogers[33] says, such an image:

> takes no account of the dependency and interdependency that characterizes human relationships, and by focusing on the individual, it excludes consideration of the moral dimensions of relationships.

It is for this reason that Wolf has serious concerns about the potential gendered dimensions of extending assisted dying. Jessica Adkins[34] explains:

> Women may feel motivated to request a hastened death, even if they do not truly want it, because they don't want to be a burden, they feel no longer valuable if they cannot act as caretakers, or they are conditioned to be self-sacrificing. When women request and have those requests approved, women would receive a credibility excess.

I suggest that these points argue against a set of criteria which, if fulfilled, automatically justify access to euthanasia. A more subtle assessment of how the decision is made might be able to take these points into account. This can be available by giving judges a broad discretion to determine whether assisted dying should be available.

D. Disability

It would be highly misleading to suggest that there is a single disability perspective on this debate.[35] Nevertheless Baroness Campbell,[36] the founder of Not Dead Yet (NDY UK), claims: 'There are no organisations in this country, of or for disabled

[32] J Parks, 'Why Gender Matters to the Euthanasia Debate: On Decisional Capacity and the Rejection of the Woman's Death Request' (2000) 1 *Hastings Center Report* 30.

[33] W Rogers, 'Feminist Bioethics' in A Garry et al (eds), *The Routledge Companion to Feminist Philosophy* (Routledge, 2019).

[34] J Adkins, 'Thinking Epistemically about Gender and Physician Assisted Death' (2018) 32 *Journal of Applied Philosophy* 197, 202.

[35] T Shakespeare, 'Just What is the Disability Perspective on Disability?' (2016) 46 *Hastings Center Report* 31; E Peel and R Harding 'A Right to "Dying Well" with Dementia? Capacity, "Choice" and Relationality' (2015) 25 *Feminism and Psychology* 137.

[36] Quoted in J Pring, 'Disabled Quartet Tell MPs and Peers Why Assisted Suicide Bill is Unsafe and Unsound', *Disability News Service*, 22 July 2021, www.disabilitynewsservice.com/disabled-quartet-tell-mps-and-peers-why-assisted-suicide-bill-is-unsafe-and-unsound/.

and terminally-ill people, who actively campaign for the law on assisted suicide to be changed. Doesn't that tell you something?' Certainly, the most vocal are groups expressing grave concern about assisted dying. They have three kinds of arguments. The first focuses on the message that is sent by legislation allowing euthanasia for those with severe disabilities, ie that the life of those with disabilities is not worth living. Second is the concern that in practice those with severe disabilities will not be able to protect themselves from being subject to assisted death. The third is that we need to appreciate the highly negative messages sent about disabled people by society and the lack of provision and opportunity given to them. This means that there is a negative context within which autonomy must be exercised.

These three points are closely linked. Gregor Wolbring[37] states:

> We believe that as long as disabled people are viewed as a suffering entity, as an object of charity, as a life not worth living, we cannot accept the broadening of our access to death. It is not without a reason that studies show that the support for euthanasia is greatest among the healthy and young and lowest among the elderly and frail and the ones with the least control over their lives. We believe that the legalization of euthanasia will force people to be euthanized in a misbegotten effort to do the right thing: save their loved ones from financial ruin, remove family members from the care taker role, cease to be a burden on the state.

This concern that disabled people will feel compelled to take up suicide is well captured by Ron Amundson,[38] who writes:

> terminally ill or disabled people sometimes do have suicidal feelings when they feel a lack of support or a shame for their own condition, or when they feel that they are a burden on their families. The desire for death under those conditions is not a free choice but a forced choice.

There are dangers in presenting disabled people as unable to make their own decisions and being easily coerced.[39] Nevertheless, is crucial to appreciate and understand the context within which autonomy is exercised and to recognise that this is different for different people. This is not to say that the reasoning of disabled people is impaired, it is that the context within which decisions are made are different.[40] As Paul Miller, law professor and disability activist, wrote, 'when people with disabilities make a "choice" to seek their right to die, they do so from

[37] G Wolbring, 'Why Disability Rights Movements Do Not Support Euthanasia: Safeguards Broken Beyond Repair', available at www.independentliving.org/docs5/Wolbringeuthanasia.html, accessed 15 December 2021.

[38] Quoted in D Scoccia, 'Physician-Assisted Suicide, Disability and Paternalism' (2010) 36 *Social Theory and Practice* 479, 481.

[39] A Silvers, 'Protecting the Innocent from Physician-Assisted Suicide' in M Battin et al (eds), *Physician Assisted Suicide: Expanding the Debate* (Routledge: 2001) 133; C Riddle, 'Assisted Dying & Disability' (2017) 6 *Bioethics* 484.

[40] B Chan and M Somerville 'Converting the "Right to Life" to the "Right to Physician-Assisted Suicide and Euthanasia': An Analysis of Carter v Canada (Attorney General), Supreme Court' (2016) 24 *Medical Law Review* 143.

the position of a society that fears, discriminates against, and stigmatizes disability as undignified … is there really a choice at all?'[41]

Our society measures people in terms of their economic productivity.[42] As COVID-19 has laid bare, society seems to place greater value on economic productivity than on the value of the 'the economically inactive', understood to be those who are disabled and aged. The markers of personhood are commonly presented to be self-sufficiency, cognition, autonomy and independence. Those who need care are a burden and a cause of worry. We are encouraged to save money or take out insurance to make sure we do not become a burden. To lose productivity is to lose value in our society.[43] Danny Scoccia[44] writes:

> Assisted dying may benefit the able (and perhaps some of those severely disabled people who would choose it), but it does so *at the expense of* the disabled as a group or class. The able can autonomously choose to end their lives if they become terminally or seriously ill and find their condition unbearable, and having that option may well be in their best interests. But – and this large causal claim is the key contention in this version of the argument – giving them that legal option has the *effect* of sustaining disability discrimination. Since providing the disabled with PAD is much cheaper than providing them the social support and antidiscrimination protections that they need to have for minimally decent lives, legalized PAD encourages the able to support PAD *rather than* the elimination of disability discrimination.

The negative messages about disability can produce a toxic mix. The messages that disabled people are a burden to others; are unproductive; are tragic and fall short of full citizens, can have a powerful impact on disabled people.[45] They fear not receiving the services they need; of being abandoned; or institutionalisation. These can have a powerful impact, promoting a person to seek assisted suicide.[46]

Paul Longmore[47] writes of Davie Rivlin, one of the first people in the US to receive court-sanctioned physician assisted suicide:

> It was not David Rivlin's respirator that 'imprisoned' him in that bleak nursing home for three horrible years. It was not his disability had reduced him to a 'cruel semblance of life.' Rivlin's freedom, and finally his life, were taken by a system that segregated him, refused him the right of self-determination (except to die), and allowed him to be exploited for the profit of the nursing home industry. The state of Michigan gave Rivlin less than $300 a month to live in his own house, but paid a nursing home $230 a day to warehouse him.[48]

[41] P Miller, 'The Impact of Assisted Suicide on Persons with Disabilities – Is It A Right Without Freedom?' (1993) 9 *Issues in Law & Medicine* 47 at 54.

[42] T de Campos (2018) 'MAiD in Canada and the Homo Economicus View of Dignity: Inclusive Enough?' (2021) 22 *Journal of Disability & Religion* 246.

[43] L Ripamonti, 'Lives Not Worth Living: Rethinking Autonomy and Assisted Dying in the Light of Profound Disability' (2018) 22 *Journal of Disability and Religion* 317.

[44] D Scoccia, 'The Disability Case Against Assisted Dying' in A Cureton and D Wasserman (eds), *The Oxford Handbook of Philosophy and Disability* (Oxford University Press, 2019).

[45] J Baer, *Ironic Freedom: Personal Choice, Public Policy, and the Paradox of Reform* (Palgrave, 2013).

[46] S Linton, *My Body Politic* (University of Michigan Press, 2006) 226.

[47] P Longmore, 'Policy, Prejudice, and Reality' (2005) 16 *Journal of Disability Policy Studies* 38.

[48] P Longmore, 'The Resistance: The Disability Rights Movement and Assisted Suicide' in P Longmore (ed), *Why I Burned My Book and Other Essays on Disability* (Temple University Press, 2003) 38–40.

Longman goes on to argue that an 'abled bodied person' who asked to die would be met with counselling and the provision of services, but that Rivlin's suicidal request was seen as understandable and rational.[49] While one may disagree about the particular case he is discussing, the broader point is a powerful one. In a society which restricts so severely the options for disabled and older people; and so poorly provides the services they need, promoting assisted dying and euthanasia is dangerous indeed.[50]

It is not difficult to find anti-disability sentiment among those who seek to promote assisted dying in the popular media. Heyer[51] is concerned with the way disability is used as a 'rhetorical tool' to drum up support for assisted suicide. She suggests that questions like 'Wouldn't you rather die than have someone else wipe your butt?' fail to recognise that many disabled people need toileting assistance, and that such questions stigmatise and shame disabled people.[52] Indeed it is unsurprising that some activists have argued that disabled people may be treated as shameful and a 'waste of space' – a message which is reinforced by offering assisted dying, particularly focused on those with disabilities.[53] It is worth recalling the common features of those who feel suicidal. These are listed by Amy Wnezel and Megan Spokas[54] as: (a) hopelessness; (b) perfectionism; (c) burdensomeness; (d) low belongingness; and (e) unbearability. They emphasise that these are perceptions, rather than necessarily reflecting reality. These features are heightened for disabled and older people, where society's attitudes to them will inevitably create these feelings.

Jonas-Sébastien Beaudry argues,[55] in an important article, that for a person to be autonomous they need to possess 'self-discovering, self-defining, and self-directing skills to a sufficient extent' and the capacity to coordinate those skills. Not only that, they must also 'possess a sufficient range of options for those skills to be meaningfully and effectively exercised'. All of these aspects of autonomy are challenges in the case of disabled people, he suggests. For example, the repeated

[49] S Malloy, 'Beyond Misguided Paternalism: Resuscitating the Right to Refuse Medical Treatment' (1998) 33 *Wake Forest Law Review* 1035.

[50] T Lemmens, 'The Conflict between Open-Ended Access to Physician-Assisted Dying and the Protection of the Vulnerable: Lessons from Belgium's Euthanasia Regime in the Post-Carter Era' in C Regis et al (eds), *Les Grands Conilits en Droit de la Sante* (Yvon Blais, 2016) 261; S Kim, 'Lives Not Worth Living in Modern Euthanasia Regimes' (2019) 16 *Journal of Policy & Practice in Intellectual Disabilities* 134.

[51] K Heyer, 'Rejecting Rights: The Disability Critique of Physician Assisted Suicide' (2011) 54 *Studies in Law, Politics and Society* 77.

[52] A Wand et al, 'The Nexus between Elder Abuse, Suicide, and Assisted Dying: The Importance of Relational Autonomy and Undue Influence' (2018) 18 *Macquarie Law Journal* 79, 86.

[53] D Coleman, 'Not Dead Yet' in D Coleman (ed), *The Case Against Assisted Suicide: For the Right of End-to Life Care* (Johns Hopkins University Press, 2002).

[54] A Wenzel and M Spokas, 'Cognitive and Information Processing Approaches to Understanding Suicidal Behaviors' in M Nock (ed), *The Oxford Handbook of Suicide and Self Injury* (Oxford University Press, 2014).

[55] J-S Beaudry, 'Somatic Oppression and Relational Autonomy: Revisiting Medical Aid in Dying through a Feminist Lens' (2020) 53 *UBC Law Review* 241.

presentation of disability as a tragedy makes self-discovering appear pointless because one is told one has no value. The shame that is attached to disability makes people withdraw and makes self-definition and self-direction impossible. As Beaudry writes:

> Death is the most expedient way to hide oneself entirely from shaming eyes, including one's own. Seeking death may itself be seen as shameful (for example, some would reject suicide because of its desperate, weak, or unhygienic connotations), but MAiD [medical assistance in dying] provides a mechanism, praised for its autonomy-enhancing and humane virtues, for ending one's life, and offers to specific groups a socially condoned sick role within one of the few institutional spaces open to them.[56]

For those who are newly diagnosed as disabled, they will immediately view their situation through the disablist lens and be overcome by the emotions society expects, of despair. The responses of fear, shame, disgust and pity which disability so often attracts reflect the message that disability must be avoided at all costs, even if that cost is death. The fact that euthanasia is often seen as particularly appropriate for those conditions for which there is no medical treatment reinforces the medicalised model of disability, that it is something to be overcome with intervention, rather than acknowledged as a difference. The wishes of disabled people to die should not be seen simply as straightforward assessments of their conditions, but as an acknowledgement of the socio-political context within which their decisions are made.[57] The wish of a disabled person to die in many cases says something utterly shameful about our society.

E. The Lessons from Overseas

The debates on assisted dying often seek to draw on evidence from jurisdictions where assisted dying has been permitted. Perhaps inevitably there is disagreement on the lessons to be learned, with supporters arguing that the message from other jurisdictions is that we can safely implement assisted dying laws, without fears of abuse, and opponents arguing that the evidence from other jurisdictions demonstrates the validity of their concerns. Lord Neuberger, referring to two sources which sought to claim that the evidence from overseas showed there was no risk of abuse, had this to say:

> 88. It is true that the Falconer Report, supported by the reports of the two Canadian panels, states that in the Netherlands, Oregon and Switzerland there is no evidence of abuse of the law, which permits assisting a suicide in prescribed circumstances and subject to conditions. However, negative evidence is often hard to obtain, there is only a

[56] ibid.

[57] E van Wijngaarden et al, 'The Social-Political Challenges behind the Wish to Die in Older People Who Consider Their Lives to Be Completed and No Longer Worth Living' (2017) 28 *The European Journal of Social Policy* 419.

limited scope for information given the few jurisdictions where assisted suicide is lawful and the short time for which it has been lawful there, and different countries may have different potential problems. In other words, the evidence on that point plainly falls some way short of establishing that there is no risk. The most that can be said is that the Falconer commission and the Canadian panels could find no evidence of abuse.[58]

I think Lord Neuberger is right to warn against exaggerating what the experience of legalising assisted dying teaches us. One key point is that the issue is greatly impacted by social mores, the provision of care in old age and for those with disabilities; and the nature of the legal systems. This means that care needs to be taken when comparing jurisdictions.

That said, there are some interesting points to note. First, only 4.2 per cent of all deaths in the Netherlands were by assisted dying in 2019.[59] However, in the case of certain neurological conditions, such as Motor Neuron Disease, some 20 per cent of those with that condition sought assisted dying. These figures indicate the relatively low numbers of those who might seek assisted dying, even in the most compelling of circumstances. A second interesting observation is that in 2019 in Canada 263 patients requested assisted dying but later withdrew their request. This highlights the need to ensure that any request is a settled one. Third, in Oregon in 2020 the majority of those seeking assisted dying gave as their primary reason not wanting to be a burden on others.[60] This highlights that it is not pain which is the majority reason people seek euthanasia. Fourth, one study found that the legalisation of physician-assisted suicide has led to an increase in suicides of around 6.3 per cent.[61] In Oregon there was a 50 per cent increase in the suicide rate of those aged 35–64 following a liberalisation of the law.[62]

VI. False Positives and False Negatives

An important issue in determining the appropriate response to debates over assisted suicide and dying are false negatives and false positives.[63] A false positive in this context would be a person who is deemed to have satisfied the requirements for assisted dying when, in fact, they have not. This would cover people who are found to satisfy the criteria even though they do not in fact autonomously (or not sufficiently autonomously) wish to die; and/or those who do not satisfy any

[58] *R (Nicklinson) v Ministry of Justice* [2014] UKSC 48.

[59] U Nath et al, 'Physician-Assisted Suicide and Physician-Assisted Euthanasia: Evidence from Abroad and Implications for UK Neurologists' (2021) 21 *Practical Neurology* 205.

[60] D Kruger, 'There's a Better Way of Dying than Assisted Suicide', *The Times*, 15 September 2021.

[61] D Jones and D Paton, 'How Does Legalization of Physician-Assisted Suicide Affect Rates of Suicide?' (2015) 18 *Southern Medical Journal* 599.

[62] D Jones, *Assisted Suicide and Euthanasia: A Guide to the Evidence* (Anscombe Centre, 2015).

[63] J Wakefield, 'False Positives in Psychiatric Diagnosis: Implications for Human Freedom' (2010) 31 *Theoretical Medical Bioethics* 5.

additional requirements (eg it is thought they have a terminal illness, when in fact they do not). A false negative would be when a person is denied the opportunity to access assisted dying when they should be allowed to do so.

Opinions on where the bar for access to assisted dying should be placed and the burden of proof required will depend on your response to these false positives or negatives. If, for example, you believe that giving euthanasia to a person without their consent is tantamount to murder and is a serious wrong, while not allowing a person to access assisting dying is only a minor interference with their rights, you are likely to have strict criteria that need to be satisfied and require strong evidence that they are met. By contrast, if you think denying a person access to assisted dying at the time of their choosing is a major wrong and that allowing a person to access assisted dying when they are not fully autonomous is not a serious wrong you are likely to have weaker criteria and be less concerned about the strength of the evidence.

In considering this, it is crucial to recall the extensive evidence of how bad we are at predicting what our response would be in a case of severe ill health or disability. Gill[64] notes that in a study of 153 emergency care workers, only 18 per cent imaged that they would be glad to be alive if they had a severe spinal cord injury. However, in fact, in a study of 128 people with high-level spinal cord injuries, 92 per cent said they were glad to be alive.

That, however, may be to oversimplify the issue. It may be that you care more about some of the conditions in place than others. Thus, while you might be horrified at the idea of a person who does not genuinely wish to die being euthanised, you might not be so horrified if a person who genuinely wanted to die was not, in fact, terminally ill, as required by the conditions. In such a case your response to the false negatives or positives might depend on which of the criteria is in issue. As there is widespread agreement that an unwanted death is the worst thing that can be happen to a person, it seems the fear of a false positive is higher. The only scenario where it might be thought that a false negative would be worse is where as a result the patient was left in considerable pain. Those are the very cases where it is unlikely a mistaken diagnosis would be made.

It might be noted that people are free to take part in all kinds of dangerous activities, from boxing to mountaineering, from hang-gliding to eating deep-fried Mars Bars, without people interfering in these choices. It might, however, be noted that there are limits to this. You cannot drive without a licence or without wearing a seat belt; you cannot consent be being given serious harm; or hand yourself over to slavery. We might ask where the law draws these lines between what appear to be equally dangerous activities. I suggest there are two matters in play:

(1) the statistical likelihood that people engaging in the activity are not acting in an autonomous way. Few people who go mountaineering are not autonomous,

[64] C Gill, 'Health Professionals, Disability, and Assisted Suicide: An Examination of Relevant Empirical Evidence and Reply to Batavia (2000)' (2000) 6 *Psychology, Public Policy, and Law* 626.

but many – if not all – who are enslaved have non-existent or impaired autonomy. Debates tend to be fierce around BDSM and prostitution, where there is a mix of people engaging in the activity who are either fully autonomous or not;

(2) the social benefit of the activity. We might see this in terms of the seat-belt rule where, for example, not wearing a seat belt is hardly key to the flourishing of people's lives or beneficial to society. By contrast, mountaineering carries risks of death and serious injury, and so outlawing it would be harder to justify than outlawing a failure to wear a seatbelt.

If we apply these in relation to suicide we might conclude that statistically few cases of suicide are richly autonomous, and most are tragic losses to the individual and their loved ones.

VII. Conclusion and the Right to Die Debate

Perhaps the primary lesson from this chapter is that so many of the debates around assisted dying have been misplaced. We have been focusing on the grand issues of autonomy and sanctity of life, and missing the reality of the cases where people want to die. There is little discussion in the academic literature of: older people dying in poverty, in freezing temperatures in utter loneliness; the abandonment of the disabled and aged by our society, too many living socially excluded lives; our care homes too often marked by abuse, neglect and over-medication, but more commonly utter boredom and absence of social interaction. No love. No tenderness. No hope.

We would see this even more clearly if we started in horror and shock at a person's wish to die. What have we done to our fellow humans that they feel this way? Is this the product of the way we have denied them the appropriate pain relief, the appropriate social provision, the appropriate affection? Instead, the proposal of many is to accept their wish and kill them, reinforcing the very messages that created those wishes in the first place.

That all said, I agree there is need to find a response to cases such as those where people have an established, settled wish to die, and attempts to provide them with meaning and sustenance have failed, such as Tony Nicklinson. I have argued above for the defence of necessity to provide that. But I do not think that this is the most significant issue raised by cases involving those who wish to die. We need to address the root causes of those wishes. We need to recognise that most suicides are tragic, wretched acts, which can and should have been stopped. The primary legal response must be to protect people from suicide. That would be all the more justifiable if there were an effective means to end their life should all attempts to dissuade them fail.

10

Conclusion

Does a person have the right to die? This is the question that is normally seen as key when thinking about the law and suicide. The cases that for academics and students come to mind are those challenging ones involving people such Debbie Purdy, Diane Pretty and Tony Nicklinson. The debates on sanctity of life, protection of the vulnerable and autonomy are much discussed in the literature.

This book has claimed that our starting point is mistaken. The primary right in this context should be protection from suicide. The vast majority of suicides are not people who are driven by careful, autonomous decisions. They are not making a grand statement about the meaning of their lives. They are not finding dignity at the end of their life. Rather they are tragic, bitter, prosaic acts, to which horror, shock and deep sadness are the only appropriate reactions.

Consider, for example, the suicides of Sam and Chris Gould.[1] The sisters took their lives aged 16 and 17, having lived with sexual abuse from the age of five. In their later teenage years they reported the abuse to the police, but found it difficult to give evidence in court. They were told by the police that victims of sexual abuse should not discuss it with anyone else, even therapists. It seemed that the focus was on avoiding anything that might jeopardise the prosecution, rather than on the wellbeing of the victims. The prosecution was dropped, causing the girls to feel they were 'invalidated and not believed'. Their suicides were not messages which express their core values and their commitment to dignity. They tell us of a failing prosecution system; a refusal to take mental health system seriously. They are a dramatic failure of the state's response to vulnerable people. The proper response should be a recognition of the duty on the state to protect people from suicide.

That leads to one of the major messages of this book. Suicide is often presented as a decision by an individual. Explanations of suicide focus on the individual: their mental health; their gender; their state of health; and their difficulty in processing the difficulties they face. This is echoed, too, in the legal responses which see suicide as raising issues around mental capacity, autonomy and mental health legislation. Reforms to assisted dying focus on individual factors: has there been an autonomous wish? Does the patient have a terminal illness? Is the patient suffering unbearably? But suicide has much to teach us about society.[2]

[1] P Shepka, 'Sam and Chris Gould: Twins' Suicides Lead to Victim Policing Change' *BBC News*, 6 August 2020, available at www.bbc.co.uk/news/uk-england-cambridgeshire-58072098, accessed 14 December 2021.

[2] M Kral, *The Idea of Suicide* (Routledge, 2020).

What kind of suicide do we have where people kill themselves when there are huge delays in them receiving the mental health treatment they need?[3] When bullying and abuse online is ignored by social media companies and governments, leading to suicide among our young? When those seeking disability benefits are treated in such degrading ways that they commit suicide in despair?[4] The language of autonomy hides the state responsibility that behind many suicides. We need to recognise the right to be protected from suicide to hold public authorities to recognising the results of their actions.

Many of those who seek a liberal approach to suicide emphasise the importance of autonomy and see suicide prevention as an improper intervention in people's own decisions. 'Whose life is it anyway?' is the question often posed. But when we look at real suicides, such language seems utterly misguided. Lex Wortley writes of his suicide attempt:

> My attempt was eight years ago this month … mine is a genetic disease. I suffer from depression, anxiety, I have some self-esteem issues. I don't do well with change …. My decision was not planned out, it was a snap decision.[5]

As argued in Chapter 3, many suicide attempts seem – like Lex's – to be impulsive and certainly lacking the kind of careful thought that deserves the protection of autonomy. Consider too the suicide of Alex Kearns,[6] who misinterpreted an investment app and wrongly believed that he owed $730,000. He e-mailed the customer service line for help but received a standard response, saying they would get back to him. Later, he killed himself. Again, that is nothing like an autonomous act. Prevention of suicide in his case would hardly be autonomy-denying. Rather it would be autonomy enhancing. If we understand autonomy as allowing people to write the stories of their lives and direct the course of their lives, intervention in suicide often helps people to do that, rather than hindering them. We know this from the vast majority of suicide attempters who are prevented from committing suicide who express enormous gratitude that they were stopped. They do not see the intervention as diverting them from their autonomous chosen track, but rather as restoring them to where they want to be. That is not, of course, to say there are not some case where a suicide can be seen as a genuinely autonomous decision, but those are rare.

Suicide prevention should be recognised as a major social justice issue.[7] The rates of suicide are a snapshot of the disadvantages with society. It is the among

[3] S Morris, 'Bristol Transgender Woman Who Took Own Life Felt Fobbed Off, Family Say', *The Guardian*, 18 October 2020, available at www.theguardian.com/society/2020/oct/18/transgender-woman-who-took-own-life-felt-fobbed-off-by-bristol-mental-health-services, accessed 14 December 2021.

[4] The Samaritans, *Dying from Inequality* (The Samaritans, 2017).

[5] S Stefan, *Rational Suicide, Irrational Laws: Examining Current Approaches to Suicide in Policy and Law* (Oxford University Press, 2016).

[6] BBC News, 'Robinhood: US Family Sue Trading App over Son's Suicide', 9 February 2021, www.bbc.co.uk/news/world-us-canada-55990461, accessed 14 December 2021.

[7] J Westefeld, 'Suicide Prevention: An Issue of Social Justice' (2020) 1 *Journal of Prevention and Health Promotion* 58.

homeless, the welfare recipients, the trans community, the lonely, prisoners and the victims of domestic and sexual abuse where we find the highest suicide rates. This does not get discussed and is hidden by the medicalisation of suicide which sees it as a problem requiring treatment, rather than a breach of human rights which requires a justice intervention.

Suicide is, then, very much the responsibility of our society. Its personal[8] and economic costs are huge.[9] Yet, suicide prevention can be easy. As we have seen in Chapter 8, restricting access to the means to commit suicide, such as putting up barriers at suicide 'hot spots'; restricting access to firearms and other materials used in suicide; and taking care in media reporting of suicide, can have striking impacts on suicide rates. Indeed, as noted in Chapter 8, dramatic interventions such as 'sectioning' people under the Mental Health Act 1983 are some of the least successful interventions available. Removing the stigma around suicidal feelings and providing properly funded mental health services are far more effective. There are also strong arguments that the current law is contrary to the United Nations Convention of the Rights of Persons with Disability.[10]

It seems that barely a day goes by when there is a not a letter in a newspaper or a lively debate on social media on the right to die. But how dare we discuss a right to die when we fail to fund mental health; welfare recipients are denied their dignity; and older people are housed in care homes with little interest in doing more than warehousing them. It seems sometimes that our response to the older person driven desperate by loneliness and boredom is to promote euthanasia. For those with disability facing repeated messages that they are not full citizens as they are not economically productive and that they are shameful and disgusting, the offer of euthanasia for those with severe disability seems to compound the stigma heaped upon them. Those seeking escape from domestic abuse need properly funded shelters, not assisted dying. We have been focusing on how to respond to the wish to die, rather than asking what in our society has been causing people to want to end their lives.

When a person expresses a desire to die they are reflecting not only – or even primarily – their own views, but the views of those around them. We noted in Chapter 8 that the most common reason given by those seeking assisted dying in Oregon is that they do not want to be a burden on others. This is a powerful indictment of our society. It is reflection of the attitude that successful citizens are competent, self-sufficient and independent; that to need the care of others, to become disabled, is a disaster and a source of shame. Yet the idealisation of autonomy and self-sufficiency is based on a fiction. It is in our caring and interdependence that we find value in our lives.[11] It is our human nature that we are

[8] For a discussion of the impact on suicide on the families left behind see S McDonnell et al, 'From Grief to Hope' (University of Manchester, 2020).

[9] Patient Safety Group, *Self-harm and Suicide in Adults* (Royal College of Psychiatry, 2020).

[10] A Nilsson, *Compulsory Mental Health Interventions and the UNCRPD* (Hart Publishing, 2021).

[11] J Herring, *Law and the Relational Self* (Cambridge University Press, 2020).

vulnerable, dependent and caring, yet we have turned these virtues into vices. As Joshua Briscoe writes:

> A yet better way of looking at it is that *people* are not burdens. Rather, they are burdened by illness and suffering. Some of that burden can be shared with others, and we bear it with them. When we deny others the opportunity to help bear our burdens, we deny them a means of loving us in our dependence, in a most profound manifestation of our humanity.[12]

As I have been at pains to point out, I am not arguing against there being assisted dying for the small number of people making a richly autonomous decision to die in a way which fits in with the values by which they have lived their life. But those are rare cases. They are important but should not dominate the legal response.

We need to recognise that people should have a right to be protected from suicide. The correct response to a person who wishes to die is for the state and those in relationships with them to do all they can to prevent suicide. The state has a duty put in place steps so that people do not reach the stage where they seek the end of their life.

The UK's suicide rates do not have to be so high. We could – and should – seek zero suicide. That requires a determined effort and it requires money. But what better thing could there be to spend money on than saving lives. Suicide prevention is, in the vast majority of cases, enormously autonomy enhancing. It puts people's lives back on track and gives them a chance to flourish. Suicide is often not so much a personal choice but a reflection of a lack of care by society, a failure of societal provision, and a refusal to take mental health seriously. Our suicide rates are a tragic indictment of societal inequality. The right to be prevented from committing suicide is being breached far too often.

[12] J Briscoe, 'Dying, But Not Alone' (2021) 65 *The New Atlantis* 40.

BIBLIOGRAPHY

'Mother cleared of ME daughter's attempted murder' *BBC Online* (25 January 2010) news.bbc.co.uk/1/hi/england/sussex/8479211.stm, accessed 5 November 2021.

'Questions about the decision to prosecute Kay Gilderdale' *CPS* (26 January 2010) www.cps.gov.uk/news/press_statements/questions_about_kay_gilderdale_decision/, accessed 5 November 2021.

Abrutyn, S and Mueller, A, 'Are Suicidal Behaviors Contagious in Adolescence? Using Longitudinal Data to Examine Suicide Suggestion' (2014) 79 *American Sociological Review* 211.

—— 'Toward a Cultural-Structural Theory of Suicide: Examining Excessive Regulation and Its Discontents' (2018) 36 *Sociological Theory* 48.

Abrutyn, S, Mueller, A and Osborne, M, 'Rekeying Cultural Scripts for Youth Suicide: How Social Networks Facilitate Suicide Diffusion and Suicide Clusters Following Exposure to Suicide' (2020) 10 *Society and Mental Health* 112.

Agerbo, E, 'High Income, Employment, Postgraduate Education, and Marriage: A Suicidal Cocktail among Psychiatric Patients' (2007) 64 *Archives of General Psychiatry* 13777.

Ahmedani, B, Simon, G, Stewart, C, Beck, A, Waitzfelder, B, Rossom, R, Lynch, F, Owen-Smith, A, Hunkeler, E, Whiteside, U, Operskalski, B, Coffey, M and Solberg, L, 'Health Care Contacts in the Year Before Suicide Death' (2014) 29 *Journal of General Internal Medicine* 870.

Aitken, R and Munro, V, *Domestic Abuse and Suicide: Exploring the Links with Refuge's Client Base and Work Force* (University of Warwick, School of Law and Refuge).

Akrama, U, Ypsilantia, A, Gardanib, M et al, 'Prevalence and Psychiatric Correlates of Suicidal Ideation in UK University Students' (2020) 272 *Journal of Affective Disorders* 191.

Alldridge, P, 'The Doctrine of Innocent Agency' (1990) 2 *Criminal Law Forum* 45.

Allen, N, 'The Right to Life in a Suicidal State' (2013) 36 *International Journal of Law and Psychiatry* 350.

Almasy, S, Segal, K and Couwels, J, 'Sheriff: taunting post leads to arrests in Rebecca Sedwick bullying death' *CNN*, 16 October 2013, www.cnn.com/2013/10/15/justice/rebecca-sedwick-bullying-death-arrests/.

American Association of Suicidology, *"Suicide" Is Not the Same as "Physician Aid in Dying"* (AAS, 2017).

Anestis, M and Anestis, J, 'Suicide Rates and State Laws Regulating Access and Exposure to Handguns' (2015) 105 *American Journal of Public Health* 2049.

Anestis, M and Houtsma, C, 'The Association between Gun Ownership and Statewide Overall Suicide Rates' (2018) 48 *Suicide and Life Threatening Behaviour* 204.

Anonymous, 'Suicide – My Story' in A Grant, J Haire, F Biley and B Stone (eds), *Our Encounters with Suicide* (PCCS Books, 2013).

Apesoa-Varano, E, Barker, J and Hinton, L, '"If You Were Like Me, You Would Consider It Too": Suicide, Older Men, and Masculinity' (2017) 8 *Society and Mental Health* 1.

Appel, J, 'Beyond Fluoride: Pharmaceuticals, Drinking Water and the Public Health' *Huffington Post*, 21 December 2009, https://fluoridealert.org/news/beyond-fluoride-pharmaceuticals-drinking-water-the-public-health/.

Appelbaum, P, 'Clinical Practice: Assessment of Patients' Competence to Consent to Treatment' (2007) 357 *New England Journal of Medicine* 1834.

Appleby, L et al, *The National Confidential Inquiry into Suicide and Safety in Mental Health. Annual Report: England, Northern Ireland, Scotland and Wales* (University of Manchester, 2021).

Arensman, E, Griffin, E and Corcoran, P, 'Self-Harm: Extent of the Problem and Prediction of Repetition' in R O'Connor and J Pirkis (eds), *The International Handbook of Suicide Prevention* (John Wiley & Sons, 2016).
Aristotle, *Nicomachean Ethics*, trans by R Crisp (Cambridge University Press, 2000 [c 330BCE]).
Australian Law Reform Commission, *Equality, Capacity and Disability in Commonwealth Laws* (Australian Government, 2014).
Baca-Garcia, E, Diaz-Sastre, D, Basurte, E et al, 'A Prospective Study of the Paradoxical Relationship between Impulsivity and Lethality of Suicide Attempts' (2001) 62 *Journal of Clinical Psychiatry* 560.
Baer, J, *Ironic Freedom: Personal Choice, Public Policy, and the Paradox of Reform* (Palgrave, 2013).
Baier, A, *Postures of the Mind* (University of Minnesota Press, 1985).
Balaguer, A, Monforte-Royo, C, Porta-Sales, J, Alonso-Babarro, A, Altisent, R, Aradilla-Herrero, A, Bellido-Pérez, M, Breitbart, W, Centeno, C, Cuervo, M, Deliens, L, Frerich, G, Gastmans, C, Lichtenfeld, S, Limonero, J, Maier, M, Materstvedt, L, Nabal, M, Rodin, G, Rosenfeld, B, Schroepfer, T, Tomás-Sábado, J, Trelis, J, Villavicencio-Chávez, C and Voltz, R, 'An International Consensus Definition of the Wish to Hasten Death and Its Related Factors' (2016) 4 *PLoS One* 11.
Bantjes, J and Swartz, L, 'The Cultural Turn in Critical Suicidology: What Can We Claim and What Do We Know' (2017) 41 *Death Studies* 512.
—— 'What Can We Learn From First-Person Narratives? The Case of Nonfatal Suicidal Behavior' (2019) 29 *Qualitative Health Research* 1497.
Baril, A, 'The Somatechnologies of Canada's Medical Assistance in Dying Law: LGBTQ Discourses on Suicide and the Injunction to Live' (2017) 7 *Somatechnics* 201.
—— 'Suicidism: A New Theoretical Framework to Conceptualize Suicide from an Anti-Oppressive Perspective' (2020) 40 *University of Ottawa Disability Studies Quarterly* 1.
Baros, M, 'The UK Government's Covid-19 Response and Article 2 of the ECHR (Title I Dignity; Right to Life, Charter of Fundamental Rights of the EU)' (2020) 9 *Laws* 19.
Barr, B, Taylor-Robinson, D, Scott-Samuel, A, McKee, M and Stuckler, D, 'Suicides Associated with the 2008–10 Economic Recession in England: Time Trend Analysis' (2012) 124 *British Medical Journal* 345.
Bartlett, P, 'The Test of Compulsion in Mental Health Law: Capacity, Therapeutic Benefit and Dangerousness as Possible Criteria' (2003) 11 *Medical Law Review* 326.
—— 'The Right to Life and the Scope of Control: Fernandes de Oliveira v Portugal' 18 March 2018, strasbourgobservers.com/2019/03/18/the-right-to-life-and-the-scope-of-control-fernandes-de-oliveira-v-portugal/, accessed 1 November 2021.
Bartlett, P and Sandland, R, *Mental Health Law* (Oxford University Press, 2007).
Battin, M, *Ending Life: Ethics and the Way We Die* (Oxford University Press, 2005).
—— 'Could Suicide Really Be a Fundamental Human Right?' in S Muders (ed), *Human Dignity and Assisted Death* (Oxford University Press, 2017).
Baumeister, R, 'Suicide as Escape from Self' (1990) 97 *Psychological Review* 90.
Bayatrizi, Z, *Life Sentences. The Modern Ordering of Mortality* (University of Toronto Press, 2008).
BBC News 'Didsbury Church's Radical Change after Gay Girl's Suicide' 23 September 2018, www.bbc.co.uk/news/av/uk-england-manchester-45615029, accessed 29 October 2021.
BBC News, 'Robinhood: US Family Sue Trading App over Son's Suicide' 9 February 2021, www.bbc.co.uk/news/world-us-canada-55990461, accessed 14.11.21.
Beaudry, J-S, 'Somatic Oppression and Relational Autonomy: Revisiting Medical Aid in Dying through a Feminist Lens' (2020) 53 *UBC Law Review* 241.
Beck, A, 'Beyond Belief: A Theory of Modes, Personality, and Psychopathology' in P Salkovskis (ed), *Frontiers of Cognitive Therapy* (Guilford Press, 1996).
Bedford, D and Herring, J, *Embracing Vulnerability: The Challenges and Implications for the Law* (Routledge, 2020).
Bélanger, J, Caouette, J, Sharvit, K, Dugas, M and King, L, 'The Psychology of Martyrdom: Making the Ultimate Sacrifice in the Name of a Cause' (2014) 107 *Journal of Personality and Social Psychology* 494, 469.

Benatar, D, 'Suicide: A Qualified Defense' in J Stacey Taylor (ed), *The Metaphysics and Ethics of Death* (Oxford University Press, 2013).
—— *The Human Predicament* (Oxford University Press, 2017).
Bennett-Hunter, G, 'Ineffability: Reply to Professors Metz and Cooper' (2016) 44 *Philosophia* 1267.
Bennewith, O, Nowers, M, and Gunnell, D, 'Effect of Barriers on the Clifton Suspension Bridge, England, on Local Patterns of Suicide: Implications for Prevention' (2007) 190 *British Journal of Psychiatry* 266.
Bering, J, *Why We Kill Ourselves* (University of Chicago Press, 2018).
Berlin, I, *Two Conceptions of Liberty* (Oxford University Press, 1968).
Bertolote, J, 'Prevention of Suicidal Behaviors' in M Nock (ed), *The Oxford Handbook of Suicide and Self Injury* (Oxford University Press, 2014).
Bertolote, J and Fleischmann, A, 'Suicide and Psychiatry Diagnosis: A Worldwide Perspetive' (2002) 1 *World Psychiatry* 181.
Bidart, C, 'How Plans Change: Anticipation, Interferences and Unpredictabilities' (2019) 41 *Advances in Life Course Research* 254.
Blikshavn, T, Husum, T and Magelssen, M, 'Four Reasons Why Assisted Dying Should Not Be Offered for Depression' (2017) 14 *Journal of Bioethical Inquiry* 151.
Blosnich, J, De Luca, S, Lytle, M and Brownson, C, 'Questions of Faith: Religious Affiliations and Suicidal Ideation among Sexual Minority Young Adults' (2020) 50 *Suicide and Life Threatening Behaviour* 1158.
Blumenthal-Barby, J-S, 'Choice Architecture: Improving Choice while Preserving Liberty?' in C Coons and M Weber (eds), *Paternalism* (Cambridge University Press, 2013).
Bojanić, L, Hunt, I, Baird, A, Kapur, N, Appleby, L and Turnbull, P, 'Early Post-Discharge Suicide in Mental Health Patients: Findings from a National Clinical Survey' (2020) 11 *Frontiers of Psychiatry* 502.
Boldt, M, 'The Meaning of Suicide: Implications for Research' (1988) 9 *Crisis: The Journal of Crisis Intervention and Suicide Prevention* 93.
Borecky, A, Thomsen, C and Dubov, A, 'Reweighing the Ethical Tradeoffs in the Involuntary Hospitalization of Suicidal Patients' (2019) 19 *The American Journal of Bioethics* 71.
Bostwick, J and Pankratz, V, 'Affective Disorders and Suicide Risk: A Reexamination' (2000) 157 *American Journal of Psychiatry* 1925.
Brailovskaia, J, Ujma, M, Friedrich, S and Teismann, T, 'Thwarted Belongingness and Perceived Burdensomeness Mediate the Association between Bullying and Suicide Ideation' (2020) 41(2) *Crisis* 136.
Brandt, R, 'The Morality and Rationality of Suicide' in R Brandt (ed), *Morality, Utilitarianism and Rights* (Cambridge University Press, 1992).
—— 'The Morality and Rationality Handbook for the Study of Suicide' in D Banatar (ed), *Life, Death and Meaning* (Rowman & Littlefield, 2010).
Breivik, G, 'Can BASE Jumping Be Morally Defended' in M McNamee (ed), *Philosophy, Risk and Adventure Sports* (Taylor & Francis, 2007).
Brennan, S, 'The Goods of Childhood and Children's Rights' in F Baylis and C McLeod, (eds) *Family-Making: Contemporary Ethical Challenges* (Oxford University Press, 2014).
Brenner, SW 'Undue Influence in the Criminal Law: A Proposed Analysis of the Criminal Offence of Causing Suicide' (1982) 42 *Alabama Law Review* 62.
Brevard, A, Lester, D and Yang, B, 'Comparison of Suicide Notes Written by Suicide Completers and Suicide Attempters' (1990) 11 *Crisis* 7.
Briscoe, J, 'Dying, But Not Alone' (2021) 65 *The New Atlantis* 40.
Broome, J, 'The Badness of Dying Early' in E Gamlund, C Tollef Solberg and J McMahan (eds), *Saving People from the Harm of Death* (Oxford University Press, 2019).
Brown, G, Beck, A, Steer, R and Grisham, J, 'Risk Factors for Suicide in Psychiatric Outpatients: A 20-Year Prospective Study' (2000) 68 *Journal of Consulting and Clinical Psychology* 371.
Brown, S and Seals, J, 'Intimate Partner Problems and Suicide: Are We Missing the Violence?' (2019) 11 *Journal of Injury and Violence Research* 53.

Burgess, P, Pirkis, J, Jolley, D, Whiteford, H and Saxena, S, 'Do Nations' Mental Health Policies, Programs and Legislation Influence Their Suicide Rates? An Ecological Study of 100 Countries' (2004) 38 *Australian And New Zealand Journal of Psychiatry* 933.

Button, M, 'Suicide and Social Justice: Towards a Political Approach to Suicide' (2016) 39 *Political Research Quarterly* 270.

Calkins, B and Swetz, K, 'Physician Aid-in-Dying and Suicide Prevention in Psychiatry: A Moral Imperative over a Crisis' (2019) 19 *American Journal of Bioethics* 68.

Callaghan, S, Ryan, C and Kerridge, I, 'Risk of Suicide is Insufficient Warrant for Coercive Treatment for Mental Illness' (2013) 36 *International Journal of Law and Psychiatry* 374.

Callahan, S, 'A Feminist Case against Self-Determined Dying in Assisted Suicide and Euthanasia' (2015) 25 *Feminism & Psychology* 109.

Campaign Against Living Miserably, *A Crisis in Modern Masculinity: Understanding the Causes of Male Suicide* (Campaign Against Living Miserably, 2020).

Camus, A, *The Myth of Sisyphus*, trans by J O'Brien (Penguin, 2000).

Canetto, S, 'Women and Suicidal Behavior: A Cultural Analysis' (2008) 78 *American Journal of Orthopsychiatry* 259.

—— 'Suicide: Why Are Older Men So Vulnerable?' (2017) 20 *Men and Masculinities* 49.

Canning, R and Dvoskinm, J, 'Preventing Suicide in Detention and Correctional Facilities' in J Wooldredge and P Smith (eds), *The Oxford Handbook of Prisons and Imprisonment* (Oxford University Press, 2018).

Case, A and Deaton, A, 'Rising Morbidity and Mortality in Midlife among White Non-Hispanic Americans in the 21st Century' (2015) 112 *Proceedings of the National Academy of Science* 15078.

—— *Deaths of Despair and the Future of Capitalism* (Yale University Press, 2020).

Centre for Disease Control and Prevention, *National Survey of Drug Use and Mental Health* (CDC, 2017).

Chadwick, R, 'Expertise Revisited' (2016) 30 *Bioethics* 549.

Chan, B and Somerville, M, 'Converting the "Right to Life' to the "Right to Physician-Assisted Suicide and Euthanasia": An Analysis of Carter v Canada (Attorney General), Supreme Court' (2016) 24 *Medical Law Review* 143.

Chan, M, Bhatti, H, Meader, N, Stockton, S, Evans, J, O'Connor, R, Kapur, N and Kendall, T, 'Predicting Suicide Following Self-Harm: Systematic Review of Risk Factors and Risk Scales' (2016) 209 *British Journal of Psychiatry* 277.

Chandler, A, *Exploring the Role Of Masculinities In Suicidal Behaviour* (The Samaritans, 2012).

—— 'Boys Don't Cry? Critical Phenomenology, Self-Harm and Suicide' (2015) 25 *Feminism & Psychology* 124.

Chesley, K and Loring-McNulty, N, 'Process of Suicide: Perspective of the Suicide Attempter' (2003) 9 *Journal of American Psychiatry Nurses Association* 41.

Chin, P, 'Detention, Capacity, and Treatment in the Mentally Ill – Ethical and Legal Challenges' (2019) *Cambridge Quarterly of Healthcare Ethics* 28.

Cholbi, M, 'Suicide Intervention and Non-Ideal Kantian Theory' (2002) 19 *Journal of Applied Philosophy* 245.

—— *Suicide: The Philosophical Dimensions* (Broadview, 2011).

—— 'Medically Enabled Suicides' in M Cholbi and J Varelius (eds), *New Directions in the Ethics of Assisted Suicide and Euthanasia* (Springer, 2015).

Christian Concern, *Euthanasia and Assisted Suicide* (Christian Concern, 2020).

Clements, C, Turnbull, P, Hawton, K et al, 'Rates of Self-Harm Presenting to General Hospitals: A Comparison of Data from the Multicentre Study of Self-Harm in England and Hospital Episode Statistics' (2016) 6 *British Medical Journal* 9749.

Clough, A, 'Mercy Killing, Partial Defences and Charge Decisions: 50 Shades of Grey' (2020) 84 *The Journal of Criminal Law* 211.

Clough, B, '"People Like That": Realising the Social Model in Mental Capacity Jurisprudence' (2014) 23 *Medical Law Review* 53.

Cohen, A, 'Must Rights Impose Enforceable Positive Duties?' (2004) 35 *Journal of Social Philosophy* 364.

Coleman, D, 'Not Dead Yet' in D Coleman (ed), *The Case against Assisted Suicide: For the Right of End-to-Life Care* (Johns Hopkins University Press, 2002).

Committee on the Rights of Persons with Disabilities, *Concluding Observations on the Initial Report of the United Kingdom of Great Britain and Northern Ireland* (2017).

Conly, S, *Against Autonomy* (Cambridge University Press, 2012).

Coroners and Justice Act 2009.

Cover, R. *Queer Youth: Suicide, Culture and Identity* (Routledge, 2012).

Cowley, C, 'Suicide is Neither Rational nor Irrational' (2006) 9 *Ethical Theory and Moral Practice* 495.

Craigie, J, 'Capacity, Value Neutrality and the Ability to Consider the Future' (2013) *International Journal of Law in Context* 4.

Craigie, J and Bortolotti, L, 'Rationality, Diagnosis, and Patient Autonomy in Psychiatry' in J Sadler, B Fulford and W van Staden (eds), *The Oxford Handbook of Psychiatric Ethics* (Oxford University Press, 2021).

Crown Prosecution Service, *Suicide: Policy for Prosecutors in Respect of Cases of Encouraging or Assisting Suicide* (CPS, 2014).

Cukrowicz, K and E Poindexter, 'Suicide' in C Richards and M O'Hara (eds), *The Oxford Handbook of Depression and Comorbidity* (Oxford University Press, 2014).

Daine, K, Hawton, K, Singaravelu, V, Stewart, A, Simkin, S and Montgomery, P, 'The Power of the Web: A Systematic Review of Studies of the Influence of the Internet on Self-Harm and Suicide in Young People' (2013) 8 *PLoS One* e77555.

Davis, A, 'The Status of Anencephalic Babies: Should their Bodies be Used as Donor Banks?' (1988) 14 *Journal of Medical Ethics* 150.

Davis, J and Mathison, E, 'The Case for an Autonomy-Centered View of Physician-Assisted Death' (2020) 17 *Journal of Bioethical Inquiry* 345.

de Albuquerque Green, C, Manthorpe, J and Martineau, S, *A Matter of Life or Death* (King's College London, 2020).

de Campos, T, 'MAiD in Canada and the Homo Economicus View of Dignity: Inclusive Enough?' (2018) 22 *Journal of Disability & Religion* 246.

De Haan, J, 'The Ethics of Euthanasia: Advocates' Perspectives' (2002) 16 *Bioethics* 154.

De Leo, D, Burgis, S, Bertolote, J, Kerkhof, A and Bille-Brahe, U, 'Definitions of Suicidal Behavior: Lessons Learned from the WHO/EURO Multicentre Study' (2006) 27 *Crisis: The Journal of Crisis Intervention and Suicide Prevention* 4.

Dees, M, Vernooji-Dassen, M, Dekkers, W, Vissers, K and van Weel, C, '"Unbearable Suffering": A Qualitative Study on the Perspectives of Patients who Request Assistance in Dying' (2011) 37 *Journal of Medical Ethics* 727.

Deisenhammer, E, Ing, C, Strauss, R, Kemmler, G, Hinterhuber, H and Weiss, E, 'The Duration of the Suicidal Process: How Much Time is Left for Intervention between Consideration and Accomplishment of a Suicide Attempt?' (2009) 79 *Journal of Clinical Psychiatry* 19.

den Hartogh, G, 'Why Extra Caution is Needed in the Case of Depressed Patients' (2015) 41 *Journal of Medical Ethics* 588.

Department of Constitutional Affairs, *Mental Capacity Act Code of Practice* (TSO, 2007).

Department of Health (Australia), *Strategic Framework* (2013).

Department of Health, *Code of Practice: Mental Health Act 1983* (Department of Health, 2015).

Department of Health, *Preventing Suicide in England* (Department of Health, 2020).

Devine, P, *The Ethics of Homicide* (University of Notre Dame Press, 1990).

Dhingra, K, Klonsky, E and Tapola, V, 'An Empirical Test of the Three-Step Theory of Suicide in UK University Students' (2019) 49 *Suicide and Life-Threatening Behaviour* 478.

Dochin, A, 'Autonomy, Interdependence, and Assisted Suicide: Respecting Boundaries/Crossing Lines' (2000) 14 *Bioethics* 187.

Dowie, S, 'What is Suicide? Classifying Self-Killings' (2020) 23 *Medicine, Health Care and Philosophy* 717.

Downie, J, 'Why Feminist Philosophy (Especially Sue Sherwin's) Matters: Reflections through the Lens of Medical Assistance in Dying' (2020) 13 *International Journal of Feminist Approaches to Bioethics* 21.

Downie, J and Sherwin, S, 'A Feminist Exploration of Issues around Assisted Death' (1996) 15 St *Louis University Public Law Review* 303.

Droge, J and Tabor, A, *A Noble Death: Suicide and Martyrdom among Christians and Jews in Antiquity* (Harper Collins, 1992).

Drummond, C, McBride, O, Fear, N and Full, E, *Alcohol Dependence* (Health and Social Care Information Centre, 2014).

Duff, A, '"Thank God I Failed"' in H Hurd (ed), *Moral Puzzles and Legal Perplexities* (Cambridge University Press, 2021).

Duff, RA, 'Socratic Suicide?' (1983) 83 *Proceedings of the Aristotelian Society* 35.

Durkheim, E, *Suicide: A Study in Sociology* (Free Press, 1951 [1897]).

Dworkin, R, *Life's Dominion* (Harper Collins, 1993).

Dworkin, R et al, 'Assisted Suicide: The Philosopher's Brief' *The New York Review*, 27 March 1997, www.nybooks.com/articles/1997/03/27/assisted-suicide-the-philosophers-brief/, accessed 13 December 2021.

Egeland, J and Sussex, J, 'Suicide and Family Loading for Affective Disorders' (1985) 254 *Journal of the American Medical Association* 915.

Elliot, C, 'Caring about Risk: Are Severely Depressed Patients Competent to Consent to Research?' (1997) 54 *Archives of General Psychiatry* 113.

Elster, J, 'The Possibility of Rational Politics' (1987) 28 *Journal of European Sociology* 67.

Esposito-Smythers, C, Weismoore, J, Zimmermann, R and Spirito, A, 'Suicidal Behaviors among Children and Adolescents' in M Nock (ed), *The Oxford Handbook of Suicide and Self-Injury* (Oxford University Press, 2014).

Eurostat, *Just over 56 000 Persons in the EU Committed Suicide* (European Commission, 2019).

Evans, R, Scourfield, J and Moore, G 'Gender, Relationship Breakdown and Suicide Risk: A Systematic Review of Research in Western Countries' (2016) 46 *Journal of Family Issues* 2239.

Fanning, J, *New Medicalism and the Mental Health Act* (Hart Publishing, 2018).

Favril, L, O'Connor, R, Hawton, K and Laenen, F, 'Factors Associated with the Transition from Suicidal Ideation to Suicide Attempt in Prison' (2020) 63 *European Psychiatry* 101.

Fawcett, J and Busch, K, 'The Pharmacologic Treatment of Suicidal Patients' in M Nock (ed), *The Oxford Handbook of Suicide and Self-Injury* (Oxford University Press, 2014).

Fearnley, D, 'The Zero Suicide Policy Challenges', available at www.england.nhs.uk/blog/david-fearnley, accessed 13 December 2021.

Feldman, F, *Confrontations with the Reaper: A Philosophical Study of the Nature and Value of Death* (Oxford University Press, 1994).

Fernandez, P, Coverdale, J and Brookbanks, W, 'Implications of Autonomy for Forensic Consequences of Extended Suicide' (2002) 9 *Psychiatry, Psychology and Law* 146.

Fiori, L, Ernst, C and Turecki, G, 'Genetic and Neurobiological Approaches to Understanding Suicidal Behaviors' in M Nock (ed), *The Oxford Handbook of Suicide and Self-Injury* (Oxford University Press, 2014).

Fitzpatrick, S, 'Re-Moralizing the Suicide Debate' (2014) 11 *Journal of Bioethical Inquiry* 223.

—— 'Epistemic Justice and the Struggle for Critical Suicide Literacy' (2020) 34 *Social Epistemology* 555.

Fitzpatrick, S, Hooker, C and Kerridge, I, 'Suicidology as a Social Practice' (2015) 4 *Social Epistemology Review and Reply Collective* 44.

Fitzpatrick, S and River, J, 'Beyond the Medical Model: Future Directions for Suicide Intervention Services' (2018) 48 *International Journal of Health Services* 189.

Fletcher, J, 'The Right to Die' (1968) April *Atlantic Monthly*.

Florentine, J and Crane, C, 'Suicide Prevention by Limiting Access to Methods: A Review of Theory and Practice' (2010) 70 *Social Science Medicine* 1626.
Fortin, J, *Children's Rights and the Developing Law* (Cambridge University Press, 2003).
Foster, C, *Choosing Life, Choosing Death* (Hart Publishing, 2009).
—— 'Suicide Tourism May Change Attitudes to Assisted Suicide, but Not through the Courts' (2015) 41 *Journal of Medical Ethics* 620.
Freeman, A, Mergl, R, Kohls, E, Székely, A, Gusamao, R, Arensman, E, Koburger, N, Hegerl, U and Rummel-Kluge, C, 'A Cross National Study on Gender Differences in Suicide Intent' (2017) 17 *BMC Psychiatry* 234.
Freeman, M et al, 'Reversing Hard Won Victories in the Name of Human Rights: A Critique of the General Comment on Article 12 of the UN Convention on the Rights of Persons with Disabilities' (2015) 9 *Lancet Psychiatry* 844.
Garcia-Vega, E, Camero, A, Fernández, M and Villaverde, A, 'Suicidal Ideation and Suicide Attempts in Persons with Gender Dysphoria' (2018) 30 *Psicothema* 283.
Gardner, S, 'Direct Action and the Defence of Necessity' (2005) *Criminal Law Review* 371.
Garfield, C, Isacco, A and Rogers, R, 'A Review of Men's Health and Masculinity' (2008) 2 *American Journal of Lifestyle Medicine* 474.
General Comment No 36 (2018) on Article 6 of the International Covenant on Civil and Political Rights, on the right to life.
Gengasamy, M, Sylvester, C, Shulman, J and Pizon, A, 'Contemporary Characteristics and Lethality Correlates of Serious Suicide Attempts in Children and Adolescents' (2020) 50 *Suicide and Life Threatening Behavior* 714.
Gergen, K, *Relational Being: Beyond Self and the Community* (Oxford University Press, 2011).
Gill, C, 'Health Professionals, Disability, and Assisted Suicide: An Examination of Relevant Empirical Evidence and Reply to Batavia' (2000) 6 *Psychology, Public Policy, and Law* 626.
Glowinski, A, Bucholz, K, Nelson, E, Fu, Q, Madden, P, Reich, W and Health, A, 'Suicide Attempts in an Adolescent Female Twin Sample (2001) 40 *Journal of the American Academy of Child and Adolescent Psychiatry* 1300.
Goldblatt, M, 'Psychodynamics of Suicide' in M Nock (ed), *The Oxford Handbook of Suicide and Self-Injury* (Oxford University Press, 2014).
Goldsmith, S, Pellmar, T, Kleinman, A and Bunney, W (eds), *Reducing Suicide* (The National Academics Press, 2002).
Goodman, J, 'The Case of Dr Munro: Are There Lessons to be Learnt?' (2010) 18 *Medical Law Review* 564.
Gormally, L, 'Two Competing Conceptions of Human Dignity' in S Muders (ed), *Human Dignity and Assisted Death* (Oxford University Press, 2017).
Greasley, K, 'R (Purdy) v DPP and the Case for Wilful Blindness' (2010) 30 *Oxford Journal of Legal Studies* 301.
Grisso, T and Appelbaum, P, *Assessing Competence to Consent to Treatment* (Oxford University Press, 1998).
Grisso, T, Appelbaum, P and Hill-Fotouhi, C, 'The MacCAT-T: A Clinical Tool to Assess Patients' Capacities to Make Treatment Decisions' (1997) 48 *Psychiatric Services* 1415.
Grzanka, P and Mann, E, 'Queer Youth Suicide and the Psychopolitics of "It Gets Better"' (2014) 17 *Sexualities* 369.
Gupta, A, 'Definitions' in E Zalta (ed), *The Stanford Encyclopedia of Philosophy* (University of Stanford, 2021).
Haas, A and Mortali, M, 'Suicidal Behavior among Sexual and Gender Minority Populations' in E Rothblum (ed), *The Oxford Handbook of Sexual and Gender Minority Mental Health* (Oxford University Press, 2020).
Hackman, R, 'Detroit Tackles Suicide Taboos Head on' *The Guardian*, 18 February 2015.
Hadlaczky, G, Wasserman, D, Hoven, C, Mandell, D and Wasserman, C, 'Suicide Prevention Strategies' in R O'Connor and J Pirkis (eds), *The International Handbook of Suicide Prevention* (J Wiley and Sons, 2016).

Hardwig, J, 'Is There a Duty to Die?' (1997) 27 *Hastings Centre Report* 34.
Harmer, B, Lee, S, Duong, T, Saabadi, A, *Suicidal Ideation* (Statpearls, 2021).
Harrington, J, 'Privileging the Medical Norms: Liberalism, Self-Determination and Refusal of Treatment' (1996) 16 *Legal Studies* 348.
Harris, J, *The Value of Life* (Routledge & Kegan Paul, 1985).
Hart, H, 'Are There Any Natural Rights?' (1995) 64 *The Philosophical Review* 131.
Hart, H and Honoré, T, *Causation in the Law* (Oxford University Press, 1985).
Haw, C, Casey, D, Holmes, J and Hawton, K, 'Suicidal Intent and Method of Self-Harm: A Large-Scale Study of Self-Harm Patients Presenting to a General Hospital' (2015) 45 *Suicide and Life-Threatening Behaviour* 732.
Haw, C, Hawton, K, Niedzxiedz, C and Platt, S, 'Suicide Clusters: A Review of Risk Factors and Mechanisms' (2013) 43 *Suicide and Life Threatening Behavior* 97.
Hawton, K et al, 'Pharmacological Interventions for Self-Harm in Adults: Three Trials Indicated No Overall Improvements' (2015) 6 *Cochrane Database of Systematic Reviews* CD011777.
Hawton, K, Casañas, I, Comabella, C, Haw, C and Saunders, K, 'Risk Factors for Suicide in Individuals with Depression: A Systematic Review' (2013) 147 *Journal of Affective Disorders* 1.
Haylen, A et al, *Suicide Prevention: Policy and Strategy* (House of Commons Library, 2020).
Hecht, J, *Stay: A History of Suicide and the Philosophies Against It* (Yale University Press, 2014).
Hendin, H, 'Psychodynamics of Suicide, with Particular Reference to the Young' (1991) 148 *American Journal of Psychiatry* 1150.
Henson, K, Brock, R, Charnock, J, Wickramasinghe, B, Will, O and Pitman, A, 'Risk of Suicide after Cancer Diagnosis in England' (2019) 76 *JAMA Psychiatry* 51.
Heron, J et al, 'Exposure to, and Searching for, Information about Suicide and Self-Harm on the Internet: Prevalence and Predictors in a Population Based Cohort of Young Adults' (2015) 185 *Journal of Affective Disorders* 239.
Herring, J, 'Entering the Fog: On the Borderlines of Mental Capacity' (2008) 83 *Indiana Law Journal* 1620.
—— 'The Legal Duties of Carers' (2010) 18 *Medical Law Review* 248.
—— *Caring and the Law* (Hart Publishing, 2013).
—— *Relational Autonomy and Family Law* (Springer, 2014).
—— 'The Disability Critique of care' (2014) 8 *Elder Law Review* 2.
—— *Vulnerable Adults and the Law* (Oxford University Press, 2016).
—— 'Peter Skegg and the Question No-one Asks: Why Presume Capacity?' in M Henaghan and J Wall (eds), *Law, Ethics, and Medicine: Essays in Honour of Peter Skegg* (Thompson Reuters, 2016).
—— *Law and the Relational Self* (Cambridge University Press, 2020).
—— *Criminal Law* (Oxford University Press, 2020).
—— *Domestic Abuse and Human Rights* (Intersentia, 2021).
—— *Law Through the Life Course* (Bristol University Press, 2021).
—— 'Relational Personhood' (2021) *Keele Law Review* 21.
Herring, J and Wall, J, 'Autonomy, Capacity and Vulnerable Adults: Filling the Gaps in the Mental Capacity Act' (2015) 35 *Legal Studies* 698.
Heyer, K, 'Rejecting Rights: the Disability Critique of Physician Assisted Suicide' (2011) 54 *Studies in Law, Politics and Society* 77.
Hill, D, 'What is it to Commit Suicide?' (2011) 24 *Ratio* 192.
Hill, T and Needham, B, 'Rethinking Gender and Mental Health: A Critical Analysis of Three Propositions' (2013) 92 Social Science *Medicine* 83.
Hillbrand, M, 'Overlap between Suicidal Behavior and Interpersonal Violence' in M Nock (ed), *The Oxford Handbook of Suicide and Self-Injury* (Oxford University Press, 2014).
Hindmarch, T, Hotopf, M and Owen, G, 'Depression and Decision-Making Capacity for Treatment or Research: A Systemic Review' (2013) 14 *BMC Medical Ethics* 54.
Hirsch, J, 'The Wish to Die: Assisted Suicide and Mental Illness' (2012) 16 *Journal of Social Work in End-of-Life & Palliative Care* 213.

Hitlin, S and Won Kwon, H, 'Agency Across the Life Course' in J Mortimer and M Shanahan (eds), *Handbook of the Life Course* (Springer, 2016).

Hjelmeland, H, 'Cultural Context is Critical in Suicide Research and Prevention' (2011) 32 *Crisis* 61.

Hjelmeland, H and Knizek, B, (2020) 'The Emperor's New Clothes? A Critical Look at the Interpersonal Theory of Suicide' (2020) 44 *Death Studies* 168.

Hjelmeland, H, Dieserud, G, Dyregrov, K, Knizek, B and Leenaars, A, 'Psychological Autopsy Studies as Diagnostic Tools: Are They Methodologically Flawed?' (2012) 36 *Death Studies* 605.

HM Government, *Preventing Suicide in England: A Cross-Government Outcomes Strategy to Save Lives* (HM Government, 2012).

—— *Preventing Suicide in England: Fourth Progress Report of the Cross-Government Outcomes Strategy to Save Lives* (HM Government, 2019).

—— *Preventing Suicide in England: FifthProgress Report of the Cross-Government Outcomes Strategy to Save Lives* (HM Government, 2021).

Holmes, J, 'Suicide and Deliberate Self-Harm' in M Popili (ed), *Phenomenology of Suicide* (Springer, 2018).

Homer, A, 'Deaths of People on Benefits Prompt Inquiry Call' *BBC News*, 10 May 2021, available at www.bbc.co.uk/news/uk-56819727, accessed 13 December 2021.

Homicide Act 1957.

Hooley, J and St Germain, S, 'Should We Expand the Conceptualization of Self-Ijurious Behavior? Rationale, Review, and Recommendations' in M Nock (ed), *The Oxford Handbook of Suicide and Self-Injury* (Oxford University Press, 2014).

Horgos, B, 'Is Physician-Assisted Suicide a Feminist Issue?' (2019) *Lady Science*, 8 October.

Horowitz, A, Berona, J, Busby, D, Eisenberg, D, Zheng, K, Pistorello, J, Albucher, R, Coryell, W, Favorite, T, Walloch, J and King, C, 'Variation in Suicide Risk among Subgroups of Sexual and Gender Minority College Students' (2020) 50 *Suicide and Life Threatening Behaviour* 1041.

https://livethroughthis.org/.

Hume, D, *Of Suicide* (Penguin, 2005 [1783]).

Hunt, I, Bickley, H, Windfuhr, K, Shaw, J, Appleby, L and Kapur, N, 'Suicide in Recently Admitted Psychiatric In-Patients: A Case-Control Study' (2013) 44 *Journal of Affective Disorders* 123.

Hunt, I, Kapur, N, Robinson, J, Shaw, J, Flynn, S, Bailey, H et al, 'Suicide within 12 Months of Mental Health Service Contact in Different Age and Diagnostic Groups. National Clinical Survey' (2006) 188 *British Journal of Psychiatry* 135.

Huxtable, R and Ives, J, 'License to Kill: A New Model for Excusing Medically Assisted Dying?' in M Cholbi and J Varelius (eds), *New Directions in the Ethics of Assisted Suicide and Euthanasia* (Springer, 2015).

Iacobucci, G, 'Suicide Rates Continue to Rise in England and Wales' (2021) 370 *British Medical Journal* 3431.

Insel, TR and Cuthbert, BN, 'Brain Disorders? Precisely' (2015) 348 *Science* 499.

International Association of Suicide Prevention, www.iasp.info/, accessed 13 December 2021.

IPSO, *Editors' Code of Practice* (IPSO, 2021).

Jackson, E, 'Secularism, Sanctity and the Wrongness of Killing' (2008) 3 *Biosciences* 125.

—— 'From "Doctor Knows Best" to Dignity: Placing Adults Who Lack Capacity at the Centre of Decisions About Their Medical Treatment' (2018) 81 *Modern Law Review* 247.

Jager-Hyman, S. and A. Cunningham, S. Wenzel, S. Mattei, G. Brown and A. Beck 'Cognitive Distortions and Suicide Attempts' (2014) 38 *Cognitive Therapy and Research* 369.

Jaworski, K, 'The Gendering of Suicide' (2010) 25 *Australian Feminist Studies* 47.

—— 'Towards Ethics of Wonder and Generosity in Critical Suicidology' (2020) 34 *Social Epistemology* 589.

Jewell, P, 'Rationality, Euthanasia, and the Sanctity of Life' (2005) *Australian Association for Professional and Applied Ethics* 1.

Johnson, K and Rhodes, R, 'Ethnicity as a Factor' in S Youngner and R Arnold (eds), *The Oxford Handbook of Ethics at the End of Life* (Oxford University Press, 2020).

Joiner, T, *Why People Die by Suicide* (Harvard University, 2005).

—— 'Scientific Rigor as the Guiding Heuristic for SLTB's Editorial Stance' (2011) 41 *Suicide and Life-Threatening Behavior* 471.

Jones, D, 'An Unholy Mess: Why "The Sanctity of Life Principle" Should Be Jettisoned' (2016) 22 *The New Bioethics* 185.

—— *Assisted Suicide and Euthanasia: A Guide to the Evidence* (Anscombe Centre 2015).

Jones, D, Gastmans, C and Mackellar, C, 'Final Conclusions on Final Solutions' in D Jones, C Gastmans and C Mackellar, *Assisted Suicide and Euthanasia Lessons from Belgium* (Cambridge University Press, 2018).

Jones, D and Paton, D, 'How Does Legalization of Physician-Assisted Suicide Affect Rates of Suicide?' (2015) 18 *Southern Medical Journal* 599.

Jordan, A, 'Postfeminist Men's Movements: The Campaign Against Living Miserably and Male Suicide as "Crisis"' in A Jordan (ed), *The New Politics of Fatherhood* (Palgrave, 2019).

Jordan, A and Chandler, A, 'Crisis? What Crisis? A Feminist Analysis of Discourse on Masculinities and Suicide' (2019) 29 *Journal of Gender Studies* 462.

Kamm, F, *Almost Over* (Oxford University Press, 2020).

Kapur, N, Clements, C, Bateman, N, Foëx, B, Mackway-Jones, K, Huxtable, R et al, 'Advance Directives and Suicidal Behaviour' (2010) 34 *British Medical Journal* 4557.

Kapur, N and Goldney, R, 'What Causes Suicidal Behaviour?' in N Kapur and R Goldney (eds), *Suicide Prevention* (Oxford University Press, 2019).

Karlsson, P, Helgesson, G, Titelman, D, Sjöstrand, M and Juth, N, 'Skepticism towards the Swedish Vision Zero for Suicide: Interviews with 12 Psychiatrists' (2018) 19 *BMC Medical Ethics* 26.

Keown, J, 'Restoring Moral and Intellectual Shape to the Law after *Bland*' (1997) 113 *Law Quarterly Review* 481.

—— 'The Legal Revolution: From "Sanctity of Life" to "Quality of Life" and "Autonomy"' (1998) 14 *Journal of Contemporary Health Law and Policy* 253.

—— *Euthanasia, Ethics and Public Policy: An Argument against Legalisation* (Cambridge: Cambridge University Press, 2002).

Kim, S, 'Lives Not Worth Living in Modern Euthanasia Regimes' (2019) 16 *Journal of Policy & Practice in Intellectual Disabilities* 134.

King, E, Baldwin, D, Sinlcair, J, Campbell, M, 'The Wessex Recent In-Patient Suicide Study, 2. Case-Control Study of 59 In-Patient Suicides' (2001) 178 *British Journal of Psychiatry* 537.

Kitchingham, L, 'World Suicide Prevention Day: Why We Should Redefine Masculinity', *Personnel Today*, 10 September 2020, available at www.personneltoday.com/hr/world-suicide-prevention-day-why-we-should-redefine-masculinity, accessed 13 December 2021.

Kleespies, PM, 'Medical Illness, Suicide, and Assisted Death' in PM Kleespies (ed), *The Oxford Handbook of Behavioral Emergencies and Crises* (Oxford University Press, 2016).

Kleinig, J, *Paternalism* (Rowman and Allanheld, 1983).

Klonsky, E and May, A, 'The Three-Step Theory (3ST): A New Theory of Suicide Rooted in the "Ideation-to-Action" Framework' (2015) 8 *International Journal of Cognitive Therapy* 114.

Knauer, N, 'Defining Capacity: Balancing the Competing Interests of Autonomy and Need' (2003) 12 *Temple Political and Civil Rights Law Review* 321.

Knizek, B and Hjelmeland, H, 'A Theoretical Model for Interpreting Suicidal Behaviour as Communication' (2007) 17 *Theory & Psychology* 679.

Korsgaard, C, 'The Sources of Normativity' (1992) 12 *Tanner Lectures on Human Values* 112.

Kral, M, 'Suicide and the Internalization of Culture: Three Questions (1998) 35 *Transcultural Psychiatry* 221.

—— *The Idea of Suicide* (Routledge, 2020).

Kreitman, N, 'The Coal Gas Story. United Kingdom Suicide Rates, 1960–71' (1976) 30 *British Journal of Preventive Social Medicine* 86.

Kruger, D, 'There's a Better Way of Dying than Assisted Suicide', *The Times*, 15 September 2021.

Kushner, H, *Self-destruction in the Promised Land* (Rutgers University Press, 1989).

Large, M and Ryan, C, 'Disturbing Findings about the Risk of Suicide and Psychiatric Hospitals' (2014) 49 *Social Psychiatry and Psychiatric Epidemiology* 1353.
Large, M, Kaneson, M, Myles, N, Myles, H, Gunaratne, P and Ryan, C, 'Metaanalysis of Longitudinal Cohort Studies of Suicide Risk Assessment among Psychiatric Patients: Heterogeneity in Results and Lack of Improvement over Time' (2016) 11 *PLoS ONE* 6.
Large, M, Ryan, C, Carter, G and Kapur, N, 'Can We Usefully Stratify Patients According to Suicide Risk?' (2017) 359 *British Medical Journal* 4627.
Large, M, Ryan, C and Nielssen, O, 'The Validity and Utility of Risk Assessment for Inpatient Suicide' (2011) 19(6) *Australasian Psychiatry* 507.
Leigh, B, 'A Bad Decision for Patients' (2012) 11 *Mind's Newsletter* 1.
Lemmens, T, 'The Conflict between Open-Ended Access to Physician-Assisted Dying and the Protection of the Vulnerable: Lessons from Belgium's Euthanasia Regime in the Post-Carter Era' in C Regis, L Khoury and R Kouri (eds), *Les Grands Conilits en Droit de la Sante* (Yvon Blais, 2016) 261.
—— 'When a Theoretical Commitment to Broad Physician Aid-in-Dying Faces the Reality of Its Implementation' (2019) 19 *American Journal of Bioethics* 65.
Lester, D, 'Can Suicide Be a Good Death?' (2006) 30 *Death Studies* 511.
Lewiecki, E and Miller, S, 'Suicide, Guns and Public Policy' (2013) 103 *American Journal of Public Health* 27.
Lewis, P, 'Informal Legal Change on Assisted Suicide: the Policy for Prosecutors' (2011) 31 *Legal Studies* 119.
Lewitzka, U, Sauer, C, Bauer, M et al, 'Are National Suicide Prevention Programs Effective? A Comparison of 4 Verum and 4 Control Countries over 30 years' (2019) 19 *BMC Psychiatry* 158.
Lin, J and Lu, T, 'Association between the Accessibility to Lethal Methods and Method-Specific Suicide Rates: An Ecological Study in Taiwan' (2006) 67 *Journal of Clinical Psychiatry* 1074.
Lindberg, J, Johansson, M and Bostrom, L, 'Temporising and Respect for Patient Self-Determination' (2019) 45 *Journal of Medical Ethics* 161.
Linehan, M, *Cognitive-Behavioral Treatment of Borderline Personality Disorder* (Guilford Press, 1993).
Linton, S, *My Body Politic* (University of Michigan Press, 2006).
Longmore, P, 'The Resistance: The Disability Rights Movement and Assisted Suicide' in P Longmore (ed), *Why I Burned My Book and Other Essays On Disability* (Temple University Press, 2003).
—— 'Policy, Prejudice, and Reality' (2005) 16 *Journal of Disability Policy Studies* 38.
Lucas, M, O'Reilly, E, Pan, A, Mirzaei, F, Willett, W, Okereke, O and Ascherio, A, 'Coffee, Caffeine and Risk of Completed Suicide' (2014) 15 *World Journal of Biological Psychiatry* 377.
Lyons, D, 'The Correlativity of Rights and Duties' (1970) 4 *Nous* 45.
Macdonald, C and Naudin, J, 'The Construction of the Suicidal Self in Phenomenological Psychology' in M-L Honkasalo and M Tuominen, *Culture, Suicide and the Human Condition* (Berghahn Books, 2014).
MacIssac, M, Bugeja, L and Weiland, T, 'Prevalence and Characteristics of Interpersonal Violence in People Dying From Suicide in Victoria, Australia' (2018) 30 *Asia-Pacific Journal of Public Health* 36.
Mackenzie, C, 'Feminist Innovation in Philosophy: Relational Autonomy and Social Justice' (2019) 72 *Women's Studies International Forum* 144.
Mackenzie, C and Rogers, W, 'Autonomy, Vulnerability and Capacity: A Philosophical Appraisal of the Mental Capacity Act' (2013) 13 *International Journal of the Law in Context* 3756.
Mackenzie, C and Stoljar, N, *Relational Autonomy* (Oxford University Press, 2000).
Madden Dempsey, M and Herring, J, 'Why Sexual Penetration Requires Justification' (2007) 27 *Oxford Journal of Legal Studies* 467.
Maghavi, M, 'Global, Regional, and National Burden of Suicide Mortality 1990 to 2016: Systematic Analysis for the Global Burden of Disease Study 2016' (2019) 364 *British Medical Journal* 194.
Malhi, G, 'The Ethics of Suicide in Mental Illness: Novel Neuroscientific Perspectives' (2019) 19 *American Journal of Bioethics* 294.
Malloy, S, 'Beyond Misguided Paternalism: Resuscitating the Right to Refuse Medical Treatment' (1998) 33 *Wake Forest Law Review* 1035.

Mallon, S, Galway, K, Hughes, L, Rondon-Sulbaran, J and Leavey, G, 'An Exploration of Integrated Data on the Social Dynamics of Suicide among Women' (2016) 38 *Sociology of Health and Illness* 662.

Mann, J, 'Neurobiology of Suicidal Behaviour' (2003) 4 *Nature Reviews Neuroscience* 828.

Maple, M, Cerel, J, Sanord, R, Pearce, T and Jordan, J, 'Is Exposure to Suicide Beyond Kin Associated with Risk for Suicidal Behavior? A Systematic Review of the Evidence' (2017) 47 *Suicide and Life Threatening Behavior* 461.

Mars, B, Heron, J, Klonsky, E, Moran, P, O'Connor, R, Tilling, K, Wilkinson, P and Gunnell, D, 'Predictors of Future Suicide Attempt among Adolescents with Suicidal Thoughts or Non-Suicidal Self-Harm: A Population-Based Birth Cohort Study' (2019) 6 *Lancet Psychiatry* 327.

Matsubayashi, T, Sekijima, K and Ueda, M, 'Government Spending, Recession, and Suicide: Evidence from Japan' (2020) 20 *BMC Public Health* 243.

McDonnell, S et al, 'From Grief to Hope' (University of Manchester, 2020).

McHugh, C, Corderoy, A, Ryan, C, Hickie, I and Large, M, 'Association between Suicidal Ideation and Suicide: Meta-Analyses of Odds Ratios, Sensitivity, Specificity and Positive Predictive Value' (2019) 5 *British Journal of Psychiatry* E1.

McKenzie, W and Wurr, C, 'Early Suicide Following Discharge from a Psychiatric Hospital' (2001) 31 *Suicide and Life Threatening Behaviour* 358.

McMahan, J, 'Our Fellow Creatures' (2005) 9 *Ethics* 353.

McManus, S, Gunnell, D, Cooper, C, Bebbington, P, Howard, L, Brugha, T, Jenkins, R, Hassiotis, A, Weich, S and Appleby, L, 'Prevalence of Non-Suicidal Self-Harm and Service Contact in England, 2000–14: Repeated Cross-Sectional Surveys of the General Population' (2019) 6 *Lancet Psychiatry* 573.

McManus, S, Hassiotis, A, Jenkins, R, Dennis, M, Aznar, C, Appleby, L, *Suicidal Thoughts, Suicide Attempts, and Self-Harm* (NHS Digital, 2016).

McTernan, N and Ryan, F, *The Harmful Impact of Suicide and Self-Harm Content Online: A Review of The Literature* (National Suicide Research Foundation, Ireland, 2020).

Meehan, J, Kapur, N, Hunt, I, Turnbull, P, Robinson, J, Bickley, H et al, 'Suicide in Mental Health In-Patients and within 3 Months of Discharge. National Clinical Survey' (2006) 188 *British Journal of Psychiatry* 129.

Mendelson, D and Bagaric, M, 'Assisted Suicide through the Prism of the Right to Life' (2013) 36 *International Journal of Law and Psychiatry* 406.

Mental Capacity Act 2005.

Mental Health Act 1983.

Mental Health Alliance, *A Mental Health Act Fit For Tomorrow* (MHA, 2017).

Mental Health First Aid, *Statistics* (Mental Health First Aid, 2021).

Mental Health Foundation, *Only One in Four Men Feel Able to Talk to Friends and Family When Feeling Stressed* (Mental Health Foundation, 2021).

Metz, T, 'Is Life's Meaning Ultimately Unthinkable?: Guy Bennett-Hunter on the Ineffable' (2016) 44 *Philosophia* 1247.

Michael, M and Miller, E 'Michelle Carter can Face Manslaughter Charge for Allegedly Encouraging Boyfriend's Suicide, Judge Rules', *Washington Post*, 24 September 2015, available at www.washingtonpost.com/news/morning-mix/wp/2015/09/24/michelle-carter-can-face-manslaughter-charge-for-allegedly-encouraging-boyfriends-suicide-judge-rules, accessed 13 December 2021.

Michaels, M, Chu, C and Joiner Jr, T, 'Suicide' in R DeRubeis and D Strunk (eds), *The Oxford Handbook of Mood Disorders* (Oxford University Press, 2018).

Miller, P, 'The Impact of Assisted Suicide on Persons with Disabilities – Is It A Right without Freedom?' (1993) 9 *Issues in Law & Medicine* 47.

Mills, C, *Decolonizing Global Mental Health* (Routledge, 2014).

—— 'Dead People Don't Claim: A Psychopolitical Autopsy of UK Austerity Suicides' (2018) 38 *Critical Social Policy* 302.

Minkowitz, T, 'Abolishing Mental Health Laws to Comply with the Convention on the Rights of Persons with Disabilities' in B McSherry and P Weller (eds), *Rethinking Rights-Based Mental Health Laws* (Hart Publishing, 2010).

Mitchell, K, Wells, M, Priebe, G and Ybarra, M, 'Exposure to Websites that Encourage Self-Harm and Suicide: Prevalence Rates and Association with Actual Thoughts of Self-Harm and Thoughts of Suicide in the United States' (2014) 37 *Journal of Adolescence* 1335.

Monkasalo, M-L, '"When We Stop Living, We Also Stop Dying" Men, Suicide, and Moral Agency' in M-L Honkasalo and M Tuominen, *Culture, Suicide and the Human Condition* (Berghahn Books, 2014).

Moore, V, 'Leaving Hospital: A Step Too Far for Risk-Based Regulation?' (2020) 28 *Medical Law Review* 675.

Morris, S, 'Bristol Transgender Woman Who Took Own Life Felt Fobbed Off, Family Say', *The Guardian*, 18 October 2020, www.theguardian.com/society/2020/oct/18/transgender-woman-who-took-own-life-felt-fobbed-off-by-bristol-mental-health-services, accessed 13 December 2021.

Moscardini, E, Aboussouan, A, Bryan, C and Tucker, R, 'Suicide-Specific Cognitions, Attentional Fixation, and Worst-Point Suicidal Ideation' (2020) 54 *Suicide and Life-Threatening Behaviour* 899.

Mośicki, M, 'Suicidal Behaviors Among Adults' in M Nock (ed), *The Oxford Handbook of Suicide and Self-Injury* (Oxford University Press, 2014).

Muehlenkamp, J, 'Distinguishing between Suicidal and Nonsuicidal Self-Injury' in M Nock (ed), *The Oxford Handbook of Suicide and Self-Injury* (Oxford University Press, 2014).

Mueller, A, 'Does the Media Matter to Suicide?: Examining the Social Dynamics Surrounding Media Reporting on Suicide in a Suicide-Prone Community' (2017) 180 *Social Science and Medicine* 152.

Mulder, R, Newton-Howes, G, and Coid, J, 'The Futility of Risk Prediction in Psychiatry' (2016) 209 *British Journal of Psychiatry* 271.

Munro, V and Aitken, R, 'From Hoping to Help: Identifying and Responding to Suicidality amongst Victims of Domestic Abuse' (2020) 26 *International Review of Victimology* 29.

Murphy, K, '"Horrific" Level of Stigma: Biggest Barrier to Suicide Prevention is Discrimination', *The Guardian*, 19 November 2019, available at www.theguardian.com/society/2019/nov/13/horrific-level-of-stigma-biggest-barrier-to-suicide-prevention-is-discrimination, accessed 13 December 2021.

Mäkinen, I, 'Social Dimensions of Suicide' in D Wasserman (ed), *Suicide: An Unnecessary Death* (Oxford University Press, 2016).

Nath, U, Regnard, C, Lee, M, Lloyd, K and Wiblin, L, 'Physician-Assisted Suicide and Physician-Assisted Euthanasia: Evidence from Abroad and Implications for UK Neurologists' (2021) 21 *Practical Neurology* 205.

National Statistics, *Safety in Custody Statistics, England and Wales: Deaths in Prison Custody to March 2021, Assaults and Self-harm to December 2020* (National Statistics, 2020).

Nedelseky, J, *Law's Relations: A Relational Theory of Self, Autonomy and the Law* (Oxford University Press, 2014).

Neimeyer, R, Klass, D and Dennis, M, 'A Social Constructionist Account of Grief: Loss and the Narration of Meaning' (2014) 38 *Death Studies* 485.

Newton-Howes, G, 'Risk in Mental Health: A Review on and of the Psychiatrist' (2018) 13 *Journal of Mental Health Training, Education and Practice* 14.

Newton-Howes, G and Mullen, R, 'Coercion in Psychiatric Care: Systematic Review of Correlates and Themes' (2011) 65 *Psychiatric Services* 465.

Ng, J, Sjöstrand, M and Eyal, N, 'Adding Lithium to Drinking Water for Suicide Prevention – The Ethics' (2019) 12 *Public Health Ethics* 274.

NHS, *Health Survey for England 2019* (NHS, 2000).

Nilsson, A, *Compulsory Mental Health Interventions and the UNCRPD* (Hart Publishing, 2021).

Nordenfelt, L, *Rationality and Compulsion: Applying Action Theory to Psychiatry* (Oxford University Press, 2007).

Nordentoft, M, 'Crucial Elements in Suicide Prevention Strategies' (2011) 84 *Progress in Neuropsychopharmacol and Biological Psychiatry* 848.

Nyttingnesa, O, Ruuda, T and Rugkasa, J, '"It's Unbelievably Humiliating" – Patients' Expressions of Negative Effects of Coercion in Mental Health Care' (2016) 49 *International Journal of Law and Psychiatry* 147.

O'Connor, R and Kirtley, O, 'The Integrated Motivational-Volitional Model of Suicidal Behaviour' (2018) 5 *Philosophical Transactions of the Royal Society of London* 373.
O'Connor, R and Nock, N, 'The Psychology of Suicidal Behaviour' (2014) *1 Lancet Psychiatry* 73.
Office for National Statistics, *Adult Psychiatric Morbidity Survey: Survey of Mental Health and Wellbeing, England, 2014* (Office of National Statistics, 2016).
—— *Self Harm and Suicidal Thoughts and Attempts* (ONS, 2017).
—— *Number of Suicides for Persons aged 10 to 17, England and Wales, Registered Years 2001 to 2016* (ONS, 2018).
—— *Drug-Related Deaths and Suicide in Prison Custody in England and Wales: 2008 to 2016* (ONS, 2019).
—— *Suicide in England and Wales 2019* (ONS, 2020).
—— *Suicide Rates for Males and Females Remain Consistent with 2018* (ONS, 2020).
—— *Adult Smoking Habits in the UK 2019* (ONS, 2021).
Okrent, M, 'To Be or Not to Be Authentic. In Defence of Authenticity as an Ethical Ideal' (2017) 20 *Ethics, Theory and Moral Practice* 567.
—— 'On Being a Human Self' in M Burch, J Marsh and I McMullin, *Normativity, Meaning, and the Promise of Phenomenology* (Taylor and Francis, 2019).
Owen, G, 'Retrospective Views of Psychiatric In-Patients Regaining Mental Capacity' (2009) 195 *British Journal of Psychiatry* 403.
Owen, G et al, 'Temporal Inabilities and Decision-making Capacity in Depression' (2013) 14 *Phenomology and the Cognitive Sciences* 163.
Owens, D, Horrocks, J and House, A, 'Fatal and Non-Fatal Repetition of Self-Harm' (2002) 181 *British Journal of Psychiatry* 193.
Palmer, H, 'Trial for Murder' (1957) *Criminal Law Review* 365.
Parker, H, 'Survivors of Suicide' in M Nock (ed), *The Oxford Handbook of Suicide and Self-Injury* (Oxford University Press, 2014).
Parks, J, 'Why Gender Matters to the Euthanasia Debate: On Decisional Capacity and the Rejection of the Woman's Death Request' (2000) 1 *Hastings Center Report* 30.
Parra-Uribe, I, Blasco-Fontecilla, H, Garcia-Pares, G, Martinez-Naval, L, Valero-Coppin, O, Cebria-Meca, A, Oquendo, M and Paolo-Vida, D, 'Risk of Re-Attempts and Suicide Death after a Suicide Attempt: A Survival Analysis' (2017) 17 *BMC Psychiatry* 163.
Patalay, P and Fitzsimons, E, *Mental Ill-Health at Age 17 in the UK* (UCL, 2000).
—— 'Psychological Distress, Self-Harm and Attempted Suicide in UK 17 Year Olds' (2021) 13 *British Journal of Psychiatry* 1.
Paterson, C, *Assisted Suicide and Euthanasia: A Natural Law Ethics Approach* (Routledge, 2008).
Patient Safety Group, *Self-Harm and Suicide in Adults* (Royal College of Psychiatry, 2020).
Peel, E and Harding, R, 'A Right to "Dying Well" with Dementia? Capacity, "Choice" and Relationality' (2015) 25 *Feminism and Psychology* 137.
Peisah, C, Sheahan, L and White, B, 'Biggest Decision of Them All – Death and Assisted Dying: Capacity Assessments and Undue Influence Screening' (2019) 49 *Internal Medicine Journal* 792.
Pilpel, A and Amsel, L, 'What is Wrong with Rational Suicide' (2011) 39 *Philosophia* 112.
Pirkis, J, Spittal, M, Cox, G, Robinson, J, Cheung, Y and Studdert, D, 'The Effectiveness of Structural Interventions at Suicide Hotspots: A Meta-Analysis' (2013) 42 *International Journal of Epidemiology* 541.
Pollard, S, Lieberman, R and Niznik, M, 'Suicide Contagion and Clusters' (2019) 47 *NSU Florida Faculty Articles* 21.
Posner, K, Brodsky, B, Yershova, K, Cuchanan, J and Mann, J, 'The Classification of Suicidal Behavior' in M Nock (ed) *The Oxford Handbook of Suicide and Self-Injury* (Oxford University Press, 2014).
Pouliot, L and Leo, D, 'Critical Issues in Psychological Autopsy Studies' (2006) 36 *Suicide and Life-Threatening Behavior* 491.
Powell, J, 'Suicide, an Issue for Feminists', available at www.thecalmzone.net/2011/04/a-call-to-feminists/, accessed 14 December 2021.

Pridmore, S, 'Mental Disorder and Suicide: A Faulty Connection' (2015) 49 *Australian and New Zealand Journal of Psychiatry* 18.
Priebe, S, 'Involuntary Hospitalization of Suicidal Patients: Time for New Answers to Basic Questions?' (2019) 19 *The American Journal of Bioethics* 90.
Priebe, S et al, 'Patients' Views and Readmissions 1 Year after Involuntary Hospitalisation' (2009) 194 *British Journal of Psychiatry* 49.
Pring, J, 'Disabled Quartet Tell MPs and Peers Why Assisted Suicide Bill is Unsafe and Unsound', *Disability News Service*, 22 July 2021, available at www.disabilitynewsservice.com/disabled-quartet-tell-mps-and-peers-why-assisted-suicide-bill-is-unsafe-and-unsound/.
Pringle, W, 'Problematizations in Assisted Dying Discourse: Testing the "What's the Problem Represented to Be?" (WPR) Method for Critical Health Communication Research' (2020) 4 *Frontiers in Communication* 58.
Public Health England, *Identifying and Responding to Suicide Clusters* (Public Health England, 2019).
Public Health England, *Preventing Suicides in Public Places* (Public Health England, 2020).
Quinlivan, L, Nowland, R, Steeg, S, Cooper, J, Meehan, D, Godfrey, J, Robertson, D, Longson, D, Potokar, J, Davies, R, Allen, N, Huxtable, R, Mackway-Jones, K, Hawton, K, Gunnell, D and Kapur, N, 'Advance Decisions to Refuse Treatment and Suicidal Behaviour in Emergency Care: "It's Very Much a Step into the Unknown"' (2019) 5 *British Journal of Psychology* 50.
Rahman, MS, Gupta, S, While, D, Windfuhr, K, Shaw, J, Kapur, N and Appleby, L, *Quality of Risk Assessment Prior to Suicide and Homicide: A Pilot Study* (University of Manchester, 2013).
Rao, A, Mahendran, N, Gopalakrishnan, C, Reddy, T, Prabhakar, E and Swaminatan, R, 'One Hundred Female Burn Cases: A Study in Suicidology' (1989) 7 *Indian Journal of Psychiatry* 330.
Raz, J, 'Right-Based Moralities' in J Waldron (ed), *Theories of Rights* (Oxford University Press, 1984).
—— *Morality of Freedom* (Oxford University Press, 1986).
—— 'Death in Our Life' (2013) 30 *Journal of Applied Philosophy* 1.
RCPCH, *Suicide* (RCPCH, 2020).
Reinders, H, 'The Power of Inclusion and Friendship' (2011) 15 *Journal of Religion, Disability & Health* 431.
Riblet, N, Shiner, B, Young-Xu, Y and Watts, B, 'Strategies to Prevent Death by Suicide: Meta-Analysis of Randomised Controlled Trials' (2017) 210 *British Journal of Psychiatry* 396.
Richardson, G, 'Mental Capacity in the Shadow of Suicide: What Can the Law Do?' (2013) 9 *International Journal of Law in Context* 37.
Riddle, C, 'Assisted Dying & Disability' (2017) 6 *Bioethics* 484.
Ridge, D, Smith, H, Fixsen, A, Ridge, D and Oliffe, J, 'How Men Step Back – and Recover – from Suicide Attempts: A Relational and Gendered Account' (2021) 43 *Sociology of Health and Illness* 238.
Ripamonti, L, 'Lives Not Worth Living: Rethinking Autonomy and Assisted Dying in the Light of Profound Disability' (2018) 22 *Journal of Disability and Religion* 317.
Roberge, E, Leifker, F, Baker, S, Rozek, D and Bryan, C, 'Suicide Following Trauma' in J Beck and D Sloan (eds), *The Oxford Handbook of Traumatic Stress Disorders* (Oxford University Press, 2019).
Roberts, S, Jaremin, B and Lloyd, K, 'High-Risk Occupations for Suicide' (2013) 43 *Psychological Medicine* 1231.
Rogers, W, 'Feminist Bioethics' in A Garry, S Khadar and A Stone (eds), *The Routledge Companion to Feminist Philosophy* (Routledge, 2019).
Rudd, M, 'Inaccurate Conclusions Based on Limited Data' Electronic letter to the (2007) 11 *British Journal of Psychiatry* 1.
Russel, J, 'Christelle and Her Baby Died at the Hands of a Callous State', *The Guardian*, 7 January 2010, available at www.theguardian.com/commentisfree/2010/jan/07/mother-suicide-welfare-state, accessed 14 December 2021.
Sanchez, D, Guija, J, Perezmoreno, P, Kelly, S, Santos, M, Oquendo, M, Courtet, P, Giner, J and Giner, L, 'Association of Religious Activity with Male Suicide Deaths' (2020) 50 *Suicide and Life Threatening Behaviour* 449.

Savage, M, 'Health Secretary Tells Social Media Firms to Protect Children after Girl's Death', *The Guardian*, 26 January 2019, available at www.theguardian.com/politics/2019/jan/26/matt-hancock-facebook-social-media-suicide-self-harm-young-people, accessed 14 December 2021.

Savulescu, J, 'Autonomy, Interests, Justice and Active Medical Euthanasia' in M Cholbi and J Varelius (eds), *New Directions in the Ethics of Assisted Suicide and Euthanasia* (Springer, 2015).

Savulescu, J and Momeyer, R, 'Should Informed Consent Be Based on Rational Beliefs?' (1997) 23 *Journal of Medical Ethics* 282.

Sawada, Y, Ueda, M and Matsubayashi, T, 'Socioeconomic Causes of Suicide' in Y Sawada, M Ueda and T Matsubayashi (eds), *Economic Analysis of Suicide Prevention. Economy and Social Inclusion* (Springer, 2017).

Scanlon, T, 'A Theory of Freedom of Expression' (1972) 1 *Philosophy and Public Affairs*, 204.

Schmidtke, A, Bille-Brahe, U, DeLeo, D, Kerkhof, A, Bjerk, T, Crepet, P, Haring, C, Hawton, K, Lonnqvist, J, Michel, M et al, 'Attempted Suicide in Europe: Rates, Trends and Sociodemographic Characteristics of Suicide Attempters during the Period 1989–1992. Results of the WHO/EURO Multicentre Study on Parasuicide' (1996) 93 *Acta Psychiatrica Scandinavica* 327.

Schrauzer, G, 'Lithium: Occurrence, Dietary Intakes, Nutritional Essentiality' (2002) 21 *The Journal of American College of Nutrition* 14.

Schuklenk, U and van de Vathorst, S, 'Treatment-Resistant Major Depressive Disorder and Assisted Dying' (2015) 41 *Journal of Medical Ethics* 577.

Scoccia, D, 'Physician-Assisted Suicide, Disability and Paternalism' (2010) *36 Social Theory and Practice* 479.

—— 'The Disability Case against Assisted Dying' in A Cureton and D Wasserman (eds), *The Oxford Handbook of Philosophy and Disability* (Oxford University Press, 2019).

Sedgwick, R, Epstein, S, Duttab, R, Ougrin, D, 'Social Media, Internet Use and Suicide Attempts in Adolescents' (2019) 32 *Current Opinion in Psychiatry* 534.

Selby, E, Joiner Jr, T, and Ribeiro, J, 'Comprehensive Theories of Suicidal Behaviors' in M Nock (ed), *The Oxford Handbook of Suicide and Self-Injury* (Oxford University Press, 2014).

Senior, M, Burghart, M, Yu, R, Kormilitzin, A, Liu, Q, Vaci, N, Nevado-Holgado, A, Pandit, S, Zlodre, J and Fazel, S, 'Identifying Predictors of Suicide in Severe Mental Illness: A Feasibility Study of a Clinical Prediction Rule (Oxford Mental Illness and Suicide Tool or OxMIS)' (2020) 11 *Frontiers in Psychiatry* 268.

Sexual Offences Act 2003.

Shah, A, 'The Relationship between the Use of Mental Health Act and General Population Suicide Rates in England and Wales' (2012) 4 *Journal of Injury and Violence Research* 26.

Shahtahmasebi, S, 'Examining the Claim that 80–90% of Suicide Cases Had Depression' (2013) 1 *Frontiers in Public Health* 62.

—— 'What Does a Statistician Know about Suicide and Suicide Prevention' (2018) 5 *Dynamics of Human Health* 1.

Shakespeare, T, 'Just What is the Disability Perspective on Disability?' (2016) 46 *Hastings Center Report* 31.

Shaw, D, Trachsel, M and Elger, B, 'Assessment of Decision-Making Capacity in Patients Requesting Assisted Suicide' (2018) 213 *British Journal of Psychiatry* 393.

Shaw, R, Cullen, B, Graham, N, Lyall, D, Mackay, D, Okolie, C, Pearsall, R, Ward, J, John, A and Smith, D, 'Living Alone, Loneliness and Lack of Emotional Support as Predictors of Suicide and Self-Harm: A Nine-Year Follow up of the UK Biobank Cohort' (2021) 279 *Journal of Affective Disorders* 316.

Shepka, P, 'Sam and Chris Gould: Twins' Suicides Lead to Victim Policing Change', *BBC News*, 6 August 2020, available at www.bbc.co.uk/news/uk-england-cambridgeshire-58072098, accessed 14 December 2021.

Shneidman, E, *The Suicidal Mind* (Oxford University Press, 1996).

Sicilianos, LA, 'Preventing Violations of the Right to Life: Positive Obligations under Article 2 of the ECHR' (2014) 3 *Cyprus Human Rights Law Review* 117.

Siegel, K, 'Psychosocial Aspects of Rational Suicide' (1986) 40 *American Journal of Psychotherapy* 405.

Sikka, T, 'Is Physician-Assisted Suicide a Feminist Issue? Barriers to Access: A Feminist Analysis of Medically Assisted Dying and the Experience of Marginalized Groups' (2021) 84 *OMEGA – Journal of Death and Dying* 4.

Silverman, M, 'Suicide and Life-Threatening Behavior' (2006) 36 *Suicide and Life-Threatening Behaviour* 519.

—— 'Challenges to Defining and Classifying Suicide and Suicidal Behaviors' in R O'Connor and J Pirkis (eds), *The International Handbook of Suicide Prevention* (John Wiley & Sons, 2016).

Silverman, S, Berman, M, Sanddal, N, O'Carroll, P and Joiner, T, 'Rebuilding the Tower of Babel: A Revised Nomenclature for the Study of Suicide and Suicidal Behaviors: Suicide-Related Ideations, Communications, and Behaviors' (2007) 37 *Suicide and Life-Threatening Behavior* 264.

Silvers, A, 'Protecting the Innocent from Physician-Assisted Suicide' in M Battin, R Rhodes and A Silvers (eds), *Physician Assisted Suicide: Expanding the Debate* (Routledge, 2001).

Singer, P, 'Is the Sanctity of Life Ethic Terminally Ill?' (1995) 9 *Bioethics* 327.

Sisask, M and Värnik, A, 'Media Roles in Suicide Prevention: A Systematic Review' (2012) 9 *International Journal of Environmental Research and Public Health* 134.

Sisti, D and Joffe, S, 'Implications of Zero Suicide for Suicide Prevention Research' (2018) 320 *JAMA* 1633.

Sjöstrand, M and Juth, N, 'Authenticity and Psychiatric Disorder: Does Autonomy of Personal Preferences Matter?' (2014) 17 *Medicine, Health Care and Philosophy* 115.

Smuts, A, 'To Be or Never to Have Been: Anti-Natalism and a Life Worth Living' (2013) 17 *Ethical Theory and Moral Practice* 711.

Spencer, J, 'Assisted Suicide and the Discretion to Prosecute' (2009) *Cambridge Law Journal* 495.

Sperling, D, *Suicide Tourism* (Oxford University Press, 2020).

Spirito, A, O'Brien, K, Ranney, M and Gomez, J, 'The Evaluation and Management of Suicide Risk in Adolescents in the Context of Interpersonal Violence' in P Kleespies (ed), *The Oxford Handbook of Behavioral Emergencies and Crises* (Oxford University Press, 2020).

St Aquinas 1271, 'Summa Theologica' in A Pegis (ed), *Basic Writings of Saint Thomas Aquinas* (Random House, 1945), part II Q 64.

St Augustine, *The Confessions of Saint Augustine* (Peter Pauper Press, 1949) book I, Chapter 20.

Standish, K, 'A Coming Wave: Suicide and Gender after COVID-19' (2021) 30 *Journal of Gender Studies* 114.

Standish, K and Weil, S, 'Gendered Pandemics: Suicide, Femicide and COVID-19' (2021) 30 *Journal of Gender Studies* 807.

Standley, C, 'Expanding Our Paradigms: Intersectional and Socioecological Approaches to Suicide Prevention' (2020) 12 *Death Studies* 1.

Stapelberg, N, Sveticic, J, Hughes, I, Almeida-Crasto, A, Gaee-Atefi, T, Gill, N, Grice, D, Krishnaiah, R, Lindsay, L, Patist, C, Van Engelen, H, Walker, S, Welch, M, Woerwag-Mehta, S and Turner, K, 'Efficacy of the Zero Suicide Framework in Reducing Recurrent Suicide Attempts: Cross-Sectional and Time-to-Recurrent-Event Analyses' (2020) 12 *British Journal of Psychiatry* 1.

Stefan, S, *Rational Suicide, Irrational Laws: Examining Current Approaches to Suicide in Policy and Law* (Oxford University Press, 2016).

Steiner, H, *An Essay on Rights* (Blackwell, 1994).

Steward, C, Peisah, C, Draper, B, 'A Test for Mental Capacity to Request Assisted Suicide' (2011) 37 *Journal of Medical Ethics* 34.

Stone, D, Jeffrey, S, Dessypris, N, Kyllekidis, S, Chishti, P. Papadopoulos, F and Petridou, E, 'Intentional Injury Mortality in the European Union: How Many More Lives Could Be Saved?' (2006) 12 *Injury Prevention* 327.

Strang, D, Molloy, D and Harrison, C, 'Capacity to Choose Place of Residence: Autonomy vs Beneficence?' (1998) 14 *Journal of Palliative Care* 25.

Stuckler, D and Basu, S, *The Body Economic: Why Austerity Kills* (Basic Books, 2013).

Suicide Act 1961.

Sullivan, P, 'Should Healthcare Professionals Sometimes Allow Harm? The Case of Self-Injury' (2017) 43 *Journal of Medical Ethics* 319.

—— 'Risk and Responding to Self-Injury: Is Harm Minimisation a Step Too Far?' (2019) 14 *Journal of Mental Health Training, Education and Practice* 1.

Sveen, C and Walby, F, 'Suicide Survivors' Mental Health and Grief Reactions: A Systematic Review of Controlled Studies' (2008) 38 *Suicide and Life Threatening Behaviour* 13.

Swaine, L, *Ethical Autonomy: The Rise of Self-Rule* (Oxford University Press, 2020).

Szasz, T, *Fatal Freedom: The Ethics and Politics of Suicide* (Syracuse University Press, 2002).

Szmukler, G, 'The UN Convention on the Rights of Persons with Disabilities: "Rights, Will and Preferences" in Relation to Mental Health Disabilities' (2017) 46 *International Journal of Law and Psychiatry* 90.

Szmukler, G and Kelly, B 'We Should Replace Conventional Mental Health Law with Capacity-Based Law' (2016) 209 *The British Journal of Psychiatry* 449.

Tack, S, 'The Logic of Life: Thinking Suicide through Somatechnics' (2019) 34 *Australian Feminist Studies* 99.

Takahashi, Y, 'Depression and Suicide' (2001) 44 *JAMA* 359.

Thaler, R and Sunstein, C, *Nudge: The Final Edition* (Penguin, 2021).

The Samaritans, *Dying from Inequality* (The Samaritans, 2017).

—— *Men Suicide and Society* (The Samaritans, 2018).

—— *Suicide Statistics Report* (The Samaritans, 2019).

—— *Media Guidelines for Reporting Suicide* (The Samaritans 2020).

The Zero Suicide Alliance, *Evidence Review: National Approaches to Suicide Prevention Strategies and Policies* (ZSA, 2020).

Tolhurst, W, 'Suicide, Self-Sacrifice, and coercion' (1983) 21 *The Southern Journal of Philosophy* 109.

Tøllefsen, I, Hem, E and Ekeberg, Ø, 'The Reliability of Suicide Statistics: A Systematic Review' (2012) 12 *BMC Psychiatry* 9.

Tolwinski, K, Nemoianu, A, Bucaloiu, A, Venditto, J, Davis, F and Wagner, J '"I Don't Want to Go on Living This Way": Desire for Hastened Death and the Ethics of Involuntary Hospitalization' (2019) 19 *The American Journal of Bioethics* 88.

Torisky, E, 'Minimally Intentional Suicide and "The Falling Man"' (2015) 49 *Journal of Value Inquiry* 69.

Townsend, E et al, 'Self-Harm and Life Problems: Findings from the Multicentre Study of Self-Harm in England' (2016) 51 *Social Psychiatry and Psychiatric Epidemiology* 183.

Tucker, J, 'The Geometry of Suicide Law' (2015) 43 *International Journal of Law, Crime and Justice* 432.

Tulloch, G, 'Feminism, Suicide and Assisted Dying: Reflections on Sandra Bem's death' (2015) 25 *Feminism & Psychology* 113.

Turvill, J, Burroughs, A, Moore, K, 'Change in Occurrence of Paracetamol Overdose in UK after Introduction of Blister Packs' (2000) 355 *The Lancet* 2048.

University of Manchester, *National Confidential Inquiry into Suicide and Safety in Mental Health Annual Report: England, Northern Ireland, Scotland and Wales 2021* (University of Manchester, 2021).

—— *National Confidential Inquiry into Suicide and Homicide by People with Mental Illness* (University of Manchester, 2017).

—— *The National Confidential Inquiry into Suicide and Safety in Mental Health* (University of Manchester, 2019).

US Department of Health and Human Service, *About Zero Suicide* (USDHHS, 2021).

US Department of Health and Human Service, Office of the Surgeon General, & National Action Alliance for Suicide Prevention, *Suicide* (DHHS, 2012).

Usborne, S, 'The Bold New Fight to Eradicate Suicide', *The Guardian*, 1 August 2017.

van Wijngaarden, E, Goossensen, A and Leget, C, 'The Social-Political Challenges behind the Wish to Die in Older People Who Consider Their Lives to be Completed and No Longer Worth Living' (2017) 28 *The European Journal of Social Policy* 419.

van Wijngaarden, E, Merzel, M, Van den Berg, V, Zomers, M, Hartog, I and Leget, C, 'Still Ready to Give up on Life? A Longitudinal Phenomenological Study into Wishes to Die among Older Adults' (2021) 284 *Social Science and Medicine* 114.

Varga, S, *Authenticity as an Ethical Ideal* (Routledge, 2012).

Verhofstadt, M, Thienpont, L and Peters, G-J, 'When Unbearable Suffering Incites Psychiatric Patients to Request Euthanasia: Qualitative Study' (2017) 211 *The British Journal of Psychiatry: The Journal of Mental Science* 238.

Vita, A, De Peri, L and Sacchetti, E, 'Lithium in Drinking Water and Suicide Prevention: A Review of the Evidence' (2015) 30 *International Clinical Psychopharmacology* 1.

von Borczyskowski, A, Hjern, A, Lindblad, F and Vinnerljung, B, 'Suicidal Behaviour in National and International Adult Adoptees: A Swedish Cohort Study' (2006) 41 *Social Psychiatry and Psychiatric Epidemiology* 95.

Wagner, B, *Suicidal Behavior in Children and Adolescents* (Yale University Press, 2009).

—— 'Nature and Scope of the Problem' in B Wagner (ed) *Suicidal Behavior in Children and Adolescents* (Yale University Press, 2009).

Wakefield, J, 'False Positives in Psychiatric Diagnosis: Implications for Human Freedom' (2010) 31 *Theoretical Medical Bioethics* 5.

Walby, S, *The Cost of Domestic Violence* (Women and Equality Unit, 2004).

Wall, J, 'Authentic Decision-Making and Depression' in C Foster and J Herring (eds), *Law and Depression* (Oxford University Press, 2018).

Wand, A et al, 'The Nexus between Elder Abuse, Suicide, and Assisted Dying: The Importance of Relational Autonomy and Undue Influence' (2018) 18 *Macquarie Law Journal* 79.

Wang, D and Colucci, E, 'Should Compulsory Admission to Hospital Be Part of Suicide Prevention Strategies?' (2017) 41 *British Journal of Psychology Bulletin* 169.

Ward-Ciesielski, E and Lindhan, M, 'Psychological Treatment of Suicidal Behaviors' in M Nock (ed), *The Oxford Handbook of Suicide and Self-Injury* (Oxford University Press, 2014).

Watt, J, *From Sin to Insanity: Suicide in Early Modern Europe* (Cornell University Press, 2004).

Webb, D, *Thinking About Suicide. Contemplating and Comprehending the Urge to Die* (PCCS Books, 2011).

Wedlake, G, 'Complicating Theory through Practice: Affirming the Right to Die for Suicidal People' (2020) 9 *The Canadian Journal of Disabilities Studies* 89.

Wente, M, 'Should Doctors Be Allowed to Kill', *The Globe and the Mail*, 19 September 2015, available at www.theglobeandmail.com/opinion/should-doctors-be-allowed-to-kill/article26428075/, accessed 15 December 2021.

Wenzel, A and Spokas, M, 'Cognitive and Information Processing Approaches to Understanding Suicidal Behaviors' in M Nock (ed), *The Oxford Handbook of Suicide and Self-Injury* (Oxford University Press, 2014).

Werth, J, Benjamin, G and Farrenkopf, T, 'Requests for Physician Assisted Death: Guidelines for Assessing Mental Capacity and Impaired Judgment' (2000) 6 *Psychology, Public Policy and Law* 348.

Westefeld, J, 'Suicide Prevention: An Issue of Social Justice' (2020) 1 *Journal of Prevention and Health Promotion* 58.

Westlund, A, 'Relational Autonomy and Practical Authority' in P Garavaso (ed), *The Bloomsbury Companion to Analytic Feminism* (Bloomsbury, 2018).

White, J, 'What Can Critical Suicidology do?' (2017) 41 *Death Studies* 472.

Wicks, E, *The Right to Life and Conflicting Interests* (Oxford University Press, 2010).

Wilks, I, 'The Debate over Risk-related Standards of Competence' (1997) 11 *Bioethics* 413.

Williams, C, Davidson, J and Montgomery, I, 'Impulsive Suicidal Behavior' (1980) 36 *Journal of Clinical Psychology* 90.

Wilson, K, 'The Abolition or Reform of Mental Health Law: How Should The Law Recognise and Respond to The Vulnerability of Persons With Mental Impairment?' (2020) 28 *Medical Law Review* 3.

Wilson, T, *Strangers to Ourselves* (Harvard University Press, 2004).

Wolbring, G, 'Why Disability Rights Movements Do Not Support Euthanasia: Safeguards Broken Beyond Repair', available at www.independentliving.org/docs5/Wolbringeuthanasia.html, accessed 15 December 2021.

Wolf, S, 'Gender, Feminism, and Death: Physician-Assisted Suicide and Euthanasia' in S Wolf (ed), *Feminism and Bioethics* (Oxford University Press, 1996).

World Health Organisation, *Suicide* (World Health Organisation, 2014).
—— *Suicide* (WHO, 2017).
—— *Suicide* (WHO, 2018).
—— *Suicide: Global Health Estimates* (WHO 2019).
Wright, J, 'The Operational Obligation under Article 2 of the European Convention on Human Rights and Challenges for Coherence – Views from the English Supreme Court and Strasbourg' (2016) 7 *Journal of European Tort Law* 58.
Yildiz, M, Orak, U, Walker, M and Solakoglu, O, 'Suicide Contagion, Gender, and Suicide Attempts among Adolescents' (2019) 43 *Death Studies* 365.
Yuill, K, *Assisted Suicide: The Liberal, Humanist Case Against Legalization* (Palgrave, 2012).
Zalsman, A et al, 'Suicide Prevention Strategies Revisted: 10 Year Systematic Review' (2016) 3 *Lancet Psychiatry* 646.
Zalsman, G, Hawton, K, Wasserman, D, van Heeringen, K, Arensman, E, Sarchiapone, M, Carli, V, Höschl, C, Barzilay, R, Balazs, J, Purebl, G, Kahn, J, Sáiz, PA, Bursztein Lipsicas, C, Bobes, J, Cozman, D, Hegerl, U and Zohar, J, 'Suicide Prevention Strategies Revisited: 10-Year Systematic Review' (2016) 3 *Lancet Psychiatry* 646.
Zhang, J, Xiao, S and Zhou, L, 'Mental Disorders and Suicide among Young Rural Chinese: A Case-Control Psychological Autopsy Study (2010) 167 *American Journal of Psychiatry* 773.
Zonana, J, Simberlund, J and Christos, P, 'The Impact of Safety Plans in an Outpatient Clinic' (2018) 39 *Crisis* 304.

INDEX

www.ingramcontent.com/pod-product-compliance
Lightning Source LLC
Chambersburg PA
CBHW071409230926
51613CB00015B/90
9781509949045